WOMEN IN TWENTIETH-CENTURY BRITAIN

Pearson Education

We work with leading authors to develop the
strongest educational materials in History, bringing
cutting-edge thinking and best learning practise
to a global market.

Under a range of well-known imprints, including
Longman, we craft high quality print and electronic
publications which help readers to understand and
apply their content, whether studying or at work.

To find out more about the complete range of our
publishing please visit us on the World Wide Web at:
www.pearsoneduc.com

WOMEN IN TWENTIETH-CENTURY BRITAIN

Edited by

Ina Zweiniger-Bargielowska

Longman

An imprint of **Pearson Education**

Harlow, England · London · New York · Reading, Massachusetts · San Francisco
Toronto · Don Mills, Ontario · Sydney · Tokyo · Singapore · Hong Kong · Seoul
Taipei · Cape Town · Madrid · Mexico City · Amsterdam · Munich · Paris · Milan

Pearson Education Limited
Edinburgh Gate
Harlow
Essex CM20 2JE
United Kingdom

and Associated Companies throughout the world

Visit us on the World Wide Web at
www.pearsoneduc.com

———————————

First published in Great Britain in 2001

ISBN 0-582-40480-0

British Library Cataloguing in Publication Data
A CIP catalogue record for this book can be obtained from the British Library.

10   9   8   7   6   5   4   3   2   1
05   04   03   02   01   00

Typeset by 35 in 10.5/12.5pt Baskerville
Produced by Pearson Education Asia Pte Ltd.
Printed in Singapore

To our grandmothers, mothers, sisters and daughters

CONTENTS

LIST OF ILLUSTRATIONS

LIST OF FIGURES

LIST OF TABLES

ACKNOWLEDGEMENTS

The publishers would like to thank the following for their permission to reproduce illustrative material: © National Library of Wales for plates 1.1, 3.1, 11.2; © Ina Zweiniger-Bargielowska for plate 1.2; © the Mistress and Fellows, Girton College, Cambridge, for plates 2.1 and 2.2; © the Centre for North West Regional Studies, University of Lancaster, for plate 3.2; © the British Library for plates 3.3, 10.2, 20.2; © the British Library/Colgate-Palmolive for plate 10.1; © the British Library/Proctor & Gamble for plate 12.1; © the British Library/*Woman*, IPC, for plate 17.2; © the Wellcome Institute Library, London/Harry Stopes-Roe for plate 4.1; © the Wellcome Institute Library, London/Family Planning Association for plate 4.2; © the Wellcome Institute Library, London/Abortion Law Reform Association for plate 18.1; © the Wellcome Institute Library, London, for plate 21.1; © Carlton International for plate 15.2; © Karen Lupson for plate 5.1; © Helen Jones for plate 6.1; © the Mary Evans Picture Library/Henry Grant for plate 6.2; © the Mary Evans Picture Library/Fawcett Library for plates 16.2 and 17.1; © Hulton Getty for plates 7.1, 7.2, 13.2, 14.1, 14.2 and 21.2; © the Photographic and Design Unit, University of Sussex for plate 8.1; © the Women and Education Newsletter Collective (Isabelle Irvine, Alison Kelly, Jill Norris, Joy Rose, Judy Samuels and Judith Summers) for plate 8.2; © Katherine Holden for plates 9.1, 9.2 and 11.1; © the University of Wales, Aberystwyth/Keith Morris for plate 12.2; © Shani D'Cruze for plate 13.1; © HM Prison and Young Offender Institution, Askham Grange, for plate 13.3; © Mills & Boon (Mills & Boon is a registered trademark owned by Harlequin Mills & Boon Limited) for plate 15.1; © the Museum of London for plate 16.1; © 'PA' Photos for plate 18.2; © the Harris Museum & Art Gallery, Preston, for plate 19.1; © Paul Mattson, Well Street, London, for plate 19.2; and © the Imperial War Museum, London, for plate 20.1.

I

INTRODUCTION

Ina Zweiniger-Bargielowska

During the twentieth century women in Britain gained control of their fertility, acquired equal access to education and, in principle, the labour market, and established their status as equal citizens. Although women widened their opportunities in many areas, traditional gender stereotypes which assumed that women's primary role is in the domestic setting continued to be influential, men held on to their dominant position in society and the double standard in sexual morality proved remarkably persistent. The history of women in the twentieth century is distinguished by this interplay of change and continuity. Ultimately, it is a question of perspective whether to stress optimism by highlighting the obvious achievements of women and advances across the century or to focus, more pessimistically, on continuing discrimination and the lack of real equality between the sexes.

Women in Twentieth-Century Britain explores transformations in the position of women during last century exemplified by changes such as the reduction in fertility or the removal of formal barriers to women's participation in education, work and public life. At the same time, the limits of formal equality are demonstrated by an examination of several indicators, including the fact that women continued to be under-represented in many areas, paid significantly less then men or subject to domestic violence and sexual exploitation. Women in 2000 have many more choices and opportunities than women in 1900 but genuine equality between men and women remains elusive. These issues are discussed from a thematic perspective. In each of the four parts of the book – *The Life Course*; *Work – Paid and Unpaid*; *Consumption, Culture and Transgression*; and *The State and Citizenship* – a number of chapters explore a particular topic throughout the century up to and including the 1990s. The three chapters dealing with the women's movement are the only exceptions, since this topic required more detailed consideration. The four parts, and the chapters within them, are linked in a variety of ways; together they provide a multifaceted picture of women's history.

This book highlights differences between women which were just as important as similarities or common experiences. Women in twentieth-century Britain were not a unified category and not all women had the same opportunities, aspirations or experiences. To give just a few examples, middle-class women above all benefited from improved female access to higher education whereas only a minority of working-class women attended universities during the late 1990s. Women's opportunities were also shaped by 'race' and ethnicity. Full-time motherhood and domesticity during the middle decades of the century was a privilege of white women whereas recent female migrants, whether European Voluntary Workers after the Second World War or West Indian and South Asian immigrants in the 1950s and 1960s, were perceived above all as workers. The experiences of young girls, on the one hand, and older women, on the other, were distinctive. The twentieth century could be seen as a period of increasing status for girls, but older women were disproportionately among the poorest members of society in 1900 and in 2000. Different generations of women had divergent aspirations and styles. The demands of feminists in the interwar years and early postwar period were relatively moderate, in contrast to both preceding and succeeding generations. Aggressive tactics were adopted by the militant suffragettes before the First World War or the activists of the Women's Liberation Movement during the 1970s. Finally, while women born around the beginning of the century had few children, those born in the interwar years again chose larger families, but their daughters, coming of age during the 1970s and later, again opted for small families.

There has been a growing interest in the history of women since the 1970s and the beginning of the new century is an appropriate opportunity to take stock and look at the history of women throughout the previous 100 years. This is important not only for women interested in tracing their own history and that of their mothers and grandmothers, but necessary in order to comprehend twentieth-century British history as a whole. As gender historians have made clear in the 1980s and 1990s, women's history is not just a sectional interest confined to ghetto status. Rather, an appreciation of women's distinctive needs and experiences is critical to understanding many social and welfare reforms during the century which were at least in part the outcome of campaigning by women's groups. Examples include the introduction of family allowances paid directly to mothers, improved maternity services, abortion rights or free access to contraception. Women made a vital contribution to the war effort during both world wars, whether in the forces, as workers in war industries, or as house-wives who were responsible for maintaining civilian health and morale. Women are central to any analysis of twentieth-century demographic patterns, such as the decline in fertility or the rise in divorce, and changes in the nature of the labour market, such as the transformation of participation rates. As we move into the twenty-first century women exert an increasingly powerful influence on the pace and direction of economic, social and cultural change.

Recently women's history has been described as outmoded as gender history has taken its place, a historiographical debate which is explored in chapter 2. Gender history differs from women's history in that it focuses not just on women, but on the relationship between women and men and, above all, on how female

Plate 1.1. Girls, *c.* 1900.
Plate 1.2. Girls, 2000.

and male identities are constructed. Arguably, the conflict between these perspectives can be resolved since a gendered approach has not necessarily supplanted women's history. Instead it has enriched women's history methodologically by drawing attention to the fluidity of gender identities and their relational characteristics. Moreover, the emphasis on gender differences and the distinctive roles and contributions of women has contributed to a growing recognition that history in general, and twentieth-century British history in particular, cannot make sense without taking women into account.

Women's Lives: 1900 vs. 2000

If we take a look at women's lives at the beginning of the twentieth century and compare this to a snapshot at the end of the century, there is little doubt about the extensive changes that have taken place. However, these changes have coincided with important areas of continuity. Frequently, dramatic changes only took off from the 1970s or even 1980s, following a period of relative stagnation for much of the century. This is true with regard to women's share of university places or women's participation rate in the labour force. Similarly, important demographic trends such as the rise in divorce, increase in cohabitation and the growing proportion of children born to unmarried women accelerated rapidly from the 1980s.

A girl born at the end of the nineteenth century could expect to live, on average, about 50 years whereas projected live expectancy at birth in 2000 is about 80 years for women – an increase of three decades in the space of three generations. A woman born in 1870 typically had between five and six children, of whom almost one-sixth died in infancy, whereas women born in 1970, on average, had approximately 1.7 children and by 1998 infant mortality stood at less than six per thousand.[1] In 1900 there were no female MPs and women were excluded from the parliamentary franchise, although about one million female ratepayers, many of whom were widows, could vote and stand for office in local elections. At the end of the twentieth century, women could vote on equal terms with men, although women remained a minority among MPs despite the massive influx of female MPs following Labour's election victory of 1997. In the late nineteenth century, girls' education was orientated towards domesticity, a small minority attended secondary schools and higher education was only just becoming available to women who had been barred from access to universities until the 1870s. In the late 1990s the overwhelming majority of girls remained in school beyond the leaving age of 16 years, girls outperformed boys at all levels from primary school tests to A level, and women accounted for a majority of undergraduates.

These educational advances were not translated fully into equal performance in the labour market in which men remained dominant and better paid. In 1900 female workers were crowded into a narrow range of occupations, above all domestic service, textiles and the clothing industries. Most were young and single whereas married women typically stayed at home – despite important exceptions such as women workers in the Lancashire cotton industry and extensive casual earnings among working-class women. Only about a third of women were in full-time employment and, lacking in skill and experience, they typically earned about half of male earnings. At the end of the twentieth century, marriage ceased to be an important factor in women's participation rate, and almost three-quarters of women were in the labour force, although frequently on a part-time basis. While many women were employed in professional and managerial occupations, clerical, secretarial and service-based jobs were the most popular and women earned, on average, about four-fifths of the male rate.

Given women's limited educational opportunities, narrow range of occupations and low wages at the beginning of the twentieth century, it is not surprising that Cicely Hamilton described *Marriage as a Trade* (indeed, the only trade open to women) in which 'she exchanged . . . possession of her person for the means of existence'.[2] Conventionally, marriage was portrayed as women's true destiny and the only respectable path to motherhood, although about one in six women never married. Spinsters were not only marginalised socially but economically vulnerable given the discrimination against women in the labour market. Divorce was costly and extremely rare and marriages were typically only terminated through death, although separation and cohabitation were not unusual among the working class according to the Royal Commission on Divorce of 1912. The final decades of the twentieth century witnessed what can be described as a demographic revolution, and in the 1990s between one-third and half of all marriages ended in divorce, re-marriage was common, cohabitation had become a precursor – or an alternative – to marriage and a growing proportion, one in six, lived alone. Almost 40 per cent of children were born outside marriage, in many cases to cohabiting parents. Nearly a quarter of all families with dependent children were headed by single parents, and more than nine out of ten by single mothers.

In 1900 Victorian sexual attitudes characterised by female chastity, ignorance and the construction of female sexuality as necessarily passive and responsive to male stimulation were well-entrenched. At the end of the twentieth century information about sex was generally available, female sexuality was more assertive, premarital sex was commonplace and generally condoned, and the rights of lesbian and gay couples were increasingly recognised. Nevertheless, despite this trend towards greater equality and liberalisation, in many important ways, sexual attitudes have remained remarkably persistent. Most notably, this is the case with regard to the double standard in sexual morality which condoned or even applauded male sexual promiscuity while condemning it among women. This double standard was not only morally unacceptable but also a danger to women's health. At the beginning of the century Christabel Pankhurst in *The Great Scourge* called for 'Votes for Women and Chastity for Men' because men who frequented prostitutes were infecting their wives with venereal diseases.[3]

Attitudes towards prostitution and the treatment of prostitutes by the state have shown a great degree of continuity – prostitutes continued to be blamed for prostitution, arrested, prosecuted and convicted while their male clients were generally able to use their services without impediment. The so-called sexual revolution of the final decades of the twentieth century has not resulted in a demise in prostitution and the sex industry which continued to flourish in the late 1990s. Likewise, with regard to crime, differences between male and female patterns of criminal behaviour or as victims of crime remained largely unchanged throughout the century. The overwhelming majority of offences were committed by men at the beginning as well as the end of the century, while women were more commonly victims of crime and sexual violence.

A central aspect of continuity was women's association with caring and unpaid domestic labour. In the early twentieth century, married women and mothers typically performed all the housework and caring duties – although middle-class women could rely on domestic service while many working-class wives and mothers had to take on casual employment to make ends meet. At the end of the century, women still performed the overwhelming majority of housework and most had to cope with a double burden. While women in the 1990s combined domestic responsibilities with paid employment there has not been a commensurate rise in men's share of domestic labour or childcare. Women have not been able to participate in a range of leisure activities, including most sports, on an equal level with men, largely because of lack of money at the beginning of the century and lack of time at the end. A final example of continuity is the enduring emphasis on physical attractiveness in representations of femininity which has stimulated the growth of body management as a central aspect of twentieth-century mass consumer culture. The following sections discuss women's control of their own fertility and the erosion of the separate spheres ideology.

Women Gain Control of Fertility

Arguably, the most fundamental change in women's lives during the twentieth century was the decline in fertility, especially when coupled with the increase in life expectancy. This transformation was summed up evocatively by Richard Titmuss in the 1950s:

> The typical working-class mother of the 1890s, married in her teens or early twenties and experiencing ten pregnancies, spent about fifteen years in a state of pregnancy and in nursing a child for the first year of its life. She was tied, for this period of time, to the wheel of childbearing. Today, for the typical mother, the time so spent would be about four years. A reduction of such magnitude in only two generations in the time devoted to childbearing represents nothing less than a revolutionary enlargement of freedom for women brought about by the power to control their own fertility.[4]

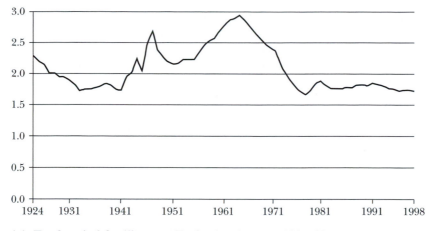

Figure 1.1. **Total period fertility rate, England and Wales, 1924–98.**

Note: The figure refers to the number of children per woman, that is, the average number of children who would be born per woman if women experienced the age-specific fertility rates of the reference years throughout their child-bearing lifespan.

Source: *Social Trends* 30 (London: HMSO, 2000), p. 17.

As Figure 1.1 shows, the decline in fertility was not a simple downward trend. Rather fertility fluctuated, although it remained below the replacement rate of 2.2 children per woman for much of the century. Fertility declined until the 1930s, rose briefly during the 1940s, and increased again from the mid-1950s until the mid-1960s. Subsequently there was a sharp decline and the number of children per woman has remained fairly stable at about 1.7 since the mid-1970s. Women from all social backgrounds experienced these trends, but professional families and Lancashire cotton workers were among the earliest social groups to restrict their fertility while coal-mining families were slow to follow the trend. Successive generations of women experienced fertility differently. Women born around the turn of the century had relatively few children, while their daughters – born during the 1930s – experienced the postwar baby boom amounting to the largest number of children born since the 1920s. By contrast, women born during the postwar baby boom again had very few children and the average age of first-time mothers also increased.

Many factors contributed to this decline in fertility, which occurred throughout the industrialised world. The phenomenon has to be understood within the context of expanding employment opportunities for women, the rising cost of children with longer school attendance and higher standards of care, the decline in infant and child mortality as well as the growth of mass consumption which meant that smaller families could expect to raise their standard of living and income per head.

Causality is complex, but a crucial determinant was the increased availability of birth control and, perhaps as importantly, the acceptance of birth control as a legitimate, respectable and indeed responsible practice among the majority of married couples. Birth control began to be practised by middle-class women from the turn of the century but it was controversial, condemned by the churches and associated with prostitution. Working-class women who wanted to control their fertility had to rely on a combination of abstinence and illegal abortion. While feminist campaigners discussed these issues from the late nineteenth century onward, birth control became widely acceptable only during the interwar years.

Marie Stopes in *Married Love* and *Wise Parenthood* – both published in 1918 and immediate best-sellers – advocated women's right to sexual pleasure in marriage for which birth control was a necessary precondition.[5] Stopes opened the first birth control clinic in London in 1921 (the origin of the Family Planning Association) which offered free contraceptive advice to married women. Stopes favoured the cap and considered spacing of births by means of birth control as critical to improving women's health and promoting happy marriages. A number of clinics were opened during the interwar years and women's ability to control their fertility increased with the advent of more reliable forms of contraception – the pill was launched in 1962 – and the legalisation of abortion in 1967. A final important turning-point was the introduction of free contraception available on the National Health Service in 1974. From the 1970s onwards, over 70 per cent were practising birth control and the pill was the most popular form of contraception used by about a quarter of women. Sterilisation was the most popular method after the pill favoured by older couples (at roughly equal proportions among men and women), while the male condom remained the most important alternative to the pill among younger people. During the twentieth century women increasingly controlled their fertility, but there is no simple connection between availability of contraception and fertility – as illustrated by the postwar baby boom and the fact that Britain during the 1990s had the highest proportion of teenage mothers in the European Union.

The Separate Spheres Ideology Eroded

Women's increased access to education, employment and politics during the twentieth century can be summed up as the erosion – erosion and not extirpation – of the separate spheres ideology. The separate spheres ideology, which originated in the late eighteenth and early nineteenth centuries, became influential in defining gender relations first, among the middle classes and subsequently in the working class. According to this ideology men and masculinity came to be associated with exclusive access to and participation in the public sphere of work and politics whereas women and femininity were perceived as confined to the private sphere of domesticity and motherhood – idealised as 'the angel in the house'. Gender roles and identities were not only distinct – with quite separate masculine and feminine characteristics – but hierarchical. Men were identified with reason, women with emotion; men were associated with action, women with passivity; and, finally, men exercised domination, while women experienced submission.

During the nineteenth century this ideology was used to justify a system of multifaceted discrimination against women buttressed by a combination of laws and customs. Married women had virtually no legal rights and were little more than chattels of their husbands for as long as their marriages lasted. They could not enter into contracts, gave up any property held on marriage and even their bodies were entirely at their husbands' disposal. The separation of the spheres had profound implications with regard to citizenship and access to the labour market. When the franchise was extended from 1832 onwards, it became a privilege associated not only with property but with a distinctive notion of masculinity – only men, primarily as heads of households, held the parliamentary franchise at the beginning of the twentieth century. Likewise, women's position in the labour market was marginalised as men, earning a breadwinners' wage, came to be seen as the quintessential workers. While men were assumed to have to support dependants – women and children – female workers frequently could not command a wage adequate to maintain themselves.

This ideology was contested and never adequately described nineteenth-century Britain. Working-class single women always had to work and wages for many working-class men were simply too low to support a family until the early twentieth century. Moreover, while working for wages was less common among middle-class single women and rare among middle-class married women until the second half of the twentieth century, this did not mean that middle-class women's lives were confined to the home. Indeed, substantial numbers were engaged in a wide range of philanthropic work, often aimed at improving the conditions of working-class women and children. The discrimination against women and their exclusion from the public sphere was continuously and extensively challenged by the so-called first wave women's movement at least since the 1860s. During the late nineteenth century these campaigns achieved considerable successes such as the expansion of female education at secondary and university level, the introduction of legislation in 1870 and 1882 protecting married women's property, the repeal of the Contagious Diseases Acts in 1883 and the expansion of female participation in local government. Despite this catalogue of achievement, women's demand for the parliamentary franchise was rejected on numerous occasions before the First World War.

The erosion of the separate spheres ideology can be traced back to the final decades of the nineteenth century, but women's claims to equal opportunity in the labour market and equal citizenship were addressed fully only during the twentieth century. Girls gradually achieved equal access to secondary education, although the education system discriminated against girls at least until the 1950s and initiatives to tackle gender inequality became central to educational policy only from the 1980s onwards. Similarly, women's presence in universities increased – if somewhat slowly – and during the final decades of the twentieth century women accounted for substantial proportions, or even a majority, of students in medicine, law or business studies. Important milestones with regard to women's role in the labour market were the lifting of marriage bars at the end of the Second World War, the introduction of equal pay in teaching and the civil service in the mid-1950s, the passage of the Equal Pay Act in 1970 (mandatory from 1975) and the Sex Discrimination Act of 1975.

These reforms were intended to end discrimination against women in the labour market, but full equality has not been achieved. The male breadwinner, female full-time housewife division of labour prevalent at the beginning of the century has been eroded, particularly with the rise of married women's employment after the Second World War. Nevertheless, gender inequalities remained entrenched in the late 1990s. Although the difference in female and male participation rates at 72 and 84 per cent respectively was smaller than ever, women still only earned about four-fifths of the male rate; men accounted for the overwhelming majority of senior staff in professions and most supervisory positions; and few men, but four out of ten women worked part-time. In sum, men were no longer the sole or even primary provider and women's contribution to household incomes increased substantially. There has been no reciprocal shift by men with regard to unpaid domestic labour and caring responsibilities and women, especially mothers working full-time, had no option but to cope with the double burden.

Women acquired the right to vote on equal terms with men during the early decades of the twentieth century. While women were finally included in a wider franchise reform in 1918, the terms of this legislation – an inevitable compromise – continued to discriminate against women in a rather peculiar manner. Although all men over 21 acquired the franchise, only women over 30 who were householders (heads of a separate household or rate payers), married to a householder, or university graduates, were allowed to vote. This reform enfranchised about two-thirds of women, but discriminated against young and single women. These distinctions based on sex were finally eliminated with the Equal Franchise Act of 1928, but in less dramatic ways women's status as second-class citizens persisted until the second half of the century. For example, until 1948 a British woman would lose her nationality on marriage to a foreigner, and women were excluded from the House of Lords until 1958.

Women were able to stand for parliament on equal terms with men since 1918, but formal equality has not resulted in equal participation. There were only a handful of female MPs and even fewer ministers after 1918, and women's share of MPs increased from about two per cent in the interwar years to about four per cent thereafter. Nevertheless, no real breakthrough occurred until the adoption of all-female shortlists by the Labour party which contributed to the election of 101 female Labour MPs and a total of 120 women in the general election of 1997. This episode illustrates the importance of positive discrimination but will not be repeated, because the policy was challenged in the courts and found to be in violation of sex discrimination legislation. A number of women achieved ministerial office after 1918 but Margaret Thatcher was unique as the only female prime minister, although her achievement was more a personal triumph than a widening of women's opportunities. Women were no longer excluded from politics and established their rights as citizens during the twentieth century, but genuine equality remained elusive.

Why Did these Changes Occur?

A number of factors contributed to this transformation in women's lives. The decline in fertility can be seen not only as a consequence of change, but also as a cause of it, in the sense that women had extra time and energy which was largely devoted to increased employment. From the end of the Second World War onwards, many married women returned to work when their children were older. This bifurcated pattern of female employment was gradually replaced by shorter periods of maternity leave and in 1997 two-thirds of professional mothers with children under five were working, mostly full-time. A second element was structural change in the economy exemplified by a decline of heavy industry – employing predominantly men – and a commensurate rise of the service sector in which women were often at an advantage. A crucial shift was the feminisation of routine clerical and administrative work and the so-called 'white blouse' revolution which began in the late nineteenth century. Domestic service declined dramatically during the Second World War and secretarial, retail and factory employment in light industries has taken its place. Women also benefited from the growth of education and welfare services which provided for the expansion of traditionally female occupations such as teaching or nursing. A further factor was Britain's membership in and closer integration with the European Union. Britain's application for membership contributed to the equal pay legislation of 1970; similarly, the Sex Discrimination Act of 1975 was partly a product of European Union requirements. From the mid-1970s onwards, European directives forced a frequently reluctant Britain to reduce gender discrimination through acts such as the strengthening of equal pay legislation in 1983 or the equalisation of retirement ages in 1992.

Nonetheless, women themselves have played a crucial role and literally millions have contributed in a variety of ways to raise women's status, expand their opportunities and generally to erode discrimination in all areas of society. Although overtly feminist organisations have often only claimed a fairly small membership, there is no doubt that the women's movement – broadly defined – was a continuous force for reform throughout the century. Since the late nineteenth century, hundreds of thousands of women have been active in a wide range of organisations from the Mothers' Union and the Women's Institutes, to the Women's Co-operative Guild, the Townswomen's Guilds, female members of political parties and affiliated women's organisations, trade unions and, finally, single-issue pressure groups. First and foremost among these were the various suffrage societies, and later examples include the Abortion Law Reform Society founded in 1936 or the cross-party Equal Pay Campaign Committee set up in 1944.

There were of course considerable differences between these organisations in terms of demands, priorities and style, but on many occasions during the twentieth century divisions coincided with broad alliances on particular issues. While the suffrage movement was deeply divided, both constitutional suffragists and militant suffragettes made a critical contribution to the final success of the women's suffrage campaign. The successors of the constitutional suffragists, renamed the National Union of Societies for Equal Citizenship, led the campaign for the equal franchise in the 1920s. A host of women-friendly reforms were introduced during the 1920s as political parties competed for the women's vote. While the women's movement during the interwar years was divided between those who prioritised egalitarian reforms and those who wanted to improve the condition of married women and mothers in the home, women from a range of organisations united in their demands for housewives' access to health care, improved maternity services and family allowances. Protests from women's campaigners ensured that family allowances were paid directly to the mother in 1944. Women acquired full access to health care after the introduction of the National Health Service in 1948. Yet again, women MPs, pressure groups and trade unions made a crucial contribution to the introduction of equal pay in the 1950s and the 1970s. The Women's Liberation Movement (WLM) of the 1970s differed from the previous generation of female activists in terms of substance and style, but it is simply wrong to suggest that the women's movement in Britain had faded away until the emergence of so-called second wave feminism. Although the WLM collapsed in the face of internal divisions at the end of the 1970s, the fact that most of the movement's core demands of 1970 – equal pay, equal education and opportunity, and free contraception – were taken for granted at the end of the twentieth century indicates the wider significance of second-wave feminism.

Throughout the twentieth century women have continuously campaigned for a better deal for women in a wide range of contexts and organisations. This campaign, and the need of political parties to appeal to female voters, has provided a crucial element in achieving the reforms detailed above. There was nothing natural or inevitable about the erosion of the separate spheres ideology and men, on the whole, have been on the defensive. Nonetheless, some men have also worked alongside women, for instance, in the suffrage campaign, and legal reforms were of course introduced by a male-dominated parliament – albeit one dependent on the women's vote.

How Should the Changes in Women's Lives Be Interpreted?

The preceding paragraphs leave little room to doubt the changes in women's status, roles and opportunities during the twentieth century. With the erosion of the separate spheres ideology, gender differences have declined, male and female roles have become increasingly fluid and ambiguous, and women have acquired greater status and power. These new-found freedoms have not been without cost in terms of increased stress and conflict exemplified, for instance in the high divorce rate. Indeed, the rapid rise in divorce rates since the 1970s, with seven out of ten decrees awarded to women in the late 1990s, could be understood as further evidence of women's greater independence since it showed that marriage was no longer the only trade open to women.

Any judgement on the impact of the twentieth century on women has to recognise, on the one hand, important elements of continuity and, on the other, the limits of change. While women's opportunities at the end of the twentieth century were more diverse than those at the beginning, many women still spent much of their lives performing unpaid caring and domestic duties or working in low-paid, low-status jobs. Class differences were also important. Middle-class women have benefited disproportionately from increased educational opportunities and access to highly-paid professional jobs, but many of these reforms have made little difference to working-class women. Moreover, the hierarchical values of the separate spheres ideology continued to be influential, illustrated for instance, by the so-called 'glass ceiling' impeding many career women who cannot reach the highest levels in their occupations, the double burden faced by working mothers – new fathers rarely experience downward occupational mobility – and the persistent double standard in sexual morality. The question whether women should be optimistic and take pride in past achievements or, more pessimistically, focus on persistent sexism and continuing disadvantages in the final analysis has no simple, conclusive answer.

According to a survey in 1995, young women (aged 18–34) supported the changes that had taken place during the previous two decades and took some pride in the achievements of women's rights activists, but most felt that

> these changes have been too slow and [they] are impatient for more changes in key areas of their lives – in attitudes to women and equal treatment at work as well as in their personal relationships. Despite this desire for change, however, they do not identify with feminists; the women's movement still suffers from an image problem with the younger generation, who see it as extreme, man-hating and separatist.

These women were concerned about the increasing 'time famine' in their lives and were looking for

> solutions to the problems of combining family and work. . . . Childcare remains the single biggest obstacle to equality. But it is not the only problem faced by working mothers. Many feel they miss out on crucial stages of their child's development and that they may be shortchanging their children.[6]

These conflicts experienced by younger women draw attention to opposing interpretations of equality which have been a recurring topic of debate within the women's movement since the late nineteenth century.

The campaign for formal equality between the sexes, promoted by liberal feminists, has been extremely influential and provided the basis for many of the legal reforms introduced during the twentieth century. However, as feminists have pointed out at least since the interwar years, this notion of equality of opportunity frequently has been of limited use to women. The right to become an MP or a barrister was of little relevance to the overwhelming majority of working-class wives and mothers working predominantly in the home. The so-called new feminists of the interwar years argued that attention should focus on housewives and mothers, even if improvements in their conditions resulted in reinforcing women's traditional roles. This dilemma of what equal rights for women actually amounted to was further complicated by notions of masculinity and femininity based on the separate spheres ideology which continued to cast long shadows. Whereas men's role as provider prevailed and, at best, a man 'helped' with domestic duties, women continued to take primary responsibility for childcare and domestic duties – regardless of employment status – because a good wife and mother still showed that she cared *about* her family by caring *for* them. At the end of the twentieth century, avoiding motherhood was one solution, and some women demanded the right to stay at home to look after their children. Such sacrifices were rarely made by men, very few chose to become so-called house-husbands and debate focused on whether men should have a right to some form of paternity leave.

These dilemmas will persist as long as gender roles remain identified with traditional notions of femininity and masculinity. A sign for optimism in the survey of young women in 1995 was that many felt that male priorities were changing, that conflicting aspirations and roles were also affecting men, and young women thought that 'men and women now need to work together for change'.[7] The history of women in the twentieth century shows that it is not sufficient for women to emulate men while, at the same time, retaining elements of traditional femininity. Without reciprocity, gender inequalities will persist – that is until men accept the need for change.

Conclusion

The history of women in twentieth-century Britain is characterised by dynamism and change, albeit change tempered by important elements of continuity. This introduction has drawn attention to the complexity of women's history and highlighted its significance to a full understanding of twentieth-century British history. The issues raised here are discussed in detail in the following chapters. The interplay of change and continuity is explored by focusing on the four key themes of the life course; paid and unpaid work; consumption, culture and transgression; as well as citizenship and the state. Emphases and interpretations are multifaceted and diverse since it would be impossible to fit the lives of over half of Britain's population in the twentieth century into one single framework.

Notes

1. For recent statistical data see *Social Focus on Women and Men* (London: HMSO, 1998); and *Social Trends* 30 (London: HMSO, 2000).

2. C. Hamilton, *Marriage as a Trade* (London, 1912), p. 14.

3. C. Pankhurst, *The Great Scourge and How to End It* (London, 1913), p. vii.

4. R. Titmuss, *Essays on 'The Welfare State'* (London, 1958), p. 91.

5. M. Stopes, *Married Love* (London, 1918); M. Stopes, *Wise Parenthood* (London, 1918).

6. H. Wilkinson, 'Truce in the War of the Sexes', *The Guardian* G2, 6 March 1995; based on research by Demos published in G. Sianne and H. Wilkinson, *Gender, Feminism and the Future* (London, 1995).

7. Ibid.

2

CHANGING THE SUBJECT: WOMEN'S HISTORY AND HISTORIOGRAPHY 1900–2000

Billie Melman

Ruminating in 1929 on the books that had not been written on women in British history, Virginia Woolf suggested that history be rewritten by the students of two women's colleges. '[W]hy not', she quizzed, 'add a supplement to history? calling it, of course, by some inconspicuous name so that women might figure there without impropriety'? Woolf's rumination, for which she had drawn on two lectures in Cambridge in October 1928 and developed into her famous essay *A Room of One's Own*, is widely cited. It is worth repeating not only because it is a classical beginning for a survey of the field of women's history, but also for her use of the term 'supplement' to describe the research and writing that would include women in 'any of the great movements which, brought together, constitute the historians' view of the past'.[1] This term, as linguists and historians have noted, is equivocal. It denotes an addition of material to the body of knowledge about the past that is relative to that body and perhaps marginal to it, but may also serve to challenge and relativise the very thing that we define as history.

The notion of the supplement may serve as a general framework to help locate women's history, as a field of study and a set of practices, in relation to modern history and to feminist politics. This is important not only for our understanding of what women's history and the history of gender have been about, but also for comprehending the development of history after 1900. What was the significance of the recovery of women as a subject of history? How did women's history relate to developments in the wider discipline? Has research and writing about women had the potential of making a difference to British history? These questions have been raised in debates, mainly among feminist historians. However, the interpretations offered have tended towards a linear description of the development of the field, according to which women's history began in the scattered efforts of individual women historians during the inter-war period, then developed towards 'politics' that is, the second wave of organised feminism accompanied by the new women's history, followed by a history of gender which studies women in relation to men and the ways in which femininity and masculinity are constructed. This last phase is either regarded as an advance for the history of women as well as for history or criticised as a retreat from feminist politics. Recently a few historians have warned against this narrative.[2] This brief survey attempts to highlight the junction of history, women's history and politics during its most dynamic periods: from 1900 to the Second World War and from the early 1970s to the present.

Early Women's History

Woolf's rumination must not be taken at face value but recognised as polemics. *A Room of One's Own* appeared during the heyday of the early or 'classical' women's history, produced by women historians inside or outside Academe, often in relation to feminist or reformist agendas. Some of these historians worked within the traditions that dominated British history: constitutional and legal history. However, it was within the emerging, relatively open and experimental fields of economic and social history with their allegiance to social policies that interest in the history of women was most developed.[3]

It is vital to stress that the idea that women had been agents in history, and therefore subjects suitable for historical research, first developed during the nineteenth century. It is equally important to stress the radical potential of this idea. Traditionally in Western thought, religion and leading modern political ideologies, women had been considered as ahistorical beings, as man's 'other', associated with nature and reproduction. Women as historical subjects were invented in the vast and varied writing of amateur female historians which during the second half of the nineteenth century ranged from histories of 'female worthies' and biographies of female monarchs, aristocrats and saints, to panoramic surveys of women in culture and society, and to travelogues. Multi-volume biographies of queens, like those produced by the yard by the sister-biographers Agnes and Elizabeth Strickland between 1830 and 1860, were accounts of female power that challenged the Victorian notion that women inhabited the private and non-political sphere. Biography however dealt with a tiny minority by no means typical of the experience of most women. It avoided direct observation and an analysis of inequalities between the genders and instead offered a 'better story' of the past that is highly nostalgic and did not analyse gender difference and hierarchies.[4]

The tradition of amateur female history did not die down with the emergence of professional women's history around the turn of the century but coexisted with, and even influenced, it. Yet professional historians broke off from the tradition in their training and relationship to what we define as 'modern' history. As developed in German universities from the 1830s and in Britain from the last quarter of the nineteenth century, history was not only a 'human science', but also a discipline or a set of practices and methods of research and writing. The stress on facts extracted from authentic documents as the basis for an 'objective' interpretation of the past marked off the new discipline from the literary tradition. True, British history was unique in that even after its pro-fessionalisation it did not develop exclusively as a scientist's craft but retained its traditional role of educating citizens, who, before 1918, by definition were ex-clusively male. Practised by historians like G.M. Trevelyan, history also retained its literary character. The trend after 1900 though was towards specialised work by professionals. Modern history was highly gendered in its selection and use of documents, privileging of subjects and even in the construction of the iden-tity of the historian. Most historians regarded constitutional and legal history and high diplomacy as particularly worthy of study, and all of these fields were related to the emergence of the nation-state from which women were excluded. Domestic and social and cultural life, in which women did figure, was deemed inferior to the affairs of the state. The identity of the professional was distinctly male. Already in 1886 the editors of the *English Historical Review*, Britain's first professional historical periodical, expressed their desire to investigate history in a 'calm and scientific spirit' and to interest 'thinking men in historical' study. As has often been noted, the new profession developed as a 'his-story' that per-ceived its practitioners as 'history men'.[5]

Yet at the same time that modern history excluded women it opened up a space for women's history and a field of opportunity for women historians. The admission of women to universities, in single-sex colleges and co-educational institutions, brought about limited access to professional training in history. Some early historians like Mary Bateson and Rose Graham concentrated on the ecclesiastical history of women. Others like Helen Maud Cam and Elizabeth Levett moved from legal history to economic history and never published pro-fessionally on women. Most of the research on women was in economic and social history, where according to Maxine Berg female production 'stands in stark contrast to their position in any time after the Second World War'.[6] This work accorded with early twentieth-century feminist interest in the condition of women, especially working-class women and in social reformism. This particular junction of history and politics may explain the main features of the explosion of writing between the 1910s and the 1930s whose subject was women as a group and the recovery of their specific experience and of their conditions of eco-nomic and social inequality. Experience was perceived first and foremost as material and was identified with work. Women's subjection was related to changes in systems of production and the division of labour wrought by the shift from a pre-capitalist economy to capitalism or to industrialisation in the second half of the eighteenth century. Alice Clark, a mature graduate student at the London School of Economics (LSE), feminist and pacifist (and later a co-director of the Clark shoe factory), saw the rise of the capitalist economy as the main reason for a deterioration in the economic position of women during the seventeenth century. Ivy Pinchbeck, another LSE graduate and later Reader in Social Studies at Bedford College, London, saw the Industrial Revolution as a disruption in the experience of working women, which nevertheless was beneficial to their economic position.

Books on, or with reference to, women's work make up the largest category in the output of the women's historians. Clark, *Working Life of Women in the Seventeenth Century* (1917), Pinchbeck, *Women Workers and the Industrial Revolution* (1930), and M. Dorothy George, *London Life in the Eighteenth Century* (1925) with its discussion of the work experience of women are classics widely in use today.[7] The focus on women's work and working-class women forms part of a general debate on the female worker who by the early twentieth century came to be the site of concerns about and criticisms of industrial society and its many problems. She was cast as the victim of industrialisation but at the same time as a social and moral problem, a danger to the working-class family and society at large. With very few exceptions, histories of the labouring classes available at the time excluded women. Early women's history did not dissociate women's work from their function as the producers of children. True, some historians adopted the maternalist stance of early twentieth-century feminism, which saw women as mothers. However, these historians denaturalised motherhood and considered it, and indeed women's work generally, as social production and not as forming part of 'nature'. The early histories expanded the definitions of work and industrialisation, making them less male-centred and less focused on factory wage-labour, as well as pointing to continuities in the work of women before and after the Industrial Revolution and to the gradual and local character of this revolution.

Women's History and History: the 1970s

The early history had no continuation. The classical writings on work were ignored by British economic and social history. The work of women historians as institution-builders in these fields was dis-remembered or trivialised. Until recently they were marginalised in the new feminist history which, it has been suggested, sought to disconnect itself from the earlier effort. Yet the two traditions share some features, not least among them the strong commitment to the study of material experience and the empiricism of social history, which I will discuss later.

The emergence of a new women's history in the late 1960s and early 1970s is related to the rise and spread throughout the Western world of an organised mass feminist movement, known as 'second-wave feminism'. One of the salient characteristics of the movement in Britain was grass-roots activism manifest in 'consciousness-raising' all-women groups, which sought to advance their own and other women's awareness of their specific experiences of marginalisation and of their separate identity. Personal experience became inseparable from the political. Indeed their overlapping was central to early feminist thinking ('the personal is political'), which refuted the nineteenth-century separation

IN FOCUS: Eileen Power (1889–1940)

The story of Eileen Edna Lepoer Power's life and her career as a historian may illustrate the gendered character of modern history during its formative decades between the wars. This story highlights the developments in economic and social history and women's history, history and feminism and of colonialism and comparative world history. Eileen Power was not a marginalised female in a male profession. She loomed large among women's historians and her contemporary practitioners of economic and social history, in which she played a major role as co-founder of the Economic History Society, founder and editor of the *Economic History Review* and, from 1934, as Chair of Economic History at the LSE. She was involved in pioneering projects such as the *Cambridge Economic History* that were the cutting edge of 'scientific' history at the time. At the same time she wrote and broadcast for wide audiences – including children. Her fame during her lifetime is comparable to that of G.M. Trevelyan, Britain's most widely read historian in the twentieth century. It was to 'the memory of Eileen Power economic and social historian' that he dedicated his *English Social History* (1942).

Her apprenticeship was different from that of men historians of her generation. It began in 1907 in Girton College, Cambridge, a female community that offered her a network of female support and connections. Upon graduation she embarked on the course of traditional training in archival research of diplomatic documents and palaeography in the *Ecole des chartes* in Paris, under the supervision of medievalist Charles-Victor Langlois, the French historian most identified with the 'scientific' and positivist tradition of history. He also, as Bonnie Smith has recently demonstrated, perceived the professional historian's craft as a masculine vocation. Significantly he assigned to Power the typical female subject, a biography of a royal woman, Isabella of France, consort of Edward II, which she abandoned upon her entry to the LSE as the holder of a women's fellowship (Shaw Fellowship). Her move to economic history was made in a women-friendly co-educational institution with a strong presence of women among both students and staff. Women trained in economic history by, among others, historian Lillian Knowles, belonged to female networks in which history and feminist Fabian politics became strongly welded in the Fabian Women's Group which had initiated historical studies of the condition of women under industrialisation.

Power's research however represents a different agenda for women's social history. *Medieval English Nunneries*, published in 1922 and establishing her reputation as a professional, was a professional's work, based on quantities of documents on female religious houses. But the book broke away from traditions of the study of women, although it retained literary strands in history. The book extracted nuns from images of female piety and spirituality and presented their everyday life in a worldly

Plate 2.2. Eileen Power in the year of her Khan Travelling Fellowship, 1920–21.
Plate 2.1. Eileen Power teaching at Girton College, 1919.

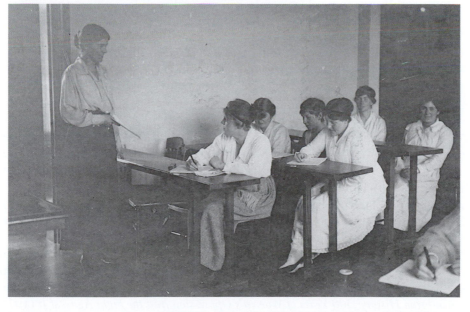

Eileen Power (1889–1940) (continued)

community, with a variety of worldly pains and pleasures like eating, dressing and sex. The book already bears the marks of her experiments with literature such as the study of character, a technique further elaborated in her popular *Medieval People* (1924), a panoramic study of social character that mixes speculation and evidence. Significantly *Nunneries* offers criticism of her male mentors, especially of Langlois and his notion of the historian as a (male) scientist and of documentary evidence as 'truth'.

Travel to South and South-East Asia as Khan Fellow in 1921 expanded Power's view on women, their status and their history. Finding an analogy between the position of medieval and contemporary Asian women, she departed from orientalist notions of the cultural 'other'. Though she 'medievalised' Asians, she did not deny them, and particularly Asian women, history. She dismissed Western notions that segregation disempowered women, stressed women's powers in Asia's nationalist movements and assigned them agency in colonial history and as authoritative interpreters of their indigenous culture. Javanese women for example were depicted in her journal as authorities on their national past. In an account on the Javanese dance of Srimpis (a military dance performed by court women) – an account that is a model of cultural relativism, Power reached the conclusion that in its female interpretation Eastern culture was superior to Western civilisation: 'I was overborne by a sense of tragic irony. We were the barbarians sitting there'. In later years she was to elaborate this early ethnographic exercise in her lecture courses and popular writing on world history and in comparative research on medieval commercial travel. In all of these she sought to redirect British history away from its national basis towards a relativist study of societies and economies. The reason for her disappearance from the history of the disciplines she practised may lie precisely in her crossing of the lines between genres, styles and subjects.

between the private and the public. Their own experience steered feminists toward investigating the historical foundation of inequality and the experiential perspective was crucial to the history produced in the 1970s. Catherine Hall, who attended the meeting of one of the first Women's Liberation Groups in Birmingham in February 1970, describes how her own work shifted from the medieval Pipe Rolls to domestic work in Victorian society as a result of her own personal and political experience.

The recovery of women developed as a 'compensatory history', seeking to amend their exclusion from the male-centred narrative. The language and metaphors of compensation are evident in key texts such as Sheila Rowbotham, *Hidden From History: 300 Years of Women's Oppression and the Fight Against It* (1973), the first crucial feminist history of the decade. Questions were formulated in a manner reminiscent of Woolf's early comment on the supplement in the narrow sense of this term, as an addition to history: 'how had women lived in the past, what had they experienced, what kinds of work had they done, in what patterns of family life had they been involved, what records had they made? How could we find out'?[8]

The 1970s have been depicted as the era of a 'herstory', a narrative cut off from the body of history, marginal and lacking organising concepts. Some critics have seen this decade as political (and therefore not professional) as well as being incubatory, leading as it were to the 'mature' women's and gender history of the 1980s. Such an approach is not very helpful because it ignores an important feature of the development of the field in Britain that marks it off from parallel ones in other Western countries, most notably the USA. British feminist history developed in relation to labour history (defined as the history of the labour movement or of social production) and to socialist-Marxist history. After the Second World War Marxist history in Britain had an authority and clout which it never exercised in the USA. The British feminist-socialist connection is evident in the commitment of feminist historians to the politics of class as well as to projects in socialist historiography like the History Workshop collective and its flagship, *History Workshop Journal*. Even more importantly, the socialist-Marxist story and interpretation of inequalities *seemed* to have offered feminist historians both subject matter and ready-made tools for theorising social difference between women and men. These historians' concentration on working-class women, sensitivity to class and use of concepts like class-struggle and the division of labour (especially in relation to capitalism) may all be attributed to Marxist influence.[9]

But the relationship between the two histories, which has been invoked in familial terms and described as a marriage, proved unhappy. In the first place, Marxist history excluded women, mainly because they could not figure significantly within its categories of class and labour or in its notion of agency, i.e. the action of individuals in history. E.P. Thompson's epochal *The Making of the British Working Class* (1963) told the story of class formation as that of the experience and emergence of the identity of working-class men. Moreover, dominant Marxist and non-Marxist labour narratives hinged on the division of labour as the primary cause for the subordination of women. Feminist historians argued that patriarchy, broadly defined as male domination in the family and society, and not capitalism, had been at the root of the subordination of women. Historians were divided on whether patriarchy was a social structure based on biological difference and cutting across societies in various times and places, or a dynamic and changing relationship. Feminist socialist historians in Britain and the USA sought to combine the category of patriarchy with an analysis of production and the division of labour and thus weld together the feminist and socialist histories and theories. In 1976 Sally Alexander and Barbara Taylor argued that the boundaries between women and men 'have been defined . . . by the capitalist mode of production as it has been made use of and strengthened the sexual division of labour and patriarchal authority'.[10] About the same time American feminist theorists attempted to develop a new analysis of patriarchy, drawing on Sigmund Freud's sexual theories, and used this analysis alongside their critique of capitalism. This 'dual system' interpretation was applied to long stretches of time at different periods to explain the ways in which class oppression and the suppression of women operated together, but since it was so generalising it was difficult to apply to actual research.

Although class and capitalism were at the centre of feminist history they were by no means its sole preoccupation. Alongside the feminist-socialist exchange there developed radical feminist historiography with a distinct agenda. This radical writing concentrated in the social sciences and engaged in topics related to female sexuality and its control: the female body, the surveillance of women's sexual behaviour and violence against them.[11] Despite the vigorousness of the debate and an impressive expansion of women's history, it had a very limited impact on history as a discipline. Both the recuperative project and the debates on theory were located in a separate space appropriated by women's historians and their female historical subjects, a space reminiscent of the Victorian 'women's sphere' which American historians in particular favoured. In the USA, where such study focused on a separate middle-class female culture, 'bonds of woman-hood' and women's empowerment, criticism of feminist history's separatism was formulated by the end of the 1970s. In Britain, with the priority given to the working class, this took a little longer. In both countries self-criticism of separatism marked the beginning of a slow, circuitous and as yet incomplete move of women's history towards mainstream history. Behind this move may be discerned the wish of historians to 'centre' their subject and use recovered materials and the emerging concept of gender to change the focus of mainstream history.

Initially gender denoted social behaviours, the relative roles of women and men and the organisation of feminine and masculine identities. It seemed to have offered historians a basis for the study of women's experience as related and relative to men's and vice versa. It also offered a category for the examination of all social relations and not just those identified with womanhood and domesticity, as explained in the editorial of the first issue of *Gender and History* in 1989, when the shift to gender was already well under way:

> we seek to examine all historical social relations from a feminist perspective to construct a comprehensive analysis of all institutions that take their gender-specific characters into account. In addressing men and masculinity as well as women and femininity, [we] will illuminate the ways in which societies have been shaped by the relationships of power between women and men.[12]

When applied to class, as in Leonore Davidoff and Catherine Hall, *Family Fortunes: Men and Women of the English Middle Class* (1987), or to the division of labour as in Sonya Rose, *Limited Livelihoods: Gender and Class in Nineteenth-Century England* (1992) gender, seen and employed as a dynamic category, proved useful for the analysis of difference and change at large.

White Women's Mythology? Gender and the Controversy Over Race

But the use of gender to denote and historically explain difference was to prove vulnerable and problematic. Until the 1980s Western historians and feminists focused on difference between women and men. 'Difference in the different', that is among women, was largely ignored. Although British feminist history was very sensitive to class it evolved around same-class binary man–woman opposites. Anglo-American feminists, who had been initiated in the feminist movement's campaigns against gender discrimination, stressed a commonality of experience and female action that implied an essentialist notion that female persons, everywhere and at all times, share a femaleness that is defined by their biological bodies and reproductive functions. Such a biological determinism led to race-blindness as well as the omission of ethnicity, nationality and religion from the discussion of gender. Moreover, the assumptions concerning commonality had clear political ramifications for feminism itself, implying that there could and should be a solidarity of women, a 'sisterhood' that could service a common struggle. This unified vision of women and of feminism drew fire from two groups of feminist critics, which came of age in two distinct historical and intellectual contexts. The first consisted of non-white feminists and feminist critics of the non-Western post-colonial world. Their work is as much a part of the process of political and cultural de-colonisation, the decline of Western hegemony in the world and the trend towards multi-racial societies as it is embedded in the feminist movement. The second group, which will be considered in the next section, consisted of historians who came under the influence of the swing, across the human sciences, away from the positivist research for objective 'truth' towards images and representations.

Non-white feminists in the West as well as non-Western feminists became alienated from the concept of sisterhood which they came to regard as exclusively white. In Britain already in the 1970s groups such as the Organisation of African and Asian Women sought to bring together women from a background that was not white. At the turn of the decade Black feminist critics contended that feminist history had been ethnocentric and white. By regarding the experience of white Englishwomen in universalist terms and applying it to women of colour and a unified entity of 'Third World' women, it had denied both these groups a history of their own. In the scathing words of British feminist Hazel Carby, British women's historians 'write their history and call it the history of women but ignore our lives . . . that is the moment in which they are acting within the relations of racism and writing history'. It is highly ironic that women's history duplicated the 'centrism' and tendency towards a universalist attitude that it had rejected in the male historical tradition. Critics of this centrism tied the exclusion from history of non-white women to British imperialism, in which women as well as men had been implicated. Interestingly ethnicity – (rather than race-) related exclusion of Scottish, Welsh and Irish women from that history was to become an issue only in the mid-1990s. 'The herstory', wrote

Valerie Amos and Prathiba Parmar, 'which white women use to trace the roots of women's oppression . . . is an imperial hisstory.' Blindness to race and ethnicity meant not only the exclusion of non-white and third world women, but also constrictions on the history of white British women. The sense of belonging to the Empire that was gender and class specific, defined both masculine and feminine identities as Catherine Hall, Antoinette Burton and myself have demonstrated. Moreover, these identities were intertwined with whiteness – as an image, discourse and set of behaviours that evolved relatively to images and perceptions of blackness which Vron Ware and Wendy Webster have explored.[13] Webster, *Imagining Home: Gender, 'Race', and National Identity 1945–64* (1996) demonstrates how white middle-class gender identities and sexualities were shaped in postwar Britain and served to define entrenched notions of Britishness. The integration of race into studies of gender, and of gender into studies of race has a great potential for the expansion and indeed revision of two fields that had developed separately.

Can Gender Kill Women as a Subject in History?
The Feminist Controversy Over Poststructuralism

An even more serious challenge to historians of gender came from feminist historians and scholars influenced by theories and methods relating to language and the production and construction of meanings in texts. This challenge was eloquently and almost simultaneously issued in two books published in 1988: Denise Riley, *'Am I That Name?' Feminism and the Category of 'Women' in History*, and Joan Wallach Scott, *Gender and the Politics of History*. Individually and together the two books fracture the categories 'women' and 'gender' and reject any sense of homogeneous female identities. Revealingly, Riley begins her book with an evocation of blackness and slavery in a reference to Sojourner Truth, an escaped slave, abolitionist and feminist who in 1851 challenged her white audience with the question 'Ain't I a woman?' which Riley follows with 'Ain't I a fluctuating identity?' This question actually sets hers and Scott's project apart from the non-white critics of feminist history who drew on differences of women's experience and identity. Riley and Scott puncture the notion that there is a retrievable experience of women and that they have a stable and definable identity. Women are 'historically, discursively constructed, and always relatively to other categories' such as the body and society.[14] Here the key terms are 'discourse' and 'construction'. They mean that we have access to women only through language that shapes the meaning of being and living as women in a particular time or place.

Of the two books it is Scott's which has received the greatest response. Probably no other single book on the concept of gender and the methodology it involves has provoked greater controversy. Her argument, and the responses of British historians to it, which illuminate notions of the relationship between a history of women, the study of gender, history and feminism, are worth elaborating on.

Clearly Scott did not invent gender as a 'useful category' in history; it had been practised by social and cultural historians by the late seventies. But she redefined it. Her definition of the term may be related to a broader shift in the very field in which Scott herself had been apprenticed: Marxist, New Left history. She had also had first-hand acquaintance with American feminist politics in the seventies and eighties. Like other social historians of her generation, she moved away from a materialist history – in her case the history of women's work and the family – and the sense that women's past is a retrievable reality that can be extracted from facts about a lived experience, towards the analysis of language and representations, known as the 'linguistic turn'.[15] In historiographical terms this turn is a revision, if not a reversal, of hierarchies in history and of the priorities of women's historians who, precisely because of their allegiance to a materialist history of class, had tended to regard language as secondary to experience and sometimes as transparent.

The turn to language was a response that cut across disciplines in the humanities to what came to be known as 'poststructuralism'. In its strictest and most helpful definition, this term describes the revision, which took place in France from the 1970s, in the theories and practices of the study of language as well as that of institutions and behaviours, and which is usually connected with the work of Michel Foucault and Jacques Derrida. Poststructuralism developed as a methodology for the reading of texts and the comprehension of their production as dynamic constructions of (often contradictory) meanings, one that rejected the previous 'structuralist' approach that had sought to unravel the structures determining linguistic behaviours. For those feminist historians who came under the influence of the new methodology, gender history meant the study of representations of women (and men) and the discourse, or knowledge, about difference between them which was constructed in a culture. History was not 'about the things that have happened to women and men and how they have related to them, instead it was about how the subjective and collective meanings of women and men as categories of identities have been constructed'.[16] Meanings, of course, include those found in the texts of feminists studied by Scott herself or by Susan Kingsley Kent in her work on British feminism and sexuality before and after the First World War. But poststructuralist feminist history has mainly had to do with the texts produced by powerful elites and institutions: economists, doctors and sexologists, the police and the state who 'constructed' the woman worker, the prostitute, the female pauper and later the female citizen, as problematic categories of difference. Language here seems to be privileged over actual women in the plural, their representation–over what they did. The past as a reality, argued Scott, was a 'linguistic event' that 'doesn't happen outside established meanings'.[17]

Response to this challenge to the assumptions and some of the basic tools in history may be summarised under four headings. First was the objection to the marginalisation of the experience of women and their place as historical agents. After all women's history had in the first place set out to study what

women do and possibly what they say. It had evolved from assumptions about
their historicity and possibilities for their action. Poststructuralist feminist study
concedes that 'experience is a subject's history' but insists that 'language is the
site of history's enactment'.[18] Second was the criticism that some of the practices
which historians had valued most were being abandoned: the search for causes
of change, the linear fashioning of narrative and the value placed on facts. The
ties between women's and social history in Britain made this objection even
stronger. Third was the concern that gender identity itself was being dissolved
into a fluctuating entity. The idea that no one can be defined by, or limited to,
a single gendered identity that is either male or female, has been put forward
by gay theorists who have argued that gender and sex are not symmetrical and
that the assumption that one's biological sex coincides with one's gender has
a heterosexual bias. Judith Butler has famously argued that there is no core
female identity and that gender is performance. Historians, including historians of lesbian identities and culture in early twentieth-century Britain such
as Martha Vicinus, have resisted this notion that women's subjectivity was constructed solely through discourse as alien to history.[19] Fourth and last, critics
have been concerned that the stress on a multiplicity of identities and difference denies women's autonomy and the possibility of feminist politics, and have
seen both as symptoms of an inherent conservatism in poststructuralism. This
apprehension went hand in hand with the political anxiety in the face of
Thatcherite policies on the family (and of the policies of Republican administrations in the USA) during the 1980s.

  Valid as each and every one of these oppositions are, the study of language
does not have to mean the surrender of experience, nor that of female agency,
to 'construction'. Recent research on gender and the two World Wars has shown
that there is space for the autonomous action of women even within and in
relation to the powerful apparatuses of the state and the law.[20] The wars were
periods in which the British state made inroads into the lives of individuals,
mobilised women and men, controlled their daily routines and their environment and subjected them to discourses of propaganda. However women, as
Penny Summerfield has demonstrated for the Second World War, could 'speak
for themselves', and sometimes robustly resisted official languages concerning femininity, work and motherhood. Indeed total modern war, one of the
hallmarks of the twentieth century and of modernity, is an exemplar of the ways
in which gender and what's seen as a 'general' history of society, the state and
the economy, may be welded together. Moreover, a gendered study of war
offers a revision of the field that had been the very stuff of traditional history:
the great dramatic event that was the scene for the ultimate action of the
nation-state. Histories of wars and of the twentieth century have for decades
excluded women, who were not soldiers. For decades feminist historiography
too had avoided the subject. Recently there has been an abundance of research
into femininity and masculinity and of male and female agency in wars that
redefines our notion of front and home, social welfare and of the very idea
of modern war that had emerged before 1914 and influenced mobilisation,

including conscription and even the organisation of the army. Nor was this a masculine experience, but rather a gendered one in which women like men had relative parts as agents.

Conclusion

This chapter has offered an outline of the history of women's history, a brief discussion of key terms it has employed and redeployed and the controversies over them – controversies that have redirected the course of study in the field. As implied in the Introduction, linear narratives of progress – from a history of women, to a feminist herstory, to social gender, to a feminist post-structuralist history, are inadequate. Equally inadequate from a historiographical point of view is the narrative of regress from a political women's history, to a 'post-feminist' and conservative study of gender. In the first place, this is the case because not all historians underwent all of these phases; and secondly because there are discontinuities between the main phases of this history as well continuities, overlapping and repetitions. One such continuity has to do with the tension between, on the one hand, the ambition of historians to decentre male history and 'centre' women and, on the other hand, the process of decentring women, propelled by the claim of different groups to be included in the new history. While the move to gender history has been driven precisely by the ambition to locate women in a 'general' history, at the same time women have become relative. This is analogous to, albeit different from, the process that occurred during the late nineteenth and early twentieth centuries, as the result of the challenge that research on women as historical subjects issued to history. Rather than being weary of this tension we should see it as a part of the dynamics of a field of research and writing. For this is the salient feature of the supplement to history suggested by Woolf – it has the potential of changing history, while itself undergoing a continual process of change.

Bibliographical Note

An accessible survey is J. Purvis, 'From "Women Worthies" to Poststructuralism? Debate and Controversy in Women's History in Britain', in Purvis (ed), *Women's History: Britain, 1850–1945* (London, 1995). C. Hall, 'Feminism and Feminist History', is an autobiographical account of the historiography, in Hall, *White, Male and Middle Class: Explorations in Feminism and History* (London, 1992). For the early historians and the relation between gender and history see B.G. Smith, *The Gender of History: Men, Women and the Practice of History* (Cambridge, MA, 1998); and B. Melman, 'Gender, History and Memory: The Invention of Women's Past in the Nineteenth and early Twentieth Centuries', *History and Memory* 5:1 (1993). On Eileen Power see M. Berg, *A Woman in History: Eileen Power 1889–1940* (Cambridge, 1996) and B. Melman, 'Under the Western Historian's Eyes: Eileen Power and the Early Feminist Encounter with Colonialism', *History Workshop Journal* 42 (1996). For women's history and class see the section on 'Gender and Class' in J. Wallach Scott, *Gender and the Politics of History* (New York, 1988) and her chapter 'Gender: A Useful Category of Historical

Analysis' together with J. Butler, *Gender Trouble: Feminism and the Subversion of Identity* (New York, 1990).

Notes

1. V. Woolf, *A Room of One's Own* (London, 1928), pp. 46–7.

2. J. Wallach Scott, 'Women's History', in P. Burke (ed), *New Perspectives on Historical Writing* (Philadelphia, PA, 1991), pp. 49–50; J. Rendall, '"Uneven Developments" in Women's History, Gender History and Feminist History in Great Britain', in K. Offen, R. Pierson and J. Rendall (eds), *Writing Women's History: International Perspectives* (London, 1991).

3. M. Berg, 'The First Women Economic Historians', *Economic History Review* 45:2 (1992), pp. 308–29; B. Melman, 'Gender, History and Memory: The Invention of Women's Past in the Nineteenth and Early Twentieth Centuries', *History and Memory* 5:1 (1993), pp. 5–45.

4. B.G. Smith, *The Gender of History: Men, Women and Historical Practice* (Cambridge, MA, 1998) for the amateur tradition, especially pp. 50–61.

5. C. Crosby, *The Ends of History Victorians and 'the Woman Question'* (London, 1991), p. 4; J.P. Kenyon, *The History Men: The Historical Profession in England Since the Renaissance* (London, 1983). For the professionalisation of history, see R. Soffer, *Discipline and Power: The University, History and the Making of English Elite 1870–1930* (Stanford, CA, 1994); A. Kadish, *Historians, Economists and Economic Historians* (London, 1983).

6. M. Berg, *A Woman in History: Eileen Power 1889–1940* (Cambridge, 1996), pp. 113–20.

7. More on their work in J. Lewis and M. Chaytor, Introduction, in A. Clark, *Working Life of Women in the Seventeenth Century* (London, 1981); Melman, 'Gender, History and Memory'.

8. C. Hall, 'Feminism and Feminist History', in Hall, *White, Male and Middle Class: Explorations in Feminism and History* (London, 1992), pp. 5–6.

9. Ibid.; A. Davin, 'Feminism and Labour History', in R. Samuel (ed), *People's History and Socialist History* (Oxford, 1981); T. Koditschek, 'The Gendering of the British Working Class', *Gender and History* 9:2 (1997), pp. 333–57.

10. S. Alexander and B. Taylor, 'Feminist History', *History Workshop Journal* (Spring 1976), p. 4. For the debate on patriarchy and capitalism, see M. Barrett, *Women's Oppression Today: The Marxist Feminist Encounter* (London, 1988); H. Hartman, 'The Unhappy Marriage of Marxism and Feminism: Toward a More Progressive Union', in L. Sargent (ed), *Women and Revolution* (Boston, MA, 1981).

11. J. Purvis, 'From "Women Worthies" to Poststructuralism? Debate and Controversy in Women's History in Britain', in Purvis (ed), *Women's History: Britain, 1850–1945* (London, 1995).

12. 'Why Gender and History', *Gender and History* 1:1 (1989), p. 1.

13. H.Z. Carby, 'White Women Listen! Black Feminism and the Boundaries of Sisterhood', in Centre for Contemporary Cultural Studies (eds), *The Empire Strikes Back: Race and Racism in 70s Britain* (London, 1982), p. 223; V. Amos and P. Parmar, 'Challenging

Imperial Feminism', *Feminist Review* 17 (Autumn 1984); Hall, *White, Male and Middle Class*; B. Melman, *Women's Orients: Englishwomen and the Middle East: Sexuality, Religion and Work*, 2nd edition (London, 1995); V. Ware, *Beyond the Pale: White Women, Racism and History* (London, 1992).

14. D. Riley, *'Am I That Name'? Feminism and the Category of 'Women' in History* (Minneapolis, MN, 1988) p. 1.

15. See T.L. McDonald (ed), *The Historic Turn in the Human Sciences* (Ann Arbor, MI, 1995); K. Canning, 'Feminist History after the Linguistic Turn: Historicizing Discourse and Experience', *Signs* 19–21 (1994), pp. 368–403.

16. J. Wallach Scott, 'Gender: A Useful Category of Historical Analysis', in Scott, *Gender and the Politics of History* (New York, 1988), p. 6; C. Weedon, *Feminist Practice and Poststructuralist Theory* (Oxford, 1987); L. Stone, 'History and Post-Modernism', *Past and Present* 113, pp. 217–18.

17. J. Wallach Scott, 'The Evidence of Experience', *Critical Inquiry* 17:3 (1991), pp. 773–97.

18. Ibid.

19. J. Butler, *Gender Trouble: Feminism and the Subversion of Identity* (New York, 1990).

20. P. Summerfield, *Reconstructing Women's Wartime Lives* (Manchester, 1998); B. Melman (ed), *Borderlines: Genders and Identities in War and Peace 1870–1930* (London, 1998), see Introduction for structure and agency during the Great War; I. Zweiniger-Bargielowska, *Austerity in Britain: Rationing, Controls and Consumption, 1939–1955* (Oxford, 2000).

Part One

THE LIFE COURSE

3

GIRLHOOD AND GROWING UP

Penny Tinkler

Typical Girls?

'Girl' is a rather slippery term variously defined by the *Oxford English Dictionary* as 'female child' or 'young woman'.[1] What it means to be a 'child' or 'woman' is, however, difficult to establish and dependent on the variables selected. Moreover, the variables are often ambiguous and contradictory in what they say about status and their relevance is frequently cross-cut by social differences such as those of class or 'race'. For the purposes of this chapter girls will be defined as females aged up to 18 years of age, although the discussion will focus specifically on girls aged between 5 and 18. Girls in the twentieth century occupied a particular space *as* girls, but were also in the process of becoming other, that is growing up into women. Girlhood, therefore, embraced a number of transitions. These included the transition from full-time schooling to full-time paid work, which had implications for girls' consumer power and status, and the socially constructed and sanctioned entrance of girls into heterosexual relationships as a prelude to marriage and motherhood. This chapter focuses on the schooling of girls and their transition from full-time education into paid work.

Histories of girls and girlhood have focused primarily on formal and informal education and popular girls' literature. Whereas this literature prioritises the female, historiographies of childhood, youth, adolescence and, more recently, the teenager have frequently presented the child, youth and adolescent as essentially masculine or as gender-neutral. Either treatment ignores the significance of the gender–age equation; age is inflected quite fundamentally by gender, and, moreover it is cross-cut by significant social differences including those of social class, 'race', ethnicity, locality, religion and sexuality.

Schooling Pre-1944

Schooling became a defining feature of girlhood over the course of the century. In 1900, full-time schooling was compulsory for all girls aged five to twelve years

Plate 3.1. Girls, *c.* 1920s.

Plate 3.2. A secondary school hockey team, Winckley Square Convent, early 1920s.

of age (although some rural school boards permitted children to leave school at ten years of age). The school leaving age was raised to fourteen in 1918, to fifteen in 1947 and to sixteen in 1972. Education beyond the compulsory school leaving age was uncommon in 1900 but in 1995 75 per cent of females remained in full-time post-compulsory education.[2] As the century progressed, girls from all social groups spent an increasing number of years in full-time education. Schooling was, however, highly variable and it prepared girls for adulthood in gender- and class-specific ways.

Prior to the Education Act of 1944, school provision consisted of elementary education for nearly all children aged between five and twelve (fourteen after 1918) and secondary education for a small minority of children from the age of eleven. Elementary schooling was at the bottom of the pyramid; it was provided by the state and it was free. Large classes predominated. In 1922, 28,000 classes in England and Wales contained 50–60 children and 5,000 had over 60 children in them.[3]

The education of most working-class girls was limited to the elementary sector. Elementary schools provided working-class girls with an education to equip them for the gender-specific work of motherhood and the care of home and family. Alongside instruction in the 3 Rs (reading, writing, arithmetic) and physical exercise, girls received compulsory education in domestic subjects such as needlework and cookery. For example, senior elementary schoolgirls in one London school in the 1930s spent two afternoons a week for two years learning cookery. Although working-class girls' education traditionally had a domestic orientation, this was intensified early in the twentieth century due to fears about the quality of the British race. These fears were prompted by the recruiting experience of the Boer War (1899–1901), in particular the high proportion of young men found to be unfit for service. An Inter-Departmental Committee of Inquiry, which was set up to investigate allegations about the 'physical deterioration' of the population, reported in 1904 that instruction in domestic subjects was being undermined by an emphasis on the 3 Rs. Following this report, teachers were reminded that girls needed a thorough training in domestic duties and that they must 'be taught "to set a high value on the housewife's position", on the grounds that national efficiency must inevitably depend upon a strong tradition of home life'.[4]

Personal testimonies reveal that the tone of instruction and academic standards varied according to individual teachers and to local traditions and conditions. Kathleen Betterton, who attended a London County Council elementary school, recalls that '[b]y the time we were half-way up the school the likely scholarship winners had been marked down, and from then on they received a quite special degree of attention'. In contrast, Winifred Foley's early education in the Forest of Dean was casual.

> As long as the pupils scraped through the low standards of learning required by the school inspector, he [the head teacher] was not much concerned with our education. . . . When he required the labour, older

pupils were sent to gather kindling wood for his home fires, sacks of bracken for his pigs' bedding, leaf-mould for his garden, and blackberries for his wife's preserves. These activities passed for nature study.

This laxity can be attributed largely to the local tradition whereby a child left school as soon as possible, girls entered domestic service while boys went down the mines. In other schools it was the bright pupils who were often offered 'privileges', which frequently meant exemption from lessons. 'Mary Smith' whose potted autobiography appeared in Pearl Jephcott's 1940s study *Girls Growing Up*, recalled that

> the teacher thought I was alright as far as History & Geography were concerned & when we used to go for these lessons she used to give me (along with three other girls) cupboards to clean, books to bind, or back, her personal writing to do, her lunch to make, & to go errands, the result was I got behind with my History & Geography while the rest of the class went ahead.[5]

While elementary schools were at the bottom of the education pyramid, secondary schooling occupied the upper sector prior to 1944. Secondary schools catered for girls up to and beyond the age of sixteen. These schools were fee-paying and they were reserved for the minority; only 14 per cent of all children obtained a secondary education prior to 1944. There were three types of secondary schooling. The first group consisted of public secondary schools that recruited most of their pupils from elementary schools at eleven years of age. The second group consisted of High Schools, Endowed Schools and large Boarding Schools, and included establishments such as the North London Collegiate School (originally established by Frances Mary Buss) and Roedean. Pupils at these schools came from diverse backgrounds including private schools and home education under a governess. The last group included Aided schools and partly or wholly municipalised Grammar schools that offered some free places to girls from elementary schools. Due to the variation in the ages at which girls were accepted into private secondary schools and the different types and standards of their primary education, the proficiency of these establishments varied greatly.

Secondary schooling was largely single-sex. Within these schools girls generally received an academic education modelled on that of the boys' public school. Grant-Aided schools, for example, offered a liberal curriculum of wide scope which included English language and literature, history, geography, mathematics, drawing, natural science, languages, games, singing and domestic subjects. Secondary schoolgirls were prepared to sit and pass the School Certificate (taken at about sixteen years of age) and the Higher School Certificate (taken at eighteen). From 1905, however, secondary schools were required to offer girls a practical training in home duties tailored to the circumstances of their own homes. In 1908, the Board of Education allowed girls over the age of fifteen to drop science in favour of domestic studies. This provision was extended in 1909 so that girls over fifteen might substitute domestic subjects for science and for mathematics other than arithmetic. Although the teaching of domestic subjects was compulsory for all girls, secondary school teachers often regarded such studies as appropriate only for less academic pupils.

Girls whose education consisted solely of elementary schooling left at fourteen; post-fourteen education was restricted to the secondary school sector. Of those working-class girls who gained access to secondary school the vast majority were the daughters of skilled manual workers, that is children from upper-working-class families. Intense competition for the limited number of places at public secondary schools clearly affected a working-class girl's chances of acquiring a secondary education. There were other factors that also impaired her prospects. Standards of elementary schooling were obviously significant as was the tone of instruction. School traditions also affected scholarship prospects and these traditions were closely correlated to social class. In Bradford, for example, only 34 per cent of schools in poor districts won scholarships compared to 75 per cent in wealthy areas.[6] Working-class girls were not only restricted by prevailing school provision, they were also hampered by the conditions in the home and family. Fatigue often impaired a girl's chances of attaining the necessary academic standard, so too did absenteeism and late school attendance. Arising from the gendered division of labour in the home, girls, rather than their brothers, assumed most responsibility for domestic chores. Moreover, for many working-class girls the role of 'caretaker' of younger siblings coexisted with that of 'schoolgirl'. These domestic commitments were seen by many education officials and teachers as impairing girls' health and their educational accomplishments. Domestic commitments were, however, frequently regarded as a valid excuse for girls' absenteeism from school. It was also common practice for girls to leave school prematurely (and illegally) to care for younger siblings.

Winning a scholarship did not necessarily mean that a working-class girl would be able to continue her education past fourteen. Parents often assumed that, if necessary, one of their daughters would leave school to help in the home. Financial constraints also prevented many working-class girls from accepting a secondary school place. Although the Free Place system was introduced in 1907 to provide free secondary education for selected able children, secondary schooling still required financial sacrifices from the family. This was partly because families had to forgo an additional wage packet if a child continued into post-compulsory education. It was also due to the many expenses incurred at secondary school; parents had to pay for their daughter's uniform, equipment, travel and items like a hymn book and church donations. The importance of maintenance grants had been recognised in 1895, but only 40 per cent of Free Place pupils received this assistance in 1919 and the value of it varied considerably between local authorities. Statistics for the period 1927–30 show that 32 per cent of annual secondary school intake left before their sixteenth birthday and presumably without a School Certificate. Personal testimonies suggest that these fifteen-year-old girls came from families who found it financially and domestically impossible to keep their daughters at school. Only a small proportion of secondary school pupils stayed on past sixteen, a few of these were upper-working-class girls who were destined to leave at seventeen for Teacher Training.

Education Post-1944

On the eve of the Second World War, education provision was clearly differentiated along the lines of social class. This parallel system of education was severely criticised for wasting potential. Following the Education Act of 1944 the education system was reorganised to provide primary schooling for all children between the ages of five and eleven and secondary education for all children over eleven in either secondary modern, secondary grammar or secondary technical schools.

The Education Act enabled a working-class girl to obtain a secondary education without having to pass a scholarship examination or having to pay fees. The 1944 Act did not make any changes to existing practices regarding maintenance grants. Subsequently the financial expenses of post-15 schooling continued to thwart the educational opportunities of many working-class girls particularly given the prevailing view that the education of girls was not as important as that of boys. Although the leaving age was raised to fifteen in 1947, the GCE examinations (which were established in 1951) could not be taken by pupils under sixteen years of age. As a result many working-class girls at secondary modern schools lost the chance of gaining GCE qualifications, so too did their working-class peers at grammar school because they often left school at the minimum age. The Robbins Report of 1963 revealed that, despite the provision of free secondary education for all, class differences in educational attainment (defined by entrance into higher education) had changed little since 1920. The report also noted that social class was a greater handicap to the education of working-class young women than to their male peers.

Preoccupation with both working-class and middle-class girls as future wives, mothers and home makers continued after the Second World War and was intensified in the immediate postwar years amidst pressures to restore prewar gender relations. Official education reports of the 1940s and 1950s repeatedly condoned the feminisation of girls' schooling even though they also acknowledged that marriage was often a break in, rather than the end of, labour market participation. Domestic subjects were presented as necessary for all girls as potential home makers. However, a differentiation was made between the academically able girl who, it was assumed, would adopt the dual role of worker and wife/mother, and the less able girl whose interests were assumed to be related mainly to herself and her future family.

Comprehensive secondary schooling was slowly introduced from 1965; by 1975, 75 per cent of secondary school children were no longer undergoing any form of selection for entry into secondary education. Social class inequalities in educational outcomes persisted. For example, a *Youth Cohort Study* of 1990 revealed significant differences in the examination results of white and

Afro-Caribbean girls from professional and manual backgrounds, although there was little difference in the performances of Asian girls from these different backgrounds. Home conditions also continued to thwart the educational performance and aspirations of working-class girls. In the late 1970s, Griffin noted that the absenteeism of Afro-Caribbean, white and Asian working-class girls was often due to housework and childcare commitments, and that this was treated less seriously than the truancy of their male peers. White middle-class girls were less likely to have domestic responsibilities due to their relatively heavy load of academic school work. Boys, she pointed out, usually did no housework. Domestic commitments also restricted girls' opportunities for continuing their education beyond sixteen. For example, 'Sandra's' hopes of further education in the 1980s were thwarted by her family's need for her to help at home.[7]

In spite of the rhetoric of equality and the wider range of curricula made available in state schools, schooling remained gender differentiated. A DES *Survey on Curricular Differences for Boys and Girls* (1975) found that formal differences in curriculum between the sexes became apparent from the age of seven years onwards. Greater differentiation occurred as pupils entered secondary school and were channelled into separate areas of the curriculum. Girls frequently took traditionally feminine subjects like cookery and feminised vocational options such as typing and shorthand; they also tended to congregate in the arts disciplines while boys gravitated towards practical, technical, mathematical and scientific subjects. Examinations taken at O and A level reflected these trends which were were also inflected by social class. The DES survey suggested that the structuring of option choice might be responsible for influencing the optional subjects taken by girls. Curricula differences had significant implications for post-school prospects; arts subjects had less occupational value relative to mathematics, the sciences and technology.

A proliferation of feminist research throughout the 1970s and 1980s offered further insights into the processes whereby schooling was gendered in unequal and discriminatory ways. It focused, for example, on sexism in children's literature; on classroom interactions; the gender differentiation of teacher expectations of pupils; the sex-typing of subjects; the differential status of female and male school teachers; and the gendering of occupations within the school. Various initiatives to challenge sex-stereotyping in the curriculum and to tackle sexism in the school environment followed from this research.

The 1980s and 1990s were also characterised by increased recognition of the heterogeneity of 'girls' arising from differences of 'race', ethnicity and religion, and by attention to differences between girls in terms of academic attainment and school experience. For example, girls (also boys) of Bangladeshi background were the most likely of all ethnic groups to leave school without any educational qualifications whereas pupils from Indian backgrounds were the least likely to leave without any qualifications. Racism, in particular, was increasingly acknowledged as a significant factor shaping the schooling of many girls. In her 1980s study Mirza noted that 33 per cent of teachers were 'overt racists'. Although the negative behaviour of teachers did not dent the positive self-esteem of the

African Caribbean girls she interviewed, Mirza found that the girls' academic energies were frequently diverted into 'the strategic avoidance of racism'.[8]

Between 1987 and 1990 considerable changes were introduced into the educational system in the form of the GCSE examination and in terms of the National Curriculum. These changes initiated a common examination for all pupils in which all levels of performance were assessed on a common scale. Although the general trend in the 1980s and1990s was for the gender entry gaps in most subjects to decrease, most subjects remained dominated either by girls or by boys. In spite of a common curriculum, gender typing continued in the 1990s with implications for academic performance and, in post-sixteen education, subject choices. At GCSE level, girls were more likely than boys to take Home Economics, Social Studies, Vocational Studies, English Literature, Modern Foreign Languages and Biology. Physics, Economics, Design and Technology (CDT) remained boy-dominated, although the gender-entry gap was decreasing in Physics and CDT. In Economics, Chemistry and Computer Studies the prevalence of boys was actually on the increase. Although, in the 1990s, girls were more likely than boys to do A levels – roughly 40 per cent of girls compared to 33 per cent of boys, girls remained concentrated in specific subject areas such as English and Modern Foreign Languages. Further, other than History, there were no major A-level subjects which were entered by equal proportions of male and female students. Reinforcing the trend apparent at GCSE level, boys predominated in A-level Mathematics and Computer Studies. During the early 1990s male dominance actually increased in Physics, Technology and Economics.[9]

The DES Survey of 1975 reopened debate about the relative merits of single-sex versus co-educational schooling. At the beginning of the century most working-class girls attended mixed-sex elementary schools, although girls and boys were often separated for part, or all, of the lessons. Secondary education, which was largely the preserve of the middle-class child, was almost invariably single sex. Seventy years later, co-education was the norm for almost all primary school children and most pupils in secondary schools. Although about a third of state secondary schools and most independent schools were still single sex in the 1970s, the number had declined significantly by the mid-1990s. In the 1990s as in the 1920s, single-sex secondary schooling remained the preserve of middle-class girls although in the 1980s they were increasingly demanded for Muslim girls. The question of whether girls perform better in single-sex as opposed to mixed-sex schools has been the subject of much controversy although it is recognised that girls in single-sex schools are more likely than their counterparts in mixed-sex schools to study traditionally masculine subjects at A level.

In many respects the education of girls changed dramatically over the course of the twentieth century. Reform of the education system and the introduction of a common curriculum for all five to sixteen year olds tackled many structural forms of gender and class inequality. Nevertheless, pockets of class privilege remained in the guise of Independent schools (also known as public, private or preparatory schools) which existed outside the maintained school system. These schools accounted for 7 per cent of UK pupils in 1991–92 drawn principally from the upper and upper-middle classes. Independent school girls enjoyed smaller classes than girls in mainstream schools (a pupil/teacher ratio of 10.6 to 1 compared to 17.1 to 1 in 1991–92) and pupils were more likely to stay on after sixteen and to do better in public examinations.[10] Forms of discrimination based on gender and class as well as 'race', ethnicity and religion also continued to characterise girls' education in the mainstream sector. Following two decades of heightened attention to girls' education, the late 1990s were characterised by a moral panic about the underachievement of boys. This panic focused attention on strategies to improve boys' academic performance. These strategies were regarded by some feminists as an obstacle to further reform and as a potential threat to some of the gains made by girls.

Transitions

The transition from full-time school to full-time paid work became an increasingly common feature of girlhood and it served as an important marker in growing up, especially for working-class girls. It is important to stress that many girls had experience of paid work prior to leaving school. For example, street trading, harvesting and paper rounds were typical schoolgirl employments in the 1920s and 1930s; and paper rounds and shop work were common in the 1980s and 1990s. Increases in the school leaving age delayed the transition to full-time paid work and those changes that followed from girls' increased economic independence. Middle-class girls, who generally remained in full-time education beyond the school leaving age, experienced this transition later than most of their working-class peers.

In 1900, most working-class girls left school at twelve and entered full-time paid work. It was common, however, for most middle- and upper-class girls to remain in the home on leaving school. The early decades of the century were, however, notable for the extension of a pattern of school followed by paid employment for the majority of girls from all social groups. Census figures show that 75 per cent of girls aged fourteen to twenty years were in the labour market in 1931. Following the raising of the school leaving age in 1947, the proportion of girls aged fifteen to nineteen in the labour market rose to 79 per cent in 1951.

On leaving school in 1921, a third of girls entered work in the textile and clothing industries and a further quarter entered domestic service. By 1951 the occupational destinations of female school leavers had changed dramatically. The most noticeable feature was the shift away from domestic service towards white-blouse work. Office work became a major employer of girls accounting for over a quarter of girl workers. Reflecting this development, employment in this sector became increasingly specialised, offering posts for typists, shorthand typists, secretaries, office machine operators, costing and estimating clerks. Working-class girls who attended elementary school invariably entered jobs that were dead-end and also short term. Secondary schoolgirls who entered the labour market at sixteen or seventeen years of age, usually for clerical or retail work, were generally not better off in terms of career opportunities than their peers from elementary schools although their jobs offered better pay and security. Only a few, mainly middle-class girls, acquired the education and training necessary for entrance into the professions where they still ranked second to their male colleagues. Although the structure of girls' employment changed drastically between 1920 and 1950, girls' options remained concentrated at the bottom of the occupational hierarchy in a narrow range of jobs.

At the end of the century, clerical and secretarial work remained 'female-dominated' and the most popular destinations for young white girls accounting for roughly 40 per cent of 20-year-olds. Personal and service occupations were also popular. Ethnographic studies from the 1970s to 1990s revealed that many young women believed that office work represented 'a nice job for a girl' and offered the possibility of a glamorous lifestyle and the prospect of promotion and success. Second-generation black women, especially working-class girls, were also attracted into office work. In contrast to their white peers, Mirza argues that black girls were attracted to this occupation by the opportunity to acquire status and career prospects. Jobs within the caring professions (nursing and social work) were, however, the most popular choice for young black women leaving school. Factories remained a significant source of girls' employment. In 1979, approximately a quarter of 16-year-old female school leavers in England and Wales entered manufacturing work; this compared to roughly half of male school leavers.[11] These young women were mainly working-class school leavers with few academic qualifications. These girls moved into a narrower range of jobs than their male peers which offered few opportunities for skilled work.

Training initiatives became increasingly significant for young girls leaving school from the late 1970s. By the 1990s, similar proportions of young men and women 'participate in Youth Training, complete their training, gain a qualification and find a job'. However, young women were more likely than men to be working towards a lower level qualification. Modern apprenticeships, like their predecessors, remained gender segregated. Girls were encouraged into traditionally feminine apprenticeships such as hairdressing, retailing, hotel and catering and also business administration. Apprenticeships in electrical installation, construction, the motor industry and engineering remained almost exclusively male.[12]

The transition from school to paid work was dramatic for most girls growing up in the first half of the twentieth century. Girls like Winifred Foley, who went into residential service in 1928, experienced a transformation both in terms of the organisation of their lives which were structured by the needs of their employer, and in terms of their new status within their families as wage earners. Rose Gamble similarly recalls of the 1920s that,

> [t]here was nothing gradual about growing up. As long as you were at school you looked like a child in short trousers and frocks, and you were treated like one, but when you left school at the end of the term after your fourteenth birthday, childhood ended. It was abrupt and final, and your life changed overnight.[13]

One way in which girls reinforced their new status was by distancing themselves from all things childish including street games and physical exercise. The street, nevertheless, remained an important site of leisure for working-class girls; over-crowded housing meant that it was rare for working-class girls to have space and privacy for leisure in their own homes. Girlfriends remained the mainstay of working girls' leisure, at least until girls started courting seriously. Dress was another important signifier of their new status as was the ability to purchase cosmetics, magazines and clothes with what remained of their wages after they had paid their 'keep'. Girls also expected to be treated differently within the home in terms of their entitlement to food.

There were, however, important continuities. Girls who lived at home were compelled to abide by parental dictates. Letters to girls' magazines indicate that this was a frequent source of tension for the young worker. The expectation that girls should undertake domestic chores and contribute to the care of siblings also continued after a girl started full-time work; boys were exempted from chores once they started full-time work. In extreme cases, where the mother was ill or had died, the eldest daughter was often expected to forgo paid employment. Girls from all social groups were bombarded with messages about the desirability of marriage and motherhood and pressures to get a boyfriend started early. Although schoolgirls often had boyfriends, 'going steady' was reserved for working girls. Middle-class girls tended to lag behind their working-class counterparts in this respect largely because of their extended schooling and the demands of homework.

IN FOCUS: Magazines for young workers in the 1920s and 1950s

Throughout the twentieth century, publishers produced a range of magazines for girls who had just left school and entered work. Young workers, also schoolgirls, were avid readers of these papers. Key to the success of these magazines was their engagement with some of the transitions which girls faced during adolescence.

In the 1920s, magazines for working-class and lower-middle-class girls commonly described their readers as 'business girls'. Typical magazines, for example *Girls' Favourite* and *Girls' Friend*, encouraged their readers to think seriously about paid employment and they offered advice on choosing a suitable job, usually office or shop work. Articles proferred guidance on how to behave in the workplace. For example, in 'Success as a Secretary', girls were firmly told that success was not reliant on a terrific speed at shorthand and typing. Accuracy, method and neatness were described as far more important. Moreover, aspiring young secretaries were advised to '[f]ind out the ways of your employer. . . . He may have little fads and fancies, such as having his blotter, pens and pencils put out on his desk ready for him when he arrives in the morning' (*Girls' Favourite*, 10 June

Plate 3.3. Cover page of *Valentine*, a teenage girls' magazine, 1957.

Magazines for young workers in the 1920s and 1950s (continued)

1922). As this quote suggests, the sexual division of labour and status in the workplace was taken for granted. Office dress was also discussed: 'Never adopt fluffy frocks or your employer may think your mind is on par with your dress' (*Girls' Favourite*, 1 April 1922).

One of the implications of readers' new-found status as paid workers was their increased economic independence. While it was the norm to pay 'keep' once earning, young workers usually had some pocket money or 'spends', although this was highly variable. Girls' magazines set themselves up as consumer guides. Articles addressed all aspects of a girls' wardrobe and encouraged girls to foster 'an eye for detail'. Correspondence editors also addressed girls' queries about how much 'keep' they should pay. They also advised on whether girls were being treated fairly by their parents now that they were contributing to the family purse. Relationships, however, constituted the main area in which girls' magazines offered advice. Indeed, much advice on paid work was tailored to the task of attracting suitable men or of equipping girls with the skills and understanding necessary to be good wives. Readers were given detailed guidance on how to manage heterosexual relationships as a prelude to marriage. This was seen as particularly crucial in the light of more relaxed courtship practices whereby a young woman did not need to be engaged before she could spend time alone with a boy.

In the 1950s, papers for young working girls or 'teenagers' continued to present finding a boyfriend as a major feminine activity once a girl had left school, and one for which readers required advice and encouragement. Whereas the workplace had been portrayed as an important site for meeting boys in the 1920s, leisure venues and social activities were popular settings in magazines of the 1950s. Indeed, leisure and consumption emerged as defining features of the young worker in magazines of the 1950s. Preoccupation with the consumer power of young workers was particularly evident in the proliferation of small adverts selling a range of products, especially clothes, records and record players, jewellery and cosmetics; it was also apparent in the appearance of a range of credit options. Visual representations of the teenager and her lifestyle offered graphic display of youthful female consumption, and stories typically portrayed girls in the most up-to-date of fashions while dancing or listening to music on the radio or record player. The combination of consumption and heterosexual romance as key to the identity of young women is clearly conveyed in the following editorial.

The keynotes of VALENTINE are Romance . . . Youth . . . Excitement! Romance which lies deep in the heart of every girl. Youth which makes her fresh and lovely – glad to be alive and to be loved. Excitement which comes from the thrill of music, dancing and song. (*Valentine*, 19 January 1957)

The significance of leaving school remained fairly constant throughout the century. As Leonard noted of young women in the 1970s, once they left school they abandoned all things that they perceived as childish and as unfeminine, for example youth clubs and other activities that did not facilitate finding a boyfriend. Commencing waged work also served to exempt many girls from some, but not all, of the domestic commitments that had characterised their school years. As with their counterparts earlier in the century, girls of the late twentieth century, especially white working-class girls, experienced an intensification of pressures to find a boyfriend and to drop girlfriends once they left school. For young workers, the types of leisure that they wished to pursue were increasingly dependent on male company. Asian and Afro-Caribbean girls tended not to experience pressures to get a boyfriend in the same way as many of their white peers and they were more likely to retain female friendships throughout their teens.[14]

During the 1980s the transition from school to paid work was disrupted. The number of young people going straight into employment at sixteen was 53 per cent in 1976 but only 15 per cent in 1986. Youth unemployment rose from 7 per cent of sixteen-year-olds in 1976 to 12 per cent in 1986: the transition from school to work had become, for many, a move from 'the classroom to the dole queue'. Increased unemployment exacerbated other forms of disadvantage. School leavers with no formal qualifications were most likely to be unemployed. Black school leavers were twice as likely as their white counterparts to go 'on the dole'. Young women with disabilities were also additionally disadvantaged. Youth training (introduced in 1978) increasingly mediated the transition of girls into the labour market; it absorbed a quarter of sixteen-year-olds in 1986. The decline of the youth labour market in the 1980s, rising unemployment and the increase in post-compulsory educational participation, meant that transitions from school to work became much more complex and protracted in the 1980s and 1990s. According to some sociologists, the lives of young people across the social classes were characterised by risks and uncertainties that were not part of day-to-day life for previous generations. The implications of these trends for girls growing up in the 1990s are still unclear.[15]

Conclusion

During the twentieth century key aspects of girlhood tended increasingly towards standardisation. The progressive raising of the school leaving age and the restructuring of education to provide primary and secondary schooling for all young people were particularly significant. Nevertheless, schooling was profoundly shaped by gender and social class, as well as by 'race', ethnicity, disability, religion, sexuality and locality. Although many structural forms of inequality and discrimination relating to gender, social class, 'race' and ethnicity, were removed in the second half of the century, inequalities persisted; these were often more subtle in form, although not insignificant. The transition from school to paid work (albeit temporary in many cases) also became established as a standard feature of growing up in the twentieth century. Trajectories through adolescence continued, however, to be significantly shaped by social differences. The transitions which had characterised adolescence for most of the twentieth century were, however, disrupted in the closing decades of the century. The paths girls took through adolescence became increasingly diverse and, for many, uncertain. Nevertheless, at the end of the century forms of post-compulsory education and training were increasingly the norm for girls from all social backgrounds.

Bibliographical Note

Carol Dyhouse, *Girls Growing Up in Late Victorian and Edwardian England* (London, 1981) provides an excellent account of the formal and informal education of middle-class and working-class girls early in the century. Anna Davin, *Growing Up Poor: Home, School and Street in London 1870–1914* (London, 1996) and the chapter on growing up in Elizabeth Roberts, *A Woman's Place: An Oral History of Working-Class Women, 1890–1940* (Oxford, 1984) offer insights into working-class girlhood in London and Lancashire respectively. The education of second-ary school girls is discussed by Penny Summerfield in 'Cultural Reproduction in the Educa-tion of Girls: A Study of Girls' Secondary Schooling in Two Lancashire Towns, 1900–1950', in F. Hunt (ed), *Lessons For Life: The Schooling of Girls and Women, 1850–1950* (Oxford, 1987). The education experiences of Welsh girls are explored in W. Gareth Evans, 'The Gendering of the Elementary and Secondary School Curriculum in Victorian and Early Twentieth-Century Wales', and G. Goode and S. Delamont, 'The Voice of the Lost Grammar School Girls of the Interwar Years', in S. Betts (ed), *Our Daughters' Land* (Cardiff, 1996). *Constructing Girlhood: Popular Magazines for Girls Growing Up in England, 1920–1950* (London, 1995) by Penny Tinkler provides a useful historical context chapter for 1920–50 as well as discussion of representations of girlhood. Education and home in the interwar years are also discussed by Deirdre Beddoe, *Back To Home and Duty: Women Between the Wars 1918–1939* (London, 1989). There are no histories of girlhood for the period 1950–70 although helpful historical overviews of girls' schooling in these decades are provided by Rosemary Deem, *Women and Schooling* (London, 1978) and by Madeleine Arnot, 'State Education Policy and Girls' Educational Experiences', in V. Beechey and E. Whitelegg (eds), *Women In Britain Today* (Milton Keynes, 1986). Notable studies of girls growing up in the late twentieth century include Christine Griffin, *Typical Girls? Young Women from School to the Job Market* (London, 1985) and, more recently, Heidi Safia Mirza's study of Afro-Caribbean girls, *Young, Female and Black* (London, 1992), and Kaye Haw, *Educating Muslim Girls: Shifting Discourses* (Buckingham, 1998).

Notes

1. The discussion focuses on England and Wales, since limitations of space make it imposs-ible to incorporate the different educational experience of girls growing up in Scotland. Useful sources on Scottish education include M. Walter Humes and Hamish M. Paterson (eds), *Scottish Culture and Education, 1800–1980* (Edinburgh, 1983); E. Turner, S. Riddell and S. Brown, *Gender Equality in Scottish Schools: The Impact of Recent Educational Reforms* (Glasgow, 1995).

2. M. Arnot *et al.*, *Recent Research on Gender and Educational Performance* (London, 1998), p. 17.

3. D. Beddoe, *Back To Home and Duty: Women Between the Wars, 1918–1939* (London, 1989), p. 35.

4. C. Dyhouse, *Girls Growing Up in Late Victorian and Edwardian England* (London, 1981), p. 94.

5. K. Betterton, 'White Pinnies, Black Aprons', in J. Burnett (ed), *Destiny Obscure: Autobiographies of Childhood, Education and Family from the 1820s to the 1920s* (London, 1994), p. 209; W. Foley, *A Child in the Forest* (London, 1977), p. 48; P. Jephcott, *Girls Growing Up* (London, 1942), p. 16.

6. K. Lindsay, *Social Progress and Educational Waste: Being a Study of the 'Free Place' and Scholarship Systems* (London, 1926), p. 8.

7. R. Deem, *Women and Schooling* (London, 1978), p. 62; Arnot, *Recent Research*, p. 70; C. Griffin, *Typical Girls? Young Women From School to the Job Market* (London, 1985), ch. 3.

8. D. Gillborn, 'Young, Black and Failed by School: The Market, Education Reform and Black Students', *International Journal of Inclusive Education* 1, 1 (1997), p. 13, cited in Arnot, *Recent Research*, p. 71; H.S. Mirza, *Young, Female and Black* (London, 1992), ch. 4, esp. pp. 57, 83.

9. Arnot, *Recent Research*, ch. 1.

10. D. MacKinnon and J. Statham, *Education in the UK: Facts & Figures* (London, 1996), pp. 184, 82–3.

11. Arnot, *Recent Research*, p. 66; Mirza, *Young, Female and Black*, ch. 5; Griffin, *Typical Girls?*, p. 135.

12. Equal Opportunities Commission, *Gender and Differential Achievement in Education and Training: A Research Review* (1999), pp. 4–5.

13. R. Gamble, *Chelsea Child* (London, 1982), p. 122.

14. D. Leonard, *Sex and Generation: A Study of Courtship and Weddings* (London, 1980), p. 88; Griffin, *Typical Girls?*, p. 62.

15. G. Jones and C. Wallace, *Youth, Family and Citizenship* (Buckingham, 1992), ch. 2, esp. pp. 25, 38–9.

4

SEXUALITY

Lesley A. Hall

'I have never met the normal woman', British feminist socialist sex-radical Stella Browne informed the 1937 Birkett committee on induced abortion. There is no normal woman and thus no single story about women's sexuality in twentieth-century Britain. This chapter paints a very general picture of some of the principal issues. The focus is on three main themes: sexual ignorance, women's own creation of sexual knowledge, and challenges to the marital heterosexual paradigm within which female sexuality was constructed. Knowledge is very incomplete. This is an area in which historical investigation is subject to particular difficulties, due to the privacy and sensitivity of the topic, and the differences between what is said or written and actual behaviour and experience. Finally, much research which can or could be done still remains to be undertaken.

Background

In 1900 Victorian sexual attitudes were still firmly in place, and behaviour, on the whole, followed suit (the illegitimacy rate in Britain was notably low). The double standard of sexual morality still reigned: sexual peccadilloes by the male were excusable, but far more serious in women. A man could divorce his wife for a single act of adultery, but even persistent adultery by a husband did not qualify a woman for a divorce unless combined with another matrimonial offence. Men allegedly 'annoyed' by prostitutes were never asked to support police testimony in court, whereas women pestered by men in the streets had little recourse. Female sexual desire was perceived as essentially responsive to the male rather than occurring independently: in 1929 a question about sexual feelings in a questionnaire on menstruation was considered inappropriate and shocking for single respondents (as 'sexual feelings were abnormal in unmarried women').[1]

Permissible sex for women was closely circumscribed by marriage, and of course motherhood, with some exceptions. Among the upper classes a certain amount of discreet adultery was accepted, for women who had already provided heirs, provided liaisons took place within the same social circle. In politically and socially progressive circles there was also a certain amount of licence and unconventionality, though sexual experimentation was not necessarily approved. The 'free love' debates within late-nineteenth socialist and freethinking groups, though horrifying to the conventional, were about committed monogamous unions rejecting the intervention of church and state. Far from being sexually unconventional, they were usually models of bourgeois respectability. The famous free union between middle-class socialist Edith Lanchester and her working-class comrade James Sullivan (which led Edith's family to attempt to incarcerate her in a lunatic asylum), was a model of stifling lower middle-class propriety.[2]

'Why, doctor? What is there to enjoy?'

At the beginning of the twentieth century women indicated sexual respectability not only by chaste conduct but by ignorance of matters sexual. Sex within marriage was, in theory, for mutual enjoyment: marriage advice literature cautioned husbands against 'excessive' indulgence, while assuming that, providing a wife was not traumatised by careless brutality during the honeymoon, sex would form a 'natural' pleasure within wedlock. Given the ignorance in which the overwhelming majority of girls of all social classes were brought up, it did not require thoughtless callousness on the husband's part for the wedding night to come as a dreadful shock.

Feminists in the social purity movement urged the sexual enlightenment of young people. However, in the case of girls even very circumscribed warnings, hygienic advice, and extremely elementary biological instruction were regarded as dangerous and contaminating. Formal sex education was in any case the exception. Some schools tentatively introduced it, sometimes with disastrous consequences, as in the case of Miss Outram, schoolmistress at Dronfield in Derbyshire, whose communication of rather innocuous biological information to her senior girl pupils aroused immense local furore. Theodora Bonwick, however, had considerable success as headmistress of an elementary school in Hackney, largely because of her well-thought-out 'outreach' policy towards local parents. However, the London County Council Education Committee found hers the only at all satisfactory scheme in the entire education authority area and effectively outlawed sex education.[3]

Well into the interwar years women of all classes reported marrying 'with the vaguest idea' as to what conjugal relations consisted of, and even going into labour without knowing where and how the baby would emerge. Mothers seldom enlightened their daughters, either giving obscure warnings, or else failing to supply any information at all, in many cases doubtless out of ignorance and shyness rather than malice. Class and educational level made little difference to this pervasive fog of ignorance. Rural Lincolnshire women reported women running home after the wedding night because husbands 'tried to do something terrible', or asking the vicar to 'unwed' them because of a husband's attempt at 'something very rude'. But a former teacher, aged 30, also found her 'first few days of married life a nightmare', and the daughter of a scientist was ignorant on 'matters of sex and birth'.[4]

While this level of ignorance dissipated to some extent as the century drew on, considerable lack of understanding of female sexuality and response continued. Many women had no idea that sex was anything but a duty to be undergone for their husbands' benefit. The disgust some women felt at conjugal relations was recounted by Leonora Eyles in *The Woman in the Little House* (1923): several women told her that 'I shouldn't mind married life so much if it wasn't for bedtime', and one was 'blooming glad the old Kayser went potty'. In the survey published as *Patterns of Marriage: A Study of Marriage Relationships in the Urban Working Classes* (1951) Eliot Slater and Moya Woodside found a pervasive view among the women was summed up in the remark 'he's very good, he doesn't bother me much'. Helena Wright wrote, in *More About the Sex Factor in Marriage* (1947), about the woman who, when asked at Family Planning clinics about the happiness or otherwise of her sex life 'looks quite blank and says nothing. The question is repeated. She realises that *something* is meant and asks "Why, doctor? *What is there to enjoy?*".'[5]

By the 1950s women were more aware that sex was meant to be pleasurable for both participants, but many still failed to achieve orgasm or much enjoyment. Investigators reported on their sense of a failure of communication when asking questions about sexual pleasure and orgasm. Helena Wright, in *More About the Sex Factor*, argued, on the basis of years of clinical experience, that women might sometimes experience some pleasure from stimulation of erogenous zones, without ever achieving orgasm. She attributed this to two main factors: a lack of appreciation of the importance of clitoral stimulation, and unexamined assumptions that the male sexual model, i.e. the achievement of satisfaction through penis–vagina penetration, would also be satisfactory for women.

Girls more frequently than boys received some formal sex education in school over several decades: however, this often concentrated on menstrual hygiene and where babies come from. The desire to prevent teenage pregnancy and sexually transmitted diseases (from AIDS to the less lethal but far more prevalent chlamydia) led to demands for and initiatives on sex education, but these were frequently stymied by 'moral panics' claiming that it will 'put ideas into children's heads' and encourage early sexual experimentation (ignoring unavoidable exposure to sex in the media). An article in the *Guardian* in 1999 suggested that sexual ignorance had not vanished in the sexually knowledgeable nineties, that for young women early sexual relationships were about 'feeling valued, loved, popular, part of the gang' rather than sexual pleasure. The majority of sex education books still ignored the clitoris and female orgasm.[6]

Women Exploring Sexuality

From the middle of the nineteenth century women resisted the attempts to keep them ignorant. Campaigns such as that to repeal the Contagious Diseases Acts enabled them to articulate critiques of male-dominated assumptions about social and sexual arrangements which oppressed women. Initially these focused around dangers associated with sexuality: arguments for the sexual enlightenment of the young were motivated by a desire to provide girls with knowledge of potential perils in place of ignorance.

Venereal diseases formed a potent metaphor for the unsuspected dangers which menaced apparently protected young women. In 'New Woman' fiction such as Sarah Grand's *The Heavenly Twins* (1893), Emma Brooke's *A Superfluous Woman* (1894) and the short stories of 'George Egerton', the theme of maritally communicated syphilis was used to critique conventional marriage, class and gender attitudes, as it blighted not only female characters' own lives but those of their children. Given increasing emphasis on the importance of motherhood to the nation and its well-being in the new century, women pointed out that women were rendered infertile or bore sickly children as a consequence of male vice, deploying medical, scientific and sociological information to demonstrate that men's insistence on extramarital sex was ruining the nation. Louisa Martindale brought the authority of a doctor as well as a suffragist to her work, *Under the Surface* (1908). She argued that venereal diseases, as the outcome of prostitution, resulted from the existing male-dominated social system. The solution was 'THE EMANCIPATION OF WOMEN'. Cicely Hamilton, actress, writer and member of the Women's Freedom League, in *Marriage as a Trade* (1909), argued that the perils of venereal infection were 'sedulously concealed' as one of the occupational risks of marriage. The subject was also alluded to in suffrage journals. Christabel Pankhurst in her famous volume *The Great Scourge* (1913) promoted 'Votes for women, and chastity for men' as the panacea for the disease which was vitiating the nation's fitness, claiming that the vast majority of men had one or another form of venereal disease. Frances Swiney in a number of publications depicted masculinity and male bodily fluids as themselves innately biologically toxic.

Not all women were happy with the simple inversion of the existing meanings of syphilis by attributing it to immoral men rather than immoral women. The idea that venereal diseases symptomatised wider imbalances and disorders in the social and sexual economy were advanced by women involved with the sex reform movement which grew up in the early twentieth century, endeavouring the difficult task of turning a rational and scientific gaze upon sexual phenomena. This generated a rather different slant to women's discussions about sexuality. In 1912 Dora Marsden founded a journal, *The Freewoman*, famous for 'its unblushingness. . . . [It] mentioned sex loudly and clearly and repeatedly, and in the worst possible taste.' It provided a space for articles and correspondence on a range of sexually related topics, most famously perhaps the debate on women and chastity (innate or acquired). During this debate Stella Browne put forward the argument, not only that women were capable of sexual pleasure, but that this was a good thing, and that the constraints on achieving it which society placed on women often had an adverse effect on their wellbeing, physical, mental and emotional. She did not, however, advocate all women plunging into a mad orgy of sexual indulgence, considering the sexual impulse in women to vary greatly both from woman to woman and within any individual woman at different times.[7]

Such ideas were becoming increasingly debated – if not necessarily put into practice – by a progressive vanguard of women. A number of women (including Stella Browne and Cicely Hamilton) were active in the British Society for the Study of Sex Psychology (founded 1914), and male suffragist Laurence Housman commended the contribution that women made to discussions of sensitive sexual topics. It was not until 1918, however, that such ideas became part of the mainstream, with the publication of Marie Stopes's path-breaking marriage advice manual, *Married Love*.

IN FOCUS: Marie Stopes (1880–1958)

Marie Stopes illuminates a number of issues discussed in this chapter. A distinguished scientist, one of the first women lecturers in science at a British university, who wrote several books and made expeditions to Japan and Canada, she declared after three years of marriage that she had only discovered herself to be still a virgin by a course of research in the scientific literature on sexology. While recent historians have been cautious about accepting this statement at face value, her story was clearly convincing to the court which granted her a decree of nullity, dissolving her marriage on the grounds of her husband's failure to consummate it. It was quite plausible for an educated woman (perhaps particularly an educated, middle-class woman) to be completely ignorant of the nature of the sexual act and where babies came from. While Stopes (and her husband, like her a botanist) knew a great deal about the reproduction of plants, knowledge of stamens and pistils, often recommended as a safe introduction to sexual reproduction for young people, did not necessarily help in understanding penises and vaginas.

While many women would have put this experience behind them, letting it remain in privatised secrecy, Stopes decided that 'knowledge gained at such a cost' should be made available for the public benefit. She therefore completed a book, which, after many difficulties in finding a publisher, was published under the title *Married Love* by the small firm of Fifield in 1918, with a contribution of £200 from Humphrey Verdon Roe, soon to become Stopes's second husband.

Married Love was a passionate plea for the recognition both of women's right to sexual pleasure (within marriage, naturally), and the differences between women's desires and those of men. Stopes emphasised the need

Marie Stopes (1880–1958) (continued)

Plate 4.1. Marie Stopes leaving the Law Courts, 1923, during her libel case against Halliday Sutherland. Although the verdict in this case and subsequent appeals were inconclusive, the proceedings were widely reported and gained valuable publicity for Stopes herself and the birth-control movement.

for a woman to be aroused as a preliminary to intercourse, and for satisfactory orgasm for both parties. She also propounded the somewhat more controversial theory that women were subject to 'sex-tides' related to the menstrual cycle, and that the apparent 'contrariety' of women was due to this fluctuation of their desires. 'Nature' and 'the natural' played an important part in Stopes's rhetoric. While making a powerful case for women as desiring sexual subjects, Stopes was careful not to violate too greatly current gender-role expectations – *Married Love* depicted women as alluring nymphs, 'always escaping'.

The book became a runaway best-seller, selling half-a-million copies by 1925 and, as copies were often circulated among family and friends, was doubtless seen by many more. It generated a huge amount of

Marie Stopes (1880–1958) (continued)

correspondence for Stopes, which still survives. Apart from giving women (and men) previously unknown information about sex, Stopes also provided them with a language for talking about their experiences and desires. She appears at her best and most sympathetic in her responses to these letters, carbon copies of which have been preserved in many cases. Although the ever-increasing amount of correspondence meant that she had resort to form letters and secretarial assistance, she continued to add personalised postscripts as well as responding at length in cases she found particularly interesting.

Heterosexuality as a beautiful, 'natural' relationship (even if one which needed working at) was at the core of Stopes's work. Prior to her marriage she had several relationships of a romantic and emotional nature with other women. However, by the time she came to write *Enduring Passion* (1928) she was implacably hostile to lesbianism, even though conceding that some women were by nature 'congenital inverts'. However, women whose husbands failed to provide them with satisfying intercourse, she claimed, were in danger of being lured into 'homosexual vice' which might soothe 'surface nervous excitement' but could not supply the profound gratifications of penetration and what Stopes believed to be the physiological benefits of semen.

Stopes is perhaps best known as an advocate for birth control, which she saw as an essential part of the erotically satisfying marriage, which could not co-exist with constant fear of unwanted pregnancy. Her eugenic views are often mentioned, but the rhetoric deployed in public arguments played remarkably little part in the practice of the birth control clinics established by Stopes, and her response to readers anxious about questions of 'breeding' was also sympathetic. Her eugenic views are often illustrated by her vitriolic assertion that her son's intended wife, who was myopic, was genetically inferior, but this has to be read in the context of her relationship with her son and her emotional response to his marriage.

As with several other writers whose work was positioned as strengthening to marriage, Stopes's own marital and emotional life was not the most shining exemplar of conjugal stability. Not only did her first marriage end in annulment, sexual problems developed in her second (possibly the delayed result of Humphrey Verdon Roe's war injuries) and a letter is extant in which Roe conceded to Stopes the right to take another lover. She had a number of relationships with younger men, although these could have been intense *amitiés amoureuses* rather than consummated liaisons.

While (and largely as a result of her path-breaking work) other authorities came to supplement and supersede *Married Love*, this, and other books of hers, continued in print until well after her death, and she continued to take an active editorial interest in reissues.

Married Love and subsequent books by Stopes and others which followed, took ideas generated within the sex reform milieu, based on the writings of sexologists such as Havelock Ellis and Edward Carpenter, and made them acceptable to a wider audience by locating them within the conventionally acceptable framework of marriage. Assertions of the possibility and desirability of female sexual pleasure, and increasingly explicit instructions as to how this might be achieved, were presented as contributions towards the preservation of the stability of marriage (and thus of society as a whole). It has been argued, principally by Sheila Jeffreys and Margaret Jackson, that during the 1920s a radical feminist critique of the patriarchal sexual institutions of society was defused by a new emphasis on the desirability, even necessity, of sexual fulfilment to women, based on the male-biased agenda of sexology. While these arguments have drawn attention to an important area for study, and have usefully generated debate and further research, they assume simplistic influences by (often rather inaccessible) texts on behaviour, and tend to neglect the wider social context which militated against the implementation of feminist reforms even after the (limited) grant of the suffrage in 1918. There is also a tendency to depict women of the earlier part of the century as wide-eyed naive dupes of conniving male 'experts', rather than feisty women who were doing their best to advance the understanding of sexuality from a woman's perspective in spite of the paucity of adequate tools and appropriate vocabulary.[8]

The resistance of women to prevalent male constructs of female sexuality can be seen in the slightly later writings of Helena Wright and Joan Malleson. Both were women doctors involved with the family planning movement, and both realised that women needed more than merely protection against unwanted pregnancy for sex within marriage to become more than something between a boring duty and a nightmare of pain and revulsion. In *The Sex Factor in Marriage* (1930) and *More About the Sex Factor in Marriage* (1947), Wright placed supreme importance on the role of the clitoris in female arousal and satisfaction. Writing during a period when it is often assumed that Freudian concepts of the supremacy of the 'vaginal orgasm' and the immaturity and general undesirability of the clitoral version were paramount (something probably anyway much truer of North America than the United Kingdom) Wright was adamant that a male penis-in-vagina model of intercourse, though it satisfied male needs, was not adequate for many women. She strongly advocated women familiarising themselves with their clitorises and finding out the best ways of stimulating them. While presented within a framework of heterosexual marriage this was still a profoundly radical approach. Malleson was perhaps less radical than Wright: in *Any Wife or Any Husband* (1950), published under the pseudonym 'Medica', she appeared to believe in the existence of the vaginal orgasm, while conceding that the most common complaint she came across among women was 'vaginal anaesthesia'. She strongly argued that women who were unable to achieve this Holy Grail would obtain a high degree of satisfaction from clitoral orgasm and that this was infinitely preferable to striving after an unobtainable ideal. Women doctors connected with the family planning movement were also instrumental in initiating the first British advances in sex therapy (some while before the work of Masters and Johnson in the USA).[9]

Meanwhile, individual women were increasingly experimenting with their own sexuality. From the 1920s women, if seldom going 'the whole way' (although this was not infrequent among couples intending marriage), were engaging in various non-coital activities ('petting'). By the 1950s sex advice literature was full of cautions about this practice, warning both of a 'slippery slope' ending in full intercourse with the risk of pregnancy, and various adverse physical and emotional outcomes from petting itself. Some women did have affairs. By the late 1950s the rise in illegitimate pregnancies and in venereal infections among young people indicated an increase in young women engaging in sexual experimentation, not necessarily with men they intended to marry, even before the advent of the Pill in the early 1960s and the 1967 Abortion Act. But until the 1970s marriage remained the central factor in female sexuality. Premarital sex was justified or condemned by relating it to the success or failure of subsequent marriage: whether 'petting' was alleged to spoil women's taste for full intercourse, or some experimentation argued to contribute to later marital stability, marriage and institutionalised heterosexuality were the criteria of judgement.

Following the so-called 'Sexual Revolution' of the late sixties, a dichotomy soon appeared between 'the liberated woman' – 'Cosmo' girl, a media image of unfettered female sexuality – and 'Women's Liberation'. The second wave of feminism soon generated critiques of male-defined models of sexuality, and queried the power-relationships embodied in heterosexual relations. Many argued for shunning heterosexuality completely, while others suggested that it was permissible if penetration was eschewed. Feminist debates on the possibility of a woman-friendly heterosexuality were occluded by feelings that lesbianism or celibacy were the genuine feminist choices. In spite of feminist literature, such as *Our Bodies Ourselves*, aimed at helping women explore their sexuality, these doubts and often heated debates fed into preconceptions about feminist 'puritanism'.

Meanwhile, increasingly explicit sexual information became available via magazines and a growing range of self-help manuals. The idea that women might be interested in improving their sex lives encouraged the commercial development of 'Ann Summers' parties where women could purchase sex toys in the privacy of their homes and the re-marketing of sex-shops as woman-friendly spaces. However, are women exploring their own sexuality, or have they simply become consumers of the products of the sexualised market-place? The contributions such sources may make to improving the lives of individual women nonetheless should not be ignored.

Beyond Phallocentric Marriage

Sexual activity did, of course, occur outside marriage. Though illegitimacy in Britain was low until the 1960s, a substantial proportion of brides were pregnant on their wedding day, from the 1930s at least. A survey of blood groups in one town revealed incidentally that a significant percentage of children were not the offspring of their purported fathers. An early 1950s survey found 40 per cent of respondents had had an extramarital liaison.[10] Some women did have affairs not meant to lead to, or substitute for, marriage, in spite of the difficulties conducting such relationships faced prior to the late 1960s: losing sexual reputation was not merely a social embarrassment, it could affect continued employment or accommodation.

Stella Browne suggested, during the *Freewoman* chastity debate, that many apparently chaste women were indulging in masturbation. She did not share contemporary stigmatising attitudes to the practice, seeing it as an inevitable, even desirable, element of sexual life. Marie Stopes, though she did not go so far in print, reassured the occasional mature unmarried woman that infrequent masturbation might be good for the nerves. The whole subject was less highly charged than male masturbation, about which Stopes received large numbers of anxious letters, while very few from women expressed equivalent concern. Given prevailing concepts of female sexuality, the whole idea must have been inconceivable to many and, while sex surveys often omitted questions on the topic altogether, modern research tends to suggest that even now female masturbation is far less universal than male. During the 'second wave' of feminism in the sixties and seventies it was recommended both as a substitute for sex with the oppressor, and as a means for women to get in touch with their own sexuality.

The major challenge to the conjugal heterosexual norm (apart from celibacy, which for probably too many women in the earlier part of the twentieth century was not a lifestyle sexual choice but a gloomy necessity) was, of course, lesbianism. This subject has been much less studied than male homosexuality, although there has been increasing historical work of recent years. The relative neglect of lesbianism is due to several factors: while male homosexuality was criminalised in many countries, generating both forensic medical discourse and the rise of sexology as an explanatory method, usually with a liberalising aim, lesbianism *per se* was never criminalised in the UK. Concepts of sex as needing a penis to be 'real' sex meant that erotic activity in which penises were by definition absent might be completely overlooked. A woman having sex with another woman did not count as adultery for the purposes of divorce (though it could count as matrimonial cruelty, and more recently 'unreasonable behaviour'). Unmarried women living together tended to be accepted as a combination of economic, social and emotional necessity: in the interwar years many women cohabiting were presumably assumed to be 'making the best of things' following the death of actual or potential mates during the First World War. Altogether lesbians, as women defined as appropriately in the private rather than the public sphere, have been less visible than male homosexuals, especially if in other respects they conformed to class and gender conventions in self-presentation.

Lillian Fadermann's influential *Surpassing the Love of Men: Romantic Friendship and Love Between Women from the Renaissance to the Present* (1981), drawing on (and tending to conflate) evidence from British, European and North American sources, argued that widespread acceptance of romantic friendship and emotional devotion between women was supplanted from the later nineteenth century by the sexological construction of the lesbian as a perverse and dangerous figure menacing heterosexuality. More recent scholarship has suggested that this over-simplifies the existence, before and after the rise of sexology, of more varied conceptualisations of women who loved other women, woman–woman affection and sexual activity, among the women concerned themselves, and observers.

Much work still needs to be done in recuperating the lives of early twentieth-century British lesbians. Upper-class lesbians, who were more able than most to lead a life of their own choosing, include the well-known Radclyffe Hall, author of the famous novel, *The Well of Loneliness* (1928), and Vita Sackville-West, who had affairs with many women, most notably Virginia Woolf, while simultaneously maintaining a successful marriage with Harold Nicolson. If few were as publicly 'out' as Hall following the publication of *The Well of Loneliness*, the inclinations of Sackville-West and others were open secrets within the circles in which they moved. There were also supportive lesbian networks among independent professional women.

But these were probably the minority. Little is known about women of other social classes lacking wealth and privilege and constrained by many factors from leading an open life. Many recognised their own feelings for other women but despaired of finding a partner or sympathetic friends. Occasional letters can be found among those received by Edward Carpenter, Marie Stopes and other 'experts' but whether the five thousand letters received by Radclyffe Hall following the prosecution of *The Well of Loneliness*, many of them doubtless from other 'inverted' women, still survive is not known.

Relationships between women seem to have been far less stigmatised than those of the male homosexual. The emphasis within marriage advice literature on sex within an emotionally important monogamous relationship as having value separate from reproduction could well be taken to justify sexual interaction within other kinds of monogamous relationship. Relationships between women (provided they were devoid of sentimentality and possessive jealousy), were often defined, even during the homophobic fifties, as not merely permissible but a good thing. An official memorandum prepared for the Wolfenden Committee on Homosexuality and Prostitution (1954–57) by the Medical Women's Federation claimed that 'a homosexual relationship between women can be a highly positive and constructive influence', that the 'promiscuous Lesbian' was rare, and the corruption of young children unknown among lesbians.[11]

During the 1970s lesbianism came to be seen as the epitome of feminism, with the rise of the concept of the 'political lesbian' who withdrew from men and put her energies into other women, even if she did not have sex with them. This led to much tension both between lesbians and women who remained heterosexual, and within the lesbian community itself over different perceptions

Plate 4.2. 'Too Great A Risk!', Family Planning Association, 1973. With the growing
acceptability of birth control, the FPA was able not only to provide a discreet service
for those who already wanted contraception but to engage in more active promotion to
particular audiences seen as in need of it – in this example, the sexually active teenager.
This leaflet, redolent of the early 1970s, deploys the stylistic conventions of strip-cartoon
stories in girls' magazines such as *Jackie* to convey its message.

Plate 4.2. (b) (*continued*)

Plate 4.2. (c) (*continued*)

Plate 4.2. (d) (*continued*)

of what it meant to be a lesbian and what were appropriate sexual practices. This tension focused on questions such as: whether there was a distinction between choosing to do without men and a positive erotic commitment to women; and whether certain practices were inevitably tainted by association with male-dominated heterosexual power relations.

Conclusion

Would an early twentieth-century feminist sex reformer (e.g. Stella Browne) who returned in the year 2000 think that Utopia had arrived? While the increased accessibility of birth control and the wider range of methods, and the legalisation of abortion, have made considerable improvements in women's control over their bodies, women still have to jump through various hoops in order to obtain morning-after contraception, specialised clinic provision has been run down and abortion is regulated by the medical profession rather than women's own needs. Sex education is still more about protecting girls from sexual dangers such as early pregnancy or venereal diseases (a worthy enough aim), than enabling them to experience sexual pleasure (with themselves or partners of either sex). Women's sexual choices can tell against them in a variety of contexts, from the raped woman who has not led a life of conventional monogamy, and the lesbian mother seeking child custody or artificial insemination, to young girls shunned as 'slags' if they pursue a sexual freedom acceptable in the male. If unwed mothers are no longer incarcerated, as occasionally happened, as 'moral imbeciles' in mental institutions, the single mother is a demonised figure in welfare policy debates. Body image dissatisfaction and eating disorders are endemic among young women in a culture which asserts, through media and advertising, that being a desirable sexual object is more important than being a desiring and confident sexual subject. Sex and the sexualised female body are commodified.

Women undoubtedly have more room for manoeuvre, sexually speaking, than they did in 1900, but a range of factors still narrows down women's choices. 'Choice' in the realm of the sexual is constrained by gender, inflected, as always, by age, class, ethnicity, economic status, educational level, contemporary models of desirable womanhood and pressures from local community mores.

Bibliographical Note

There are still many gaps in the history of sexual behaviour and attitudes in Britain during the twentieth century and much research remains to be done. Lesley Hall, *Sex, Gender and Social Change in Britain since 1880* (Basingstoke, 2000) provides an overview. Jeff Weeks, *Sex, Politics and Society: The Regulation of Sexuality since 1800* (London, 1981) remains a useful introduction. Paul Ferris, *Sex and the British: A Twentieth Century History* (London, 1993), though written for a popular audience, is soundly researched and helpful. On the sexual knowledge available and how accessible it was to the general public, see Roy Porter and Lesley Hall, *The Facts of Life: The Creation of Sexual Knowledge in Britain, 1650–1950* (New Haven, CT, 1995) and, for the influence of sexology, see Lucy Bland and Laura Doan (eds) *Sexology in Culture: Labelling Bodies and Desires* (Oxford, 1998). Oral histories which illustrate sexual ignorance include Steve Humphries, *A Secret World of Sex: Forbidden Fruit: The British Experience 1900–1950* (London, 1988); Nicky Leap and Billie Hunter, *The Midwife's Tale: An Oral History from Handywoman to Professional Midwife* (London, 1993); Maureen Sutton, *'We Didn't Know Aught': A Study of Sexuality, Superstition and Death in Women's Lives in Lincolnshire during the 1930s, '40s, and '50s* (Stamford, Lincs, 1992). Lucy Bland, *Banishing the Beast: English Feminism and Sexual Morality 1880–1914* (London, 1995) is already recognised as a classic work on this topic. Liz Stanley, *Sex Surveyed, 1949–1994: From Mass Observation's 'Little Kinsey' to the Hite Reports* (London, 1995), not only includes the text of Mass Observation's 'Little Kinsey' survey but a useful analysis of other British sex surveys. On Marie Stopes, see Ruth Hall, *'Dear Dr Stopes': Sex in the 1920s* (London, 1978) for a selection from letters to her, June Rose, *Marie Stopes and the Sexual Revolution* (London, 1992) and Robert A. Peel (ed), *Marie Stopes, Eugenics, and Birth Control* (London, 1997). Stopes's copious papers are in the Department of Manuscripts at the British Library, and the Contemporary Medical Archives Centre, Wellcome Institute for the History of Medicine (which holds the vast bulk of letters from her grateful public). Lesley A. Hall, *Hidden Anxieties: Male Sexuality 1900–1950* (Oxford, 1991), draws extensively on the Stopes correspondence to consider conjugal relations in interwar Britain. On lesbianism, see relevant essays in Bland and Doan (op. cit.); Emily Hamer, *Britannia's Glory: A History of Twentieth Century Lesbians* (London, 1996), Liz Stanley, *The Auto/biographical I* (Manchester, 1992) and Jeff Weeks, *Coming Out: Homosexual Politics in Britain from the Nineteenth Century to the Present* (London, 1977). On Radclyffe Hall, *The Well of Loneliness* and its influence, see Rebecca O'Rourke, *Reflecting on 'The Well of Loneliness'* (London, 1989). The history of sex education remains to be written, but Carol Lee, *The Ostrich Position: Sex, Schooling and Mystification* (London, 1983), is a vivid account by a sex educator.

Notes

1. R.A. McCance, M.C. Luff and E.E. Widdowson, 'Physical and Emotional Periodicity in Women', *Journal of Hygiene* 37 (1937), pp. 571–611.

2. E. Lanchester, *Elsa Lanchester Herself* (London, 1983), pp. 34–5.

3. F. Mort, *Dangerous Sexualities: Medico-moral Politics in Britain since 1830* (London, 1987), pp. 153–63; H. Kean, *Deeds not Words: The Lives of Suffragette Teachers* (London, 1990), pp. 60–2.

4. M. Sutton, *'We Didn't Know Aught': A Study of Sexuality, Superstition and Death in Women's Lives in Lincolnshire during the 1930s, '40s and '50s* (Stamford, 1992), pp. 43, 50; Mrs EH, Miss MH, letters to Marie Stopes, Stopes papers in the Contemporary Medical Archives Centre, Wellcome Institute for the History of Medicine, London, CMAC: PP/MCS/A.114, A.118.

5. M.L. Eyles, *The Woman in the Little House* (London, 1922), pp. 129–32; E. Slater and M. Woodside, *Patterns of Marriage: A Study of Marriage Relationships in the Urban Working Classes* (London, 1951), pp. 165–76; H. Wright, *More About the Sex Factor in Marriage. A Sequel to the Sex Factor in Marriage* (London, 1947, second edition 1954), pp. 11–19.

6. B. McConville, 'Mission Position', *Guardian G2* (17 May 1999), p. 6.

7. *The Freewoman* and Stella Browne are discussed at greater length in L.A. Hall, 'The Next Generation: Stella Browne, the New Woman as Freewoman', in A. Richardson and C. Willis (eds), *The New Woman in Fact and Fiction* (forthcoming) and L.A. Hall, '"I Have Never Met the Normal Woman": Stella Browne and the Politics of Womanhood', *Women's History Review*, 6 (1997), pp. 157–82.

8. S. Jeffreys, *The Spinster and Her Enemies: Feminism and Sexuality 1880–1930* (London, 1985); M. Jackson, *The **Real** Facts of Life: Feminism and the Politics of Sexuality c.1850–1940* (London, 1994); L.A. Hall, 'Feminist Reconfigurations of Heterosexuality in the 1920s', in Lucy Bland and Laura Doan (eds), *Sexology in Culture: Labelling Bodies and Desires* (Oxford, 1998), pp. 135–49 presents a critique of their position.

9. H. Wright, *The Sex Factor in Marriage: A Book for Those Who Are or Are About to Be Married, with an Introduction by A. Herbert Gray MA DD* (London, 1930) and *More About the Sex Factor, op. cit.*; 'Medica' [J. Malleson], *Any Wife or Any Husband* (London, 1950); P. Tunnadine, *The Making of Love* (London, 1985), pp. 11–14.

10. G. Gorer, *Exploring English Character* (New York, 1955), pp. 144–61.

11. Medical Women's Federation, 'Female Homosexuality', Medical Women's Federation Archives in the Contemporary Medical Archives Centre, Wellcome Institute for the History of Medicine: Wolfenden Committee on Homosexuality and Prostitution: MWF Evidence for: Memoranda and drafts, CMAC: SA/MWF/H.9/2.

5

MARRIAGE

Jane Lewis

The twentieth century has seen profound changes in marriage and the 'marriage system', indeed it is tempting to argue that we have seen the 'rise and fall' of marriage. This would be premature, behaviour in relation to such a long-lived institution is notoriously hard to predict. However, there have been major changes in terms of how many people get married, when they do so, how many have children outside marriage, how many divorce and how many cohabit. The meaning of marriage has also changed. The reasons for these changes are matters of huge debate among historians and social scientists, although marriage in and of itself has been a relatively neglected subject. Commentary on it is all too often confined to what happens after it ends in divorce.

In 1909, the feminist Cicely Hamilton published *Marriage as a Trade*, which deplored the fact that women had so few means of financial support other than husbands. How far the changes in marriage can be attributed to the changing status of women is a source of particular controversy. Women are no longer obliged to marry in order to survive economically, although the wages of many are extremely low. In the case of women who are mothers, the absence of a male breadwinner because of divorce or unmarried motherhood usually means reliance on welfare benefits in addition to, or instead of earnings, because the woman must do unpaid caring work for her child. Some have therefore argued that there is a causal relationship between the 'welfare state' and changes in the marriage system. Others point to the relaxation in divorce law as an explanation for the much greater frequency in marriage breakdown, especially during the last quarter of the twentieth century.

Sociologists have suggested that we can understand the changes in marriage as a movement from 'institution to relationship'. However, marriage has always been both. Still, this does point us towards the importance of considering mentalities and meanings both for ordinary people and for policy makers: are we seeing evidence of a movement away from obligation and duty, born of a shared morality and possibly of material and emotional dependence, and towards greater individualism that may or may not also be selfish?

Plate 5.1. A young couple getting married, 2000.

Patterns of Marriage, Divorce and Cohabitation

Marriage has been part of the typical experience of the vast majority of women throughout the century, although there are signs at the end of the century that this is ceasing to be the case. John Gillis has called the period 1850–1960 'the long era of mandatory matrimony'.[1] The first marriage rate per 1,000 women over 16 rose from just over 57 at the beginning of the century to a high of 98 in 1971 (see Table 5.1). There were nevertheless many women at the beginning of the century who never married. This was partly due to the imbalance in the sex ratio, which increased steadily from the late nineteenth century to 1911. This 'surplus woman problem' caused considerable anguish, particularly in the late nineteenth century, because it became inevitable that some women would not be able to fulfil their 'natural destiny' of marriage and motherhood. The 'excess' of women increased dramatically again as a result of the First World War. Of those women who were single and in their late twenties in 1921, 50 per cent

Table 5.1. **First marriage by age and sex, England and Wales, 1901–95**

Year	All ages thousands	rate*	Mean age
Men			
1901	233.9	59.6†	26.7
1911	251.7	61.8†	27.4
1921	290.6	63.5†	27.5
1931	285.5	59.7	27.3
1941	357.1	78.3	26.9
1951	313.5	76.2	26.7
1961	308.8	74.9	25.6
1971	343.6	82.3	24.6
1981	259.1	51.7	25.4
1985	253.3	46.6	26.0
1991	222.8	37.0	27.5
1995**	198.5	31.8	28.9
Women			
1901	240.6	57.4†	25.3
1911	257.5	58.7†	25.8
1921	290.4	55.2†	25.5
1931	294.1	54.7	25.4
1941	365.0	74.5	24.6
1951	319.2	76.3	24.4
1961	312.2	83.0	23.1
1971	347.4	97.9	22.6
1981	263.4	64.0	23.1
1985	258.1	58.2	23.8
1991	224.8	46.0	25.5
1995**	198.5	40.1	26.9

* Per 1,000 single persons aged 16 and over

** Provisional

† Quinquennia rates 1901–05, 1911–15, 1921–25

Source: OPCS, *Marriage and Divorce Statistics: Historical Series 1837–1983*, Table 3.2a and b, 3.5a and b, 3.7a and 3.7b, FM2 No. 16 (London: HMSO, 1995); ONS, *Population Trends* 88 (Summer 1997).

remained unmarried a decade later, compared with a figure of 30 per cent for men. After the Second World War, women married for the first time at increasingly younger ages and marriage became virtually universal in the 1960s, a decade usually associated with student revolt against established institutions. At the end of the century, marriage remains popular, but increasing numbers of marriages are remarriages after divorce. If we look at first marriage rates, the decline at the end of the century is particularly dramatic. Age at first marriage also began to rise again from the 1970s. At the end of the twentieth century, fewer people were getting married in the first place and they were marrying later.

Two major developments have transformed the marriage system: the rise in the divorce rate and of cohabitation. Prior to 1914, divorce was largely confined to the middle and upper classes. Changes in aid given to poor petitioners in 1914, together with the effects of the First World War, produced an increase in the divorce rate after 1918, but it was not until 1946, when legal aid became freely available that divorce petitions began to come from a cross section of the population. Prior to the Second World War, working-class couples made use of the judicial separation machinery administered by the magistrates' courts rather than divorce, although the number of informal separations was probably larger than the number of cases that came to court. Whereas only 7 per cent of all matrimonial proceedings in the courts were divorces in the early 1900s, this figure jumped to 55 per cent by the early 1950s. The role of the magistrates' courts in granting maintenance and separation orders remained important until a major reform of the divorce law was implemented in the early 1970s. Prior to 1923, when the grounds for divorce were equalised for men and women, women had to prove another fault in addition to adultery, which constituted a ground for divorce for male petitioners. In 1937 the grounds were extended to include desertion, cruelty and insanity, and in 1969 a major relaxation of the divorce law took place. The divorce rate increased dramatically in the 1970s and 1980s (see Table 5.2) and has continued to rise slightly during the 1990s. As the divorce rate rose, so did the proportion of divorcing couples with young children. In 1971 divorcing couples with children of four or younger accounted for 25 per cent of the divorce population, by 1991 this figure had risen to 47 per cent.

Patterns of cohabitation are harder to document for the whole century. There is evidence to suggest that cohabitation was common in the early part of the century when divorce was rare. Members of the Royal Commission on Divorce that reported in 1912 were certainly very concerned about the number of working people who were 'living in sin' because they had separated, were unable to get a divorce and had therefore decided to live informally with someone else. When separation allowances were provided for the wives of servicemen during the First World War, special provision had to be made for 'unmarried wives'. Cohabitation probably reached its nadir in the 1950s and 1960s when marriage was almost universal. Living together as a prelude to marriage began in the 1970s. In the 1990s, typically 70 per cent of women who marry for the first time have cohabited with their husbands, compared with 58 per cent of those marrying

Table 5.2. **Divorce rate per 1,000 married population, England and Wales, 1950–95**

Year	Rate
1950	2.8
1960	2.0
1965	3.1
1970	4.7
1975	9.6
1980	12.0
1985	13.4
1990	13.0
1995	13.6

Source: OPCS, *Marriage and Divorce Statistics, Historical Series 1837–1983*, Table 5.2 FM2, No. 16 (London: HMSO, 1995); OPCS, *Marriage and Divorce Statistics 1837–1983*, Table 2.1, FM2, No. 21 (London: HMSO, 1995); ONS, *Marriage, Divorce and Adoption Statistics*, 1995 series FM2, No. 23 (London: The Stationery Office, 1997).

between 1985 and 1988, 33 per cent marrying between 1975 and 1979, and 6 per cent marrying between 1965 and 1969. The proportion of spinsters who were cohabiting more than trebled between 1979 and 1993, from 8 per cent to 24 per cent. Additionally, in 1993, 25 per cent of divorced women were in cohabiting unions. Indeed, during the last quarter of the century, the increase in cohabitation has affected the remarriage rate after divorce. The remarriage rate for divorced women halved between 1980 and 1993. Cohabitations in the postwar period have tended to be short-lived and childless, but from 1980 children were increasingly born within these relationships. The changing patterns of birth registration (see Table 5.3) provide some evidence of this. Of the 77 per cent who jointly registered their babies in 1994, 58 per cent lived at the same address.

Table 5.3. **Registration of births outside marriage, 1964–97 (percentages)**

	1964	1971	1981	1994	1997
Sole registration	60	54.5	41.8	22.7	21.3
Joint registration	40	45.5	58.2	77.3	78.9
Births outside marriage as a percentage of all births	7	8.4	12.8	32.4	37

Source: OPCS, *Birth Statistics, Historical Series 1837–1983*, Tables 1.1 and 3.7, series FM1, No. 13 (London: HMSO, 1987); ONS, *Population Trends* 93 (Autumn 1998), Table 10 (London: Government Statistical Service, 1998).

At the beginning of the century the vast majority of people married before they had sex, had their children inside marriage and stayed married. At
the end of the century people's family arrangements looked increasingly messy.
Cohabitation and childbirth may proceed marriage, which may be followed
by divorce and possibly another cohabitation, another marriage and more
children.

The Story Behind the Statistics

Politicians expressing anxiety about marriage and the family in the 1990s have
tended to locate the beginnings of dramatic change in family structure in the
'permissive' 1960s. However, the story is more complicated than this. The 1960s
were in fact a decade of near universal marriage.

The most profound change to have taken place in the twentieth century is
the collapse of the assumption that childbirth will take place inside marriage.
There were always births to unmarried women. However, the extramarital birth
rate was relatively stable until the 1960s, with the exception of two peaks during
the world wars, when wartime disruption stopped many marriages that would
have taken place following the discovery that the woman was pregnant. Until
the 1930s illegitimacy was primarily a rural phenomenon, although there were
wide differences in the extramarital birth rate between regions and between
different groups of women. A 1911 survey showed that 46 per cent of the
illegitimate children in Britain were born to women who had worked in domestic
service. John Gillis's study of a London Foundling Hospital in the nineteenth
century showed that this group of women experienced profound contradictions
in attempting to combine customs of courtship and marriage appropriate to
women of their class backgrounds with the standards of conduct expected by
their employers.[2] Sexual intercourse did not take place until marriage was promised, and marriage failed to take place usually because of job difficulties on the
part of the man. The point is that it was expected that marriage would follow
the discovery of pregnancy. In 1938 the Population Statistics Act required the
age of the mother at the birth of the child to be recorded for the first time, and
these new data revealed that one seventh of all children born between 1938 and
1939 were premaritally conceived.

There is evidence that sexual activity among the young increased during the
1960s; the growing use of the contraceptive pill from the beginning of the
1970s exacerbated this trend. Sex was increasingly separated from marriage and
increased sexual activity resulted in a rise in both the extramarital and marital
birth rates. This contrasts with both the First and Second World Wars, when the
extramarital birth rate rose faster than the marital rate, and with the period
since 1985, when the extramarital rate has risen and the marital rate has fallen.
While in the late 1950s and 1960s more and more sex took place outside marriage, there was still a tendency for pregnant women to marry. Slightly over
20 per cent of women marrying for the first time in the late 1960s were pregnant,

compared to 10 per cent in 1992. Furthermore, there is room for speculation that many of these young, 'shotgun weddings' from the 1960s ended up fuelling the divorce rate in the late 1970s and 1980s. Nevertheless, the point remains that during the 1960s it looked as though the conventions were being observed. In 1969, 55 per cent of conceptions outside marriage were legitimised by marriage, 32 per cent resulted in extramarital births and 14 per cent were aborted (the law on abortion was liberalised in 1967).

Social scientists writing about marriage and the family in the 1960s were optimistic about the future. Ronald Fletcher concluded that, although there was real change, there was no sign of moral decay. Marriage rates were high and divorce rates were low. Geoffrey Gorer's study of sex and marriage published in 1971 concluded that England was still chaste, 26 per cent of married men and 63 per cent of married women in his sample were virgins at marriage. Compared to his earlier survey, published in 1955, he found that the main change was the increase in the proportion of those who thought sexual experience had a good effect on the person's character.[3]

The changes in the marriage system taking place during the last quarter of the century represent a real break. Increases in divorce, cohabitation and childbearing outside marriage have contributed to the separation of marriage and parenthood. The result has been a trebling in the percentage of lone mother families between 1971 and 1994 (see Table 5.4). The commentary by academics, politicians and policy makers has also grown more pessimistic. In particular, British research followed the American in providing increasing evidence of the detrimental impact of divorce and lone parenthood on the educational achievements, employment and personal relationships of children and young adults. There is a *fin de siècle* anxiety about the future of marriage.

Table 5.4. **Distribution of lone-mother families with dependent children according to marital status, 1971–94 (percentage of all families with dependent children)**

	1971	1974	1981	1984	1991	1994
Single lone mothers	1.2	1.0	2.3	3.0	6.4	8.0
Separated lone mothers	2.5	2.0	2.3	2.0	3.6	5.0
Divorced lone mothers	1.9	2.0	4.4	6.0	6.3	7.0
Widowed lone mothers	1.9	2.0	1.7	1.0	1.2	1.0
All lone mothers	7.5	7.0	10.7	12.0	17.5	21.0

Note: Estimates are based on three-year averages except 1994.

Sources: Haskey, J., 'Trends in the Numbers of One-Parent Families in Great Britain', *Population Trends* 71 (1993), pp. 26–33; OPCS, *Living in Britain* (London: HMSO, 1996), Table 4.

How Do We Explain the Changes?

The theory of a second demographic transition beginning in the 1960s with the separation of sex and marriage followed by the emergence of cohabitation has stressed the importance of the accompanying belief in the rights of the individual, especially in respect of personal and career development. Many sociologists, especially in the USA, have also argued strongly that love and marriage have increasingly come to be seen primarily in terms of personal gratification, which threatens their older social function of providing people with stable, committed relationships that tie them into the larger society. Explanations have focused primarily on the changes in the economic organisation of the family, involving a shift from the male breadwinner to a dual-earner model and with it greater female autonomy; on legal reform and in particular successive relaxations of the law of divorce; and on an increase in what is perceived as individualistic behaviour, which is sometimes also deemed to be selfish.

The Decline of the Male-Breadwinner Family Model

The assumption that families would be based on a husband responsible for earning and a wife responsible for caring and household work was both strong and long-lived in Britain. It also played a major part in shaping understandings of marriage.

It has often been pointed out that this male-breadwinner model did not fit the social reality of early twentieth-century Britain. While the 'separation of spheres' was relatively complete for middle-class women, working-class women engaged in a large amount of casual labour as and when the state of the family economy demanded it. However, the ideal of the male-breadwinner model and the family wage that accompanied it were broadly shared by working-class men and women, as well as by middle-class observers and policy makers. Respectable male workers expected to earn enough to 'keep' a wife. Women, who faced the prospect of repeated pregnancy and hard household labour, were to be pitied if they also had to go out to work full-time. Ellen Ross has reminded us that the marriage contract did not enjoin romantic love or verbal or sexual intimacy, but required financial obligations, services and activities that were gender-specific.[4] The Fabian Women's Group's investigation of working-class women's lives in Edwardian Lambeth reported that wives judged husbands according to how much money they were allowed. In instances where the husband proved unwilling to provide, the wife might look elsewhere for support. The 1912 Royal Commission on Divorce took copious evidence to this effect. Miss E. Lidgett, a poor law guardian, described a case where the Guardians had taken a whole family into the workhouse, the father being 'hopelessly out of work'. Eventually the wife was allowed out to try and build up a home again. She immediately began to live with another man and had more children by him, complaining to Miss Lidgett that the Guardians would not allow her to visit her children by her first husband who remained in the workhouse. She 'stoutly defended' her new home, saying that the first husband 'was no husband for her and one that worked for her she respected'.[5]

The element of solid calculation in early twentieth-century working-class marriage can be over-stressed at the expense of evidence of domestic affection, revealed by both historians and contemporaries. However, as evidence to the 1912 Royal Commission on Divorce showed, between 50 and 80 per cent of couples obtaining legal separations were reconciled, usually as a result of an improvement in the husband's financial position. The meaning of early twentieth-century marriage for working people and the justification for cohabitation were intimately linked to ideas about the male breadwinner model with its concomitant gendered division of labour.

The position of better-off women was somewhat different. Many feminists, like Cicely Hamilton, deplored the fact that there were so few opportunities for women to live independently and railed against the way in which women forfeited the power to control their own lives. Nevertheless, others defended marriage as the basic unit in society. Millicent Garret Fawcett, the constitutional suffragist, viewed marriage as a discipline and an order. As an institution it imposed rational bonds on irrational sexual urges. Marriage was also viewed as a necessary protection for women in a world where they had few other options. Thus Lady Acland, who campaigned for women to have the legal right to a share of their husbands' income, defended marriage on the grounds that women would be yet worse off without it. Women who relied on marriage for the means to subsistence had a vested interest in defending the institution and the traditional pattern of obligations within it.

When other options for women to live independently opened up, arguably marriage became more of a choice. But 'getting married' was by no means a matter of solely economic rational decision-making that neo-classical economists have tried to make it out to be. Indeed, how to understand marriage – as institution, contract, or 'a law unto itself' with a sacred, magical status – has always been a matter of considerable debate. Nevertheless, declining birth rates (from the late nineteenth century in the case of middle-class families, and from the interwar period in the case of most working-class families), together with the changing economic position of women after the Second World War, made possible a much more fluid approach to marriage. In particular, exit via divorce became more possible. Economists have argued that, as women's capacity to support themselves increased, so they have become less willing to put up with unsatisfactory marriages.

However, women's capacity for financial independence can be overstated. Virtually all of the postwar increase in women's labour force participation has been accounted for by part-time work. In addition, a majority of women found themselves in low-paid work. It is likely that the rise in women's employment had not been a cause of the increase in divorce, but has rather had the effect of making it easier. In other words, it has facilitated, not caused family change. Some sociologists have suggested that, whereas women who were wholly dependent on men for economic support used to abandon their hopes, they are now able to abandon their marriages. On average, their standard of living declined following divorce. But income from paid employment and/or state benefits has made independent living possible both for unhappily married women and for women who find themselves pregnant but who do not wish to marry the fathers of their children.

French data have also suggested that it is not the increase in paid employment *per se* that is responsible for women's greater readiness to abandon marriage, but the awareness it creates of tensions within the marriage. During the 1970s, sociologists were optimistic that marriages were becoming more 'symmetrical'. Just as women were entering the workforce in greater numbers, so it was predicted that men would gradually do more unpaid caring and domestic work. However, the empirical sociology of the 1980s showed that this had not happened, leading Arlie Hochschild to identify the enormous dissatisfaction of women with 'the double shift'. As a dual-earner model has increasingly replaced the male-breadwinner model, so women's expectations of marriage have changed radically. The proportion of household income contributed by men has fallen steadily in the 1980s, and Oppenheimer has suggested that a new collaborative model of marriage has begun to replace the old specialisation of men as breadwinners and women as housewives and carers. In this new form, marriage is based on the ability of each partner to make a contribution, unique or similar, and to pull his or her weight in the relationship. The commitment of each partner to the relationship is contingent on this happening.[6] While the male-breadwinner model family was marked by clear-cut obligations, the dual-earner family of the late twentieth century is not. Obligation has given way to a commitment that is more personal and contingent.

Law and Behaviour

The relationship between changes in the law of marriage and divorce and changes in marital behaviour has been another area of huge debate. Rheinstein's comparative socio-legal study argued that marital breakdown could be high even in the absence of divorce. Similarly, Phillips's comparative historical study of divorce insisted that levels of marital breakdown have not been dependent on legal change.[7] As the 1912 Royal Commission on Divorce observed, the impossibility of divorce did not prevent large numbers of people separating and then cohabiting. Some social scientists have argued that economic variables, such as female labour market participation; demographic variables, such as young marriage and premarital pregnancy; and individual characteristics, such as emotional immaturity have all been more important in accounting for rates of marital breakdown than legal change. On the other hand, in a cross-national study of divorce between 1976 and 1983, Castles and Flood concluded that the presence or absence of liberal divorce law reform was the most important variable explaining differences in divorce rates.[8] However, politicians have always believed that law makes a difference. Interestingly, the major relaxations of the divorce law in 1937 and 1969 were accompanied by statements assuring the public that the intention of reform was to strengthen marriage. By the 1990s, politicians were more concerned about the way in which legal reform may have encouraged high levels of marital breakdown. Thus the 1996 Family Law Act was the first major piece of legislation in the field to make provision for attempts at 'marriage saving' before the granting of divorce.

In 1912, a majority of the members of the Royal Commission on divorce accepted the arguments in favour of liberalising the grounds for divorce, the hope being that, if divorce was made more accessible, those 'living in sin' would be able to remarry:

> So far from such reforms as we recommend tending to lower the standard of morality and regard for the sanctity of the marriage tie, we consider that reform is necessary in the interests of morality, as well as in the interests of justice, and in the general interests of society and the state.[9]

The recommendations of the Royal Commission were not implemented until 1937, the immediate cause being the publicity A.P. Herbert gave to the hypocrisy attaching to divorces granted on the basis of carefully staged hotel scenes, designed to provide evidence of adultery. However, reform in the interwar period was also an attempt to make the law consistent with changes in the ideal of marriage. While the male-breadwinner model was not questioned, there was much more emphasis placed on 'companionate marriage' (which helped to justify the equalisation of the grounds for divorce in 1923), and on the importance of the quality of marital relationships, particularly in terms of sexual relationships. In 1937 the grounds for divorce were extended to desertion, cruelty and insanity, none of which could be considered compatible with a properly companionate marriage.

IN FOCUS: Reforming the Law of Marriage and Divorce in the Postwar Period

---

During the 1920s and 1930s there was a strong current favouring reform, but this largely disappeared during the 1940s and 1950s. The Second World War gave rise to a moral panic about family disintegration that strengthened the determination of those opposed to any further reform of the divorce laws. Rebuilding the family became part of the more general impetus to postwar reconstruction.

In 1951 Mrs Eirene White MP attempted to introduce a Bill to make marriage breakdown a new ground for divorce. Reiterating the concerns of the 1912 Royal Commission, Mrs White wanted to enable those people who had been separated for a number of years to remarry. The Bill failed, but a Royal Commission on Divorce was set up which reported in 1956 (Cmd 9678). A majority of the Commissioners were concerned above all to protect marriage as an institution, their concerns echoing those of Victorian and Edwardian moralists:

Reforming the Law of Marriage and Divorce in the Postwar Period (continued)

It is obvious that life-long marriage is the basis of a secure family life, and that to ensure their well-being children must have that background. We have therefore had in mind throughout our inquiry the importance of seeking ways and means of strengthening the resolution of husbands and wives to realise the idea of a partnership for life (para. 37).

Yet, within a decade a major reform had been passed in the form of the 1969 Divorce Law Reform Act. A challenge to the conservatism of the 1956 Royal Commission came in 1963, when Leo Abse reintroduced Eirene White's Bill. The Archbishop of Canterbury responded by setting up a group to review the secular law of divorce. Its report, published in 1966, took a radically different position from that adopted by the church ten years before, recommending that the concept of marital breakdown replace that of fault. But because the Church still refused to countenance divorce by consent, it favoured 'breakdown with inquest'. In other words, because marriage was considered a matter of public concern, the Church wanted the couple's declaration of breakdown to be investigated. The Law Commission also reported in 1966 and also favoured the abandonment of fault-based divorce, the aim being to enable 'empty shell' marriages to be ended with the maximum fairness and the minimum bitterness. The new legislation did not require the kind of 'inquest' favoured by the Church, but nor did it wholly abandon fault. People wishing to divorce had to prove that their relationship had broken down, either as a result of one of the old 'faults', or something new: separation for two years with the respondent's consent, or five years without consent being required. Most people wanted a quick divorce and therefore opted to use adultery or unreasonable behaviour as a proof. Not until the 1996 Family Law Act did fault-based divorce disappear, but in 1999 the Labour Government announced that this part of the legislation was not going to be implemented.

In the postwar period, the law of divorce continued to rest on the proof of fault, which had much to do with the way in which marriage was defined by Church and state. A second Royal Commission on divorce, which reported in 1956, refused to contemplate any further reform to allow the idea of 'breakdown' rather than 'fault' as a ground for divorce. According to the Archbishop of Canterbury in his evidence to the 1956 Royal Commission, divorce could only be justified morally if one or more of the 'purposes' of marriage were frustrated. This was why 'fault' had to be proved:

The purposes of marriage are the procreation of children, natural relations and the comfort that one ought to have of the other. Adultery breaks the

union of man and wife. Desertion deprives him [sic] of the partner, one
of the purposes of marriage. Cruelty frustrates one of them, also insanity,
and sodomy and bestiality. I think you could say, could you not, that they
all frustrate one or more of the purposes of marriage.[10]

The Church saw marriage as a vocation. A marriage came into being when the
parties exchanged vows, which could be viewed as the making of a contract. But
in the Church's view the exchange of vows was merely a means of bringing the
marriage into existence. As a vocation, marriage had no other properties of
contract and could therefore not be dissolved by the parties themselves. There
had always to be a judgement by a third party in a court of law as to whether
some fault had been committed. Anything resembling divorce by mutual consent could not be countenanced because it would have effectively undermined
the Church's understanding of the whole nature of marriage.

The debate over the law of divorce in the twentieth century has therefore
also been a debate about the nature of marriage. In 1969 fault was partially
abandoned. The legislation was a compromise between Church and state. The
willingness of the Church to move towards no-fault divorce resulted in large
measure from the rethinking of sexual morality during the 1960s, a decade in
which, as we have seen, it was possible to remain optimistic about the state of
the family. At the extreme, and most influentially, the Bishop of Woolwich
rejected the traditional moral code governing marriage and divorce and advocated a position 'based on love', whereby nothing could be labelled as 'wrong' –
not divorce, nor premarital sex – unless it lacked love. The aim of the Bishop
and many other churchmen was to rely on a morality that came from within,
rather than on a morality that came from without. The argument was that this
would make for more honest, more loving, higher quality personal relationships,
but the logical end point of this position was that only people themselves could
decide if their relationship was loving and worth maintaining. Once the priority
accorded marital stability was abandoned in favour of securing better personal
relationships, there was little left by way of defence against sexual relationships
outside marriage, so long as they were based on love and mutual respect.

While it is very difficult to say how far legal reform led to or how far it
reflected behavioural change, the trend has been clearly towards treating marriage as a private contract and allowing individuals to make decisions about
their personal lives. As changes in marital behaviour became more dramatic in
the last quarter of the century, so policy makers had to decide whether to
recognise and work with them or whether to try and put the clock back. On
the whole, legislation has endeavoured to do the former, with the emphasis of
the 1996 Family Law Act on saving marriage standing as an exception. Both the
1989 Children Act and the 1991 Child Support Act (which has substantially
failed in its implementation) endeavoured to enforce the responsibilities of
men and women in intimate relationships as *parents* rather than as husbands
and wives. This recognised the social reality in terms of the increase in lone-
mother families and in cohabiting relationships.

Plate 5.2. Still from David Lean's classic film *Brief Encounter* (1945). Set in the 1930s, the film explores the subject of marital infidelity through the example of a married English middle-class mother and housewife's repressed desire. For a discussion of *Brief Encounter*, see chapter 15, p. 239.

Increasing Individualism?

Those who have been active in thinking about and analysing family change particularly in respect of the rapid changes of the last quarter of the century, have highlighted the importance of what is perceived as growing 'individualism'. In the longer historical perspective, this view presents some problems. The work of Alan Macfarlane has argued that individualism also characterised behaviour in a much earlier historical period.[11] Nevertheless, sociologists in particular have presented evidence to suggest that twentieth-century society has become increasingly individualistic. Whether or not individualism at the end of the century is also essentially selfish is a matter of more debate.

Bellah *et al.* sounded a trumpet call in their account of middle-American life with the statement: 'We are concerned that this individualism may have grown cancerous'.[12] They identified two forms of individualism in the postwar period: the utilitarian, which amounted to the traditional American desire to 'get ahead' and to be self-reliant, and the expressive, which emphasised self-expression and the sharing of feelings rather than material acquisition. The perception of these American writers was that the values of the public sphere – the 'coolly manipulative style' (p. 48) that is required to 'get ahead – were invading the private world of the family. Such an anxiety has a long history. The ideology of separate spheres, whereby the ruthless competition that was thought necessary for the successful operation of the market was balanced by the haven of the family where women would care for husbands and children was central to the thinking of late nineteenth-century liberal social theorists such as Herbert Spencer and underpinned the male breadwinner model. In the view of Bellah *et al.*, the contractual structure of commercial and bureaucratic life threatened to become an ideology for personal life. Obligation and commitment were being replaced by an ideology of full, open and honest communication between 'self-actualising' individuals. In the socio-legal literature and in the history of ideas arguments have emerged that also stress the implications of 'the rise of psychologic man', and of the shift towards emphasising personality and with it self-expression and self-gratification.

The argument has been expressed more polemically in terms of people becoming less willing to invest time, money and energy in family life and turn instead to investment in themselves. The strong inference being that individualism is also essentially selfish, a charge that was taken up in the British Parliamentary debates over the 1996 Family Law Act. In the House of Lords, Baroness Young said that 'for one party simply to decide to go off with another person . . . reflects the growing self-first disease which is debasing our society'.[13]

In particular, the dramatic late-twentieth-century rise in cohabitation has been interpreted as signalling a more individualistic approach to private life. According to British Household Panel data, cohabitation is four times more unstable than marriage. The concern that cohabitation may increasingly be an alternative to marriage has been heightened by the anxiety that it also appears to be a much less committed form of relationship. Some demographers have suggested that high rates of cohabitation have been produced by increasing individualism and secularisation, and that these values are carried over into marriage, involving the spread of an individualistic outlook on intimate relationships.

The idea that there has been a growth in individualism in respect of personal relationships bears some relation to the long-held notion that marriage has moved from being an institution to a relationship. Inherent in both sets of ideas is the notion that those involved in intimate relationships have become less conscious of their 'public', social dimensions – in terms of the duties owed to one another, to children and to the wider kin group – and have increasingly limited their attention to the quality of the relationship itself and the calculus of benefits and dis-welfares to themselves as individuals. Giddens called this the emergence of the 'pure relationship'.[14] However, in Giddens's interpretation, while love has become contingent rather than 'forever', it has also become more democratic, which constitutes a much more optimistic view of the growth of individualism.

Conclusion

Both pessimists and optimists in the debate over the growth and influence of individualism have a vision of people freed from externally supplied norms and morality. For example, the erosion of the male-breadwinner model and the removal of the idea that people must justify to a third party their wish to end a marriage mean that people must negotiate the way they structure their intimate relationships for themselves. Many academics and policy makers fear that in the absence of such frameworks, people behave selfishly. Others argue that people are negotiating their relationships more democratically and indeed that they are continuing to exercise moral responsibility. Much of this fierce debate arises from the rapid pace of change in the last quarter of the century. Indeed, it is tempting to write of the 'rise and decline of marriage' in the twentieth century. Any such judgement would be premature. Nevertheless, it is the broad trends associated with the decline of marriage and the rise of cohabitation that have promoted the *fin de siècle* anxiety about the future of marriage.

Bibliographical Note

Marriage has not been the subject of very much interest on the part of historians or sociologists, and most of the work on it has been attempted via an analysis of divorce. However, this means that there is little by way of sustained comment on changes in practices within marriage. An early and interesting feminist commentary on marriage is: M. Caird, *The Morality of Marriage and Other Essays* (London, 1897); see also D. Clark (ed), *Marriage, Domestic Life and Social Change* (London, 1991).

Useful studies of divorce include: L. Stone, *The Road to Divorce, 1530–1987* (Oxford, 1990); J. Burgoyne, R. Ormerod and M.P.M. Richards, *Divorce Matters* (Harmondsworth, 1987); O.R. McGregor, L. Blom-Cooper and C. Gibson, *Separate Spouses* (London, 1970). The Reports of the two major Royal Commissions in 1912 and 1956, together with their minutes of evidence are important and accessible sources.

Notes

1. J. Gillis, *For Better, for Worse: British Marriages: 1600 to the present* (Oxford, 1986), p. 259.

2. J. Gillis, 'Servants, Sexual Relations and the Risks of Illegitimacy in London, 1801–1900', *Feminist Studies* 5 (1979), pp. 142–73.

3. R. Fletcher, *The Family and Marriage in Britain* (Harmondsworth, 1966); G. Gorer, *Sex and Marriage in England Today: A Study of the Views and Experience of the under-45s* (London, 1971).

4. E. Ross, *Love and Toil* (Oxford, 1993).

5. PP., Cd. 6480, Minutes of Evidence to the Royal Commission on Divorce and Matrimonial Causes (London, 1912), Q. 20120.

6. A. Hochschild, *The Second Shift: Working Parents and the Revolution at Home* (New York, 1989); V. Oppenheimer, 'Women's Rising Employment and the Future of the Family in Industrialised Societies', *Population and Development Review* 20 (1994), pp. 293–342.

7. M. Rheinstein, *Marriage, Stability, Divorce and the Law* (Chicago, 1972); R. Phillips, *Putting Asunder: A History of Divorce in Western Society* (Cambridge, 1988).

8. F.G. Castles and M. Flood, 'Why Divorce Rates Differ: Law, Religion, Belief and Modernity', in F.G. Castles (ed) *Families of Nations: Patterns of Public Policy in Western Democracies* (Aldershot, 1993).

9. PP., Cd. 6478, Report of the Royal Commission on Marriage and Divorce (London, 1912), para. 50.

10. Royal Commission on Marriage and Divorce, *Minutes of Evidence* (London, 1956), p. 155.

11. A. Macfarlane, *Marriage and Love in England, 1300–1840* (Oxford, 1986).

12. R. Bellah, R. Madsen, W. Sullivan, A. Swidler and S.M. Tipton, *Habits of the Heart: Middle America Observed* (Berkeley, CA, 1985), p. 48.

13. *Hansard*, House of Lords, 29/2/96, col. 1638.

14. A. Giddens, *The Transformation of Intimacy* (Cambridge, 1992).

6

HEALTH AND REPRODUCTION

Helen Jones

This chapter sets out the general trends in women's health over the course of the twentieth century, and it reviews the explanations which historians have presented for changes in women's health and reproduction. This overview is supplemented by two case studies which examine controversies over women's health. The first concerns the relationship between women's health, their paid work, and the economic and military strength of the country in the early years of the century; and the second discusses the relationship in the 1930s between health and poverty. The changing health care services, in particular those relating to women's reproductive roles, are also explored. Finally, differences between female and male standards of health, and between different groups of women are discussed.

Trends

A girl born in 1901 could expect to live to the age of 49 whereas a girl born in 2001 can expect to live to the age of 81. The reasons for this increased longevity are complex and contested. First, from the second decade of the century more babies and children have survived into adulthood. The infant mortality (death in first year of life) rate has fallen from 105 per thousand births in 1910 to 6 per thousand in 1994. Second, there has been a decline in deaths from infectious diseases. Historians do not agree over why this is so. It has been argued that infectious diseases have become less virulent; that there has been a rise in human genetic resistance; and that vaccinations have reduced deaths, although, in fact, the decline in deaths from infectious diseases began before the introduction of vaccinations. Lastly, it is argued that humans are better able to resist infections because they are healthier.

  Why are we healthier at the end of the century than at the beginning? One explanation lies in the health services and medical interventions which have improved over the century, but one should not lay too much emphasis on medical services. For the first half of the century poorer women had minimal

Table 6.1. **Life expectancy, 1901–2001 (total number of years which a female might expect to live)**

	1901	1931	1961	1991	2001
at birth	49	62	74	79	81
	(46)	(56)	(68)	(73)	(75)
At age					
1 year	59	65	75	79	81
	(55)	(62)	(70)	(74)	(76)
10 years	63	68	75	79	81
	(60)	(65)	(70)	(74)	(76)
20 years	64	69	76	80	81
	(62)	(66)	(70)	(74)	(76)
40 years	68	72	76	80	82
	(66)	(69)	(71)	(75)	(77)
60 years	75	76	79	82	83
	(73)	(74)	(75)	(78)	(80)
80 years	85	85	86	88	89
	(85)	(85)	(85)	(86)	(87)

Note: Figures for males in brackets.

Source: *Social Trends* 27 (1997).

services, and it is still the case that areas of the country with the best services do not have the best health: Scotland has enjoyed especially good maternity and child care provision but not maternal and child health. Second, standards of living have risen; in particular, nutrition has improved and this means that people are far better able to resist infections in the year 2000 than a century ago. Third, women have benefited from fewer pregnancies and, after the first three decades of the century when the maternal mortality (death) rate (MMR) was very high, a declining risk of death in childbirth.

One of the most striking changes in women's lives over the course of the century has been the decline in the number of children they have borne. Fewer children have contributed to, and been a reflection of, a woman's greater control over her body and her lifestyle. Fertility (the number of children born, not the biological capacity to bear children) has varied between classes and between regions, but these variations have been less significant than overall trends. From the 1870s the middle class, then a minority of the population, began to control their fertility effectively; from the turn of the century the working class, which comprised the bulk of the population, also began to space their children and

Table 6.2. **Annual average crude birth rate, 1900–90**

Year	England & Wales	Scotland
1900	29	30
1910	25	26
1920	26	28
1930	16	20
1940	14	17
1950	16	18
1960	17	20
1970	16	17
1980	13	13
1990	14	13

Source: N.L. Tranter, *British Population in the Twentieth Century* (London, 1996).

choose the size of their families. A woman born in 1870 had an average of 5 to 6 children. As middle-class couples began to control their fertility, the average number of children which middle-class and working-class women bore diverged considerably so that in the first decade of the twentieth century the wife of a professional man averaged 3 to 4 children while the wife of working-class man could average 7 children. By 1920 there was greater class convergence with women in all classes having, on average, two children. The average number of children born to women has continued to decline: a woman born in 1936 has an average of 1.9 children whereas a woman born in 1966 has an average of 1.3 children.

Historians do not agree over the reasons for the declining birth rate; they argue over a combination of the following possibilities. First, as the infant death rate declined in the early part of the century more babies survived into adulthood, thus fewer pregnancies produced more surviving offspring, so it was not necessary for parents to have more children than they expected to survive into adulthood.

Second, as methods of efficient birth control improved, access to contraceptives became easier and knowledge of them spread; how this dissemination occurred is not clear. At first it was assumed that in the early decades of the century information gradually seeped down from the middle class to the working class, but more recently it has been argued that knowledge spread as women's employment changed: from the First World War more young women found employment in factories rather than as domestic servants and they picked up information about birth control from workmates.[1]

Third, there has been a greater willingness to use contraceptives. Early on in the century contraceptives were still associated with immorality and prostitution;

and they were opposed by the Church and the bulk of the medical profession. From the First World War campaigners managed to break the link between immorality and birth control. Women were more easily won around to the idea of using birth control than men, many of whom resolutely refused to use contraceptives, even if this meant running the risk of making a single, or married but ill, woman pregnant. It has been suggested that men's attitudes towards women have softened so that they have become more willing to use contraceptives in order to help relieve women of the health risks of frequent and closely spaced pregnancies, and the hard work associated with a large family. What brought about this apparent change of heart is not clear. As well as women and men wanting to relieve women of the ill health associated with large families, changing attitudes towards children and family leisure time is also thought to have contributed to smaller families. It has been suggested that with ever-lengthening formal education; child psychologists advocating child-centred activities; young people's lessening respect for authority; and fears for the safety of children, children have become more financially and emotionally costly, and more time-consuming. At the same time, the costs of contraceptives relative to incomes have dropped, and growing leisure and multiple ways of spending more disposable income have made smaller families more attractive. Finally, it is argued that, with state and occupational pensions and various other forms of welfare provision, children are no longer the only insurance against a poverty-stricken old age.

While the trend towards women having fewer babies has continued throughout the century, the proportion of unmarried women having babies declined for the first half of the century and then gradually started to rise again, until the 1980s when the proportion of unmarried to married mothers shot up. Again, historians are not agreed over the reasons for these changes. First, it has been argued that in the early part of the century, as working-class standards of living rose and as the employment alternatives to domestic service multiplied, fewer girls and young women had to leave home and enter domestic service. When girls had to move away from home there were possibly not only more opportunities for them to choose to have sex, but also a greater risk of exploitation and rape from men in the households in which the girls worked. As fewer girls moved away from home the opportunities for premarital sex declined and parental protection increased. Second, contraceptives became more widely available. It should be remembered, however, that it was not until the mid-1970s that contraceptives became easily available on the NHS to unmarried women, and by then the trend towards a higher proportion of unmarried mothers had already begun.

The growth in the proportion of unmarried mothers, particularly at the very end of the century, reflects changing social attitudes. Public attitudes towards premarital sex and the institution of marriage have changed. Feminists have highlighted the negative and abusive side of marriage, and women now expect more from a marriage than in the past. Fewer women have to tolerate miserable marriages because there are economic alternatives to dependence on a husband,

and at the end of the century it is socially acceptable for women in all classes to be separated or divorced. In the past, unmarried mothers were widely regarded as immoral women who should be punished. Now that the stigma has largely disappeared more women are choosing to be single mothers, whether previously, or never, married, and many more women than in the past openly cohabit.

It has also been argued that young people have thrown off their parents' norms of behaviour; they are more concerned with meeting their own individual wishes than those of their families or their communities. This holds true up to a point. Afro-Caribbean women who came to Britain in the 1950s and 1960s led the trend towards unmarried motherhood, so their daughters are not rejecting their mothers' behaviour, but following in their footsteps. White young people are behaving in a fashion which would have been largely unacceptable to their parents' generation when young, but a higher proportion of Asian mothers are married than white or Afro-Caribbean ones, which suggests that fewer Asian young women are willing, or able, to fly in the face of their community's mores. While a higher proportion of women are choosing to be unmarried mothers than earlier this century, the extent to which teenagers are making a rational choice to become mothers is not so clear. While there is some evidence that some teenagers make a positive choice to become pregnant, for others it is the result of a lack of knowledge of contraception, or of misjudging the risks of pregnancy.

Despite the apparently easy availability and reliability of contraceptives, in the late 1990s one in a hundred girls under the age of 16 became pregnant. Half of all pregnancies occurred outside marriage, and in some inner-city areas the figure was nearer two-thirds. A rapid change took place over the 1980s and 1990s: in 1986 nearly two-thirds of all conceptions were within marriage; a decade later only a half were within marriage. Of all conceptions outside marriage just over one third were terminated by abortion, and of all conceptions roughly one fifth were terminated by abortion. The absence or failure of sex education for young people has been pointed to for many years, but sex education for children and young people has always been constrained by critics who have argued that it encourages promiscuity among the young. The teenage pregnancy rate at the end of the 1990s in Britain – especially in relation to comparable countries which have extensive educational programmes and easily available contraceptives and far lower teenage pregnancy rates – has aroused such alarm in the media and in political circles, that government action has finally been taken.[2]

IN FOCUS: Controversies Over Women's Health: War, Work and Empire

---

In the opening years of the twentieth century there was widespread concern over Britain's ability to defend its economy and empire. Fears of poor, and apparently declining, standards of health which were assumed to be

Controversies Over Women's Health: War, Work and Empire (continued)

undermining Britain's competitiveness turned public attention to the way in which working-class mothers bore and reared their children, the future workers in industry and soldiers in the field. Mothers' ability to look after their own, and their families', health transformed the issue from a private domestic matter to a public and imperial one. There was a focus not only on the social, economic and environmental conditions in which families lived, but also on the behaviour of working-class mothers. It was assumed that a mother had a duty to the nation to look after the health and well-being of herself and her family. During the Edwardian years disagreements existed over whether a mother who undertook paid work was undermining her own and her family's health, or whether by bringing much-needed cash into the home, she was improving the family's standard of health.

Once war broke out and there was a demand for women's labour to replace that of men who had joined the Armed Forces, less was heard of the deleterious effects of women's paid work outside the home on the health of the nation. Both the First World War and the Second World War prompted concerns over women's health: one concern related to working-class women's allegedly immoral behaviour which was supposedly leading to the infection of the fighting forces with venereal disease (VD) and to a rise in the illegitimacy rates. Women's morals became the subject of public debate, and in both wars the government initiated investigations into the sexual morals of women in the auxiliary forces. In the Second World War the question took on another twist because of British women's liaisons with black American troops, of which the American authorities disapproved, and the birth of mixed race babies to British unmarried women. In an effort to appease the American authorities, without upsetting Britain's allies in the black empire, efforts were made to frighten British women away from black American soldiers by spreading rumours that they were riddled with VD.

A second wartime concern was over the health of women who undertook vital war work, especially in munition factories. In both wars standards of health and safety for women in industry initially plummeted as women worked excessively long hours in poor conditions. Official interest developed when married women had high absenteeism rates, and this prompted concern about their health. While some women in both wars worked in extremely dangerous conditions, and the health of women who worked with TNT which turned their skin yellow and led to the nickname 'canaries' was especially poor, married women – of whom more undertook paid work in the Second World War than in the First World War – had high absenteeism rates for reasons other than ill health brought on by their place of work. Married women had the burden of paid and unpaid work, and the latter was especially stressful in wartime because of rationing, queuing and the lack of adequate nursery schools and child-care provision.

Health Services

Throughout the first half of the twentieth century health care for women was patchy and much less adequate than for men. It was rare for women, unlike men, to be covered by friendly societies for General Practitioner (GP) or hospital care. Voluntary hospitals required payment; some women were covered by a hospital insurance, but the cost of voluntary hospitals was beyond the reach of most women. Poor Law, from 1929 known as local authority, infirmaries provided lower standards, and carried the stigma of their long association with the Poor Law. Women were subjected to a means test before free treatment was offered. Hospitals ran outpatient clinics and dispensaries where women could receive treatment. The costs and inconvenience of formal health services meant that most women treated themselves or relied on advice from family and neighbours. At the end of the 1930s it was noted that 'The woman comes onto the map of the public conscience only when she is performing the bodily function of producing a child.'[3]

From 1911 national health insurance (NHI) covered working-class men through their employment – but almost no women – for GP and hospital treatment, and for financial support when they were off work through ill health. The bulk of married women did not undertake paid work in the formal economy so they did not pay into NHI or receive its benefits. Those women who were covered paid in at a lower rate and consequently received lower benefits, which were cut in 1915 and again in 1932. Any woman claiming NHI was closely monitored. There was a 30s maternity payment which all those who were part of the scheme could claim: men in the scheme could claim it for their wives, as could women who paid NHI.

Up until the Second World War women's organisations demanded free medical treatment for women to no avail. Public health and maternity provision was the responsibility of local authorities so provision varied from place to place, and was usually worse in poorer areas where it was most needed. From the 1920s infant and maternal welfare clinics, as well as a health-visiting service to visit mothers after the birth of a baby, spread unevenly around the country, relying on local resources and initiatives. Clinics and health visitors could only offer advice not free treatment or, more importantly, cash support. In the early years of the century, most women gave birth at home, with the help of family or neighbours, or a midwife who may or may not have received any training. A midwifery service developed across the country, but it was not until after 1936 that a national and trained service was put in place. Over the course of the 1920s and 1930s a growing number of women entered hospital to give birth, but because of the problems of cross-infection this was not a safe option and contributed to the high maternal mortality rate. From the First World War the slow spread of voluntary birth control clinics meant that some women had access to contraception, but too many closely spaced pregnancies were the scourge of poor women.

Plate 6.1. School nurse, mothers and children outside a school clinic, Plymouth, Devon, late 1930s.

IN FOCUS: Poverty and Women's Health in the 1930s Depression

Throughout the 1930s arguments raged over the relationship between poverty and poor health. Women were at the centre of the argument for two reasons. First, the persistently high maternal mortality rate prompted research which produced conflicting evidence. Government reports blamed women and their relatives for their irresponsibility in not taking medical advice and in not using the available maternity services. Maternity services, however, varied between local authorities which in practice meant that poorer women received the poorest service. In 1930 an experiment by Rochdale's Medical Officer of Health to improve obstetric care led to an impressive fall in the MMR. Yet, schemes in the Rhondda area of Wales to improve maternity services made little difference to the MMR. Instead, food was distributed to women at clinics and this did lead to a fall in the MMR, which suggested that women without enough money for an adequate diet suffered from malnutrition which affected their health and even their life in pregnancy. For contemporary critics of government policies the root of the problem lay in women's poverty. Yet, until 1935 the MMR remained

Poverty and Women's Health in the 1930s Depression (continued)

high for poor and rich alike, which points to another piece in the puzzle. One possible further contributory explanation is that the MMR remained high because of the trend towards women giving birth in hospitals, where infection spread like wildfire. It was not until after 1935 when sulphonamides were used to treat puerperal fever that the MMR showed a real improvement.

Second, women were at the centre of the controversy over the relationship between poverty and the poor health of their families. Government sources identified women's lack of skills in the kitchen as the cause of poor nutrition. Ranged against the government was a growing dossier of evidence pointing to poor families, especially among the unemployed in the depressed areas, simply having too little money for the mother to buy enough food for an adequate diet. Mothers, moreover, suffered most because they would cut back on their meals for the sake of the husband and children. The contribution of diet to health was found to be even more important than housing: when families moved to new housing estates as a result of slum clearance programmes, mothers had even less money in their purses because of higher rents, and health deteriorated. The poor health of many women is documented in a survey conducted by the Women's Cooperative Guild (WCG) which details in women's own words their experience of ill health, diet and housing. For many women 'good health is any interval between illnesses, or at best the absence of any incapacitating ailment. They consider themselves not only fortunate, but well, as long as they can keep going and can get through the work that must be done.'[4]

While public controversy over the link between poverty and ill health focused on families, the plight of many single women without employment and a man to support them financially, at a time when there was no free health service, was dire:

> Among the older age groups the health of the women interviewed was very poor. A large number of our applicants suffer from rheumatism, bronchitis, nerve, bad eyes, bad teeth and a host of minor ailments. Some have [had] severe operations from which owing to the absence of after care there has been no complete recovery. It is the exception, not the rule, to hear a woman say her health is good. Nervous strain is common, due to unemployment, unsatisfactory home conditions and insufficient food. Anxiety about the future prays on their minds. . . . The medical aspects of these women is most unsatisfactory. The majority have long since exhausted their health benefit and do not know where to turn for medical aid. . . . a mass of illness remains untouched and unrelieved.[5]

Poverty and Women's Health in the 1930s Depression (continued)

The National Government, and the Ministry of Health in particular, belittled as unreliable and politically inspired, or ignored, independent research which drew links between poverty and ill health. The Ministry of Health put out misleading aggregate statistics which covered up poor standards of health and high mortality rates in areas of high unemployment, fobbed off its critics and even threatened the livelihood of doctors who spoke out against it. The Ministry alleged that poor women's bad household management, lack of hygiene and poor cooking aggravated the effects of low incomes on their families and caused ill health. The Ministry claimed that poverty was not the cause of ill health, but rather mothers caused their own ill health through ignorance and irresponsibility.

The government refused to accept the arguments of its critics for a number of reasons. The implications of poverty causing ill health were that the government should spend more money on providing poor families with higher incomes and with better welfare services, in order to counter the effects of the depression. The National Government, however, was driven by a policy of balancing the budget and of keeping down taxation and spending, in order to create an economically stable environment for trade. Unemployment was not evenly spread around the country, and the government wanted people in the depressed areas to move elsewhere for work, and for employment always to be more attractive than unemployment. Thus, research which unearthed evidence of poor health and malnutrition in the depressed areas struck at the very heart of the National Government's economic strategy. As with the pre-First World War controversy over the health of the nation, the row in the 1930s over the relationship between poverty and poor health, linked the role of working-class mothers in maintaining the health of their families with the future prosperity of the country.

The introduction of the NHS, which came into operation in 1948, providing a range of services free at the point of use, had the biggest impact on married women. Free GP and hospital treatment, along with rising standards of living contributed to women enjoying better health. Although a free contraceptive service was not introduced until the 1970s women could more easily limit the size of their families – due to a greater knowledge of contraception than in the past, and more easily purchased contraceptives such as condoms – which also contributed greatly to their improved health. The NHS was essentially a curative service, it was many years before it developed a stronger preventative role, so many of women's health needs relating to reproduction were not well catered for in the NHS's early years.

The introduction of the contraceptive pill in 1962 has helped women to avoid unwanted pregnancies, to plan their families with greater sureness than ever before and has therefore increased the control which women exert over their lives to a greater extent than in the past. Its impact has been felt well beyond the confines of the home. The pill, nevertheless, is not an unmitigated benefit to women. There are health risks associated with the pill for women, so that contraception still remains a health risk for women, but not for men, and a greater burden for women than men. From time to time health scares break out over the pill, although its safety has improved over the years so that at the end of the century it is mainly a health risk for women with high blood pressure and smokers. While increasing the risks of strokes, thrombosis and certain cancers, it has a protective effect against ovarian cancer. The major alternatives to the pill available to women included the coil, which also carried health risks, or barrier methods such as the cap or condom. Women were forced to weigh up the advantages of the condom, easy availability, no health risk and protection against sexually transmitted diseases, with lower levels of reliability as a contraceptive.

In 1967 abortion was legalised, but was dependent on two doctors certifying that a pregnancy to full term would harm the woman; it was not abortion on demand and for this reason the law on abortion has been criticised by those who have argued that it reinforces male doctors' control over women rather than enhances women's control over their bodies. The way in which the law operates in practice, with varying abortion rates around the country, which reflects the differing attitudes of doctors both towards abortion in principle and towards different groups of women (young or old, middle class or working class, mothers or not mothers) has also been a source of distress and criticism.

A further controversy over women's reproduction joined that of abortion in 1978 following the birth of a healthy baby after *in vitro* fertilisation (IVF), a technique for getting around problems of infertility. As well as questions about the ethics of 'test-tube babies' as the popular press dubbed them, there have been disagreements over whether the NHS should fund such treatment; IVF treatment on the NHS is not a woman's right, and depends on the funding policy of the local health authority, and thus where a woman lives. Doubts have also continued about its efficacy: there are those who claim that it is increasingly successful while others claim that it is not significantly more successful than spontaneous pregnancy.[6]

The prewar trend towards hospitalisation at childbirth continued under the NHS: in the 1950s roughly two-thirds of births took place in hospital, by 1990 barely one per cent of babies were born at home. Hospitalisation at childbirth was widely regarded as safer than a home birth and, while this is certainly true when there is a complication, hospital births are as much a matter of convenience and efficiency for medical and nursing staff as a safety issue for mothers and babies when the birth is a straightforward one. In the last quarter of the century medical interventions, such as inductions and caesarian sections, shot up. At the same time researchers uncovered widespread dissatisfaction with maternity services among mothers who complained above all about the lack of communication and continuity of care, and about long waits.[7] How far women were less satisfied than in the past is, however, impossible to judge as there is no comparable qualitative research from earlier in the century.

A large body of different feminist critiques on the NHS now exist. Earlier in the century women criticised the absence of general and specific services for women, and presented women's health needs in a rounded fashion, rather than in distinct compartments of life. Feminists have developed these earlier critiques, pointing to women's continued lack of control over their bodies and their health. Control over women's bodies continued to lie with a male-dominated medical establishment which has favoured ever-increasing medical intervention in women's lives, turning 'normal' life events into medical ones.[8]

From the outset the NHS was gendered in meeting health needs, and contained a sexual division of labour with men dominating medicine. Problems of low pay and poor working conditions, which had always existed in nursing, continued to dog the service and contributed to the acute shortage of nurses, which from the 1950s prompted the government to recruit women from Asia and the Caribbean to work in the NHS. Although the NHS was disproportionately staffed by poorly paid women recruited from countries of the former British empire, their health needs did not receive sympathetic attention. At the end of the century it was still the case that a higher proportion of NHS employees were women than men, and of the female employees a high proportion were ethnic minority women.

Differences Between Women and Men, and Between Women

There are two striking, and consistent, differences between women and men: women are apparently less healthy than men but then live longer. At the same time, both women and men have benefited from increased life expectancy over the course of the century. Trends in death rates and their causes can be charted over the century although it is harder to provide consistent evidence for illness, and attitudes towards health and illness, because of the absence of information culled by the same methods throughout the century. Ideas about what it means to be 'ill' or 'healthy' have changed, and vary between women and men, and between ethnic groups. Attitudes towards 'health' and what symptoms require treatment as well as financial, social and psychological barriers to seeking treatment all affect both women's experiences of health and illness, and the statistics which are then used to draw conclusions about women's health. Statistics on mortality are never entirely accurate because causes of death are not always clear cut, and the reasons for the greater longevity of women is still speculative. Is it because women are genetically stronger than men and better able to resist diseases, or is it because men live more risky and dangerous lives, which is reflected in a higher death rate from accidents?

Whether women really are less healthy than men is debateable. It has been argued first, that women live more stressful lives than men which leads to more ill health among women; second, that throughout the century women have

Plate 6.2. Healthy young women enjoying their leisure time in the 1950s.

borne the brunt of poverty, and as there is a close relationship between poverty and ill health this explains why women's health is worse than men's health, and third, that in the first half of the century health care and treatment was less easily accessed by women than men. Yet, it is possible that women are not actually less healthy than men, but only appear statistically so. Stereotypes of women and men created in the nineteenth century, but still current in the twentieth century, project women as the weaker sex; the medical profession has more readily labelled women as mentally ill than men, and it is possible that women express stress through illness while men express stress through violence. Finally, research for the latter part of the century indicates that when reproductive-related reasons for the use of health services are removed, women hardly make any more use of health services than men.[9] The jury is still out, therefore, on whether there are differences between women and men's stand-ards of health. Just as problematic are the causes of health differences between women.

Inequalities between women have been little researched, and most of the evidence relates to the latter part of the century. The categories, such as occupa-tion for determining social class, which researchers have used for investigating social inequalities in standards of health are not very illuminating for women. Despite a higher proportion of women than men living in poverty throughout the century, most earlier research focused on the links between men's, rather than women's, health and poverty. Attempts to develop more appropriate measures of women's socio-economic inequalities indicate that women in manual occupations, single women in manual occupations, women living in rented accommodation and women with no access to a car suffer high mortality rates. When women suffer from all these disadvantages combined, their death rates are two to three times higher than for women in non-manual occupations and with access to a car.[10] Research shows that women living in the most disadvantaged circumstances are likely to behave in a less healthy way – in terms of diet, exercise, alcohol consumption and smoking – than women in more socially and economically advantaged situations.

Ethnic minority women are especially likely to suffer from the multiple disadvantages listed above. Women born in Africa, the Caribbean or the Indian subcontinent and now living in Britain, as well as their daughters born in Britain suffer from higher death rates, including maternal mortality rates, than other women in Britain. From the 1980s there is evidence that black women are under greater economic pressure to work during pregnancy, and to return to paid work soon after childbirth.[11] Despite indicators of ethnic minority women's poorer health, research into the health of ethnic minority women is very limited. Many publications on the health of ethnic minorities do not distinguish between women's and men's health, and the research that has been undertaken has various methodological flaws. The apparently poorer health of particular ethnic minority groups could be explained by a range of factors which include racism and discrimination leading to stress, lower educational attainment, poor employment prospects, poor housing, an unhealthy environment, as well as health services not tailored to the needs of each group of women. It is impossible to discuss trends between ethnic groups over the century because of the way in which the composition of ethnic minority groups has changed, from predominantly Irish and Jewish to predominantly Irish, black and Asian.

Conclusion

Throughout the twentieth century official concern over women's health has been intimately concerned with women's behaviour and reproductive role. In the early years of the century arguments raged over the links between women's paid work and their reproductive capacity. Working-class women in particular were singled out for criticism of their lifestyles which, it was argued, were undermining the health and well-being of the next generation, a matter of national concern because of the belief that a healthy and efficient working class was required to maintain Britain's edge over economic competitors and defence of the empire. Official gaze and action therefore focused on the needs of children rather than the mothers and led to the opening of infant welfare clinics offering advice to mothers but no financial assistance, medical aid or contraceptives, the very things required to improve their health.

While the infant mortality rate declined (for reasons unrelated to infant welfare clinics) the MMR remained persistently high in all classes, a subject of grave concern to women's groups who campaigned, with only a modicum of success, for a range of benefits to improve the health and MMR of working-class women. Arguments over the causes of the high MMR and the poor health of poor women, well documented by contemporaries who adopted a broad, holistic approach, peaked in the 1930s when campaigners roundly condemned governments' narrow, behavioural analyses of women's ill health. The exclusion of the vast majority of women from the national health insurance scheme does not indicate that women's health was a priority for governments.

In the early postwar years women's health issues were subsumed under general concerns and assumptions about the impact of the NHS on different classes. When women's health again came to the fore in public discussion it was in the context of the alleged social and sexual revolution of the 1960s, the legalisation of abortion and the introduction of the family planning service. The huge contribution made by poorly paid women to the NHS went largely unacknowledged, and it was some years before the varied needs of different ethnic groups were recognised, let alone acted upon.

At a time when feminists alerted the public to particular failings of the health care system for women, and to women's formal and informal contribution to other's health, women's standard of health was higher than it had ever been in the past. How far the health services and particular medical interventions contributed to those rising standards is a matter of debate. Controversy also existed over why women appeared to have higher morbidity rates than men, but yet lived longer than men. The behaviour of particular groups of women, in particular unmarried teenage mothers, continues to be seen as a threat to society.

Throughout the twentieth century women's health has been closely related to social and economic relationships and political imperatives, and as such was integral to the social and political history of the century. The mix of determinants of patterns of women's health is as unclear in 2000 as it was at the beginning of the twentieth century. While women's day-to-day health reflected their gender and sexuality, it also reflected their age, class background and ethnic origin.

Bibliographical Note

A huge amount has been written about women's health and reproduction. The best general survey is N.L. Tranter, *British Population in the Twentieth Century* (London, 1996). The Office for National Statistics annually publishes *Social Trends* which provides up-to-date information on current social issues, including health, and places them in the context of long-term trends. Also useful from the same publisher is F. Drever and M. Whitehead (eds), *Health Inequalities: Decennial Supplement* (1997). For details and further references to many of the issues raised, see H. Jones, *Health and Society in Twentieth-Century Britain* (London, 1994).

Women's voices on their health can be heard in M. Pember Reeves, *Round About a Pound a Week* (London, 1979), first published 1913; M. Llewelyn Davies, *Maternity: Letters from Working Women* (London, 1978), first published 1915; and M. Spring Rice, *Working-Class Wives: Their Health and Conditions* (London, 1981), first published 1939.

Useful historical approaches to women's health are A. Digby and J. Stewart (eds), *Gender, Health and Welfare* (London, 1996); and L. Davidoff, M. Doolittle, J. Fink and K. Holden, *The Family Story: Blood, Contract and Intimacy, 1830–1960* (London, 1999). On the debate over women, health and poverty in the 1930s, see C. Webster, 'Healthy or Hungry 30s?', *History Workshop Journal* 13 (1982); C. Webster, 'Health, Welfare and Unemployment during the Depression', *Past and Present* 109 (1985); M. Mitchell, 'The Effects of Unemployment on the Social Conditions of Women and Children in the 1930s', *History Workshop Journal* 19 (1985); J. Winter, 'Unemployment, Nutrition and Infant Mortality in Britain, 1920–50', in J. Winter (ed), *The Working Class in Modern British History* (Cambridge, 1983); and J. Winter, 'Infant Mortality, Maternal Mortality and Public Health in Britain in the 1930s', *Journal of European Economic History* 8 (1979).

In addition to works cited in the Notes, general issues around women's health in the latter part of the century can be followed up in M. Blaxter, *Health and Lifestyles* (London, 1991); H. Roberts (ed), *Women's Health Matters* (London, 1992); and A. Miles, *Women, Health and Medicine* (Buckingham, 1991).

Notes

1. D. Gittins, 'Married Life and Birth Control Between the Wars', *Oral History* 3 (1975), pp. 55–6.

2. The above section draws heavily on N.L. Tranter, *British Population in the Twentieth Century* (London, 1996), especially pp. 72–115.

3. M. Spring Rice, *Working-Class Wives: Their Health and Conditions* (London, 1981) [first publ. 1939], p. 18.

4. Spring Rice, *Working-Class Wives*.

5. H. Jones (ed), *Duty and Citizenship: The Correspondence and Political Papers of Violet Markham, 1896–1953* (London, 1994), p. 137. Unemployment Assistance Board memo., 31 May 1937.

6. J. Harris and S. Holm, *The Future of Human Reproduction: Ethics, Choice and Regulation* (Oxford, 1998).

7. C. Martin, 'How Do You Count Maternal Satisfaction? A User-commissioned Survey of Maternal Services', and A. Oakley, 'Who's Afraid of the Randomized Controlled Trial?', in H. Roberts (ed), *Women's Health Counts* (London, 1990), pp. 147–94.

8. A. Oakley, *Essays on Women, Medicine and Health* (Edinburgh, 1993); P. Foster, *Women and the Health Care Industry: An Unhealthy Relationship* (Buckingham, 1998).

9. A. MacFarlane, 'Official Statistics and Women's Health and Illness', in Roberts, *Women's Health Counts*, p. 45.

10. H. Graham, 'Behaving Well: Women's Health Behaviour in Context', in Roberts, *Women's Health Counts*, p. 201.

11. S. Payne, *Women, Health and Poverty: An Introduction* (London, 1991).

7

AGEING – OLDER WOMEN

Pat Thane

The Ageing of British Society

By the mid-twentieth century, for the first time in history, almost everyone in Britain could expect to live out a full lifespan from birth to old age. This was due, above all, to the rapid decline in death rates among infants and young children and, to a lesser extent, to falling death rates in middle age. Over time it became normal to expect to grow old and more people were living to later ages than ever before. This is clear from Table 7.1. However, this table, like all statistical tables, should be read with care. In everyday discourse it is often asserted that in 'the past' most people lived only into middle age, to their thirties or forties. So it appears, at first glance, from the table. But what it shows is only life expectancy *at birth*. Infant mortality was at very high levels in the

Table 7.1. **Expectation of life at birth for generations born 1841–1991, United Kingdom**

Year of birth	Males	Females	Year of birth	Males	Females
1841	39	42	1921	61	68
1851	40	43	1931	66	72
1861	42	45	1941	69.6	75.4
1871	44	49	1951	72.7	78.3
1881	47	52	1961	73.6	79.1
1891	48	54	1971	74.6	79.7
1901	51	58	1981	75.5	80.4
1911	56	63	1991	76	80.8

Source: Office of Population Censuses and Surveys (OPCS), *National Population Projections 1989 Based*, series PP2, No. 17 (London: HMSO, 1991), Table 2, p. 5, from P. Johnson and J. Falkingham, *Ageing and Economic Welfare* (London, 1992), p. 23.

nineteenth century and at the beginning of the twentieth century and deaths at very early ages pull down the average life expectancy of the whole birth cohort. At the beginning of the twentieth century, and before, those who survived the early years of life in fact had a good chance of living to old age.

Why Do Women Outlive Men?

Table 7.1 also shows that throughout the century, as for long before, women have outlived men. Table 7.2 demonstrates that women keep this advantage even at later ages. This table also shows that among those who survive to the latest ages the gap in life expectancy between men and women has grown over the century. Why do women live longer than men? From birth, females are more effectively physically conditioned for survival than males. They start life with a longer life expectancy. Through their lifetimes females are less frequently exposed to, and are less likely to expose themselves to, conditions which hasten death, such as physically heavy or dangerous occupations, or activities, or heavy smoking or drinking, though there are signs in the later decades of the century that the gender gap in these respects is diminishing.

Yet, though women live longer, they are not necessarily healthier than men of comparable ages. Older women suffer more illness and longer periods of disability than men of the same ages. In many cases this is due to the long-term effects of childbirth. Also, the menopause is a stage of ageing which for some women is physically debilitating. But since this can occur at ages varying from the late thirties to the late fifties it is not a simple marker of the onset of old age. It has become still less so for some women with the introduction of Hormone Replacement Therapy (HRT) in the 1980s. HRT was widely used by post-menopausal women in the 1990s. This may ease the transition and diminish the likelihood of certain physical ill effects which can result from the menopause,

Table 7.2. Expectations of life at birth, at 65 and at 80 for men and women, Great Britain, 1906–85

	At birth		At age 65		At age 80	
	Men	Women	Men	Women	Men	Women
1906	48	52	11	12	5	5
1961	68	74	12	15	5	6
1985	72	77	13	17	6	8
2011*	75	80				

* projected.

Source: CSO (1989), Table 7.2, from S. Arber and J. Ginn, *Gender and Later Life* (London, 1991), p. 9.

such as osteoporosis (the thinning of bone-mass causing breakages and spinal curvature). Also menopause is a highly variable experience. In the later twentieth century about one-third of all women experienced significant health problems associated with it and another third none at all. Very little is known about the experience of menopause in the past, other than anecdotally.

A more important cause of ill health among older women has been poverty. Throughout the twentieth century the social group experiencing the greatest poverty in Britain has been women past the age of 60. The reason is that women have had fewer opportunities through their lifetimes to accumulate savings or other assets due to their generally more limited employment opportunities and incomes. Some have been supported by, or inherited assets from, prosperous husbands, but most have not. Poverty is a major cause of ill health for males and females in all age groups.

One outcome of the longer lives of older women is that a high proportion of them live alone. Table 7.3 could be interpreted to mean that a very high, and especially in the second half of the century an increasing, proportion of old women were isolated and lonely. But, again, the table can be interpreted differently. There is much evidence throughout the century, and for earlier centuries, that older people preferred to keep their independence and to control their own lives, to living in the homes of others, even of their own adult children. They were aware of the tensions that can result when the generations share a home. As the century has gone on more older people have been able to afford to

Table 7.3. **Proportion of elderly men and women reported as living alone, United Kingdom, 1684–1985 (percentages)**

1684–1769	Males	Females	All
1684–1769	6	14	10
1891	10	16	13
1901	7	13	10
1911	8	9	9
1921	10	18	14
1951	8	16	13
1962*	11	30	22
1980*	14	38	28
1985	20	47	36

* refers to those over 60 years of age.

Sources: J. Falkingham and C. Gordon, 'Fifty Years on: The Income and Household Composition of the Elderly in London and Britain', in W.B. Bytheway and J. Johnson (eds), *Welfare and the Ageing Experience* (Aldershot, 1990), Table 12.4, p. 157; and OPCS, General Household Survey, 1985 (London, 1987).

maintain their own households and lead their own lives. Older women were more likely to live alone than older men because they outlived their male partners.

But living alone is not the same as being lonely. Again, the evidence is strong that old people who lived alone were generally in regular contact with their children and with other relatives and friends. Although society in the later twentieth century was more mobile than in earlier generations still a majority of older people who have surviving children lived within easily accessible distance of at least one child. Also as modern communications have developed – the telephone, motor, air and rail transport, e-mail – the generations have been enabled to maintain contact and to exchange support over much longer distances than in the past. And older people were more likely to have surviving children than in earlier centuries or at the beginning of the twentieth century when high death rates meant that many people outlived their own children. Though families were smaller, on average, at the end of the century than at the beginning, higher survival rates meant that children were more likely to be alive when their parents grow old. At any time up to the 1970s at least one-third of people aged 75 and over had no surviving children. In the 1990s this was true of less than 20 per cent. At all times some older people have been lonely and neglected, but most have not. Many have lived with adult children or other relatives especially at the very end of life if they become disabled and dependent (as most older people do not). The fact that throughout the century older people resident in institutions – workhouses earlier in the century, for poor old people, private residential homes for the better off; public and private residential homes since the Second World War – have been disproportionately those without close relatives and that they have never numbered more than 5 per cent of the older population, suggests the reality and importance of family relationships in old age.

These relationships have not simply taken the form of the young supporting the old. The reality is best conveyed by examples.

IN FOCUS: Old Women's Relationships and Survival Strategies

---

1. Middlesbrough, 1907

At the beginning of the century Lady (Florence) Bell, the wife of a local manufacturer explored working-class life in Middlesbrough, a heavy industrial town in north-eastern England. She reported that:

> One constantly finds on going into a cottage where the young wife is ill, or her children are ill, her mother managing the situation, the competent motherly old woman sitting by the fireside with one or more of the babies in her arms and seemingly steering the whole household.[1]

Old Women's Relationships and Survival Strategies (continued)

2. York, 1936

When Seebohm Rowntree surveyed poverty in the northern town of York in 1936 he found older people exchanging mutual support. For example an unmarried woman aged 59 was deaf and could not work:

> Has father aged 80 living with her, who pays 20 shillings weekly out of his pension of 24. Another spinster aged 57 (a lifelong friend) lives with her. She is in poor health but manages to earn a little by cleaning. She pays 12 shillings for her keep. They were very poor.[2]

3. Wolverhampton, 1947

A survey in Wolverhampton, in the Midlands, shortly after the Second World War uncovered many examples of 'the extent to which old people who are ostensibly living alone . . . are in actual fact by no means living alone but are in close and regular contact with their children'. For example:

> A widow aged 70 lives by herself. She habitually spends the day with a married daughter living in the same street and helps to look after the grandchildren, which she greatly enjoys and at which she is very useful. She only uses her own home for bed and breakfast. In case of illness, of either the subject or the daughter, each would look after the other.[3]

4. Bethnal Green, 1955

A decade later Peter Townsend found similar relationships in East London. For example:

> Mrs Hopkins, a widow in her early sixties, lived alone in a new council flat. She did most of her own shopping, cooking, cleaning and washing, although she had some help with errands from one of her daughters-in-law, a grandson and one of her two sons, all of whom lived in an adjoining borough. In the day she looked after a grandson, aged six, and at midday her son came for a meal and so did her other son's wife. She charged them 2s each for the meal. 'I wouldn't cook for myself. That's why I like them coming.' She spent her weekends with one or other of her sons.
>
> A woman and her married daughters living nearby were able to organise domestic work and care of the children in such a way that each of them was able to maintain a part-time job. The grandmother went off to work as an office cleaner at 6 in the morning, returning home at 10 am. She then had the care of the grandchildren while two married daughters went out to work. . . . The daughters did her shopping on their way home from work.[4]

What Do We Mean by 'Old Age'?

When do people become 'old'? It is conventional at the end of the twentieth century to define old age as beginning around the ages of 60 or 65. This is because these are the ages at which state old age pensions are paid (60 for women, 65 for men). These ages were fixed earlier in the twentieth century when pensions were first introduced: 65 was established as the pensionable age in 1925; it was reduced to 60 for women in 1940. At these dates these were generally felt to be the ages at which men and women found it difficult to work to support themselves due to physical decline caused by ageing and so needed support from elsewhere. The very first state pensions were in fact paid at age 70, to men and women, from 1908, but this age was chosen in order to limit the cost of pensions and was generally believed to be too high. Very many old people died or suffered severe poverty before living to be old enough to draw the pension: 65 was widely thought to be a more appropriate age. For most pensioners this became the pensionable age in 1925. The pension age for women was reduced again to 60, in 1940, mainly because some women protested that, regardless of their physical fitness, women found it more difficult than men to find paid work as they grew older, due largely to prejudice against employing older women. Employers, for example, preferred young to older women as secretaries. This continued to be an issue after the Second World War. The Sex Discrimination Act, 1986, made it illegal for men and women to be made to retire at different ages. The European Commission ruled that from 1992 the gender difference in pension ages must gradually be eliminated, though it could be argued that this is a rare instance of discrimination in favour of women. Such a differential was increasingly unusual elsewhere in Europe by the 1990s.

It is questionable whether pension ages set so long ago still define the beginning of old age at the end of the twentieth century, following decades in which improved living standards and improved medical care have resulted in more women and men living longer and, on the whole, remaining healthier until later ages. Medical opinion in the year 2000 suggests that 75 is a more appropriate age at which to place the onset of old age, in terms of the physical capacities of women and men. But even this cannot be an invariable rule. People 'age' at variable paces. Some are very active in their eighties, others are sadly decrepit. There is greater variety in the condition and circumstances of older than of younger age groups, and the difference is greatest among women, since they include the poorest and the frailest old people. People can be described as 'old' at ages from the fifties to past 100. They can include some of the richest and the poorest, the very fit and the extremely frail. This variety has been evident throughout the century and has increased over the second half of the century as Britain itself has become a more varied society. In particular it has become increasingly multi-cultural and the first generation of migrants from the Commonwealth, who arrived in the 1950s, were among the elderly at the end of the century. The different life experiences and different cultural expectations of diverse cultural groups influence their experiences of ageing. For example

Asian elders expect to live with their married children, as, historically, ageing British people have not.

'Old age', then, is not a category, or an experience, which is fixed and un-changing over time or among different social groups at the same time. Also, the example given above of pension ages suggests that old age is not defined simply by biology, that is by physical characteristics. Old age is popularly believed to begin at the pension age, even though physically many people are no longer 'old', as they were earlier in the century, when they reach those ages. The reduction of women's pension age in 1940 suggests that women were then defined as 'old' at earlier ages than men and were perceived by employers as incapable of work at earlier ages (though they themselves felt able to work) for reasons which had more to do with prejudice and employers' preference for employing younger women who were thought to be more decorative, than with the actual physical condition of the older women.

'Old age' unquestionably is a physical experience: hair becomes grey, the skin becomes wrinkled, limbs stiffen. It is not simply a cultural construct. But ideas of who is old and of what old people can do and how they should behave are often culturally conditioned, products of perception and prejudice rather than of objective assessment. Cultural groups may have fixed expectations of what people should wear and how they should behave at certain ages. Older women themselves, both now and earlier in the century, also vary immensely in how they define old age and assess and experience it. Their own comments show that old age is not always a sad or a pitiable condition, though for some it may be.

IN FOCUS: Older People Describe Old Age

Beatrice Webb (1858–1943) the writer and social reformer wrote in her diary about her own old age and that of her husband Sidney Webb, a Labour Party politician and her co-author. In 1933 when she was 73 and Sidney aged 74 she reported:

> Watching the milestones of departing strength. For the first two or three years of our life here – 1924–6 – the longest walk was eight miles or a little over; for the next five or six years, six to seven remained my limit. Yesterday I dared for the first time in six months the shorter round, which is five miles and was overtired in heart and muscle. Sidney can do more than I, but he claims he is tired at five or six miles.

But she remained optimistic:

> Still I have my eyesight and my hearing; I can go for a three or four mile walk: sort material, read and talk, listen to my wireless; above all I have the companionship of my beloved.

Older People Describe Old Age (continued)

Plate 7.1. Beatrice Webb aged 83 at home in Liphook, Hampshire, 1941.

And Beatrice described the old age of her youngest sister, Rosy, who as a young woman had been a highly problematic anorexic. At almost 70 she was enjoying greater independence than ever in her life. She had visited for a week:

> between her voyage to the Arctic regions around Spitzbergen and returning to Majorca for the winter . . . at 70 Rosy is happier and healthier than I have ever known her during her youth and prime of life . . . she has become a globe-trotter with a purpose . . . her husband and children are more or less dependent upon her for subsidies and she certainly is generous with her limited income – travelling third class or cheap tourist, staying at cheap lodgings . . . the secret of her happiness is her art, her freedom to go and do as she likes and make casual friends.[5]

In 1992 the Mass Observation archive[6] collected the views of a variety of people about 'Growing Older'. A 67-year-old housewife from Kent wrote:

> These days you aren't classed as old until you are 80. I don't feel old, with fashions very flexible you can look fashionable up to any age. My mother is 95 and she wears very fashionable clothes.

A 74-year-old retired barmaid wrote:

Older People Describe Old Age (continued)

> Titles of age, young, middle age, etc. really don't mean much, do they? I know young people of 25 who are 90 in their heads and 90 year olds who are young and outgoing. I decide how to age people by their behaviour . . . I think a lot of age is in your own head . . . unless you are unfortunate enough to have ill health, even then keeping your mind lively helps.

Some thought that women aged faster than men while other older women believed:

> Men would seem to stay younger until they retire when often they settle down to old age, whereas women have a slow decline. . . . Women look younger and stay younger because they take more pride in their appearance. They enjoy looking nice, buying clothes, using cosmetics, having their hair done, all this makes for ageing for women to be superficially slower than men. . . . [and] There are some cases where men seem to age rapidly on retirement and seem to feel their lives are over, whilst women if they survive the transition from mother to 'mother-whose-children-have-left-home' often seem to gain a new lease of life.

Is Old Age Different for Old Women and Old Men?

The quotations from Mass Observation suggest that the experience of old age is different between men and women. It is sometimes thought, as we have seen in the debate about women's pensionable age, that women may be defined as old at earlier ages than men and are more likely to be socially marginalised in 'old age'. To a great extent this is the extension into old age of the marginalisation experienced by women at all ages. Also for much of the century women have been defined by contemporary perceptions of physical attractiveness to a greater extent than men and so they have probably been more prone to social exclusion when that attractiveness is perceived to have waned. Older women have been less likely to exert the economic or cultural power that ensures social inclusion for many older men. It is often suggested that negative stereotypes of older women are reinforced by negative representations in the media, e.g. in soap operas or in advertisements. This has rarely been studied and where it has the results do not clearly support this interpretation.

The Mass Observation comments suggest that older women do not always feel that old age is a more negative experience for old women than for old men. Perceptions may be changing by the end of the twentieth century as some older women acquire more powerful positions and more women have the capacity to disguise ageing by the use of HRT, cosmetics and cosmetic surgery. A significant change over the course of the century, associated with rising living standards and the growing range of consumer goods and services, was the range of such aids and of the numbers of women making use of them. Such practices are sometimes criticised as cultural impositions upon older women (and increasingly, men) arising from a youth-dominated culture which inculcates a desire to prolong youth rather than 'growing old gracefully' and 'naturally' as, it is assumed, was once the norm. But such criticisms can be another form of cultural domination, restatements of old assumptions that older people should conform to a uniform stereotype. Growing old 'naturally' in previous centuries without the aid of modern medicine and artifice was by no means invariably 'graceful', and it is not obvious why at a certain age women who have coloured their hair and experimented with cosmetics since their youth should cease to do so.

Survival

Work – Paid and Unpaid

At the beginning of the century older women, like older men, if they needed to do so for survival, worked for pay until as late ages as possible. Such work is often hard to trace in the sources, because it was often part-time and casual and not reported in such sources as the census. This was especially true of women whose work was often domestic and hidden from official statistics, such as cleaning or childcare. Census statistics however provide a minimum level of involvement in the paid labour force. They show that around 21 per cent of women aged 55–59 reported themselves as employed in the 1911 census, about 11 per cent past that age. Table 7.4 shows the pattern thereafter. At the beginning of

Table 7.4. **Labour force participation in older men and women, United Kingdom, 1911–89 (percentages)**

	Men					Women				
	45–54	55–59	60–64	65–69	70+	45–54	55–59	60–64	65–69	70+
1911	—	94.1	—	56.8	—	—	21.6	—	11.5	—
1921	96.8	91.9	—	79.8	41.2	20.7	19.1	—	15.1	6.5
1931	96.7	94.1	87.6	65.4	33.4	21.0	18.8	16.3	12.2	5.5
1951	97.9	95.4	87.8	48.7	20.9	34.0	27.7	14.4	9.0	3.2
1961	98.6	97.1	91.0	39.9	15.2	43.3	36.9	20.4	13.0	3.1
1970	97.5	95.3	86.7	20.1	—	59.4	50.1	27.9	6.4	—
1985	92.1	81.8	54.5	8.2	—	69.1	51.6	18.6	3.0	—
1989	89.4	77.4	53.5	8.8	—	70.0	52.3	22.3	3.3	—

Source: P. Johnson and J. Falkingham, *Ageing and Economic Welfare* (London, 1992), p. 90.

the century it was thought that women were able to stay in some form of employment to later ages than men due to the high demand for their domestic skills, such as child care. Also, their greater poverty may have increased their need to seek work, though the work available was poorly paid. Many earned livings in their own homes: letting out rooms, taking in washing, caring for children. Rowntree described how, in York in 1936, some impoverished old women struggled to make a living:

> A few for instance keep a lodger, others earn a few pence or are paid in kind for rendering small services. To 'mind the baby' for a neighbour when the mother is out, or to wheel one in a pram on washing day and do any necessary errand, will probably mean a square meal or a 'mash of tea' and some coppers, as well as discarded garments, if the neighbour's husband is in good work.

Throughout the century at all ages women have been employed at low-paid, casual work, but have found it difficult to find work at other levels. Table 7.4 suggests a decline in such work among older women from the 1960s at the same time that men were also increasingly withdrawing from the labour force around the age of 65. The apparent rise in numbers of women aged 65–69 in the paid workforce between 1951 and 1961 was mainly because more women were in the labour force in the 1940s and 50s rather than due to a greater willingness of employers to keep older women at work.

Earlier retirement by both men and women was due to the increased value of pensions, and greater prosperity, which ensured that more older people had savings and that their children could give them more support than before. But increasingly from the 1970s an outcome of growing unemployment and restructuring of the labour force was even earlier retirement, sometimes voluntary, sometimes not, of both male and female workers. An effect of the economic recession was that increasing numbers of women and men were retiring even before the age of 60. However the extent of unrecorded part-time work by older women throughout the century remains uncertain.

Older like younger women continued through the century to work hard at caring for themselves and others in the household and the community: for spouses while they survived and for children, grandchildren, friends and neighbours. As life expectancy rose, women past the age of 60 increasingly were carers of older people still. Examples of older women's unpaid work can be seen in the descriptions of their family relationships above.

Welfare

Throughout the century older women were more vulnerable to poverty than men of comparable ages and more of them survived. In consequence as the scope of state welfare grew through the century more of them were dependent upon it and gained from it. At the beginning of the century the Poor Law was

Plate 7.2. 'Holiday Kicks'. Older women enjoying the seaside, 1955.

the only source of state welfare. The majority of recipients of poor relief (paupers) were people aged over 65; a majority of them were female, but only a small minority (about 5 per cent) of all older men and women were paupers. When state pensions were introduced in 1908 the main reason why they were 'non-contributory' and financed wholly from taxation, rather than, as some proposed, on a national insurance basis as they later became, was that they were designed above all to relieve severe poverty and it was recognised that the greatest need in old age was among women who were too irregularly employed and poorly paid to contribute to an insurance system. These first pensions were of limited amount (up to 5s a week), which was insufficient for survival without further assistance. They were means-tested and targeted upon the very poor. A higher proportion of old people applied for them than had applied for poor relief, which carried far greater social stigma. Sixty-three per cent of the first pensioners who qualified under the rigorous tests were women, though they were only 58 per cent of the over 70 age group. The kind of life they led was described by two old women to a government investigation in 1919. One of them, Mrs Caroline Thompson, was a widow aged 73. Her total income was 9s 6d a week: her pension (which had risen to 7s 6d during the First World War) plus 2s from a charity. Of this 3s was spent on rent, 3s 8d on lighting, fuel, laundry and insurance; 2s 10d remained for food. The only meat she could afford was four ounces of bacon each week. She drank no fresh milk and a single tin of milk lasted a fortnight. Four ounces of butter, one loaf of bread, 2 ounces of tea and a little coffee formed the bulk of her diet. Sometimes she felt weak from lack of food. In winter she had a fire only every other day. She had a son who, she stated, 'used to allow me something up to his illness . . . if he had it he would be very, very good to me'. Some friends passed on their used clothes to her and 'a bit of food', but no cash 'because they are not well off'. She did her best to repay them, saying 'I try to make it up to them, but not what they give me'. So about twice a week she did some tidying and washing up for them and 'a bit of sewing'. She could not manage anything heavier.[7]

National insurance pensions were introduced in 1925. They were paid at age 65 and benefited mainly men. Women were rarely regularly employed in the kind of jobs which enabled them to pay the weekly contributions. They qualified for the pension either as wives of insured men at age 65 or continued to receive just the non-contributory pension at age 70. As already described, women successfully campaigned for pensions at 60 which they gained in 1940. Still immense poverty remained, as was revealed in shocking wartime surveys. A typical enough case was an old lady who confessed, reluctantly and with dignity, that 'she had only what she stood up in . . . an old, thin skirt, a torn cardigan and no blouse – and slept under a single tattered blanket and meagre cotton coverlet'.

Partly in consequence of these wartime revelations the Beveridge Report in 1942 recommended the increase and universalisation of pensions. This was introduced in 1948, although most married women remained dependent upon their husband's insurance contributions and the pension alone has never provided an adequate income without supplementation from means-tested state benefits or other sources. This has been revealed by a succession of surveys. Townsend found in the 1960s that the largest group 'in poverty' in Britain were women aged 65 and above.[8] The Joseph Rowntree Foundation similarly showed in 1995 that very old women were especially vulnerable to severe poverty. Younger women were benefiting from the spread of second (employer or private) pensions, but more slowly than men.[9]

Women of all ages gained immeasurably from the introduction of the National Health Service in 1948. Poorer women had previously had least access to free health care despite their relatively poor health. 'Rationing' has discriminated against the health needs of older people throughout the history of the National Health Service, and before. Even William Beveridge in his famous Report on Social Insurance of 1942 endorsed this when he commented that: 'It is dangerous to be in any way lavish to old age until adequate provision has been assured for all other vital needs, such as the prevention of disease and the adequate provision of the young.'[10] Nevertheless health care for older women under the NHS has been better than the very poor standards available before for most people.

Conclusion

It is important not to perceive older women, and men, primarily as receivers of welfare or in other respects as dependents upon the community. As we have seen, not all were poor or dependent. Many more than ever before enjoyed active lives, holidays, sports and entertainment. Throughout the century older people have been givers as well as receivers, to their families and to society and the economy at large.

Bibliographical Note

P. Thane, *Old Age in England: Continuity or Change in English History* (Oxford University Press, 2000) puts issues about older women in the twentieth century into a wider perspective. S. Arber and J. Ginn, *Gender and Later Life* (London, 1991) provide a sociological analysis of these issues in the later twentieth century. P. Thompson, C. Itzin and M. Abendstern, *I Don't Feel Old: Understanding the Experience of Later Life* (Oxford, 1990) uses oral accounts of the experience of ageing combined with contemporary and historical documents to provide a valuable history of ageing in the twentieth century. P. Johnson and J. Falkingham, *Ageing and Economic Welfare* (London, 1992) provide essential facts, figures and analyses about the demography, social policy and the incomes, health and work of older people in twentieth-century Britain.

Notes

1. Lady Bell, *At The Works* (London 1907, reprinted 1985), p. 115.

2. B.S. Rowntree, *Poverty and Progress: A Second Social Survey of York* (London, 1941), p. 72.

3. J.H. Sheldon, *The Social Medicine of Old Age* (Oxford, 1948), p. 140.

4. P. Townsend, *The Family Life of Old People* (London, 1957), pp. 45, 150.

5. N. and J. MacKenzie (eds), *The Diaries of Beatrice Webb* vol. IV (London, 1986).

6. Housed in the University of Sussex Library.

7. *Report of the Departmental Committee on Old Age Pensions* (Cmd. 1919), Questions 5737 ff.

8. P. Townsend, *Poverty in the United Kingdom* (Harmondsworth, 1979), p. 285.

9. Joseph Rowntree Foundation, *Inquiry into Income and Wealth* (York, 1995).

10. *Social Insurance and Allied Services,* Report by Sir William Beveridge (Cmd. 1942), p. 92.

Part Two

WORK – PAID AND UNPAID

8

EDUCATION

Carol Dyhouse

Women's access to higher education has always been a key issue for feminists. Nineteenth-century feminists fought for higher education as proof of women's mental and intellectual capacities, to enable them to practise medicine and to better their chances in teaching. Changes in educational provision for middle-class girls and women in the late Victorian period were intimately connected with the rise of 'first-wave' feminism and with the demand for suffrage. It can be argued, similarly, that the rising levels of educational aspiration and achievement among women, which followed extensions of secondary schooling after 1944 and of university education during the 1960s, and particularly following the Robbins Report of 1963, were crucial precursors of the rise of 'second-wave' feminism and the Women's Liberation Movement in the 1970s.

Opening Doors?

By 1914 women could study in all British universities although some departments or faculties (medicine, divinity and engineering) resisted accepting them as students, and neither Oxford nor Cambridge would allow them to graduate. Oxford conceded degrees to women in 1920, following the Sex Disqualification (Removal) Act of 1919, but Cambridge withheld graduation (and full membership of the University) from its female students until 1948.

Although the desire to study medicine had accounted for some of women's earliest attempts to gain access to university education in the nineteenth century, medical schools and faculties were often among the last to concede entrance to female students. Most of the 'provincial' medical schools admitted women by 1914, but the situation in Edinburgh, Oxford, Cambridge and London was less clear cut. In Edinburgh women students were confined to 'extra-mural' schools, the University itself would make no provision for their teaching and acted as an examining body only. In London, at the time when war broke out in 1914, women were confined to a separate school, the London (Royal Free Hospital) School of Medicine (before 1897, The London School of Medicine for Women).

The University of London found itself in an anomalous and somewhat embarrassing position in that it prided itself on having been the first British university to have opened its degrees to women (in 1878), and yet none of the medical schools of the university except the Royal Free would actually admit them as students.

The First World War brought changes here, not least because it depleted the medical schools of their male students. The University of Edinburgh decided to accept responsibility for the education of women medical students in 1916, and between 1916 and 1917 both Oxford and Cambridge opened their medical examinations (though not yet their degrees of course) to women. In London, King's College agreed to accept a number of female students in the Department of Anatomy in 1916, and University College opened its Faculty of Medicine to women in the following year. By 1918 seven of the London medical schools were admitting women students, although four more (St Bartholomew's, Guy's, St Thomas's, the Middlesex) remained staunchly all-male.

Lest this catalogue should convey an impression of steady and inexorable progress in the opening of doors to women, it should be pointed out immediately that several of them were soon to slam shut again. By 1928 five of the London medical schools had reversed their policy and decided not to admit any more women. At the same time both University and King's College London had determined to restrict their admission of female students to a tiny number (10–12 annually). The reasons given for reimposing these barriers and restrictions varied from the assertion that the presence of women undermined the morale of male students to the accusation that the female presence had destroyed the schools' reputation for rugby. The fear that women students threatened the status of elite institutions in higher education was not limited to the London medical schools. Writers in university journals in Edinburgh, Aberdeen and Durham, for instance, could be found protesting against the 'invasion' of the groves of Academe by women, who 'infested' the cloisters and male precincts. The imagery was territorial; the universities were to be guarded as male territory. Cambridge's rejection of women's claim to degrees in 1920 has been seen by the historian Rita McWilliams-Tullberg as best summed up in the sentence used in the Report of the Royal Commission on Oxford and Cambridge in 1922, 'we desire strongly that Cambridge should remain mainly and predominantly a "men's University" though of a mixed type'.[1] To this end a limit of 500 was placed on the number of women students in residence in Cambridge (a ratio of one woman to eight or nine men).

Cambridge's determination to stay male caused heart-searching in Oxford, particularly among those who feared that 'the best men' would be lured by the virility of the rival institution. Joseph Wells, Warden of Wadham, warned that unless Oxford followed by taking steps to limit numbers of women students, 'our young men will prefer the other place'.[2] In June 1927, Oxford voted in favour of limitation: the number of women students was not to exceed 840 (a ratio of one female student to about six men).

There was some debate in other universities in the 1920s and 1930s about whether the numbers of women students had risen too quickly and should be limited, but most Vice-Chancellors were against the idea: universities needed students and only the elite could afford to be so selective. Sir Alfred Ewing, from Edinburgh, argued in 1927 that the advantages of admitting women outweighed any disadvantages. He pointed out that, while the proportion of women students was high in Edinburgh, their presence had 'in no way altered the character of the teaching', nor could he detect 'any trace of any tendency towards feminine government'.[3] This of course was precisely what worried many academic women and feminists, and is a point to which I shall return later.

Women began to graduate, in small numbers at first, in the last two decades of the nineteenth century. Their presence in universities originally attracted a good deal of attention and merriment from male students who tended to refer to them as 'Lady-students', 'sweet girl graduates' (after Tennyson) or 'undergraduettes'. When the first female student was presented to Joseph Chamberlain at Birmingham University's first degree day procession in 1901 it is recorded that male students shouted out 'Go on, Sir, kiss her', although Chamberlain did not oblige. The numbers of women students in universities in Britain began to increase rapidly after the 1890s with the development of teacher education in the newly established 'day training departments' attached to universities, the precursors of the modern university departments of education. Mabel Tylecote observed that the advent of the day training college in Manchester in 1892 effectively doubled the number of women undergraduates in that university between 1891–92 and 1892–93, and from 1899 to 1914 one-third (or in some years nearly a half) of all Manchester's women students were members of the day training college.[4] Figures from the University Grants Committee (UGC) show that women represented 16 per cent of the student population of Great Britain in 1900: this proportion rose to 24 per cent in 1920, 27 per cent in 1930 and registered a slight decline on the eve of the Second World War. The proportion of women was higher in the Scottish Universities and in the University of Wales. By 1937–38 the UGC figures show a total of 11,299 full-time women students enrolled in British universities (including Oxford and Cambridge). There were 37,890 men, so women represented over a quarter of the total.

It was much harder for girls to secure the financial support necessary for a university education than it was for boys. Parents were often less willing to make the financial sacrifices necessary to send daughters to college than they were sons. G.S.M. Ellis, who reported on the availability of scholarships in a publication entitled *The Poor Student and the University* (1925), emphasised that, even before the First World War, 'the supply of public scholarships for women was lagging behind the demand for higher education in a most alarming manner'. There were many reasons for this. Far fewer of the girls' secondary schools were in a position to be able to offer scholarships to leavers. The universities themselves offered far fewer scholarships and bursaries to girls. State Scholarships were first introduced by the Board of Education in 1920, but they were very few in number (200, originally). There was a good deal of controversy about how these should be divided between boys and girls and, in any case, they tended to go to pupils whose sights were set on Oxford and Cambridge. This left two other important sources of funding: local authority awards and Board of Education Grants. The system of local authority awards, municipal and senior county scholarships, was extremely patchy and girls were almost everywhere at a disadvantage. In 1911–12, of the 464 university scholarships made by these authorities, 373 went to boys and only 91 to girls. For girls the Board of Education scholarships were crucial throughout the interwar period. They covered both fees and maintenance, although girls received less of a subsidy than boys (from 1911 a male student living in recognised accommodation received £35 per annum, whereas girls received only £25). However, to qualify for one of these Board of Education awards required a commitment or 'pledge' to teach, usually for a period of at least five years after graduation.

There can be no doubt that many women embarked upon degree courses with a schoolteaching career in mind. Many others went into teaching by default, at a time when there were limited career options available to them. It is also clear, as many contemporaries commented, that some women were only very reluctantly driven into 'signing the pledge' to teach, simply because the chance of securing financial assistance from a Board of Education award represented their only hope of going to university.

Most of the women who graduated before 1939 did go into schoolteaching: probably as many as 70 per cent or even three-quarters of them. Those who were most able (or fortunate) managed to secure jobs in girls' high schools or the newer municipal secondary schools for girls. Others found themselves teaching in elementary schools. Michael Sanderson has commented on 'the flavour of the insecurity, poverty, fly-by-night quality of life of women graduates who tried to break out of the well-worn path to teaching in the 1920s'.[5] However, significant inroads were made into other occupations. There had been only about 1,000 women doctors registered in Britain just before the First World War; the war encouraged many more to qualify and the number doubled to 2,100 by 1921. By 1939–40, the figure stood at about 6,300. Some women went into social and welfare work, librarianship, advertising and marketing. A few pioneers took up scientific research and engineering: their careers were important as a demonstration of what women could achieve. Sanderson draws our attention to Margaret Partridge BSc, who set up a lighting and heating firm in Exeter as early as 1922, dealing with large-scale contracting, and to Pearl Swan, Liverpool University's first female graduate in engineering, who went to Metropolitan Vickers. To appreciate the climate these women were working in, it is salutary to be reminded that the idea that women should study engineering at King's College London provoked outrage and a furore in 1932.

Women first gained appointments in universities either in women's colleges, or by taking up posts with pastoral responsibilities for female students as 'lady superintendents', 'women's tutors' or wardens of women's hostels. Women lecturers proper were few and far between, although the development of the day training departments in the 1890s led to the appointment of the quaintly titled 'Mistresses of Method' responsible for pedagogy on 'the girls' side'. The first woman professor in Britain was probably Millicent Mackenzie, previously 'Normal Mistress' in the training department at the University of Wales (Cardiff), who became Associate Professor in 1904 and a full professor of education in 1910. According to the British Federation of University Women there were 13 women professors in England and Wales in 1931 (compared with 829 men) and 583 women lecturers and demonstrators (compared with 3,103 men). Women who were teaching in the universities in this period often experienced very difficult careers: discrimination was both overt and covert. The career of Edith Morley (Professor of English Language in Reading in 1908) got off to less than a good start when the college authorities assured a young male lecturer in her department that they planned to appoint a male professor as soon as possible: he would not long have to suffer the ignominy of being subordinate to a woman.

Expanding Opportunities?

In the aftermath of the Second World War there was strong government awareness of the need for long-term planning in education at every level. The rising birth rate, together with extensions in secondary education following the Butler Education Act of 1944 and plans for the raising of the school leaving age from 14 to 15, made it urgent to increase the supply of teachers. There was also a sense of urgency about the need to encourage technical and scientific education. Between 1942 and 1946 the McNair Committee addressed teacher supply, the Percy Committee looked at technical education, and the Barlow Committee concerned itself with scientific 'manpower'. It is important to capture the sense of optimism that accompanied this sense of urgency; this was above all to be a period of expansion and of social transformation. The Barlow Committee estimated a need for 70,000 student places in the universities by 1950 and 90,000 by 1955. Between 1947 and 1952 the UGC grant to universities was to increase massively, by 90 per cent. Existing universities expanded, and five further institutions achieved their charters: Nottingham (1948), Southampton (1952), Hull (1954), Exeter (1955), and Leicester (1957). Between 1954 and 1961 the student population in universities rose from 82,000 to 113,000, more than doubling the figure for 1939.[6]

How did women fare in this expansion? By 1939 there had been clear signs that the supply of highly educated women exceeded the opportunities for their employment even in teaching. The war allowed many of these women access to employment, training and experience that would not have been available in peacetime. Women had been urged to regard teaching as a form of national service during the war and were specifically targeted in the emergency training programme which followed it. The number of students in colleges trebled, to 30,000 by 1958. Even so, teacher supply remained a pressing problem for the government which, as Christine Heward has remarked, 'found itself in the position of Canute, attempting to stem the rising tide of children to be taught with a supply of predominantly young women teachers, who promptly left the profession to have children'.[7] The expansion of the training colleges had obvious significance for women, not least because many of them were single-sex institutions. The academic reputation of these colleges was not always high, and they have been seen as a cheap form of higher education for women. For example, it was estimated in 1963 that a university student cost £660 per annum, whereas a student in a training college cost only £255. Up until the mid-1960s, far more women went to teacher training college, taking a two-year certificate course (the BEd was not introduced until after the Robbins report of 1963) than to university.[8] However the women's training colleges did at least afford reasonably high-status jobs in teaching and educational management to some women, jobs which were usually lost to men when the colleges were later merged into larger coeducational institutions and polytechnics.

Women were the beneficiaries of educational expansion at all levels in the 1950s. The numbers of women entering the universities continued to rise, although it is interesting to note that they still represented only 24 per cent of the university student population in 1958: the same proportion as in 1920. More bastions had fallen. Following the Goodenough Report on medical education in 1944, the all-male medical schools were cornered into accepting 'a reasonable proportion' of women students as a condition of receiving Exchequer subsidy. In Cambridge – at long last – women were allowed to graduate (in 1948).

In 1958 the question of student grants was referred by the Ministry of Education to the Anderson Committee. Their report, published in 1960, recommended a national scheme, to be administered by local educational authorities. Every student enrolling on a degree course for the first time became eligible for a grant toward tuition fees and maintenance, the actual level of grant depending on parental income. The report specifically rejected any argument in favour of discriminating against women students on the grounds of their likelihood of marrying early and 'wasting' their education and training. It was suggested that it would be a mistake to measure the benefits of a university education solely in terms of earning capacity, and that 'A sustained increase in the number of highly educated mothers, as well as fathers, would benefit the nation to an extent that is not yet generally appreciated'.[9]

The 1950s can most usefully be seen as a decade of contradictions for women: these contradictions were not easily resolved and were if anything to sharpen and deepen over the following decade. Amidst the widening of opportunities for further and higher education, women were exhorted to train as teachers, scientists and technologists. 'Manpower' was not to exclude 'womanpower'. The country's need for highly educated workers contributed to the lifting of formal marriage bars in occupations such as medicine and teaching. But the fact remained that the majority of even highly educated women married, and the trend towards earlier marriages went hand-in-hand with a growing emphasis on the importance of motherhood and domesticity. Educational policy and discourse both reflected and reinforced these contradictory messages.

Plate 8.1. Women students at Sussex University in the 1960s and the 1990s.

In 1948 John Newsom published a highly controversial essay on *The Education of Girls*, in which he argued that 'the home-making mission' was the major goal of almost all women. Feminists bent on proving women's capacity for an academic education had distorted the whole system of provision for educating girls by seeking to emulate men. Women teachers, many of them 'involuntary virgins' too often represented 'a drab and depressing spinsterhood' and were the wrong kind of role models for young girls. Education should celebrate rather than ignore femininity, and for 'non-academic' girls particularly the curriculum should be based on the home. Even degree courses should be modified; 'I do not mean that the young women of Somerville or Girton should take degree courses in dietetics or *haute couture* instead of modern history or economics, [but] . . . there should be subjects more suited to the particular intellectual abilities of women.'[10]

In spite of its angry reception in some feminist quarters, Newsom's book provoked much discussion and debate, and echoes of the idea that women's education had 'gone too far' in emulating 'male' academic values can be heard in much of the educational discourse of the 1950s and 1960s. Participants in a study group on the education of girls held at the University of Newcastle in 1952 emphasised the importance of giving girls a 'dual education' to prepare them for home and family as well as careers, and suggested the need for new research on the differences between men and women which might usefully inform policy. The controversy about whether social change necessitated 'a complete rethinking' of girls' education was also reflected in the Women's Group on Public Welfare's study, *The Education and Training of Girls*, published in 1962. This group took a more robustly feminist stance on these issues, urging the need to increase women's share of university education. While conceding that women needed to be educated for 'the dual role', they drew attention to the inspiring speech given by no less a person than Queen Elizabeth the Second on a visit to Oxford in 1960. Her Majesty, having expressed her delight in the fact that the women's colleges now had equal status with the men's, announced that nowadays 'A woman need not barter her intellectual life for the happiness and deep satisfaction of bringing up a family'.[11]

A slightly more defensive tone had been apparent in Judith Hubback's study, *Wives Who Went to College*, which appeared in 1957. Were 'the university women of today better equipped to become wives and mothers than their less academic sisters?' asked Hubback, or was their higher education 'merely a liability which arouses ambitions never-to-be-fulfilled?' Was a university degree 'wasted and forgotten among the cares of domesticity'? Was it possible 'to combine marriage and motherhood with a job and do justice to all three'? Hubback concluded that it was, but only if a woman's husband gave his wholehearted support: 'With his love, his trust and his help' a woman could 'do great things.'[12]

Provision for higher education expanded still more rapidly in the 1960s and 1970s than it had in the previous decade. The need for teachers continued unabated in the 1960s and the training colleges expanded rapidly, trebling their numbers a second time, from *c.* 30,000 in 1958 to over 107,000 in 1970. More of these colleges were becoming coeducational institutions, and the two-year certificate course increasingly gave way to the three-year degree (the BEd).

Teacher training colleges continued to absorb far more women than the universities: in 1965 first-year full-time university entrants included 15,000 women and 38,000 men. The comparable figures for training college entry were 26,000 women and only 10,000 men. However, the late 1970s saw sudden and savage cuts in teacher education in response to a falling birth rate. A period of dramatic reorganisation saw colleges merged and amalgamated, many of them into the new, local-authority controlled 'Polytechnics'. Many women principals and lecturers lost their jobs or found themselves displaced by men in senior and managerial positions in the process.

Even before the Robbins Report on higher education in 1963, the UGC had planned for unprecedented expansion in the universities. The 'civic' or 'redbrick' universities had been referred to as the 'modern' universities before 1939. With the advent of the 'new', or 'plateglass' universities of the 1960s and 1970s the redbricks became the 'older' universities (as indeed the 'new' universities were in their turn to become the 'old' universities when the Polytechnics achieved university status in the 1990s). Sussex received its charter in 1961, Keele in 1962. These were followed by York and East Anglia (1963), Essex and Lancaster (1964), Kent and Warwick (1965), and Stirling in 1967.

According to some observers, the new universities, with their innovative and less specialised curricula exercised a particular appeal to girls. The Women's Group on Public Welfare study mentioned above singled out Keele, with its foundation year of general studies, and Sussex, where Schools of Study rather than traditional departments emphasised 'integration and cross-fertilisation, not the fragmentation of knowledge' as particularly noteworthy in this respect. Kathleen Ollerenshaw went so far as to suggest that the older civic universities had always exercised a limited attraction for women: the new universities, especially Sussex (only one hour's train journey from 'the swinging city') had much more appeal for 'bright and lively girls who have good brains but do not see themselves devoting their lives to academic study'. She contended that Sussex University had proved so attractive to women that there had to be 'discriminatory selection in the arts subjects to prevent the student population from being predominantly female'.[13] The undergraduate might still be referred to as 'he' in much of the educational discourse of the period, but the proportion of women in the student population was at last beginning to rise: to 28 per cent in 1968, to 38 per cent in 1980 and to 40 per cent in 1984. Another significant trend was the increase in the number of mature women students entering the universities from the 1970s; the generation of women who had missed out on higher education in the 1950s and early 1960s was now more likely to seek a second chance of graduating as mature returners. The Open University, founded in 1969 with flexible requirements for entry and home-based study, played an important pioneering role in this context.

The new confidence of 'youth' in the 1960s had its impact on social arrangements in the universities. In particular, the lowering of the age of majority from 21 to 18 in 1969 meant that university authorities were no longer *in loco parentis* in relation to students, which allowed for a relaxation of their disciplinary function, particularly in respect of policing the sexual morality of undergraduates.

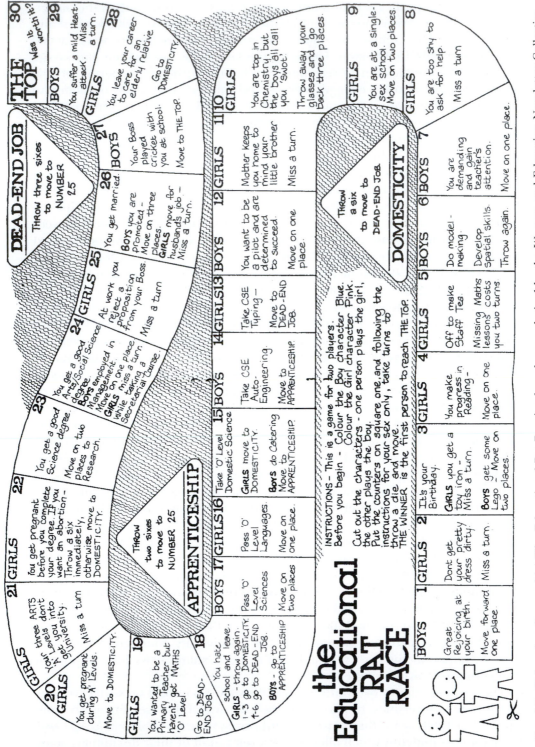

Plate 8.2. Girls as handicapped in 'The Educational Rat Race', a board game devised by the Women and Education Newsletter Collective, 1980.

More 'permissiveness' often followed lively and sometimes disruptive expressions of student unrest. A relaxing of rules in hostels concerning residence had important implications for women, who had previously experienced rather more restrictions on their behaviour and freedom than the men. Impatience with the standards and strictures of traditional authority probably contributed towards frustration with single-sex institutions and fuelled the tendency towards co-education. Bedford College, originally founded for women in 1849, took in men from 1963. In the 1970s many previously all-male colleges in Oxford and Cambridge began admitting women. Mixed student residences – unimaginable at the beginning of the century – became acceptable.

But, in spite of rising aspirations and a new confidence among women graduates in the 1960s, careers advice remained rather rudimentary and the availability of career options lagged behind educational achievement. One of the female graduates with whom Judith Hubback had corresponded in the 1950s had wondered ruefully whether her five daughters, who wanted to become doctors and teachers, would eventually find that their careers, like her own, would 'end at the kitchen sink'. The conflict between motherhood and employment had not diminished for the women of 'the bulge generation', as Mary Ingham found in her study of the predicaments faced by her contemporaries at the end of the 1970s, *Now We are Thirty* (1981). However, there was a less defensive tone about the discussion of these problems than there had been among the graduate wives of the 1950s. This was partly because the rise of 'second-wave' feminism, or the Women's Liberation Movement, in the early 1970s encouraged women to see the conflicts less in terms of personal failings and more as the consequence of social conditions that called for rearrangement.

Autobiographies provide useful insights into these changes. Ann Oakley was born in 1944 and grew up in a middle-class family with a conventional sexual division of labour between her housewife mother and her eminent academic father (Richard Titmuss). Her autobiography, *Taking It Like a Woman* (1984), describes her student years in Oxford, where she entered Somerville College in 1962. Women were outnumbered by men in Oxford by eight to one: 'Being female, we had to make our way in a man's world.' Ann Oakley found the curriculum in Oxford disappointing in many ways, arguing that it failed to help her understand the way society worked. She married in 1964. Her husband went on to a DPhil and a university lectureship, she tried to apply herself to housework and motherhood but fell into severe depression. Salvation came through sustained intellectual analysis of her own – and other women's – social situation and the conflicts around women's work and motherhood. Inspired by her reading of Betty Friedan's *The Feminine Mystique* (1963) and Hannah Gavron's *The Captive Wife* (1966), Oakley completed her own doctoral thesis on housework and went on to write several books on the subject of women's social position, which were widely used on women's studies courses over the following decade.

The women's movement of the 1970s and 1980s was associated with a sustained critique of education at every level. There was a burgeoning of text and publications: newsletters, articles in popular and academic journals (the specialist journal *Gender and Education* was instituted in 1989) and books. Eileen Byrne's *Women and Education* (1978) and Rosemary Deem's *Women and Schooling* (1978) and *Schooling for Women's Work* (1981) were particularly widely read, but there were many similar publications. Educational provision was seen to have fallen short of having offered equal opportunities, of having perpetrated 'sexual stereotyping', of not being 'girl friendly' and of having taken for granted the 'under-achievement' of girls. The period was one in which affirmative action initiatives proliferated: New Opportunities for Women programmes (NOW), Girls into Science and Technology (GIST), Women into Science and Engineering (WISE).

A notable feature of Eileen Byrne's analysis was its concern with women's position in further education. The Women's Group on Public Welfare had pointed out in 1961 that girls received much less post-school education than boys: employers were far less willing to offer day and block release training schemes to girls. Byrne pointed out that, although statistics in the 1970s showed a higher proportion of girls going on to FE than boys, girls were mainly confined to skills-based, lower-level courses. These courses were not career-orientated and, given many girls' deficiencies in science, maths and technical studies, the majority were all too likely to end up 'on the inexorable tramline to training over a hot stove or a cold typewriter'. Byrne made an eloquent plea for extra resources to be made available, and emphasised a need for radical change if girls were to benefit fully. Helena Kennedy's report on Further Education in 1997 suggests that the case for radical change in this sector, in the interests of disadvantaged groups generally, was still strong at the end of the century.[14]

The feminist critique of universities in the 1970s and 1980s had many dimensions. There was concern over the fact that so few university teachers – especially at the higher levels of the profession – were female. A report published by the Hansard Society in 1990 argued that women suffered from a double disadvantage in British university life: they constituted only a minority (14 per cent) of full-time, tenured university teachers, and this minority were concentrated in lower-grade posts. Strikingly, 97 per cent of university professors and 94 per cent of readers and senior lecturers were male. Figures from the Higher Education Statistics Agency in 1999 reveal that male professors still outnumbered female professors by ten to one.[15] Feminists began to ask questions about what was taught in higher education and indeed about the nature of knowledge itself. To what extent was knowledge 'gendered'? Was there a need for 'Women's Studies' or should feminists focus their attention on trying to modify the subjects and structures of a male-defined curriculum?

Conclusion

Changes in women's education in the twentieth century have been gradual but, taken cumulatively, dramatic. There were 14 universities in England, Wales and Scotland in 1920 and women represented 24 per cent of the student population. In the late 1990s there were around 130 universities, and women represented just over 50 per cent of the undergraduate entry. Women performed well at every educational level, and in the late 1990s there was alarm about 'under-achievement' by *boys* rather than girls at the secondary school level. Women continued to be under-represented in higher education in some of the physical sciences, particularly in engineering. They obtained fewer first-class degrees in Oxford and Cambridge than their male peers – an issue which is currently attracting interest and research. Despite signs that the number of women gradu-ates taking up some forms of professional employment exceeded the number of men, it was still possible to argue at the end of the century that the overall educational achievements of women have yet to be fully reflected in their position in the labour market. Men continued to dominate 'top jobs'. Cultural and ideo-logical factors, and the continuing conflicts between employment structures and motherhood, undoubtedly played their part here. There are also grounds for concern about whether changes in educational policy in the late 1990s will impact disproportionally on women. The abolition of grants for tuition fees in higher education and the replacement of maintenance grants with student loans may discourage women more than men (especially mature women and those from working-class and ethnic-minority backgrounds) from going to university.

IN FOCUS: Women's Colleges and Halls of Residence

Single-sex colleges and halls of residence played a crucial role in the early phases of women's entry into higher education. Girton and Newnham in Cambridge (beginning in 1869 and 1871 respectively), Somerville and Lady Margaret Hall in Oxford (from 1879), Bedford (1849), Westfield (1882) and Royal Holloway (1886) in London were all pioneering institutions, bent on establishing women's claims to learning. Women's colleges were also founded in the late nineteenth century in Glasgow (Queen Margaret's College) and Durham (St Mary's). Most universities had their women-only halls of residence (not colleges in the fullest sense in that they did not actually provide teaching). Examples of these were Ashburne Hall in Manchester, Clifton Hill House (Bristol), Alexandra Hall (Aberystwyth) and Aberdare Hall (Cardiff). These were established in the main from the 1890s, owing much to those sympathetic to the women's cause, but also backed by authorities uneasy about the idea of young women living in unsupervised lodgings.

Virginia Woolf emphasised the need for 'a room of one's own' if girls were to be freed from domestic responsibilities for study and self-development. The feminist historian, Martha Vicinus, has argued that between 1850 and 1920 the women's colleges provided crucial space for intellectual development and for the cultivation of friendship among women students and teachers. It should be remembered that before the Second World War the majority of students outside Oxbridge lived at home or

Women's Colleges and Halls of Residence (continued)

in lodgings. The fact that a greater proportion of women than men lived in halls or hostels could be seen as having offered the women more opportunity of benefiting from the social and cultural advantages of a full 'collegiate' life.

Some saw disadvantages in this, in that women students might be hedged in by a plethora of rules and regulations devised to 'protect' them from danger and temptation. Mounting criticism of traditional forms of authority in the 1960s, the lowering of the age of majority in 1969 (redefining 18-year-old students as adults), and a new liberalism in educational thinking, all contributed to a mood of impatience with single-sex provision and an optimism about the potential of coeducation. As said above, Bedford College admitted men from 1963. Amid much heart-searching (plenty from the men and probably more from the women), the majority of the colleges in London, Oxford and Cambridge began to admit students of the opposite sex, a process which accelerated in the 1970s. However a research project focusing on the experience of women students in King's College, Cambridge, which was published in 1990, suggested that it was not always easy for women to work in an environment still dominated by male academic traditions and values. Some argued that the benefits which single-sex colleges had offered to women were too easily forgotten. They had (for instance) provided women with important avenues for promotion. When Somerville decided to admit men in 1992 (a particularly controversial decision), Joan Thirsk (formerly Reader in Economic History at Oxford) reminded the Principal of what had happened at Westfield and Bedford when they had done the same. 'In no time at all, they were taken over by men, and the women yet again featured in the lowlier academic ranks', she contended, adding gloomily that 'Those who cannot remember the past are condemned to repeat it.'[16]

Bibliographical Note

There are numerous histories of individual universities and university colleges. Few of the former devote more than the odd page or two to women's experiences. The volume edited by Brian Harrison (vol. VII, *The Twentieth Century*), part of *The History of the University of Oxford* (Oxford, 1994) is an exception, and contains an excellent chapter on women by Janet Howarth. More focused studies of women in individual universities include M. Tylecote, *The Education of Women at Manchester University, 1883–1933* (Manchester, 1941); Rita McWilliams-Tullberg, *Women at Cambridge: A Men's University, Though of a Mixed Type* (London, 1975); W. Gareth Evans, *Education and Female Emancipation: The Welsh Experience, 1847–1914* (Cardiff, 1990); and L. Moore, *Bajanellas and Semilinas: Aberdeen University and the Education of Women, 1860–1920* (Aberdeen, 1991). Histories of individual women's colleges include M. Tuke, *A History of Bedford College for Women, 1849–1937* (Oxford, 1939); C. Bingham, *The History of*

Royal Holloway College, 1886–1986 (London, 1987); and P. Adams, *Somerville for Women: An Oxford College 1879–1993* (Oxford, 1996). M. Vicinus, *Independent Women: Work and Community for Single Women, 1850–1920* (London, 1985) is excellent on the historical importance of the women's colleges. The most general survey of women in universities outside Oxbridge is C. Dyhouse, *No Distinction of Sex?: Women in British Universities, 1870–1939* (London, 1995). M. Sanderson, *The Universities and British Industry, 1850–1970* (London, 1972) contains an extremely useful chapter on 'The University Woman in Business and Industry before 1939'.

There has been very little historiography focusing on women in universities generally during the postwar period, although as this chapter has indicated, there is a large feminist literature on equal opportunities (or the lack of them). Useful starting points include S. Acker and D. Warren Piper (eds), *Is Higher Education Fair to Women?* (Guildford, 1984) and M. Masson and D. Simonton (eds), *Women and Higher Education: Past, Present and Future* (Aberdeen, 1996). S. Delamont, *Knowledgeable Women, Structuralism and the Reproduction of Elites* (London, 1989) provides intriguing sociological insights.

Notes

1. R. McWilliams-Tullberg, *Women at Cambridge: A Men's University – Though of a Mixed Type* (London, 1975), p. 199.

2. J. Wells, 'Statement of Support for Limitation Statute', July 1927 (Limitation of numbers file, Somerville College Archives).

3. 'Girl Students in the Universities: Should Their Numbers be Limited?', *Sheffield Evening News*, 29 October 1927.

4. M. Tylecote, *The Education of Women at Manchester University, 1883–1933* (Manchester, 1941), pp. 47, 53–4.

5. M. Sanderson, *The Universities and British Industry, 1850–1970* (London, 1972), pp. 325, 336.

6. W.A.C. Stewart, *Higher Education in Postwar Britain* (Basingstoke, 1989), p. 57.

7. C. Heward, 'Men and Women and the Rise of Professional Society: The Intriguing History of Teacher Educators', *History of Education*, 22, 1 (1993), p. 23.

8. R. Crompton and K. Sanderson, *Gendered Jobs and Social Change* (London, 1990), pp. 55–6.

9. Ministry of Education, *Grants to Students* (London, 1960), p. 3.

10. J. Newsom, *The Education of Girls* (London, 1948), pp. 116, 146.

11. Women's Group on Public Welfare, *The Education and Training of Girls* (London, 1962), p. 95.

12. J. Hubback, *Wives Who Went to College* (London, 1957), p. 159.

13. K. Ollerenshaw, *The Girls' Schools* (London, 1967), p. 67.

14. E.M. Byrne, *Women and Education* (London, 1978), pp. 186–210; H. Kennedy, *Learning Works: Widening Participation in Further Education* (Coventry, Further Education Funding Council, 1997).

15. Hansard Society, *Women at the Top* (London, 1990), p. 65; *Guardian* (Higher Education section), 13 April 1999, p. i.

16. J. Thirsk, *Observer*, 16 February 1992, quoting George Santayana.

9

FAMILY, CARING AND UNPAID WORK

Katherine Holden

Margaret is an academic living alone with total responsibility for her young daughter aged three. At the end of a very busy term a male colleague asks how long it will take her to finish an article which she needs to submit to fulfil her quota for the Research Assessment Exercise, upon which her promotion prospects will partly depend. She replies: 'if I didn't have to look after Emily, about a fortnight. In reality I'd be lucky to finish it in six months.'

Julie is married with two school-age children. Her husband John is a self-employed plumber and she does shift work as a nurse which she tries to fit in with school and her husband's working hours. She points out how pleased she is that John now takes the children to school *for her* once a week.

Grace, now in her late 60s, spent much of her life caring for both her parents and subsequently her husband, all of whom had long-term illnesses. She was helped by her unmarried daughter Sally, aged 45, who currently works as a low-paid care assistant in a nursing home. Grace who is well past retirement age can now only survive by working as a cleaner in the nursing home and in private houses in addition to doing all the cooking and cleaning in her own home.[1]

Each of these examples points to the fact that, despite major cultural and economic shifts during the twentieth century, the nature and meaning of work for most women in Britain has continued to be linked with their positions within household, family and kinship networks and shaped by an injunction to care. Neither Margaret, Julie, Grace nor Sally could dissociate their paid work from their responsibilities as unpaid carers. Margaret had a potentially prestigious career ahead of her, but the physical and emotional 'work' of being a single mother had compromised her prospects. Grace's paid work had always taken second place to her role as family carer and both she and Sally were only qualified to do low-paid caring work. Despite women's improved pay and job prospects in the late twentieth century, Julie's career still took second place to her role as mother and she considered caring for the children to be her job. She gratefully received John's occasional help with the children even though he was in control of his own working hours, while she was not.

These seemingly unbreakable connections between work and home life point to some level of continuity with women in previous centuries. It is still difficult for women living in an advanced capitalist society to draw boundaries between public and private aspects of their lives, and to detach themselves from the identity of carer or from paid and unpaid work in service positions. This chapter explores continuities and change in women's position as carers and unpaid workers during the twentieth century both within and outside the home.

IN FOCUS: Caring and Service Work

What has it meant to be cared for or be a carer in twentieth-century Britain? It is a relationship of power and dependence: between the weak and the strong, children and adults, the old and the young, the sick and healthy, the master or mistress and servant. For those who did the caring it also involved relentless physical and often messy tasks which overlapped with and shaded seamlessly into housework and domestic service. To care for someone meant preparing and giving them food and/or medicines; lifting, carrying, washing and dressing their bodies; and clearing up the dirt and mess they created: changing and washing their clothes or cleaning up bodily products. It has also included giving them attention: keeping them warm and away from harm; stopping them falling down stairs or out of bed, responding to and anticipating their wants, listening to their woes; and, especially in the case of children, teaching them to care for themselves. While carers often exercised considerable power, they were also tied to their work and often depended on those for whom they cared for subsistence and/or a sense of self-worth.

Caring is of vital importance for the survival of the human race, yet it has never been highly valued in monetary terms. Neither has it been seen as the work of men, although a minority of men have performed caring work, for example, in the nursing and ambulance services. It is somewhat paradoxical that, despite the common association of femininity with weakness and dependence, it has been overwhelmingly women who have carried out this hard physical work and been depended upon as carers. During the course of the twentieth century technological advances have lessened some of the physical burdens. The introduction of state welfare services has substituted some paid for unpaid labour, while at the same time largely removing the paid personal servant. Scientific discoveries and changing ideas about sickness and health, the value of children and length of childhood, and the relative numbers of young, elderly, married and single in the population, have all served to alter the nature, situation and timing of care-giving. Yet gender divisions within caring have not fundamentally changed.

Caring and Service Work (continued)

Why is this so? Feminist work has pointed to the dual meanings of the term 'care' and their association with core female and familial identities. 'Good' mothers and 'dutiful' daughters give service to and care *for* their family because they care *about* them. The problem of valuing caring work lies in the fact that women's love and service cannot be costed. Within the boundaries of the family women are supposed to work not for money but for love. But in reality love is also tied in with other familial and contractual obligations, including investment in the future and long-term reciprocity. Caring relationships can also be productive of guilt, resentment, feelings of being trapped and considerable material loss.

There has often been a tension between mothers' emotional bonds with their children and the unwritten contract they hold with the state to produce and maintain future citizens. This maternal duty was made explicit in the first half of the century during periods of concern about the falling birth rate and the importance of maintaining the health and fitness of the British race. Daughters also often maintained their parents in old age, not just out of love but out of duty, obligation and perhaps in the hope that they would receive similar services from others. As argued in chapter 7 the retirement and nursing homes which in the latter half of the century replaced workhouses and hospitals have not replaced familial care.

Not all caring work has been unpaid nor in family settings but, where caring work has been done by paid employees, once again these were and are still usually women. Women in caring work, such as nurses, nannies and domestic servants (the major occupations for women in the early part of twentieth century), have had to negotiate a particularly difficult boundary, one which fits uncomfortably with masculine values and identities and which most men have preferred to avoid. Not only did the associations of caring with love, duty and obligation mean that it was easier to attach to it a low monetary value, but women who were paid employees often did get attached to the people for whom they cared causing deep emotional conflicts. The comforting myth of the nanny supported as an old retainer in her old age was in reality a rarity and many carers had to suffer sometimes agonising partings when their services were no longer required.

Thus caring and service work create conflicts. These lie at the boundaries of the public and private and as such are a neglected aspect of women's history.

Gendered Work

How has the work of caring been negotiated by women historically? In the earlier part of the century some of the arguments outlined above were used to exclude women from the labour market. The idea that a wife's primary work was to serve her husband and a mother's to care for her children justified the widespread marriage bars during the 1920s and 1930s in many occupations (including teaching, the civil service and some factories) forcing women to resign their jobs on marriage. Although in reality such rulings were linked to economic factors such as a depressed labour market and high male unemployment, they fitted well with the cult of home and domesticity which characterised the interwar years.

However women's caring responsibilities stretched beyond the ubiquitous model of the nuclear family with a male breadwinner and young children. The notion of 'family responsibility' was built into the nineteenth-century Poor Law, requiring families to support their dependent members, including grandparents and grandchildren. Although the Poor Law was gradually dismantled during the 1930s, legal definitions of what exactly constituted a family were avoided by authorities such as the Ministry of Health and the Unemployment Assistance Board. While only unmarried women were legally required to support their parents financially, assumptions were made that, in the absence of the mother, grandparents or aunts would care for children, and, in the event of illness or disability, daughters would care for parents and other elderly relatives.

The demographic surplus of women which prevailed in the first half of the century meant that it would often be single women who cared for elderly mothers or fathers. Daughters sometimes were deliberately discouraged from marrying by parents who wanted them at home as an 'insurance policy' for their old age. The fact that many women saw these tasks as obligations to their family enabled the state to make considerable savings in providing for the needs of its dependent members.

Although after 1948 responsibilities attached to relationships lying outside the nuclear family were no longer legally defined, the advent of the welfare state has not fundamentally changed women's responsibility for care of the sick and rising numbers of elderly people. It was estimated in the late 1980s that there were more than a million carers of aged and disabled relatives without state or charitable assistance.[2] Not all these were women and fewer were single than at the start of the century, a change reflected in the change of name during the 1980s of the 'National Council for the Single Woman and her Dependant' (set up by Mary Webster in 1965 to recognise the caring responsibilities of single women who were often on very low incomes) to the National Association of Carers. The greatly reduced numbers of unmarried women now tend to have higher career aspirations. However married women like Julie and Grace, often with part-time jobs, still do much of the caring both for their own and their husband's kin, sometimes simultaneously for older and younger generations.

The postwar welfare state, which was regarded as a 'safety net' for families, relieving them of total responsibility for their dependent members, created jobs in caring occupations for women (many of them part-time) and was partly responsible for the demise of living-in domestic service. These jobs ranged from social work, health visiting and nursing to home helps or untrained care assistants in institutions. Yet it was not always possible for women doing this kind of work to separate their job from their home. This is apparent from the diary of Jane, a social worker in the early 1970s. Her home life included managing an over-worked husband in poor health and the conflicts of several teenagers and young adults in various stages of leaving home. Many of these familial crises were reproduced in her professional life and, finding the stresses of her dual role too onerous, she eventually gave up paid work.[3]

Caring and Unpaid Work within the Home: Supporting Children and Husbands

Women's position as carers and unpaid workers within the home, while it may have remained a constant general feature of female experience, has shown many different faces. External factors such as demographic change and the fluctuating demands of the labour market influenced women's experience of domestic life. So did variables within individual experience such as age, class, 'race', marital status, family and/or household composition, geographical and social mobility. The next chapter looks at the status of housework which forms a large proportion of the unpaid work in the home done by women. The other equally significant components discussed here are care for children, and the unpaid support wives give husbands in their jobs.

The examples at the start of this chapter have shown that responsibility for childcare has generally been expected to fall onto the shoulders of mothers. Nevertheless middle and upper-class women at the beginning of the century did little of the physical work of caring, while in working-class families responsibilities were often shared with other family members. Born in the first decade of the century, Charlotte's description of her relationship with her mother (who came from a military family) might be more typically applied to fathers. Brought up by a nanny, she only saw her mother for two hours every day from 5 to 7pm, when she and her brothers and sister would wear silk frocks and dance or play games, and remembered her mother telling a visitor 'it's not a party it's just my family'. By contrast Molly, born in 1899 the eldest daughter of a large working-class family in Bath, moved between her parents' and grandmother's homes. As she grew older she took the part of a responsible adult woman. She was expected not only to contribute to the care of her nine younger siblings, but was also paid to mind a neighbour's children.

Key factors influencing the extent and nature of mothers' involvement with child care during the twentieth century were falling birth and mortality rates, the rising divorce rate and changes in married women's and young people's participation in the labour market. Both the above examples of childhood experience in the first two decades of the century came from families with seven or more children, which, although above average at this time, was by no means unusual. By the end of the century, the great majority of marriages produced only one or two children; families with three to four children (the average size for marriages at the beginning of this century) were considered large.[4] Thus the length of time most mothers were involved in the care of young children and the need to draw upon the services of older siblings declined.

Child mortality rates are also important here. Two of Molly's nine siblings died before the age of 15 months. The number of children born to a marriage declined coinciding with rapidly improving levels of infant survival after the First World War, obviating the necessity to replace children who had died. At the same time the perceived value of children increased, influenced both by pro-natalist social policies and at mid-century by psychoanalytic theories which stressed the importance of the mother–child bond and warned women against leaving their young children in the care of others. Not only were mothers encouraged to spend more time nurturing their children but, with an increased value being set on education and successive rises in the school leaving age from twelve to fourteen in 1918, to fifteen in 1944 and to sixteen in 1972, childhood itself was extended into the new category of adolescence. By the end of the century the length of time children remained dependants living within the parental home was much greater than in 1900. Working-class girls were no longer sent into residential domestic service at the age of twelve or younger and upper and middle-class children much less likely to be sent away to boarding school from the age of seven, though the latter practice still continued.

In what ways have these factors affected the amount of time mothers actually spent caring for children? The equation is not simple nor is progress unidirectional. During the interwar years very few married women were in paid employment and most saw their primary task as caring for a smaller number of children than a generation previously. However the demographic surplus of women over men also meant that they could often draw upon the services of the single to give them support. Servants and nannies were still available and aunts were a valuable source of unpaid child care particularly for the colonial middle classes. Jane Reid wrote of her Aunt Gwen, who cared for her in the late 1930s when her parents were abroad, that she was the most important person in her life, 'In the man-short aftermath of the War [she] can never have had any real hope of marriage, the only way for a girl of her class to get away from home. My arrival and the special charge she had of me must have made a world of difference.'[5]

The minority of working-class married women who were employed full-time in the interwar years often used networks of neighbours and kin to care for young children, particularly important in Elizabeth Roberts's study of three Lancashire towns where married women's full-time employment was more usual. The widespread mobilisation of married women into employment during the Second World War was accompanied by the provision of state day nurseries. But, although married women continued to be recruited into part-time employment to fill the postwar labour shortage, encouraged by the government to play a 'dual role' in the economy and the home, childcare options for women gradually shrank, with day care places dropping from 62,000 at the end of the war to 22,000 in the 1960s.[6] The lower age at marriage, coupled with smaller families, of the post-Second World War generation also meant that women were more likely to return to work after their children had grown up and as grandmothers were less likely to be available for childcare. The average age at which women born after the Second World War had their last child was 28, more than ten years earlier than women in the mid-nineteenth century.

The demise of domestic service after the Second World War meant that middle-class women, who generally gave up work on the birth of their first child, could no longer rely on nannies or daily servants for support with childcare. It has been suggested that the women's movement of the late 1960s may have grown out of the frustrations experienced by servantless middle-class women whose burden of unpaid work, as Ina Zweiniger-Bargielowska shows in chapter 10, had substantially increased.[7] Fears of family breakdown and juvenile delinquency in the 1950s and 1960s which would result from large numbers of 'latchkey children', projected blame onto working-class mothers, encouraging feelings of guilt in mothers who worked. However Wendy Webster has argued that the meanings attributed to work and domesticity were specific to white middle-class English women. Black women recruited from the Caribbean to fill the postwar labour shortage were denied a domestic and maternal identity and defined as 'workers' not 'working wives': 'There was no expectation that they

Plate 9.1. An extended family group, early 1950s. The mothers in this group (far left and third from right) experienced the postwar baby boom. They each had four children and husbands who were frequently absent or worked long hours. Neither were in paid employment when their children were young but they relied on the other women in the photo (unmarried aunts and a grandmother) to give them unpaid help with the childcare.

would subordinate their employment to the needs of the family.'[8] Children were sometimes sent away to their parents' country of origin to be cared for by grandparents or other family members.

The lack of familial support systems for many mothers could also be intensified by geographical and social mobility. The movement of families from the inner cities to the suburbs has been a continuing trend throughout the century, making it less likely that female relatives will be living near enough to offer regular care. The revolution in work of the 1980s and 1990s, which has increased job insecurity and mobility, has also reduced the availability of unpaid care from relatives, although there is evidence that wider kin do still offer support even if living at a distance. As more women in the 1980s and 1990s went into full-time work, their dependence on paid childminders and day nurseries increased. At the end of the twentieth century in many families both parents had full-time jobs and increasing numbers of men did some proportion of child-care. Yet, as Julie's experience suggests, women overwhelmingly still took the main responsibility for looking after children. Not only did they have to plan complicated rotas for picking up children from childminders and arranging after-school care, but, in the event of illness, school holidays, etc., predominantly women took time off work (often unpaid) and as a result were disadvantaged in the labour market.

Other factors which have changed the nature of childcare in the late twentieth century have been increased road traffic and a growing level of organisation of children's lives. This has been prompted partly by fears of child-abduction, intensified by the media spotlight on child-abusers and paedophile rings. Children who earlier in the century played out in the street unsupervised or watched by older siblings and neighbours were more closely guarded and remained within the confines of house and garden in the 1990s. This coincided with increasing reluctance to take responsibility for other people's children, particularly by men who feared false accusations of abuse. Such fears were well-founded as suggested by a case of a single man fostering a teenage boy, whose neighbour called the police when she noticed a string of teenagers entering his house.[9]

Lack of family and community support poses particular problems for single mothers today. Until the 1970s single (unmarried) mothers, if not sent away to institutions, most commonly worked and relied on their families to care for their children, often passing them off as nephews, nieces or younger siblings. Illegitimacy no longer exists as a legal category and the stigma of single parenthood has shifted to concern about their widespread dependence on the state for support. At the end of the century, single (now mainly divorced) mothers were more likely to care for their children alone, making paid work more difficult than earlier in the century.[10] By contrast unmarried fathers have rarely taken responsibility for their children, while widowers earlier in the century either remarried or, like unmarried mothers, often drew upon the support of female relatives. A not uncommon pattern was the experience of Dora, an unmarried youngest daughter born in 1903, who was kept at home to look after

Plate 9.2. A woman with her great-nephew, early 1980s. Grandmothers and great-aunts were an important resource for childcare throughout the century but more likely to be in paid employment after the Second World War.

her ailing mother and also cared for her 10-year-old niece after her brother's wife died.

The meteoric rise in the divorce and remarriage rates over the last three decades has led to a greater number of single (mainly divorced) fathers doing a proportion of childcare. However since higher numbers of divorced men than women remarry or cohabit they too often rely on a new partner as stepmother to help with childcare. This trend is not entirely new but has taken a new form. High maternal mortality rates at the beginning of the century also frequently led to complex family groups containing stepmothers. However the lack of a living birth mother meant that these relationships generally had a different emphasis. In the late twentieth century children often divide their time between two family groups with consequent tensions arising between birth mothers and stepmothers in negotiating care.

A final area of unpaid work within the home which is rarely considered has been highlighted by Janet Finch in her book *Married To The Job*. This is the unpaid labour wives give to their husbands' work. The business of being a wife is by no means confined to giving domestic support and childcare although these factors are crucial in enabling men both to work long hours and help bring up children. Wives have contributed to their husbands' enterprises in a variety of ways both within and outside the home. These include cleaning offices (when the business is transacted directly from home), entertaining customers and clients, taking phone calls, making appointments, acting as secretary, bookkeeper, proofreader or amanuensis (now less common with the advent of the computer), and deputising in a husband's absence. For example in Mitchell's study of police wives in the 1970s, 34 per cent said they played an active part in police work, while one respondent in another study of the police said this included cooking dinner for prisoners in police cells.

Just as wives often did unpaid secretarial and clerical work in the home, so also did secretaries and personal assistants (one of the main growth areas in women's employment in the early twentieth century) become 'the office wife'. They often performed domestic and emotional work for their bosses by doing tasks normally expected of wives: making their tea, booking hotels and restaurants, listening to their problems and sometimes even remembering birthdays and buying presents for relations.

Finch pointed out that the investment wives make in their husbands' jobs was logical in that it offered a comprehensible way of being a wife which conformed to commonly understood cultural and linguistic forms and also made economic sense. She argued that dual-career marriages are less likely to survive precisely because separation is more possible. It is not yet clear how far women's progress towards economic and career parity with men will change the meaning of being a wife, and the extent to which women invest in their husbands' and bosses' careers rather than their own.

Unpaid Work Outside the Home

The idea that, while men work for money, women work out of love and duty, may also be linked to the latter's prominent position in voluntary, charitable and philanthropic work outside the home, another legacy from nineteenth-century Britain. Victorian middle-class women's movement into philanthropy was prompted partly by their exclusion from paid work and justified by the idea that it was a 'woman's mission' to work with the poor and needy and to rescue her suffering 'brothers' and 'sisters'. Despite the increasing involvement of the state during the twentieth century in areas that had previously been the province of charitable and voluntary institutions, the voluntary sector has adapted rather than diminished its role and many organisations have remained heavily dependent on women's labour power.

Religion and Philanthropic Work

With declining church attendance and the adoption of scientific standards and methods in areas such as health care and education, religious institutions, which were at the centre of the Victorian philanthropic impulse, became less prominent in the twentieth century. Yet they continued to be the focus for a significant proportion of the voluntary charitable work done by women in the first half of the century, both in convents and in organisations such as the Girl Guides, the Girls' Friendly Society, the Church Army, the Mothers' Union, the Young Wives and numerous missionary societies and parish-based charities, many of which were still active in the late 1990s.

The significance of marital status is particularly interesting. For unmarried women taking religious orders or going into missionary work had long been seen as a way of leaving home and gaining independence from their families. However those who entered convents, usually to engage in educational, charitable or rescue work, lived and worked within structures modelled closely upon families and reproducing family nomenclature and hierarchies. Unmarried women working in religious orders and communities received no direct financial payment but were supported by the community in return for their labour. Nuns who were 'sisters' worked under the immediate authority of a 'mother superior' who was herself subject to the higher authority of a 'father' who was an unmarried male priest. Familial hierarchies continued to be reinforced in convent schools, whose pupils were closely protected from contact with the opposite sex and in convent-based homes for unmarried mothers, who were rescued and sent into domestic service.

In nineteenth-century missionary work abroad, the presence of wives as models of domestic virtue was seen as desirable and the unpaid work of wives, sisters and daughters in missionary families to teach 'native' girls and women greatly valued. However the increasing recruitment of single women as missionaries in the early twentieth century provoked debates about marital status. Although missionary wives still provided unpaid labour in teaching or support work, there was no question of either paying them directly or giving their husbands a higher salary. Single women were required to undertake not to marry for a period of up to five years as it was assumed that if they married the missionary societies would lose trained workers. Although by the early 1990s The Church Missionary Society recognised husbands and wives as equal partners with a joint allowance payable, wives' incorporation into their husband's job still continued in some societies. For example the United Society for the Propagation of the Gospel paid a single salary to the husband and, although wives might not be seen as missionaries themselves, they were still expected to participate in the training of all outgoing missionaries.[11]

Thus churches' expectations of women's work in the community, either as nuns or missionaries, have remained rooted in nineteenth-century middle-class domestic ideology and the images of the virtuous wife, holy mother, dutiful daughter and supportive sister, models which they have sought to impose on other classes and cultures. But how far were women themselves inspired either by such imagery or by religious zeal? Did they have other reasons for engaging in charitable and philanthropic work?

Women who did not have (or whose husbands did not have) a religious vocation still also often used church-based groups as a basis for philanthropic work. The most widespread of these were the mothers' meetings established from the mid-nineteenth century with the aim of getting poor women together outside the home to engage in needlework, prayer and good works. Mothers' meetings both drew upon the symbolic power and imagery of the mother to mobilise support and fulfilled an important social function for isolated women in the home. They remained a significant community base for philanthropy until the Second World War.

The best known of these organisations was the Mothers' Union which in 1914 had 8,000 branches and 400,000 members attending weekly meetings and remained one of the foremost philanthropic organisations into the late twentieth century. In line with state policy these and other groups adopted maternalist philosophies in the early twentieth century with a particular emphasis on child health, yet Frank Prochaska points out that, because they did not take up state assistance, they have been neglected in 'whiggish' histories of child welfare, despite a long history of lobbying the government on social policy. Through the endless round of jumble sales, coffee mornings and local fêtes, mothers' meetings and young wives' groups have also formed an essential role in fund-raising upon which local and national charities have heavily depended.[12]

Secular Women's Groups and Unpaid Work

The early twentieth century also saw the creation of a number of secular mainly middle-class women's organisations in the wake of the suffrage movement such as the National Federation of Women's Institutes (WI) formed in 1915 which by the 1970s had 9,000 branches and the National Union of Townswomen's Guilds (TG) in 1928. These groups combined social, domestic and leisure activities with work perceived as being of benefit to the community. For example the WI was formed for food production during the First World War for which they initially received grants from the Ministry of Agriculture. While the first stated aim of an early TG leaflet was to 'improve the science and practice of home-making' they also wanted 'to enable women as citizens to make the best contribution to the common good' and took up causes such as the anti-litter campaign 'Keep Britain Tidy' and the provision of public lavatories in the 1950s.[13]

Here too women have drawn upon the language of family and home. The philanthropic image of women extending family values to the nation in their role as social housekeepers remained active, particularly during the Second World War when, in addition to growing food, TG members did domestic work in hospitals and provided a mending service for factory workers' clothes. Wartime governments drew heavily on the unpaid services of women, linking love of home and family with women's patriotic duty to serve on the 'home front'. Similarly Herbert Morrison praised the achievements of the Women's Voluntary Service (later the WRVS), formed in 1939 for the purposes of civil defence, which became an auxiliary of over twenty government departments. He saw them as 'applying the principles for good housekeeping to the job of helping run their country in its hour of need.' The difficulties women's voluntary organisations have continued to face in escaping such domestic metaphors parallel those of the 'office wife'. This is evident in a 1990s leaflet which insisted: 'WRVS members have worked in all disasters from 1939 to the present day – and *we don't just make tea*'.[14]

Women and Voluntary Work after 1945

Several factors have altered women's relationship to charitable and voluntary work outside the home since the Second World War. More women moving into full-time employment and the rise in average working hours, their continuing primary role in household and familial care coupled with the demise of living-in domestic service, have combined to reduce the time women have available to work for voluntary organisations and led to a crisis in recruitment in organisations such as the WRVS and the Red Cross.

In 1948 it was optimistically assumed that the welfare state would remove the need for charitable work and voluntary action, but this has been far from the case. Expanded demand on health and welfare services caused partly by the increase in numbers of the elderly and reluctance by governments in the 1980s and 1990s to meet the costs from state funds have increased the demand on voluntary organisations to meet the shortfall. However, although many women may have less time to give to voluntary and charitable organisations, pressure is still put upon mothers who work part-time to contribute unpaid work to their children's schools in areas such as fund-raising, helping in the class-room and organising after-school care.

Conclusion

It is apparent from this discussion that at the end of the twentieth century the burden of caring still falls much more heavily on women than on men and it is clearly in the interests of the latter to perpetuate this division of labour. Women's progress towards equality in the labour market has not been matched by a parallel movement of men taking an equal responsibility for caring and unpaid family work. The injunction to care is still perceived and experienced as integral to women's identity but sits uncomfortably with late twentieth-century notions of masculinity. The advent of men's groups and the 'new man' stereotype in the late 1970s, and the popularity of films highlighting men's relationship with children in the 1980s and early 1990s such as *Three Men and a Baby*, have done little to change this position. More fathers may be picking up children from school, but women still do most of the 'emotion work' within marriages and take responsibility for the physical and emotional needs of dependent family members.[15]

The gender ratio in voluntary and charitable work was more equally balanced in 2000 than it was at the start of the century. Working women had less time to give to charitable causes and this change has been matched by an increase in the number of retired men who were volunteering. Greater longevity, improved health and earlier retirement by the middle classes were important factors here. In the over-75 age group men in organised voluntary work now outnumbered women. Yet the overall balance of unpaid work outside the home still favoured women, just as it did within the home and family. It remains to be seen how far changes in women's economic role and in state family policy in the twenty-first century will alter this gender divide.

Bibliographical Note

Unattributed examples used in this chapter are taken from oral history interviews conducted by the author for her PhD thesis, K. Holden, 'The Shadow of Marriage: Single Women in England, 1919–1939', (University of Essex PhD, 1996). Names have been changed to preserve anonymity. Texts which discuss the connections between public and private and familial ideologies include L. Davidoff, *Worlds Between: Historical Perspectives on Gender and Class* (Cambridge, 1995); L. Davidoff, M. Doolittle, J. Fink and K. Holden, *The Family Story: Blood Contract and Intimacy: 1830–1960* (London, 1999); D. Gittins, *The Family in Question: Changing Households and Familiar Ideologies* (London, 1985); and S. D'Cruze, 'Women and the Family', in J. Purvis (ed), *Women's History: Britain, 1850–1945* (London, 1995). For helpful feminist and sociological perspectives on caring and relationships between kin, which also cast light on the late twentieth-century patterns of care, see J. Lewis and B. Meredith, *Daughters Who Care: Daughters Caring for Mothers at Home* (London, 1988); J. Finch and D. Groves, *A Labour of Love: Women, Work and Caring* (London, 1983); and J. Finch, *Family Obligations and Social Change* (London, 1989). Several chapters in J. Lewis (ed), *Labour and Love: Women's Experience of Home and Family* (London, 1986); and J. Lewis, *Women in Britain since 1945* (London, 1992) provide historical perspectives on caring and unpaid work. E. Roberts, *A Woman's Place: An Oral History of Working-Class Women 1890–1940* (London, 1984); and E. Roberts, *Women and Families: An Oral History, 1940–1970* (London, 1995) give useful but regionally specific evidence of women as carers in working-class families based on oral history interviews. For the unpaid work of wives see J. Finch, *Married to the Job: Wives Incorporation in Men's Work* (London, 1983). On demographic change see D. Gittins, *Fair Sex: Family Size and Structure 1900–1939* (London, 1982); and M. Anderson, 'The Social Implications of Demographic Change', in F.M.L. Thompson (ed), *The Cambridge Social History of Britain*, vol. 2: *People and their Environment* (Cambridge, 1990). While there are a number of individual histories of women's voluntary organisations, no general historical text specifically on women and voluntary or philanthropic work in the twentieth century exists. F. Prochaska, *The Voluntary Impulse: Philanthropy in Modern Britain* (London, 1988) remains a useful if limited source of information.

Notes

1. See Bibliographical Note for references for these and later examples.

2. F. Prochaska, *The Voluntary Impulse: Philanthropy in Modern Britain* (London, 1988), p. 19.

3. Diary of Jane Hill held by author.

4. See D. Gittins, *Fair Sex: Family Size and Structure 1900–1939* (London, 1982).

5. J. Reid, unpublished autobiography, 1998.

6. J. Lewis, *Women in Britain since 1945* (Oxford, 1992), p. 75.

7. L. Davidoff, *Worlds Between: Historical Perspectives on Gender and Class* (Cambridge, 1995), p. 12.

8. W. Webster, *Imagining Home: Gender, Race and National Identity, 1945–64* (London, 1998), p. 147.

9. BBC Radio 4, 'Home Truths', 3 July 1999.

10. For very useful discussions on the changing position of lone mothers in the twentieth century see K. Kiernan, H. Land and J. Lewis, *Lone Mothers in Twentieth Century Britain* (Oxford, 1998).

11. D. Kirkwood, 'Protestant Missionary Women: Wives and Spinsters', in F. Bowie, D. Kirkwood and S. Ardener (eds), *Women and Missions: Past and Present* (Oxford, 1993).

12. Prochaska, *The Voluntary Impulse*, pp. 52–8.

13. M. Stott, *Organisation Woman* (London, 1978).

14. L. Westwood, 'More than Tea and Sympathy', *History Today* 48, 6 (June 1998) [my emphasis].

15. J. Duncombe and D. Marsden, 'Love and Intimacy: The Gender Division of Emotion and "Emotion Work": A Neglected Aspect of Sociological Discussion of Heterosexual Relationships', *Sociology* 27, 2 (May 1993).

10

HOUSEWIFERY

Ina Zweiniger-Bargielowska

This discussion of housewifery explores women's roles within the family by focusing on the home which provides a site where gender identities are forged and reaffirmed through the division and allocation of labour, time, space and material resources. Gendered divisions of labour and women's association with tasks such as cooking and laundry date back many centuries. By contrast, the identification of married women with full-time housewifery is a much more recent phenomenon. The nineteenth century witnessed the emergence of the male breadwinner earning a family wage and increasingly elaborate domestic rituals, first within the middle class and later the working class.

Despite the power of the ideal of male breadwinner and female full-time housewife in Western society and its association with a nuclear family as the norm, this form of household formation and gendered division of labour in fact flourished for only a brief historical period. The family wage remained an aspiration rather than a reality for the working class until well into the twentieth century. At the same time, the middle class relied heavily on domestic servants until the 1930s and only from the Second World War onwards did middle-class women perform the bulk of domestic work themselves.

Marriage provided the major turning point in most women's lives from worker to housewife during the first half of the century. More recently, the birth of the first child has precipitated a reorientation in women's roles and sense of identity from worker to homemaker. While full-time housewifery was a typical experience during the middle decades of the century, from the 1950s onwards married women's employment increased dramatically. At the end of the century, the traditional nuclear family accounted for only a small minority of households. Most married women were in employment, albeit frequently part-time, the male breadwinner role had been eroded and there were a wide range of household patterns, including a growing proportion of single-parent families headed by women. These developments are traced within the context of changing employment opportunities, the transformation of the home and the domestic technology revolution of the twentieth century. First of all, it is necessary to define the term 'housewife'.

What or Who is a Housewife?

A housewife is anybody who does housework – shopping, cooking, cleaning, washing for themselves and for others.

The absurdity of the above statement highlights the powerful social and cultural associations of the concept housewife. Doing housework does not turn a person into a housewife. Domestic servants are not housewives, because they get paid for their labour whereas the work of the housewife is unpaid. She is the mistress of the house and responsible for the direction of housework, which she may perform exclusively or delegate to servants and other family members. A man cannot be a housewife and the small number of men who have done more than help with the housework fly in the face of conventional masculine roles and aspirations. So-called house-husbands were not unheard of in the late twentieth century but, even in families where the woman was the primary or exclusive earner, traditional gender roles were not simply re-versed as most women continued to perform domestic chores after work while men, for example, used hobbies to define their identity and role. A woman living alone is not a housewife. Women become housewives in the context of marriage, motherhood and economic dependency. While not all housewives are married – in the early decades of the century, many women kept home for other relatives – and cohabitation has partially replaced marriage since the 1980s – the notion of a housewife is firmly located within conventional gender hierarchies.

Allen's analysis of debates establishing categories which exempted women from conscription during the Second World War is interesting here. Domestic duties which could exempt women from conscription included looking after a man such as a widowed father, but by contrast, women looking after female relatives such as a widowed mother did not qualify. The domestic ideal was essentially preserved, even in the context of total war, and housewives were

> women who were identified with, and seen as necessary for, the continuation of a 'home', [but] a woman alone could not constitute a 'home'. Neither could men by themselves, make a 'home'. Home-making was shown basically to be something which women did for men or children.[1]

A housewife is assumed to be heterosexual as Oerton makes clear in her discussion of 'queer housewives'. Studies of lesbian households, therefore, strike at the heart of how gendering processes are constituted since these households could contain two housewives or none. Housewives receive a housekeeping allowance from the main provider, usually the husband. The division and allocation of economic resources frequently causes conflict in a context where the housewife is likely to be the weaker party. Housewives' part-time or casual earnings are often treated as a household as opposed to a personal resource

– housewives do not have pocket money while breadwinners do. A similar point could be made with regard to time. Seymour highlights that the housewife has 'no time to call my own'; she cannot clock off or separate work and leisure like the breadwinner.[2] A housewife's time is a resource at the disposal of the entire household and this applies particularly to women in employment who spend their 'free' time catching up on chores. In sum, a housewife is typically a woman living in a heterosexual cohabiting relationship whose identity is defined in terms of her ultimate responsibility for keeping house and servicing the family regardless of employment status. Being a housewife, therefore, for many women is not simply about what they do but strikes at the heart of who they are.

Housewives' Status: Patriarchy or Pride?

The conventional and still influential approach to the study of housewifery in Britain is based on the work by Ann Oakley written at the height of the second-wave feminist movement in the early 1970s. Oakley's polemical book *Housewife* is bristling with anger at the limited opportunities open to women, who are forced into full-time housewifery and enslaved by narrow domestic roles under patriarchy. She deplores housewives' low status, and draws attention to the demeaning nature of housework as well as the boredom, monotony and frequent social isolation experienced by many housewives. In order to liberate women, Oakley declares, 'The housewife role must be abolished. The family must be abolished. Gender roles must be abolished.'[3] This account of housewifery was written by a woman representing the generation reaching adulthood in the 1960s and 1970s who were better educated and had greater employment opportunities than women in the past. Among the middle class, they were also among the first generations expected to cope with housework and childcare single-handedly with virtually no help from domestic servants and few modern domestic appliances. This was frequently a difficult, frustrating and lonely experience and it is interesting to note that Ann Oakley's wish list written in 1968 included modern domestic durables and 'a cleaning lady'.[4]

This chapter aims to historicise the experience of housewifery, the nature of housework and women's attitudes and aspirations. While Oakley's analysis struck a chord in the specific circumstances of the late 1960s and early 1970s, particularly with regard to middle-class women, there is no reason why this approach should be equally valid or relevant at other historical periods or with regard to working-class or black women. Full-time housewifery was a popular aspiration for many working-class women in the face of low-status, low-paid employment opportunities which were not perceived as liberating but as additional burdens. However, this aspiration was beyond the reach of many working-class women until the interwar years and beyond. Similarly, Webster argues that the idealisation of the home managed by the housewife on a full-time

Lucy and Ajax Liquid versus kitchen grease

Lucy learns how Ajax with Double Ammonia takes the hard work out of even the toughest kitchen jobs!

2. "Monday didn't get off to a good start either. Burnt milk all over the cooker."

3. "...So I got down to it with just a little Ajax on a sponge."

4. "Those burnt-on stains I was dreading came off just like that."

5. "While I was at it, a quick wipe over the worktops to get rid of the stains and marks."

1. "Cooking on Sunday always means grease on Monday. Wasn't I glad Ajax was there to help!"

6. "Ajax with Double Ammonia really does take the hard work out of my kitchen, leaves everything spotlessly clean!"

Cleans like a white tornado

(Also new Ajax Pine Cleaner with a fresh disinfectant).

93

Plate 10.1. 'Lucy and Ajax Liquid Versus Kitchen Grease', *Woman*, April 1972. Modern domestic appliances did not eliminate women's responsibility for housework as illustrated by this detergent advert from the early 1970s.

basis during the early postwar years was a privilege enjoyed by white women only and black women, including recent immigrants to Britain, were effectively excluded.

Among the middle class housewifery had been associated with the employment of domestic servants – at least a maid-of-all work – until the interwar years. This situation changed dramatically from the Second World War onwards when domestic servants – except in very wealthy households – ceased to be part of normal middle-class life leaving the housewife to deal with every aspect of domestic work and childcare, with no more than occasional help for those who could afford it. This situation was perceived as degrading, boring and isolating by those women whose aspirations conflicted significantly with the narrowly prescribed domestic role they were expected to fulfil giving rise to the angry explosion of the second-wave feminist movement.

Recent historical work presents a more positive interpretation and maintains that housewives took pride in their work which was of major economic, social and cultural significance. Davidoff highlights the cultural importance of housewives' role in providing the framework within which social life was conducted. Housework was basically concerned 'with creating and maintaining order in the immediate environment, making meaningful patterns of activities, people and materials'. Cooking, 'the transformation of raw ingredients into a new substance . . . [was] used in family or social ritual' in the sense that 'proper' meals had to adhere to 'ritually prescribed patterns' and their consumption demarcated 'the boundaries of the household, of friendship patterns, of kinship gradations'. Cleaning played a similar role in marking boundaries by imposing and maintaining order.[5]

Housewives' skills and priorities were of great economic value and defined not only women's sense of identity, social status and aspirations but those of the family as a whole. The distinctive features of the home, the preparation and presentation of food, and the maintenance of clothing provided the means by which the family presented itself to the world. Bourke criticises feminist scholarship and conventional economic history which undervalues housewives as supposedly non-productive by stressing the significance of housewifery in converting cash into domestic comforts. Women's transition towards full-time housewifery from the late nineteenth century onwards was a popular aspiration and a rational choice. Full-time housewifery, as Bourke argues, provided women with a power base since husbands were as dependent on female domestic skills as women were on male earnings. Roberts and Ross emphasise the contribution of housewifery skills in raising family living standards, along with the high status in family and community that working-class women derived from their success in making ends meet and holding the family together. This dominant position of the housewife in the family was eroded with rising prosperity from the middle of the twentieth century onwards.[6] The following paragraphs discuss housewives' efforts to maintain customary domestic comforts during the exceptional circumstances of the Second World War and postwar austerity.

IN FOCUS: Citizen Housewife: Housewives under Austerity during the 1940s

In the Second World War the civilian population had to cope with extensive rationing of food and clothing as well as severe shortages of most other consumer goods as economic resources were diverted towards the war effort.[7] The end of the war did not mark any relaxation and, indeed, food rationing was more extensive and ration levels were lower and more volatile during the late 1940s than in wartime. Total prewar consumption levels were reached again at the end of the decade, but for many foodstuffs and domestic consumer goods prewar consumption levels were not surpassed until the mid-1950s.

During this period of austerity, housewifery acquired an enhanced sense of national importance since the successful implementation of rationing and other domestic economy measures was vital in maintaining civilian health and morale. Housewifery was no longer regarded as a private concern but rather as a central component of the war effort and postwar reconstruction. Thus the housewife's daily battle on the kitchen front was as critical to victory as that of the soldier or the worker in essential industry. Housewives, who accounted for the majority of the adult female population even at the height of mobilisation, did most of the queuing, contriving and making do in order to preserve, as much as possible, customary culinary traditions and domestic rituals. Housewives' disproportionate sacrifice frequently shielded men and children from the full impact of the reduction in consumption.

This pivotal female contribution was recognised by the government during the war, resulting in an unprecedented outpouring of propaganda – such as recipes, nutritional advice and economy measures disseminated in leaflets, booklets, short films and above all the radio – which aimed to help women adapt their housewifery skills to wartime conditions as well as to raise standards generally. For example a Ministry of Food leaflet declared,

> The line of Food Defence runs through all our homes. . . . It may seem so simple, this urgent duty, that we may tend to overlook its full meaning. A little saving here and there – how can that really help us to win the war? A little here and there, with our 45 million people all contributing, becomes an immense amount. . . . *The woman with the basket* has a vital part to play in home defence. By saving food you may be saving lives.[8]

Housewives' reaction to austerity measures varied depending on the policy. Moreover, their attitudes changed over time and wartime patriotic acceptance gave way to disillusionment and discontent among many housewives during the late 1940s. Housewives welcomed the introduction of a comprehensive food policy and supported food rationing enthusiastically during the war. By contrast, clothes rationing was widely resented, the difficulties of clothing children under rationing became a continuous source of grievance, and queuing was a persistent problem on

Citizen Housewife: Housewives under Austerity during the 1940s (continued)

Plate 10.2. Cartoon illustrating housewives' frustration after the war, *Sunday Dispatch*, June 1946.

the home front. Nevertheless, female morale was generally high during the war, the overwhelming majority of housewives considered themselves to be well fed and accepted the necessity of sacrifice for the duration.

The continuation of austerity after the war was hard to bear in the face of high expectations engendered by victory and a majority of the entire population thought that their diet was insufficient to maintain good health and that lack of food adversely affected their ability to work during the late 1940s. There was little readiness to tolerate further hardships but the situation became more difficult as a result of ration cuts and continuous shortages. These cuts bore particularly heavily on housewives who frequently gave up some of their rations to other members of the family. During this period of crisis, the flexibility of female consumption standards served as a buffer in the family economy and a disproportionate share of the burden resulting from the postwar recovery policy based on domestic austerity and the export drive was borne by women and especially housewives. This sacrifice extended well beyond the poorest income groups, many women were fatigued and female morale was generally low. A good example is Mrs Jones, a typical, if fictional, housewife in *Picture Post's* special issue on the economic crisis of April 1947.

Citizen Housewife: Housewives under Austerity during the 1940s (continued)

> Mrs Jones doesn't care a damn for economics. . . . She is too busy with
> the urgent considerations of living. . . . She is absorbed every hour of the
> day in the task of feeding her family . . . shopping, scrubbing, cooking,
> mending – and making the money go round. And she finds the job a
> hard one. Harder than before the war. Harder, even, than during the
> war. She is utterly weary. . . . her prevailing mood is one of profound
> disappointment. We won the war. We expected an easier time. Why is
> it so much worse? . . . She finds there is less food for the family . . . that
> there are less goods in the shops . . . She is fed up with queuing . . . This
> is her general attitude to life today.[9]

Women did not accept this situation passively. The problems of
the housewife became a major political issue as women registered their
dissatisfaction in protests organised, for example, by the British Housewives'
League and, more importantly, through the ballot box. The postwar
Labour's government's collectivist, producerist agenda remained popular
among men whose discontent about shortages and low rations was
outweighed by an appreciation of gains such as full employment and
higher wages. These gains were not necessarily translated into increased
housekeeping money and women were greatly concerned about the high
rate of inflation during the late 1940s and early 1950s.

Labour's appeal to women which highlighted fair shares, food subsidies
and welfare reform, was not without support but these policies failed to
arrest the erosion of female support for the Attlee government. Many came
to favour the Conservative party which fashioned itself as the champion
of the female consumer by recognising the burden borne by women
under postwar austerity and promising relief in the form of decontrol,
the restoration of the price mechanism and increased supplies of
consumer goods. The Conservative party's skilful exploitation of widespread
dissatisfaction with persistent shortages and ration cuts was instrumental
to its electoral recovery during the late 1940s. The Conservative victories
in the general elections of 1951 and 1955, when the party polled a
disproportionate share of the female vote, indicate that the appeal to
housewives brought extensive rewards in terms of electoral success.
Housewives' central role in the austerity policy contributed to raising
women's status and consolidated their citizenship. The citizen housewife
was a significant political force during the 1940s and Labour's failure to
listen to her voice enabled the Conservative party to reconstruct an electoral
majority which, if initially fragile, was consolidated following the abolition
of rationing and unleashing of the postwar consumer boom when affluence
became a byword of political success.

The Rise and Decline of Full-time Housewifery

Paid work is discussed in the next chapter and the following paragraphs briefly sketch the dramatic transformation of female participation rates which has to be understood within the context of marriage and motherhood. From the late nineteenth century until just after the Second World War, women accounted for just under one-third of the total labour force. This figure gradually rose to 40 per cent in 1981 and stood at about 45 per cent in 1998.[10] During the twentieth century, the proportion of women of working age in employment increased from about one-third in the first half of the century to about half in 1971 and 70 per cent in 1996. These trends mask the continuing significance of gender differences in employment patterns which are illustrated, for example, by looking at part-time employment. In 1998 four out of ten women were employed part-time, whereas among men part-time work accounted for only one in twenty, the overwhelming majority worked full-time, and frequently for longer hours than female full-time employees.

Married women's participation rate declined in the second half of the nineteenth century and by the turn of the century marital status was the most important determinant of female employment patterns. Figure 10.1 shows that

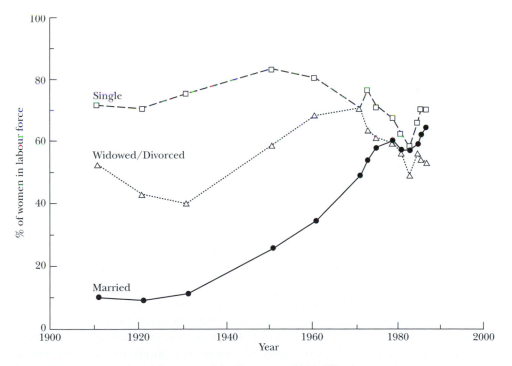

Figure 10.1. **Female labour force participation rates, 1911–87.**

Source: D.A. Coleman and R. Salt, *The British Population: Patterns, Trends and Processes* (Oxford, 1992), p. 141.

the bulk of single (and usually younger) women were in paid employment during the first half of the century, as was a substantial proportion of widowed or divorced women. By contrast, almost nine out of ten married women were full-time housewives until the 1930s. However, these statistics have been criticised since they generally omit married women's casual earnings, for example, from cleaning, washing, child-minding or taking in lodgers. According to Roberts this was a widespread practice which could augment the budget of a working-class family substantially. The overwhelming identification of married women with full-time housewifery declined rapidly from the Second World War onwards as a result of a dramatic rise of married women's employment, albeit frequently on a part-time basis. At the same time, employment among single women, the widowed and divorced fell slightly and by the 1980s marital status had ceased to be the dominant factor influencing women's employment status.

In the final quarter of the century motherhood – and particularly the age of the youngest child and the number of children – became the central deter- minant of female participation rates. While a dual pattern of married women's employment – including a period of full-time housewifery and caring for young children – was typical from the 1950s to the 1970s, the final decades of the century have witnessed a decline of full-time housewifery even among mothers with children under five years. At the same time, a gap emerged between mar- ried and lone mothers.

Full- and part-time employment among married women with dependent children increased between 1977 and 1996 from 15 and 36 per cent to 24 and 42 per cent respectively. The most dramatic changes have taken place among mothers with children under five years. In 1977 only 5 per cent were working full-time (22 per cent part-time). In 1996 less than half stayed at home with 18 and 36 per cent respectively in full- and part-time employment. The transforma- tion is even more dramatic if occupational status is taken into account and two- thirds of professional mothers with children under five were in employment in the 1990s – most of them full-time – while part-time work was most popular among semi-skilled and unskilled mothers with young children. In contrast with the increasing erosion of full-time housewifery among married and cohabiting women, the experience of lone mothers has remained relatively stable since 1977. Just under one-quarter were in part-time employment and the propor- tion of lone mothers in full-time employment has actually declined from just over 20 per cent to about 15 per cent. Indeed, fewer than one out of ten lone mothers whose youngest child was under five worked full-time during the 1990s.

Full-time housewifery was the typical experience of married women in the first half of the twentieth century – even if tempered by casual earnings among the working class. In the second half of the century married women increasingly combined housewifery with employment. This was so particularly among middle- class professional women, a majority of whom remained in employment in the 1990s even when their children were very young. In this sense, women's improved education and higher qualifications have partially addressed the dis- content of middle-class housewives highlighted by Ann Oakley in the early 1970s.

However, this experience has not been an unqualified success story as working wives – and above all full-time working mothers of young children – have had to cope with the double burden discussed below. By contrast, working-class married women with young children were more likely to stay at home during the 1990s but, above all, lone mothers became the final bastion of full-time housewifery at the end of the twentieth century.

Housework and the Domestic Technology Revolution

The housewife's environment was transformed dramatically during the twentieth century as a result of extensive house building and the rapid spread of utilities coupled with the emergence of mass-produced consumer durables.[11] Piped water became generally available in towns just before the First World War but about a third of the rural population did not have access to piped water until after the Second World War. In 1971 one-eighth of dwellings still lacked at least one of the basic amenities – kitchen sink, bath or shower, wash hand basin (all with hot and cold water) and an indoor WC – but in 1996 this figure had fallen to less than one per cent. About two-thirds of households were wired for electricity in 1938, in the late 1940s four out of five had gas supplies and over 95 per cent of households were wired for electricity in the late 1950s. As a result of these developments, coupled with the expansion of mass-production techniques and hire-purchase facilities, the middle decades of the century witnessed a revolution in domestic interiors transforming kitchens and bathrooms as well as lighting and space heating. Gas and electric cookers replaced the cooking range, solid fuel was supplanted by gas or electric fires and later central heating, and electrical appliances became standard features.

From the interwar years onwards, a range of new so-called labour-saving devices such as vacuum cleaners, washing machines, cookers and heaters were marketed as reducing the housewife's burdens particularly in the new middle-class servantless home. According to advertisements, these appliances transformed the housewife into a home-technician who merely had to push a few buttons instead of spending long hours on demanding jobs such as washing, cooking or cleaning.

Whatever the merits of these marketing campaigns, the overwhelming majority of women in Britain had to do without until the 1950s. Due to the relatively high cost of these appliances only lighting, radios and electrical irons were widely available before the Second World War. The diffusion of washing machines, refrigerators and vacuum cleaners as well as water and space heaters took off in Britain only from the mid-1950s onwards. The proportion of households owning a washing machine increased from two-thirds to 90 per cent between 1972 and 1996. Deep freezers became commonplace during the 1980s, microwave ovens during the 1990s, about half of all households owned a tumble drier in the mid-1990s but only one in five owned dishwashers which failed to attract buyers beyond the middle classes.

There is no doubt about the arduous and time-consuming nature of house-work during the first half of the century when women had to manage without piped indoor water supplies, running hot water, washing machines, vacuum cleaners or fridges and cope with open coal fires and gas lighting. Zmroczek graphically describes the laborious process of washing with little change in technology until the 1960s. Washing involved carrying water which was heated in a copper boiler, the mangling of washing between rinses and elaborate starch-ing and ironing. Children had to help and many middle-class housewives sent their washing out while working-class women frequently took in washing to earn extra cash. Nevertheless, modern domestic appliances did not always reduce the housewife's burdens. In practice, labour-saving appliances fell well short of the promises of advertisers since their introduction tended to coincide with rising standards such as washing more frequently. The rapid diffusion of domestic appliances did not reduce the amount of time women spent doing housework as illustrated by a number of surveys conducted between the 1930s and the 1970s. There was also a convergence between working- and middle-class women in the amount of time spent doing housework. Schwarz Cowan draws attention to the withdrawal of domestic help by other family members, most notably children, and concludes that there was

> more work for a mother to do in a modern home because there is no one left to help her with it . . . although the work is more productive (more services are performed, and more goods are produced for every hour of work) and less laborious than it used to be, for most housewives it is just as time-consuming and just as demanding.[12]

The Double Burden

Most women in the late twentieth century had to cope with a double burden since modern domestic technology did not eliminate housework and the dramatic rise in female employment was not accompanied by a fundamental reallocation of domestic labour. Men's participation in domestic chores did not increase in line with female employment and the gendered division of housework remained remarkably resilient. In surveys of social attitudes conducted in the 1980s and 1990s a small majority of respondents rejected the traditional bread-winner model, which was most disliked by women, the young, those with higher qualifications and especially women working full-time.[13] These surveys also pointed towards a considerable gap between aspiration and experience. While single people anticipated greater equality and couples felt that tasks should be shared more equally, in practice this was not the case. For example, in 1987 41 per cent among single people expected washing and ironing to be shared equally and about a quarter of couples thought it should be, but only 9 per cent actually shared this task equally. In the same survey, among households where the man was the main provider, 88 per cent of women who worked part-time and 91 per cent of women not employed were mainly responsible for household duties. Even when both partners worked full-time, 72 per cent of women were still mainly responsible for housework and only just over one in five shared out duties equally. Five years later, there had been a slight shift in the allocation of housework but 67 per cent of women remained mainly responsible for housework within households with both partners in full-time employment while about a quarter shared domestic chores equally. Between 1984 and 1991 the gap between 'should' share equally and 'do' share equally widened with regard to many tasks – especially cooking, cleaning and washing – suggesting that women's expectations of male participation as well as male guilt had increased.

The so-called 'New Man' remained relatively rare and a 1996 survey of the division of household tasks among parents shows that mothers spent almost three times as many hours as fathers on household and family responsibilities. Not only did mothers do most of the cooking, cleaning and washing, but they also spent more time playing with children, shopping, washing up and driving children to school. The only categories where fathers spent more time were gardening and 'other household tasks' – presumably minor repairs – both traditional male domestic duties. This evidence suggests that the transformation of female participation rates and more egalitarian attitudes have not altered behaviour substantially. At the end of the century housework continued to be allocated according to traditional gender norms and most women were confronted with the double burden since they were unable or unwilling to shed their primary responsibility for cooking, cleaning and caring for their families.

Conclusion

The ideal of the male breadwinner remained influential throughout the twentieth century but full-time housewifery as the typical experience of married women was a relatively brief phenomenon. It emerged in the late nineteenth century and was eroded in the second half of the twentieth in the wake of declining fertility, improved access to education and changing female employment opportunities. Second-wave feminist writers have portrayed housewives as bored, isolated, exploited victims forced into a narrow role under patriarchy. By contrast, recent interpretations see the housewife as a central figure who defined the family's social status and aspirations and whose skills at making ends meet could contribute substantially to family living standards. Housewifery was a laborious task – especially in the first half of the century when modern domestic appliances were not generally available – and successful household management gave the housewife a power base *vis-à-vis* the breadwinner who was as dependent on her skill of converting cash into domestic comforts as she was on the housekeeping allowance.

The experience of housewifery in the twentieth century has to be understood within the context of changing circumstances and aspirations among different generations of women and between social classes. Full-time housewifery was a rational choice for many working-class women, especially in the first half of the century. After the war, full-time housewifery was rapidly eroded as married women entered the labour market but this did not apply to mothers of pre-school children. During the 1960s and 1970s full-time housewifery and mother-hood was a stressful experience for middle-class women who – in contrast with their mothers' generation – had no domestic help and whose aspirations in career terms were frequently thwarted. Professional women have increasingly been able to combine career, marriage and motherhood since the 1980s, but full-time employment, and to a lesser extent part-time employment, has led to the double burden of work and housewifery for most women. At the end of the century, there was no equality between the sexes in the labour market or in the home and women workers did not adopt the breadwinner's approach to dividing work and leisure. Even among full-time employees, women continued to retain their housewife role – partly because men refrained from taking women's place but also because managing the home and servicing the family remained central foci of women's sense of identity.

Bibliographical Note

The literature on housewifery is usefully surveyed in S. Jackson, 'Towards a Historical Sociology of Housework: A Materialist Feminist Analysis', *Women's Studies International Forum* 15, 2 (1992), pp. 153–72. A special issue of *Women's Studies International Forum* 20, 3 (1997) on 'Concepts of Home' raises many important points and the *International Review of Social History* Supplement 5 (1997) focuses on the theme of 'The Rise and Decline of the Male Breadwinner Family?'. S. D'Cruze, 'Women and the Family', in J. Purvis (ed), *Women's History: Britain, 1850–1945* (London, 1995), pp. 51–83, is useful for the earlier period; and L. Davidoff, 'The Rationalisation of Housework', in her *Worlds Between: Historical Perspectives on Gender and Class* (Oxford, 1994) raises major conceptual points in a piece first published in the mid-1970s. For the classic feminist approach see A. Oakley, *Housewife* (London, 1974); and A. Oakley, *The Sociology of Housework* (London, 1974). A slightly earlier and hugely influential American study is B. Friedan, *The Feminine Mystique* (London, 1963). This feminist approach is criticised in J. Bourke, 'Housewifery in Working-Class England 1860–1914', *Past and Present* 143 (1994), pp. 167–97; and J. Bourke, *Working-Class Cultures in Britain 1890–1960: Gender, Class and Ethnicity* (London, 1994). Important local studies of working-class housewives and mothers in London and Lancashire are E. Ross, *Love and Toil: Motherhood in Outcast London, 1870–1918* (New York, 1993); E. Roberts, *A Woman's Place: An Oral History of Working-class Women, 1890–1940* (Oxford, 1984); and E. Roberts, *Women and Families: An Oral History, 1940–1970* (Oxford, 1995). Classic contemporary accounts of working-class housewives' conditions and survival strategies are M. Pember Reeves, *Round About a Pound a Week* (London, 1979) [first published 1913]; M. Llewllyn Davies (ed), *Maternity: Letters from Working-Women* (London, 1978) [first published 1915]; and M. Spring Rice, *Working-Class Wives: Their Health and Conditions* (London, 1939). For the postwar debate on working mothers see A. Myrdal and V. Klein, *Women's Two Roles: Home and Work* (London, 1956). On the revolution of domestic technology and the transformation of the housewife's environment see C. Davidson, *A Woman's Work is Never Done: A History of Housework in the British Isles, 1650–1950* (London, 1982); C. Hardyment, *From Mangle to Microwave: The Mechanization of Household Work* (Cambridge, 1988); and R. Schwarz

Cowan, *More Work for Mother: The Ironies of Household Technology from the Open Hearth to the Microwave* (New York, 1983). The slow diffusion of domestic appliances is traced by S. Bowden and A. Offer, 'Household Appliances and the Use of Time: The United States and Britain since the 1920s', *Economic History Review* 47 (1994), pp. 725–48; and C. Zmroczek, 'Dirty Linen: Women, Class and Washing Machines, 1920s–1960s', *Women's Studies International Forum* 15, 2 (1992), pp. 173–85.

Notes

1. M. Allen, 'The Domestic Ideal and the Mobilisation of Womanpower in World War II', *Women's Studies International Forum* 6 (1983), pp. 401–12.

2. S. Oerton, '"Queer Housewives?": Some Problems in Theorising the Division of Domestic Labour in Lesbian and Gay Households', *Women's Studies International Forum* 20 (1997), pp. 421–30; J. Seymour, '"No Time to Call My Own": Women's Time as a Household Resource', *Women's Studies International Forum* 15, 2 (1992), pp. 187–92.

3. A. Oakley, *Housewife* (London, 1974), p. 222; A. Oakley, *The Sociology of Housework* (London, 1974).

4. Quoted in W. Webster, *Imagining Home: Gender, 'Race' and National Identity, 1945–64* (London, 1998), p. 165, see also pp. 161–5; a good example of sheer bewilderment at the transition from student to full-time housewife and mother is, S. Gail, 'Housewife', in R. Fraser (ed), *Work* (Harmondsworth, 1968), pp. 140–55.

5. L. Davidoff, *Worlds Between: Historical Perspectives on Gender and Class* (Cambridge, 1995), pp. 75–6.

6. J. Bourke, 'Housewifery in Working-class England 1860–1914', *Past and Present* 143 (1994), pp. 167–97; E. Roberts, *A Woman's Place: An Oral History of Working-class Women, 1890–1940* (Oxford, 1984); E. Roberts, *Women and Families: An Oral History, 1940–1970* (Oxford, 1995); E. Ross, *Love and Toil: Motherhood in Outcast London, 1870–1918* (New York, 1993).

7. This topic is discussed in I. Zweiniger-Bargielowska, *Austerity in Britain: Rationing, Controls and Consumption, 1939–1955* (Oxford, 2000).

8. Ministry of Food, *Wise Housekeeping in War-time*, n.d. [approximately 1940], in Mass-Observation Archive, Sussex, Topic Collection Food, Box 2/C (emphasis in original).

9. *Picture Post*, 19 April 1947.

10. See S. Horrell and J. Humphries, 'Women's Labour Force Participation and the Transition to the Male-breadwinner Family, 1790–1865', *Economic History Review* 48 (1995), pp. 89–117; J. Lewis, *Women in England 1870–1950: Sexual Divisions and Social Change* (Brighton, 1984), pp. 145–55; J. Lewis, *Women in Britain since 1945* (Oxford, 1992), pp. 65–78. For the 1990s and comparative trends going back to the 1970s, see Office for National Statistics: Social Survey Division, *Living in Britain: Results from the 1996 General Household Survey* (London, 1998), pp. 52–73; *Social Trends* 29 (London, 1999), pp. 71–7.

11. C. Davidson, *A Woman's Work is Never Done: A History of Housework in the British Isles, 1650–1950* (London, 1982); C. Hardyment, *From Mangle to Microwave: The Mechanization of Household Work* (Cambridge, 1988); R. Schwarz Cowan, *More Work for Mother: The Ironies of Household Technology from the Open Hearth to the Microwave* (New York, 1983); C. Zmroczek,

'Dirty Linen: Women, Class and Washing Machines, 1920s–1960s', *Women's Studies International Forum* 15 (1992), pp. 173–85; S. Bowden and A. Offer, 'Household Appliances and the Use of Time: The United States and Britain since the 1920s', *Economic History Review* 47 (1994), pp. 725–48. For developments since the 1970s see *Social Trends*, 19 (1989), p. 104, 27 (1997), p. 112, 29 (1999), p. 175.

12. Schwarz Cowan, *More Work for Mother*, p. 201.

13. See R. Jowell *et al.* (eds), *British Social Attitudes: The 1984 Report* (Aldershot, 1984), pp. 133–6; R. Jowell *et al.* (eds), *British Social Attitudes: The 5th Report, The 9th Report* and *The 15th Report* (Aldershot, 1988, 1992, 1998), pp. 182–5; pp. 89–103; pp. 30–3; *Social Trends* 19 (1989), pp. 20–1; 26 (1996), p. 216; 27 (1997), p. 215.

11

PAID WORK

Deirdre McCloskey

The story of women in paid work in the twentieth century is that until the 1950s and especially the 1970s they mainly didn't have it. In Britain and in most rich countries until late in the century women worked first and often last at home. The question is, why were British women so largely homemakers in 1900 and why did they emerge in the last quarter of the twentieth century from the home?

In 1900 about 30 per cent of women over age 10 worked for wages, at wages half those of men. This labour force participation rate stagnated for decades, as did the wage gap. Yet by the 1990s the labour force participation rate of women (aged 15–64) had risen to around 65 per cent (the men's rate was 85 per cent, and falling); wage rates had risen from half up to three-quarters of men's. In other words, women rose from being only 14 per cent of the nation's wage bill around 1900 to 36 per cent in the 1990s. In a commercial society honour and power attends on money. Women by the 1990s earned more of it for themselves. They went out to work.

Why, then? Because, as we shall see, life expectancy rose and the number of children fell; and because women wanted it to be so, an ideological change that swept the Western world. The same answer can be given, with small lags or anticipations relative to the British story, about the United States, the Netherlands, Scandinavia or Japan. A Brito-centric view would be a mistake.

Bourgeois Women Kept from Work for Wages

Like much in British history during the past two centuries, women's work was influenced by social class. The bourgeois Victorian family separated the spheres, and kept its women out of the marketplace. Florence Nightingale's unpublished *cri de coeur*, *Cassandra* laments that her upper middle-class sisters 'sink to living from breakfast till dinner, from dinner till tea, with a little worsted work, and looking forward to nothing but bed'.[1] The bar to work was even stronger against *married* bourgeois women, and hysterical against *mothers* of any class working outside the home. The bourgeois pattern was imitated when possible among the middle-and-upper working class, the wives of engine drivers and clerks and cabinetmakers. The Victorian strength of feeling against wives and mothers working in the labour market shows in a Mrs Bayley's paper to the National Association for the Promotion of Social Science, in 1864:

> the wife and mother going abroad for work is, with few exceptions [presumably Mrs Bayley herself, on the lecture platform], a waste of time, a waste of property, a waste of morals and a waste of health and life and ought in every way to be prevented.[2]

So it was in 1900. The distance that educated women of the upper middle class had yet to go may be seen in the list of The First British Woman As: school board member (1870), mayor (1908), chartered accountant (1910), banker (1910), elected MP (1918 – an Irish revolutionary), sitting MP (1919 – an American heiress), barrister (1921), cabinet minister (1929), president of the Trade Unions Congress (1943), prison governor (1945), diplomat (1946), King's Counsel (1949), life peer (1958), bank manager (1958), ambassador (1964), High Court judge (1965), member of the Stock Exchange (1973), leader of a political party (1975), prime minister (1979), Lord Mayor of London (1983). These of course are not dates of equality. By the 1950s only a handful of women had in fact become chartered accountants; by the 1990s women were pouring into the profession.

Working-class Women: The Disemployment Down to 1900

In the lower but respectable working class before the Great War, earning 'round about a pound a week', the margin was narrow, and the wife often worked for pay. Even an unexpected funeral, for example, was a disaster:

> For months afterwards the mother and remaining children will eat less in order to pay back the money borrowed. The father of the family cannot eat less. He is already eating as little as will enable him to earn the family wage. To starve him would be bad economy.[3]

Families falling into Seebohm Rowntree's category of 'primary poverty,' that is 'earning insufficient to obtain the minimum necessaries for the maintenance of mere physical efficiency' needed women to go out to work, or to engage in homework for pay. In Elizabeth Roberts's great survey of memories in Barrow, Lancaster and Preston

> we need look no further than men's earnings [in the first decades of the twentieth century] ... to find the explanation why so many women had

to go out to work. . . . It was rare for a family where the father's wage was near the poverty line, not to have the mother and later the children in paid employment.[4]

For the rest, few women worked in 1900, or 1930, and very few married women. As Eric Richards argued in 1974,

Karl Marx and R.M. Hartwell may well be correct in saying that the Industrial Revolution created the possibilities for emancipation [from household tyranny by working for pay]. . . . but for the overwhelming majority of women this particular benefit of industrialization did not accrue until the middle of the twentieth century.[5]

The rise of industrial employment and decline in agriculture, 50 years earlier in Britain than in America or France, left married women alone in city rooms with the children, more or less removed from the workplaces of the men, and sometimes from other women, too. In the countryside women helped with the harvest, tended the animals, gathered wood, crossing the men at work all day. In the older cities the bourgeois wife lived over the shop, and helped in it. By 1900 the women did much less beyond their housework.

The disemployment of women in the nineteenth century can be overstated: official, market jobs are what we count, and we do not count even all the work for pay that women did – minding a working neighbour's children, for example. Non-bourgeois women engaged in much by-employment poorly accounted in censuses. John Benson argues that 'penny capitalism', legal and illegal, some of it women's work – clothes washing, taking bets, sewing, gardening, running a dram shop on the side – was the chief support of one in ten working-class families and the partial support of four in ten by the late nineteenth century.[6] Yet on balance it seems that Eric Richards was correct in claiming that there was a U-shaped movement of women's market employment, perhaps flatter than he claimed: high in the rural economy of the eighteenth century, falling in the nineteenth (despite the importance of female textile workers), and slowly rising in the twentieth.

By 1900 jobs for women were constricted more than at any time before or since, and except in textiles and pottery (big exceptions but regionalised) and clothing at the sewing machine, their jobs were not of the First Industrial Revolution. Two in every five women in market work in 1901 were employed in domestic service. There were few changes in domestic technology and a maid-servant in 1900 was making beds, serving meals and polishing silver in much the same way she would have done two centuries before. The workers of the newly prominent trades of industrialisation – coal miners and iron puddlers and railway workers – were men. Richards speaks of a 'cumulative differentiation of employment' down to 1900 or so. In 1900 men did men's paid work, women did women's paid work, and little enough of that.

War and the Composition of Industry?

Why then over the next century did it change? The wars are commonly noted: women first went on the buses as conductresses during the First World War; the airplanes for the Battle of Britain against Hitler were assembled by women. War was the great social solvent, it is said. But like its effect on improving technology, war's effect on liberating women can be exaggerated. Labour force participation was hardly affected by the First War: when the boys came home, the girls went home, too. The Second War had more lasting effects, but not as revolutionary as popularly believed, Penny Summerfield has argued.

The jobs changed during the early twentieth century in a way that favoured women a little. Fewer coalminers and more light assembly workers, and then at the end of the century more brain workers, meant more work for women. In the 1920s and 1930s (a desperate time for shipbuilding, coal, steel, textiles) the Second Industrial Revolution of motors, glass, plastic, oil and electrical appliances gave work to women, in the Midlands and around London (though Richards points out that the sharp decline in domestic service during and after the Great War meant that in total no higher percentage of young women went out to work).

Longer Lives and Fewer Children

The pattern of family histories was more important than war or the structure of industry. It is this, not the direct effect of the Second World War, that explains most of the tripling of married women's labour force participation, between 1931 and 1961, from 10 to 32 per cent.

For one thing, life expectancies rose over the twentieth century. By the 1960s a 20-year old young woman could expect to live to 76 years (see Table 6.1, p. 87). That meant a longer period of childlessness in middle age than her great grandmother could have expected at age 20 in 1900, and more time therefore for a second serving of market work. And slowing population growth meant more older women, a narrowing of the age pyramid.

For another, families became smaller. In 1900, as at the end of the century, most British women married and most had children. Marriage was a given constraint on the labour force participation of most British women until the 1970s. The power of this constraint depended on the prevailing ideology of the 'home'. If you married you had children, and women of course were presumed to bear the weight of care. Completed family size fell sharply, from a little over four children for women married in the 1890s to a little over two children for women married in the early 1930s (see Figure 1.1, p. 7). Despite the temporary rise in the postwar baby boom, the constraint of childcare declined dramatically since the 1960s resulting in women's increased ability to go out to work.

In short, rising life expectancies and falling size of families left millions of British women by the 1970s with labour years on their hands. A 'typical' great-grandmother of a 15-year-old British woman in 1970 had worked in the mill from age 13 to 25, married with four children to take care of from 25 to 45, died at age 55 – supplying 15 or 20 years of work for pay. By contrast the great-granddaughter could expect to work from 17 to 25, marry but have only two children, carefully planned, and go back to work at age 38, working full or part-time until age 65, and then have a long retirement financed by a work-related pension: 35 years of work for pay, double her great-grandmother's supply. Half as many children; twice as much market work. The upshot was at first a rise in part-time paid work among women who would not earlier have worked for pay at all. In 1980 44 per cent of working women were part-timers (which can be viewed as a scandal or a 'good thing', as a measure of the subordination of women or a tribute to their good sense in a rich and postindustrial age). By the 1990s in any case the work had become more full-time.

The Ideological Change, 1965–80

But there was an unexpected social earthquake during the 1960s and 1970s which drove these figures higher than the demographics would have led one to expect. In 1965, before the earthquake had been truly felt, though the new arithmetic of family size and survival had become clear, Viola Klein could write

> It is not suggested here that it is – or likely to become so in the near future – the general practice for married women to accept employment away from their homes. Housewives without outside jobs, after all, still [in 1957, it would appear, when the survey was first taken] outnumber those in employment by 2 to 1.[7]

Yet that 'general practice' is precisely what happened in the 'near future'; in fact, while she was writing. The labour force participation of British women aged 25–34 (the prime years for having pre-school children) rose from 29.5 per cent in 1961 to 38.4 per cent in 1971 to 48.6 in 1981 – think of it as 1 percentage point of rise each year, after 60 years of no change outside of war work. The ratio of 2 to 1 in 1957 reversed: working for wages rapidly became the 'general practice' of married women. By 1980 of every 100 women married or cohabiting, 60 were working (over half part-time) as against 35 'economically inactive' (with 5 per cent reporting themselves as unemployed and therefore part of the workforce).

In other words, women decided they were market workers. So did their husbands. Between two large-scale surveys of British opinion about women's work, in 1957 and 1980, married women reported a shift in their husbands' attitudes, from definite opinions (for instance, 58 per cent of housewives reported in 1957 that their husbands did *not* want them to work) to a much larger percentage of hands off: it's her decision. Women still quit work to have children. In 1981 among 25–34 year olds, married women's participation was in the high 40s out of a hundred while that of single women was in the low 80s. But they went back to work after the children went to school in unprecedented numbers: in 1951 only a quarter of married women aged 35–54 worked for wages; by 1981 64 per cent did. The age group 35–54 had by then the highest rather than the lowest labour force participation rate before retirement.

The way to judge whether a labour force participation rate is high or low is to put it into comparative or historical perspective. In 1992, for example, the UK's rate of 64.8 was a little below the 68.9 of the USA and well below the rates of 79 per cent attained in Denmark and Sweden (one might take 80 per cent as a practical limit nowadays; it approaches the falling rate of men). Out of 24 economically advanced countries the British rate was eighth, and at about 65 per cent was far above the 40 per cent in the Irish Republic, or the 34 per cent of Turkey – or the 30 per cent of Britain in 1900.

What had happened? In a phrase, ideological change. It is ideological as much as demographic change that sent women out to work late in the century. Still in 1955 the model was Grace Kelly, as a pop tune put it, 'Marry the Prince of Monaco'. Give up your career as a movie actress to have the marriage of your dreams. Such attitudes changed during the next decade and a half among progressive women with astonishing speed. It was part of the break of the 1960s, 'between the end of the *Chatterly* ban/And the Beatles' first LP' and what followed from it. In the fictional 1971 of Fay Weldon's satirical novel, *Big Women*, everyone agreed that:

> Obviously women need men. Everyone needs men. Masculinity is all. Armies need men, and government and business and technology and high finance. . . . Offices, except for the typing pool, which is female, need men. It's homes which need women, except for the lawn which is male. . . . Layla and Stephie, friends, mean to change all this. *A Woman Needs a Man like a Fish Needs a Bicycle.*[8]

Weldon's narrator later reflects 'How fast things change. . . . all it takes is a handful of determined and energetic women; big women not little women'. By 1979, 61 per cent of women of working age worked, up from 54 per cent eight years before, again about a 1 percentage point increase every year. And the trend continued, if less dramatically, for the remainder of the century.

Of course material conditions mattered to the ideological change of the 1960s and 1970s. The weight of childcare fell as the postwar baby boom subsided. The longstanding equality in secondary education and the burst of new universities in the 1960s open to women created more 'human capital', unwasteable. By 1976, 27 per cent of the female labour force was already 'professional and scientific', two-thirds of people with such occupations, though nearly half of these were part-time and therefore subordinate on the job. A breakout had occurred of educated women after the war.

But there was something remarkable, and international, about the ideological shift. A higher percentage of American women went to university, and so it is no surprise that the revolt against the *Feminine Mystique* began there.[9] Worldwide during the 1970s the ideological shift was ratified in legal change. Britain's Equal Pay Act of 1970 (in force in 1975; made necessary by Britain's entry into the Common Market) made a legal case for equal pay for (exactly) equal work. It was amended under pressure from the European Court in 1983 as work of equal 'value' – even if the man's and the woman's job were different. Under pressure from the European Court the labour market that British women faced was affected by the international current of ideas. The Sex Discrimination Act of 1975, introduced by a Labour government, was directed against discrimination in education, advertising and public facilities, enforced by an Equal Opportunities Commission able to investigate. In the same year (more Labour progressivity) the Employment Protection Act prevented the sacking of women for pregnancy, instituted maternity leave and mandated that a woman could return to the same job within four months of giving birth.

The ideological nourishment supporting such laws was of course long in the baking. Middle-class women worked without pay as volunteer social workers *c.* 1900 (we hear the poor largely because middle-class women spoke for them, and spoke because the speakers needed more of life than 'a little worsted work'). After the First World War the bourgeois bar to paid work was slowly, slowly breaking down, and advanced thinkers commenced sneering at domestic science. Winifred Holtby, a feminist writer of interwar England, declared 'The consciousness of virtue derived from well-polished furniture or rows of preserving-fruit bottles is too lightly acquired'. And yet Cambridge did not admit women to equal degrees until 1948, and the character of a Cambridge scientist Rosalind Franklin (1920–58), the co-discoverer of DNA, 'has been used – vastly warped to fit the purpose – to provide reasons why men who work with intelligent women should resent them'.[10]

In the 1930s the equal-rights feminism of the bourgeois women seemed foolish to many working-class women with an unemployed husband and five children: for them the problem was getting *any* job, and keeping it; and minding the children; and preventing being viciously exploited on the job. The issue was 'protection': laws that forbade the employment of women at night or long hours; that required humane conditions; that protected, to use an image popular then, the mothers of the race.

The problem was that a protected woman was someone who could not be a supervisor (because she could not be there after the last subordinate had gone home). She could not work at night because she could not be on the streets, or else would be treated as a prostitute. In the 1930s Helena Swanwick wrote in her autobiography that she was of course as a girl not allowed to walk about at night: 'When it was explained to me that a young girl by herself was liable to be insulted by men, I became incoherent with rage at a society which, as a consequence, shut up girls instead of the men.'[11] Middle-class women, for example members of the National Union of Societies for Equal Citizenship, were

Plate 11.1. A nanny with child, early 1920s. Domestic service was the largest occupational category for women until the Second World War.

opposed to protection. By such 'protection', said the bourgeois Equal Right feminists, freedom of competition was abridged: we ask merely to be able to compete in the same field as men.

The women's trade union movement by contrast favoured protection. In conditions of mass unemployment the working-class case seemed more relevant. Such 'welfare feminism', protecting women and the 'family [that is, the man's] wage', characterised the 1920s and 1930s and 1940s, creating a body of law and custom that needed to be broken in the 1970s. Working-class women before the last war were not on the whole indignant about the resulting inequality of wages: 'I don't remember any of our women ever raising the issue of equal pay', recalled the (female) personnel manager of an English shoe factory in the 1930s. 'There was the general view that the man was the breadwinner and that it was therefore reasonable that he should have more money than a woman.' Trade unions approved marriage bars, that is, dismissal of a woman on her wedding day. As Carol Dyhouse notes, 'Labour politics and the emergence of social welfare in early twentieth-century Britain certainly served to institutional-ize a conservative vision of family life.'[12]

IN FOCUS: Images and Sounds of Working-Class Emancipation

Working-class women eventually benefited from the ideological change after 1965. A photograph in Angela Holdsworth's book of the BBC series *Out of the Doll's House* (1988) captures the optimistic story of increasing human capital: the matriarch was a domestic servant, hired at a fair in 1905; her daughter was a shop assistant; hers a typist; hers a shipyard engineer (p. 60). The great-granddaughter in Holdsworth's photo, to be sure, is an *apprentice* engineer. But she is the only one of the four generations, this last in 1988, who intends to keep her job on marriage.

The engineer in the photograph parallels the heroine of Peggy Seeger's serio-comic ballad of 1971, 'I'm Gonna Be an Engineer' (Seeger was an American married to the Scottish folksinger Ewan McColl):

> When I went to school I learned to write and how to read,
> Some history, geography, and home economy,
> And typing is a skill that every girl is sure to need,
> To wile away the extra time until it's time to breed,
> And then they had the nerve to say, 'What would you like to be?'
> I says, 'I'm gonna be an engineer!'
> > 'No, you only need to learn to be a lady,
> > The duty isn't yours for to try and run the world,
> > An engineer could never have a baby,
> > Remember, dear, that you're a girl.'
>
> ....
>
> As soon as Jimmy got a job, I studied hard again,
> Then busy at me turret-lathe a year or so and then
> The morning that the kids were born, Jimmy says to them,
> 'Kids, your mother was an engineer.'
> > 'You owe it to the kids to be a lady,
> > Dainty as a dishrag, faithful as a chow,
> > Stay at home, you got to mind the baby,
> > Remember, you're a mother now.'
>
> ....
>
> But now that times are harder and my Jimmy's got the sack,
> I went down to Vicker's, they were glad to have me back,
> I'm a third-class citizen, my wages tell me that,
> But I'm a first-class engineer!
> > The boss he says, 'I pay you as a lady,
> > You only got the job because I can't afford a man,
> > With you I keep the profits high as may be,
> > You're just a cheaper pair of hands!'

Peggy Seeger
© Copyright 1976, 1979 by STORMKING MUSIC, INC.
All rights reserved. Used by permission.

The Gap that Remains: 1980 until 2000

The ideological change is not of course complete. Women were still paid less than men: that 'wage gap'. The traditional wage gap was 50 per cent of the male wage. The Second World War resulted in a 40 per cent gap, that is, a female wage amounting to 60 per cent of the male, maintained down to the 1970s. Equal pay for women in British teaching came in the mid-1950s (the marriage bar for teachers had been abolished in 1944), as in the civil service and local government, after decades of agitation. The wage gap then narrowed from 40 per cent of the male wage in 1967 to 28 per cent in 1994 (most of the change was a burst in the 1970s, after the Equal Pay Act). The US gap narrowed by about the same amount over the same period (38 to 24 per cent), though most of its change was in the 1980s. Both were still well below Swedish or Australian or Norwegian gaps of only 10 or 12 per cent, and well above the Japanese, stagnant since 1967 at about the traditional 50 per cent of the male wage.

Various studies have concluded that 'human capital', that is, educated skill, explains *only* half of the male–female wage gap. But half is a lot, showing it is wrong to ignore economic productivity as an explanation of wages. The woman in Seeger's song does not expect equal pay unless she's equally skilled as men are at the turret-lathe.

Yet a portion of the gap unjustified by productivity remains: 'I'm a third-class citizen, my wages tell me that.' Why? The gap arises, and arose, from segregation of jobs and the ideological convictions that support it. Women were long forbidden to become airline pilots, for example (stewardess, yes, at a quarter of the pay). The justifications were once frankly sexist: 'No, you only need to learn to be a lady,/The duty isn't yours for to try and run the world,/An engineer could never have a baby,/Remember, dear, that you're a girl.' A woman who had learned welding in the shipyards of the Second World War was rebuffed for *thirty years* afterwards in repeated attempts to get back into the trade: 'I wonder what the boys would say', one of the bosses said on rejecting one of her applications, 'if I employed a woman.'[13] The Sex Discrimination Act finally got her the job.

Cynthia Cockburn observes that 'In a world where so many things are gendered, from shampoo and deodorants to entire environments as local as the "ladies toilet" and as large as the North sea oil rig, it is not surprising that occupations are often gendered too'.[14] Down to the 1960s there was little change in the amount of occupational segregation. In an imagined world in which there were literally no occupational segregation, or differences in human capital (setting aside therefore the dispute about which it is), all the following in the 1986 occupational categories in Britain would have been 50 per cent instead of what they were: managerial, high level, 11 per cent women; clerical, 74 per cent; construction and mining, 0.4 per cent; catering, cleaning, hairdressing and other personal services, 76 per cent.

One can generalise such figures by thinking of an 'index of gender segregation' – simply the percentage of women in an occupation that would need to

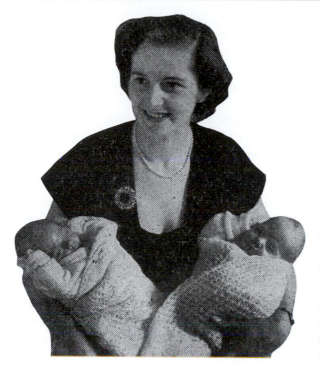

Plate 11.2. Margaret Thatcher aged 28, with her twins, 1954. Recently called to the Bar, she defended the rights of the working mother in *Onward*, a Conservative party monthly magazine, April 1954; 'it all depends on the woman'. While domesticity will suit some women, 'if she has a pronounced bent in some other direction in which she has already achieved some measure of success then I am sure that it is essential both for her own satisfaction and for the happiness of her family that she should use all her talents to the full. With a little forethought she will find that most things are possible.'

take over men's jobs to bring the share to the perfect 50 per cent. An occupation with all women (virtually, pre-school childminding) would imply an index of necessary shifted workers of 50 per cent; an occupation with 50–50 women an index of zero. In America the average segregation index by major occupation (such as executive, or service, or operators, i.e. machine minders) fell from 41.8 to 33.8 between 1972 and 1995. That is, by 1995 *only* one-third of the women would have to replace men to bring employment to parity. Similar trends occurred in Britain and elsewhere.

Yet still one-third. As Cockburn puts it, 'If we think of occupations as being separate cells, each with its own cell wall, men reach out and penetrate into more of them. We could say that women do not "defend" their cell walls'. The radical question posed by Walby is: Is gender segregation, 'a rational economic practice (as conservative economists argue) or . . . a patriarchal protection racket'? Economists of all schools would have to concede that it is for the most part a patriarchal protection racket. 'If a man shares an occupation with a woman he feels his status tremble', writes Cockburn. She found cutters in the clothing trades who 'felt the industry had lost its masculinity', that is, the men-only spaces. A mail order firm was letting men resign with a large severance package rather than take up 'women's work'. 'They couldn't bring themselves to work alongside women. One said the idea made him feel giddy.'[15]

The economist Myra Strober argued in 1976 that 'occupational segregation has been maintained because all other systems in the society have so strongly supported it' and that what is needed to break out of the mutually reinforcing system is a 'jolt'.[16] She mentions the shift of clerical work, the jolt being the coming of the typewriter. By 1911 women were 20 per cent of clerks in Britain, by 1931, 46 per cent, by 1971, 72 per cent. But of course this gets us nowhere: all-male jobs became all-female, and the social system that kept men and women separated in the office was maintained.

The story of women's market employment since 1900 shows in short what economic sociologists call 'embeddedness'. That is, the economy is 'embedded' in the wider society, like flowers in their beds. As the economic historian Claudia Goldin put it in describing her work on the gender gap, 'The [strictly economic] framework had to be bent to fit the historical reality. We economists still don't know how to incorporate changing norms, and I was researching a subject in which norms played a major role.'[17] This does not mean, however, that economics is mistaken or useless and that sociology reigns. A sociologist will reckon she has rejected economics by showing that markets are not 'smoothly' functioning. But perfection is not needed for markets to have force. Supply and demand 'works', even if roughly. A cleaner with widely available skills earns less than a barrister. In the years before 1914 in which the career choice for a girl was service or some factory work, *and nothing else*; or the 1950s in which it was nursing, typing, teaching, *and nothing else*, supply and demand suggests that wages in such fields would be crowded down. Or quality would be crowded up: many a nurse recruited in 1960 would have become a business executive in 1990.

But the embeddedness point is that supply and demand happen within a society. The demand for pork products is low (officially zero) in many Muslim countries. The culture matters. The employment of married women at all, and the employment of single women in most occupations, was for much of the twentieth century like eating pork: taboo. Yet the interaction is two-way. For example, whether or not the family wage happens – the assignment of men to the paid workforce exclusively – will depend strongly on the traditions of female work. In Blackburn in the 1930s, it was said, 'wages have always been fixed . . . on the assumption that several members of the family will be working'. In Preston the wages of male weavers were so low that virtually all women worked; one of the women, a ring spinner, reported that 'I never wound a clock up in all my married life, I never made a fire and I never chopped wood and I never made a bed. . . . [My husband] would look to the boy and I would look to the girl'.[18] In other words, the culture affected whether women worked, but the economic decision to work outside the home fed back into the cultural assumptions about men's and women's housework. As Roberts concludes, 'patterns of women's employment [that is, the economics] cannot be ignored in the study of role-relationships [that is, the sociology] with marriage'.

For a long time, and still at the end of the century, some men won't work with women, as for a long time whites wouldn't work with blacks in the United States. The pronounced taste of half the population gives an incentive for bosses to hire men into segregated workplaces, which keeps the nurse's aide separate from the road worker. Gender anxiety on the part of men can explain the long life of gender ghettos on the job – lorry drivers just *are* men, the male workers declare, and make it so. Some occupations come to be valued more than others even when there is no more training or strength or intelligence involved. New jobs get categorised as 'male' and then get paid more. The history of women's work makes vivid the dance between attitudes and conditions: embeddedness.

And it raises an old set of questions about our economy. Is the market enslaving or emancipatory? Was capitalism good for women? Or was it socialism that saved us? The answers are not open and shut: we don't know enough (Janet Thomas concluded in 1988). Unions and the welfare state long supported the family wage and segregation of women. Yet it was the state, supported by some of those very unions (though compelled by the European Community), that began the dismantling of discrimination in the 1960s and 1970s. Employment for women has widened, but some of the wage gap remains. Some women are fulfilled in market jobs, some are still drudges. Capitalism leaves women with a second shift of housekeeping; or does it lead them out of the home entirely?

Conclusion

The upshot will please neither side in the deeper questions – about the ultimate sources of women-hating or the ultimate role of capitalism in emancipation – though it leaves plenty of research to be done: a Scottish verdict, 'unproven'. What is proven is the constraint on women's work for wages and the reasons for its partial relaxation: longer lives, fewer children and above all a new social attitude towards women on the job.

Bibliographical Note

Elizabeth Roberts has done crucial surveys of working-class memories, including work experience: *A Women's Place: An Oral History of Working-Class Women 1890–1940* (Oxford, 1984); and *Women and Families: An Oral History, 1940–1970* (Oxford, 1995). At the other end of the qualitative/quantitative methodological divide is H.E. Joshi, R. Layard and S.J. Owen, 'Why Are More Women Working in Britain?', *Journal of Labour Economics* 3, 1 (1985), pp. 147–76. J. Martin and C. Roberts, *Women and Employment: A Lifetime Perspective: The Report of the 1980 Department of Employment/Office of Population Censuses and Surveys Survey* (London, 1984) is essential. The situation in the 1990s is covered in *Social Trends* and *Living in Britain: General Household Survey*, from the government, as is *Social Focus on Women and Men* (London, 1998), which brings together data from recent official sources. An earlier survey is V. Klein, *Britain's Married Women Workers* (London, 1965). A good resource for comparative statistics and for insights into the economics involved is F.D. Blau, M.A. Ferber and A.W. Winkler, *The Economics of Women, Men, and Work* (Upper Saddle River, NJ, 1998). C. Goldin, *Understanding the Gender Gap: An Economic History of American Women* (New York, 1990) is fundamental.

Still valuable, though its conclusions have been softened by later work, is E. Richards, 'Women in the British Economy since about 1700: An Interpretation', *History* 59 (1974), pp. 337–57. A more recent survey of the longer story is J. Thomas, 'Women and Capitalism: Oppression or Emancipation? A Review Article', *Comparative Studies in Society and History*,

28 (1988), pp. 534–49. C. Dyhouse, *Feminism and the Family in England 1880–1939* (Oxford, 1989) is social history at its best. An older work still useful is M. Hewitt, *Wives and Mothers in Victorian Industry* (London, 1958) and the popular book by A. Holdsworth on the condition of women generally in the twentieth century, *Out of the Doll's House: The Story of Women in the Twentieth Century* (London, 1988) is finely done.

The surprisingly small role of the wars in getting permanent work for women is argued in P. Summerfield, 'Women and War in the Twentieth Century', in J. Purvis (ed), *Women's History: Britain, 1850–1945* (London, 1995). The decidedly mixed role of unions is examined in S. Lewenhak, *Women and Trade Unions* (London, 1977); and K. Purcell, 'Militancy and Acquiescence among Women Workers', in S. Burman (ed), *Fit Work for Women* (London 1979).

The recent history of segregation of the workplace is well treated in C. Cockburn, 'The Gendering of Jobs: Workplace Relations and the Reproduction of Sex Segregation', in S. Walby (ed), *Gender Segregation at Work* (Milton Keynes, 1988); and C. Hakim, *Occupational Segregation* (London, 1979). Resegregation at the typewriter is discussed in M. Zimmeck, 'Jobs for the Girls: The Expansion of Clerical Work for Women, 1850–1914', in A. John (ed), *Unequal Opportunities: Women's Employment in England 1800–1918* (Oxford, 1986).

Notes

1. Quoted in C. Dyhouse, *Feminism and the Family in England 1880–1939* (Oxford, 1989), p. 9.

2. Quoted in M. Hewitt, *Wives and Mothers in Victorian Industry* (London, 1958).

3. M. Pember Reeves, *Round About a Pound a Week* (London, 1913), p. 68.

4. E. Roberts, 'Working Wives and Their Families,' in T. Barker and M. Drake (eds), *Population and Society in Britain, 1850–1980* (London, 1982), pp. 144, 146.

5. E. Richards, 'Women in the British Economy since about 1700: An Interpretation', *History* 59 (1974), pp. 348, 352.

6. J. Benson, *The Penny Capitalists: A Study of Nineteenth-Century Working-Class Entrepreneurs* (Dublin, 1983).

7. V. Klein, *Britain's Married Women Workers* (London, 1965), p. 21.

8. F. Weldon, *Big Women* (London, 1997), pp. 5–6, 66, 226.

9. B. Friedan, *The Feminine Mystique* (New York, 1963).

10. Quoted in Dyhouse, *Feminism and the Family*, p. 48; A. Sayre, *Rosalind Franklin and DNA* (New York, 1975), p. 197.

11. Quoted in Dyhouse, *Feminism and the Family*, p. 21.

12. Quoted in A. Holdsworth, *Out of the Doll's House* (London, 1988), pp. 74–5; Dyhouse, *Feminism and the Family*, p. 5.

13. Quoted in Holdsworth, *Doll's House*, pp. 78, 82.

14. C. Cockburn, 'The Gendering of Jobs: Workplace Relations and the Reproduction of Sex Segregation', in S. Walby (ed), *Gender Segregation at Work* (Milton Keynes, 1988), p. 38.

15. Cockburn, 'Gendering of Jobs', p. 38; Walby, *Gender Segregation at Work*, p. 2.

16. M. Strober, 'Toward Dimorphics: A Summary Statement on the Conference on Occupational Segregation', in M. Blaxall and B. Reagan (eds), *Women and the Workplace* (Chicago, 1976), p. 295.

17. C. Goldin, 'The Economist as Detective', in M. Szenberg (ed), *Passion and Craft: Economists at Work* (Ann Arbor, MI, 1998), p. 107.

18. Roberts, 'Working Wives', pp. 151, 152.

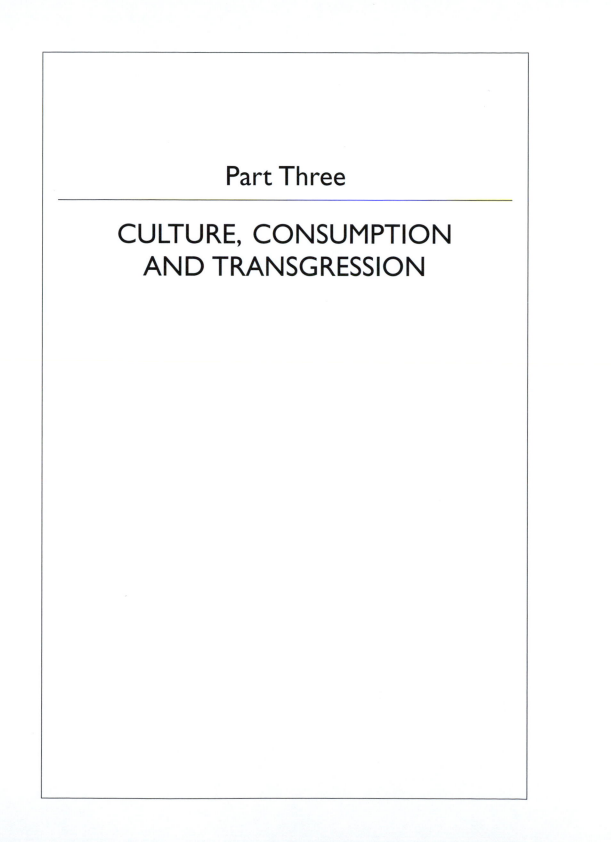

Part Three

CULTURE, CONSUMPTION AND TRANSGRESSION

12

THE BODY AND CONSUMER CULTURE

Ina Zweiniger-Bargielowska

The expansion of mass consumer culture during the twentieth century had a profound impact on the female body. It resulted in shifts in the way bodies were represented and in women's attitudes towards their bodies which, in turn, transformed the body itself. During the last 100 years female appearance has changed dramatically – women in the late 1990s looked very different from women at the turn of the century, the 1920s, 1950s or 1970s. Each of these periods is associated with distinctive images based on changing fashions in clothing, hair styles and use of cosmetics. However, the transformation has gone beyond mere adornment and included manipulating the weight and shape of women's bodies. Examples are the accentuation or concealment of waists, breasts or legs. Clothes and, especially, underwear played a major role and the hourglass figure of the Edwardian era was based on tight corsets. Nevertheless, foundation garments were of limited use to acquire the youthful, slender body popular in the interwar years and since the 1960s. This was based on a so-called 'internal corset' achieved through dieting and exercise. A recent phenomenon, dating from the 1980s, is the growing emphasis on body-shaping exercise to develop muscles in female bodies.

In order to appreciate the implications of the commercialisation of the body it is necessary to distinguish, on the one hand, ideal beauties or stereotypes and, on the other, ordinary women's responses to these changing images which have become increasingly pervasive. The main priority of this chapter is not to chart changing ideals but to trace how women responded. Throughout the century substantial numbers of women have aimed to emulate ideal beauties with the help of rapidly growing industries selling an ever wider range of beauty aids – including clothes, hair care products, cosmetics, exercising equipment and fitness videos as well as services such as cosmetic surgery – to an ever wider audience at a wide range of prices. An underlying message with which many of these products are marketed is that anybody could and should aspire to emulate the contemporary ideal and that consumption of beauty aids will achieve the required results.

From the interwar years onwards demand for beauty products was high, especially among younger women from all social backgrounds. Of course not all

Plate 12.1. 'You Too Will Look Lovely with Colour Harmony Make-up', *Woman*, June 1938. This example neatly illustrates the link between film stars, Hollywood and self-improvement through the purchase of consumer goods common in interwar advertising.

women were equally concerned about their appearance and income levels continued to be significant. From the 1920s onwards, a majority of young women have spent substantial amounts of money, energy and time in order to manipulate their bodies and change their looks to copy the ideal beauty of a particular era. This emphasis on perfect bodies and particularly on self-improvement through the purchase of consumer goods is a central feature of twentieth-century mass consumer culture.

This mass consumer culture is distinguished by an ever more pervasive representation of increasingly stylised beauty ideals which coincided with the emergence and expansion of a range of industries whose products supposedly enable every woman to emulate these ideals. Mass consumerism has expanded dramatically since the late nineteenth century based on rising real wages and increased female employment. Most consumer goods have become cheaper with the rapid spread of mass production and modern forms of retailing. This trend gathered speed in the interwar years and has accelerated again since the consumer boom of the 1950s.

As a result of these developments, a growing range of consumer goods and services intended to manipulate the body was no longer an exclusive privilege of the wealthy but within general reach. At same time, demand has been stimulated by aggressive advertising by the fashion and beauty industry, for example in women's magazines. Based on an editorial formula of beauty, romance and domesticity, both adverts and features continuously advised women on how to look beautiful and improve their appearance to emulate a contemporary ideal which was within reach of anybody who purchased the beauty products and followed the beauty regimes. The images of ideal beauty to be emulated have also been propagated through the new mass media of the twentieth century, the cinema since the interwar years and more recently television. Hollywood films have been especially influential throughout the period and in recent decades the music industry has provided a further source of inspiration.

The Importance of the Visual Image and the Construction of the Body

The visual image is of considerable importance to women and the representation of the body reflects different notions of femininity. These illustrate the transformation of and continuing tension surrounding women's roles throughout the century. The cultural construction of the body has varied between social groups and changed over time. While the underlying theoretical issues are complex, generally speaking the visual representation of the body has provided a site for the construction of identity. Physical appearance has never been trivial but rather has indicated social status as well as cultural and individual identity. For women, approximating or rejecting a given beauty ideal has provided a response to competing feminine roles and has had major implications in terms of social capital and self-esteem.

There is no natural way to look and the presentation of the body is culturally constructed and historically contingent. Conformity to prevailing beauty ideals has been the aspiration of women (and men) for many centuries. Visual sources illustrate the great changes in ideal body images in Western culture and historians have documented the extensive effort women in particular have undertaken in order to approximate these ideals in the last few centuries. The critical transformation during the twentieth century has been that these aspirations, and the means to fulfil them, are no longer confined to a narrow elite but have become a mass phenomenon.

At the same time, there has been a shift in perceptions of the body with the result that physical appearance rather than character or virtues have been increasingly emphasised as representing 'the self'. Therefore, an individual's response to contemporary body ideals is not only of aesthetic significance but has emotional and moral implications. For example, success in achieving a fit, slim body denotes prized characteristics such as willpower, energy and control over impulses whereas obesity indicates laziness, greed and lack of control in the face of temptations. In short, failure to conform to narrowly prescribed body ideals has become not merely aesthetically disagreeable but more importantly morally deficient.

Rather than being self-indulgent and narcissist, emulating an ideal body-type by following various beauty regimes and purchasing beauty aids is of considerable social benefit expressing status, identity and self-worth by defining an individual's 'exchange value'. A number of commentators have stressed the link between beauty, pleasure, desire, love and happiness in the sense that beauty is an invaluable aid in getting and keeping 'your man'. Steele emphasises the connection between fashion and sexual pleasure and Lake argues that women's enthusiastic response to beauty products represents an assertive female sexuality. In short, the successful manipulation of the body is central to the 'life and death game of compulsory heterosexuality'. Since modern consumer culture proclaims that beauty is within reach of all who purchase its products, 'body maintenance' becomes a social obligation and an individual responsibility. Every woman has the duty to 'make the most of herself' – and those who do not or cannot conform must face up to the consequences in social interaction.[1] Appearance is a critical determinant of social success which, according to Featherstone

> depends upon the preservation of the body within a culture in which the body is the passport to all that is good in life. Health, youth, beauty, sex, fitness are the positive attributes which body care can achieve and preserve. With appearance being taken as a reflex of the self the penalties of bodily neglect are a lowering of one's acceptability as a person, as well as an indication of laziness, low self-esteem and even moral failure.[2]

The advantages of emulating beauty ideals are considerable. Arguably women who spend time and money on 'body maintenance' behave rationally within a clearly understood market, although critics have claimed that the 'beauty system' does not lead to love and happiness but rather to narcissist preoccupations which can undermine the possibility of close relationships. Another area of debate is whether women are passive victims of a 'beauty myth' imposed by patriarchy to women's disadvantage by undermining female claims to greater equality and even women's health. Alternatively, the cult of thin bodies since the 1960s could be interpreted as women rejecting a femininity based on reproduction and domesticity. Likewise, the accentuation of muscles since the 1980s implies an erosion of gender differences and women's appropriation of masculine characteristics.[3]

'Building the Body Beautiful': The Interwar Revolution[4]

During the interwar years female appearance was revolutionised. This revolution affected ideal images as well as ordinary women with the result that the 'modern body' became a mass phenomenon. The hourglass figure of the Edwardian era rapidly gave way to the boyish, youthful look of the 1920s characterised by a slim silhouette in which neither breasts nor waists were emphasised.

Long skirts disappeared and, with hem lines just below the knee, women's legs were visible for the first time. Simultaneously, hair was cut short, makeup became socially acceptable and suntans were actively cultivated. Fashion during the 1930s focused on glamour and elegance, and the female silhouette was distinguished by broad shoulders and a return of waists. The new fashionable clothes were quickly mass-produced and cosmetics were widely available. The simple styles were easy to copy and, with home dressmaking flourishing, fashion was no longer confined to the higher income groups but within reach of all.

This transformation of women's appearance was noted by contemporary commentators such as J.B. Priestley who in *English Journey* observed the influence of Hollywood on young women in provincial towns and highlighted the democratic effects of mass production with 'factory girls looking like actresses' which meant that 'for the first time in history Jack and Jill are nearly as good as their master and mistress . . . Jill beautifies herself exactly as her mistress does'. George Orwell in *Road to Wigan Pier* maintained that the

> two things that have probably made the greatest difference in . . . [helping people cope with the depression were] the movies and mass-production of cheap smart clothes. . . . You may have three halfpence in your pocket and not a prospect in the world . . . but in your new clothes you can stand on the street corner, indulging in a private daydream of yourself as Clark Gable or Greta Garbo, which compensates for a great deal.[5]

The following paragraphs focus on two aspects of this transformation, namely cosmetics and body culture.

Makeup had been applied by a minority of women for centuries but its use and meaning changed dramatically with the rise of mass consumer culture. Before the twentieth century makeup functioned as marker of rank, confined to the highest social groups, and at the other social extreme it was associated with prostitution. Cosmetics were generally shunned since painted faces amounted to an invitation to lust which was unacceptable for respectable women. This situation was transformed during the interwar years when makeup became not only respectable but, indeed, an indispensable signifier of dominant heterosexual femininity. Makeup was popularised by the cinema and aggressively marketed by rising manufacturers with the result that painting faces became an essential practice. Women were increasingly obliged to use makeup and a female face without makeup came to symbolise a rejection of conventional femininity.

On the eve of the Second World War, the message that women had a duty to beautify themselves had been thoroughly absorbed. The most popular items, namely lipstick and powder and to a lesser extent mascara and rouge, had become necessities for the majority of women, especially younger women. Wartime survey data shows that two-thirds of women applied cosmetics regularly and they were used by 90 per cent of the under-thirties but only 37 per cent of women over forty-five. Cosmetics use was high among working women and lowest among housewives, the retired and unoccupied. During the war, the duty to beautify was promoted in advertising as vital to morale. The Board of Trade, which was responsible for the production of consumer goods, considered makeup to be a necessity rather than a dispensable luxury and high demand for cosmetics gave rise to an extensive black market.[6]

The interwar years also witnessed a dramatic transformation in attitudes towards the female body. A slender, supple and youthful body became the ideal which was to be achieved by following beauty and exercise regimes. This development resulted in the emergence of a slimming industry and slimming diets on a mass scale for the first time. The period is distinguished by the growing popularity of physical culture and activities such as hiking, swimming, dancing and gymnastics were practised on an unprecedented scale.

The most successful example of this physical culture was the 'Women's League of Health and Beauty' founded by Mrs Bagot Stack, which boasted 170,000 members in 1939, while even greater numbers attended 'keep fit' classes run by the league. As with cosmetics, there was a major shift in attitudes and the cultivation of a beautiful body became a legitimate part of ideal femininity – a right and increasingly a duty – rather than being associated with narcissism, temptation and sexual abandon. The beautiful, sexually controlled female body became socially respectable and seemingly available to all. In this sense, the beautiful body became a site of 'modern' femininity which was healthy, respectable and fun.[7]

The transformation of women's appearance during the interwar years reflected the emergence of an assertive femininity which arguably was more liberated than nineteenth-century constructions but, more importantly, which emphasised heterosexual physical attractiveness and was democratically available to all by means of cheap mass-produced consumer goods. Wartime austerity, and particularly clothes rationing, reduced supplies and a military style with a square silhouette and economy in materials were characteristic of fashion during the Second World War. Women's desire to retain a heterosexually attractive femininity focused on elaborate makeup and hairstyles to counterbalance the limitations of their wardrobe. The combined effect of rationing and state regulation of consumer industries, including government-sponsored guidelines on design, generated greater uniformity in women's appearance. This provided the basis for the homogeneous mass market of the postwar consumer boom.

After the war, women rebelled against this regimentation and the severe, functional styles by rapidly adopting the New Look during the late 1940s. Characterised by long, flowing skirts and a return of the hourglass figure, the New Look dramatically transformed the female silhouette and during the 1950s ideal beauties accentuated curves and particularly breasts. The consumption trends established during the interwar years accelerated following the onset of the consumer boom from the early 1950s onwards. Surveys on the use of cosmetics during the late 1940s and early 1970s show that over two-thirds of women and up to 90 per cent of young women used makeup regularly. Especially young women were highly fashion-conscious with regard to clothes, although they did not follow fashion slavishly and looked for styles that suited them as individuals. The relative stability of these figures suggests that market saturation had already been achieved by late 1930s.[8]

Thin and muscular! Growing Pressures Since the 1960s

Since the 1960s the ideal female body has been redefined yet again. The change from the voluptuous figure of the 1950s is illustrated by the success of Twiggy (Leslie Hornby) who weighed $6\frac{1}{2}$ stone (41 kg) in the mid-1960s. American data since the 1960s points towards a decline in weight among models, beauty queens or actresses who frequently weigh less than 85 per cent of their expected body weight norms. Body weights below this figure provide a major criterion for anorexia nervosa and many models, dancers and actresses are presumed to suffer from eating disorders. The low weight, for example, of Kate Moss and Victoria Adams Beckham has received attention in the 1990s. This decade has seen a levelling off in weight reductions since models could not get any thinner without dying and muscles have become increasingly prominent in women's ideal bodies. Perceptions of slimness are contingent and it is worth noting that the three ideal beauties of the interwar years cited by Matthews would be classed as normal to slightly overweight by late twentieth-century standards.

The upshot of this transformation towards a very thin ideal was a growing divergence between ideal and reality. Moreover, a normal or even desirable body-shape at mid-century was re-defined into an unsatisfactory 'fuller figure' demanding remedial measures. Some feminist critics have argued that the new body ideal amounts to a patriarchal conspiracy to debilitate women by forcing them to spend energy controlling their weight, undermining their confidence and literally reducing the space women's bodies command to almost childlike proportions.

A more positive interpretation suggests that a thin body implies a re-definition of femininity which rejects women's traditional reproductive role. The thin ideal denies most 'normal' female attributes, particularly hips, breasts and more generally fat. Female fat, which is physiologically imperative in order to maintain women's reproductive capacity (women cease menstruating if body fat falls below a certain level) has been redefined, in Wolf's words into 'expendable female filth' which has to be fought. Women who approximate this ideal can find satisfaction not only because they are conforming to a dominant aesthetic but also because this illustrates their self-control. By contrast, overweight women are not only discriminated against on aesthetic grounds but perceived as morally deficient since being overweight is seen to indicate greed and indulgence.[9]

The ever-increasing social and cultural pressures on women to emulate the thin ideal have stimulated a range of industries and services marketing slimming, dieting and fitness products intended to 'remedy' the growing gap between ideal and reality for many women. An extreme example is the rising popularity of cosmetic surgery with liposuction one of the most common operations in the 1990s. The following paragraphs discuss two aspects of this consumer culture, namely dieting and exercising.

Since the 1970s popular slimming diets have been endlessly reproduced in books, magazines and television programmes, not to mention slimming clubs such as Weight Watchers or slimming foods. Critical analysis dismisses slimming foods as expensive, often unhealthy, at times dangerous and generally ineffective. A similar verdict applies to many of the vast range of diet books, some of which have sold several million copies, for frequently making false claims, being based on misleading nutritional premises and providing a potential health hazard, for example by encouraging rapid weight loss or yo-yo dieting (i.e. repeated cycles of weight loss and gain).

Paradoxically, the expansion of the slimming industry coincided with an increase in average weight and obesity among British women. The mean Body Mass Index (ratio of height to weight, generally used to classify obesity) has increased considerably since the 1970s. The figure stood well below the 'overweight' limit of 25 in 1970 and has gradually crept to about 26 in the mid-1990s. The proportion of women classed as obese (BMI of over 30) has more than doubled during the same period, and in the mid-1990s just over half of women were above the 'normal' BMI measure of 25 (34 per cent were overweight and 18 per cent obese).

Irrespective of these trends, the slimming industry has been flourishing. Despite the fact that many of its products fail to achieve lasting, if any, results, the industry has continued to expand by trading on hope and promise rather than performance and product success. The pressures resulting from the gap between ideal images and real bodies are illustrated by a recent survey of young women, aged 16–24 years, which noted that 8 per cent were obese, 19 per cent overweight, 56 per cent normal and 17 per cent underweight. Questions relating to these women's dieting habits revealed that 'almost half were trying to lose weight. Young women tended to perceive themselves as overweight when they were not: among those with desirable BMI, 20 per cent said they were too heavy and 45 per cent were trying to lose weight, and even of underweight young women 10 per cent were trying to lose weight.'[10]

Since the 1980s the ideal female body was not only thin, but also muscular and the last two decades of the twentieth century have been marked by a rise of participation in 'keep fit' classes, especially among women under 30. Recalling the fitness culture of the interwar years, the primary purpose of these classes has been to work towards an aesthetic ideal body although promoting and maintaining health has also been an element. The late twentieth century workout is more intense than its interwar counterpart and aimed at developing not just a thin and supple but also a muscular female body.

Beginning with Jane Fonda whose influential *Workout Book* was published in 1981, the 'workout' has been aggressively promoted in a range of books and videos, requiring the purchase of specialised equipment, clothes and membership of fitness clubs with local leisure centres catering for the budget end of the

Plate 12.2. Women working out, late 1990s.

market. In 1998 the gym and health club business was estimated to be worth £1bn, accounting for a 58 per cent increase in five years. Data from the *General Household Survey* shows that sporting activities among women have become increasingly popular in the final quarter of the century and there has been a dramatic shift towards the more intense 'workout'. In 1977 walking and swimming were the most frequent forms of exercise among women with 'gymnastics/yoga/keep fit' practised by only 2 per cent. This figure rose to 12 per cent in 1987 and stabilised at 17 per cent in 1993 by which time the 'workout' had become the most popular activity after walking. In the mid-1990s one third of women under 30 from non-manual occupations worked out regularly.[11]

The rapid rise of the 'workout' and the prevalence of dieting suggests that women were not immune to contemporary representations of idealised bodies. This evidence draws attention to the social and cultural pressures faced especially by young women. Unrealistic expectations coupled with a widening gap between ideal and reality frequently resulted in extremely negative body images. These contributed towards unhappiness, low self-esteem and in extreme cases major health problems or even death, for example as a consequence of eating disorders.

IN FOCUS: Eating Disorders

Late twentieth-century body culture provides a context in which to explain the rise of eating disorders – anorexia nervosa and bulimia nervosa – particularly among teenagers and young women. While anorexia was extremely rare and bulimia virtually unknown before the 1970s, both phenomena have become increasingly prevalent during the last quarter of the century. Male sufferers are not unheard of but women account for well over 90 per cent of clinically diagnosed cases. This gender imbalance is the most extreme among a range of gender-sensitive psychological disorders. Despite the differences between anorexia and bulimia, both share common features such as a pathological fear of being or becoming fat along with obsessive concern with food, body weight and shape.

The causes of eating disorders are complex. Physiological factors play a part – especially after the onset of the disease – but familial as well as social and cultural factors are particularly significant. Many commentators highlight the stresses and ambiguities of female roles in the late twentieth century as a major element accounting particularly for the rise of eating disorders. According to Gordon, eating disorders are an 'ethnic disorder', that is a culture-based syndrome providing an extreme expression of the dilemmas of feminine identity comparable to hysteria in the late nineteenth century. Orbach sees the anorexics' *Hunger Strike* as a *Metaphor for Our Age.*[12]

Anorexia nervosa is distinguished above all by a self-imposed starvation diet leading to rapid weight loss and refusal to maintain weight above a bare minimum, intense fear of weight gain, a distorted body image according

Eating Disorders (continued)

to which highly emaciated women consider themselves to be fat and, finally, amenorrhoea (cessation of menstrual periods). The phenomenon is not without historical precedent exemplified by the so-called fasting girls or miraculous maids of the medieval and early modern periods. Anorexia was first described in the 1870s and typical sufferers are adolescent girls, who are frequently high achievers from socially conservative and restrictive backgrounds among the higher socio-economic groups.

This stereotype is still valid, but the literature draws attention to the great variety of sufferers in terms of age and social background, including girls under 10 years as well as older women and men. Anorexia affects about 1 per cent of those most at risk (girls and women aged between 15 and 30 years) although, with regard to some of the symptoms of subclinical severity estimates range between 5 to 10 per cent among those most at risk. While treatment appears to be relatively successful and between one half and three quarters of patients regain at least some weight, psychological and physical health problems frequently persist and, including suicide, between 5 and 10 per cent of diagnosed cases are fatal.

In contrast with anorexia, bulimia nervosa is a much more recently diagnosed phenomenon, first written about in the 1970s. Bulimia is characterised by recurring episodes of excessive bingeing and purging, typically by means of self-induced vomiting or laxative abuse. Bulimics, like anorexics, are intensely preoccupied with weight, body shape and appearance. They may be of normal weight and considerable weight fluctuations are not unusual. The practice is highly secretive. Bulimics appear successful and disguise their suffering behind a façade of outward perfection while tension is released through the combination of bingeing and purging.

Bulimics are generally older than anorexics, the onset is typically during late adolescence and early adulthood. Bulimia is particularly prevalent among women in prestigious college settings and high-status careers, circumstances which place women under enormous stress, including pressure to maintain weight and an immaculate appearance. While bulimia is rarely fatal, treatment is difficult and many sufferers are never diagnosed at all. The rise of bulimia was even more dramatic than that of anorexia and milder versions of bulimia are considerably more common than anorexia. While 2–3 per cent of younger women are severe bulimics, estimates of subclinical incidence range from 10 to 20 per cent among those aged 15 to 30 with groups such as female university and college students particularly at risk.

The late Diana, Princess of Wales provides the most famous example and, according to her biographer, fits the pattern of outward success coinciding with great unhappiness remarkably well. She vividly describes her bulimia which started during her engagement, remembering 'the first time I made myself sick. I was so thrilled because I thought this was the release of

Eating Disorders (continued)

tension.' She lost weight rapidly and a binge on the night before her wedding set the tone for her honeymoon when the 'bulimia was appalling, absolutely appalling. It was rife, four times a day. . . . Anything I could find I would gobble up and be sick two minutes later.' The bulimia, depression and suicidal episodes carried on for several years, although her condition improved after she received treatment from a specialist in eating disorders.[13]

The statistical data is limited and it has been suggested that the prevalence of eating disorders was diminishing during the 1990s. However, the figures cited above relating to the high number of young women dieting and especially the 10 per cent of young underweight women on a diet, based on the Health Survey for England conducted during the mid-1990s, provide little indication that eating disorders were on the decline. One danger, especially with regard to vulnerable young women, was the widespread media practice of glamorising anorexia with emaciated fashion models, actresses or celebrities becoming the ideal emulated especially by teenage girls.

Anorexics have been, albeit grudgingly, admired for their sheer willpower. Their extreme thinness is both envied and condemned and anorexics themselves take considerable pride in their achievement. According to some feminists, their refusal to eat amounts to a protest against the expectations imposed upon women, they are hunger strikers in Orbach's imagery. By contrast, bulimia lacks this touch of glamour and celebrity. The condition is dismissed as disgusting, perceived as cheating and instead of being a source of pride and status, however misguided, generally held to be secretive and shameful.

A number of commentators reject the notion of perceiving these eating disorders as separate, clearly defined diseases and instead suggest that they are part of a continuum. In other words, severe eating disorders represent very extreme manifestations of the stressful and ambivalent attitudes to food and bodies which are prevalent among many, if not most women. This is illustrated by extensive evidence of dieting, negative and distorted body images and the range of more or frequently less effective methods to lose weight and maintain an ideal body. While vulnerable teenagers and young women in extreme cases develop the full clinical symptoms of anorexia or bulimia, many 'normal' women are on a diet, coming off a diet, or adopting a range of measures to acquire the ever-elusive ideal body as the key to a better life. A good, if fictional, example is Helen Fielding's best-selling *Bridget Jones's Diary* published in 1996. Bridget Jones, a thirty-something single professional charts her success from day-to-day in terms of alcohol, tobacco and calories consumed. One of her New Year's resolutions at the beginning of the book was 'Reduce circumference of thighs by 3 inches (i.e. $1\frac{1}{2}$ inches each), using anti-cellulite diet.' At the end of the year she had gained 5st 2lb and lost 5st 3lb which was 'excellent' progress.[14]

Conclusion

The increasingly pervasive representation of an idealised female body and the rise of a beauty industry enabling women to emulate these ideals were a central feature of twentieth-century mass consumer culture. The implications of this commercialisation of the female body are controversial. Critics maintain that women have become virtual slaves of a 'beauty myth' or 'beauty system' which is exploitative and destructive. According to Wolf the virtually unattainable thin ideal promoted since the 1960s amounts to a deliberate ploy by patriarchy in response to the second-wave feminist movement to undermine women's confidence and their health. This interpretation which portrays women as victims is not fully acceptable despite the undeniably destructive potential in terms of mental and physical health of women's quest for beauty. In this context Bordo usefully points out than an oppressor–oppressed model is too simple and that the quest for beauty can be creative or subversive. Are women undergoing cosmetic surgery victims, or are they taking control and improving their lives? Are women pumping iron at the gym manipulated, or are they building confidence and strength as well as muscles?

Women can and do make choices and the demand for beauty products and services is not just artificially manufactured by commercial forces controlled by patriarchal, capitalist interests. As Featherstone argues, the success of consumer culture is based on its ability to harness and channel genuine bodily needs and desires. Women's ever-growing use of beauty products to emulate changing ideal body images can be interpreted positively as an increasingly democratic assertion of female sexuality. The thin ideal could be perceived as women debilitated by the continuous need to control their hunger. Alternatively, it could be interpreted more positively as women adopting a femininity which rejects traditional reproductive and domestic roles. Similarly, the rise of muscles can be seen as part of the wider erosion of gender differences and women's appropriation of essentially masculine attributes which enhances women's physical strength and symbolises female power. Since the notion of a 'natural' body or 'natural' beauty is an illusion and some form of visual presentation is inevitable, emulation of contemporary ideals should not be casually denigrated as trivial or idle self-indulgence but rather understood as capable of offering important rewards in terms of self-esteem, personal happiness and economic security.

Bibliographical Note

Many of the issues raised in this chapter have been relatively neglected in the literature, and the history of women's bodies in twentieth-century Britain still remains to be written. Rather more work has been done on North America or Western culture more generally and the following references do not focus exclusively on Britain. For a general introduction to the body as a historical topic see R. Porter, 'History of the Body', in P. Burke (ed), *New Perspectives on Historical Writing* (Oxford, 1991). Rising living standards and the emergence of mass consumer culture since the late nineteenth century are discussed in P. Johnson (ed), *Twentieth*

Century Britain: Economic, Social and Cultural Change (London, 1994); J. Benson, *The Rise of Consumer Society in Britain, 1880–1980* (London, 1994); G. Cross, *Time and Money: The Making of Consumer Culture* (New York, 1993); J. Obelkevich, 'Consumption', in J. Obelkevich and P. Catterall (eds), *Understanding Postwar British Society* (London, 1994). For a gendered perspective see V. de Grazia and E. Furlough (eds), *The Sex of Things: Gender and Consumption in Historical Perspective* (Berkeley and Los Angeles, CA, 1996). Changing fashions and body images are traced in E. Wilson and L. Taylor, *Through the Looking Glass: A History of Dress from 1860 to the Present Day* (London, 1989); and M. Thesander, *The Feminine Ideal* (London, 1997). While there is little British research, the rise of cosmetics is analysed in K. Peiss, *Hope In A Jar: The Making of America's Beauty Culture* (New York, 1998). On the visual representation of the female body and women's quest for beauty in a longer term perspective see N. Zemon Davies and A. Farge (eds), *A History of Women In the West III. Renaissance and Enlightenment Paradoxes* (Cambridge, MA, 1993). The leading accounts of women's magazines are C.L. White, *Women's Magazines 1693–1968* (London, 1970); and M. Ferguson, *Forever Feminine: Women's Magazines and the Cult of Femininity* (London, 1983). For changing beauty ideals, women's attitudes towards beauty culture and female consumption of beauty products see V. Steele, *Fashion and Eroticism: Ideals of Feminine Beauty from the Victorian Era to the Jazz Age* (New York, 1985). M. Lake, 'Female Desires: The Meaning of World War II', *Australian Historical Studies* 24 (1990), pp. 267–84, provides an Australian case study. J.J. Matthews, 'Building the Body Beautiful', *Australian Feminist Studies* 5 (1987), pp. 17–34 explores British developments during the interwar years; and R. Scott, *The Female Consumer* (London, 1976) provides a snapshot of the mid-1970s. Theoretical issues are discussed from rather different perspectives by M. Featherstone, 'The Body in Consumer Culture', *Theory, Culture and Society* 1 (1982), pp. 18–33; and A. Offer, 'Epidemics of Abundance: Overeating and Slimming in the USA and Britain since the 1950s', *University of Oxford Discussion Papers in Economic and Social History* no 25 (November 1998); published in A. Offer, 'Body-Weight and Self-Control in the USA and Britain since the 1950s', *Social History of Medicine* 14: 1 (2001–forth-coming). For feminist analyses on beauty and the body see D. MacCannell and J.F. MacCannell, 'The Beauty System', in N. Armstrong and L. Tennenhouse (eds), *The Ideology of Conduct: Essays in Literature and the History of Sexuality* (London, 1987); and N. Wolf, *Beauty Myth: How Images of Beauty are Used Against Women* (New York, 1990). For a more nuanced approach see S. Bordo, *Unbearable Weight: Feminism, Western Culture and the Body* (London, 1993). Wolf and Bordo also deal with eating disorders which are discussed in S. Orbach, *Fat Is A Feminist Issue and Its Sequel*, new edn (London, 1998); S. Orbach, *Hunger Strike: The Anorectic's Struggle as a Metaphor For Our Age*, second edn (Harmondsworth, 1993); and A. Gordon, *Anorexia and Bulimia: Anatomy of a Social Epidemic* (Oxford, 1990). For a critical analysis of dieting and the slimming industry see T. Sanders and P. Bazalgette, *You Don't Have to Diet* (London, 1994).

Notes

1. See M. Featherstone, 'The Body in Consumer Culture', *Theory, Culture and Society* 1 (1982), pp. 18–33; V. Steele, *Fashion and Eroticism: Ideals of Feminine Beauty from the Victorian Era to the Jazz Age* (New York, 1985); M. Lake, 'Female Desires: The Meaning of World War II', *Australian Historical Studies* 24 (1990), pp. 267–84; J.J. Matthews, 'Building the Body Beautiful', *Australian Feminist Studies* 5 (1987), pp. 17–34.

2. Featherstone, 'The Body in Consumer Culture', p. 26.

3. A. Offer, 'Epidemics of Abundance: Overeating and Slimming in the USA and Britain since the 1950s', *University of Oxford Discussion Papers in Economic and Social History* no 25

(November 1998); published in A. Offer, 'Body-Weight and Self-Control in the USA and Britain since the 1950s', *Social History of Medicine* 14: 1 (2001–forth-coming); D. MacCannell and J.F. MacCannell, 'The Beauty System', in N. Armstrong and L. Tennenhouse (eds), *The Ideology of Conduct: Essays in Literature and the History of Sexuality* (London, 1987); N. Wolf, *Beauty Myth: How Images of Beauty are Used Against Women* (New York, 1990); S. Bordo, *Unbearable Weight: Feminism, Western Culture and the Body* (London, 1993).

4. M.M. Bagot Stack, *Building the Body Beautiful: The Bagot Stack Stretch-and-Swing System* (London, 1931).

5. J.B. Priestley, *English Journey* (London, 1934), pp. 376, 401–2; G. Orwell, *The Road to Wigan Pier* (London, 1937), p. 89.

6. Public Record Office, Kew, RG 23/17, Wartime Social Survey: Retail Services and Short-ages, May 1942–March 1943; see I. Zweiniger-Bargielowska, *Austerity in Britain: Rationing, Controls and Consumption, 1939–1955* (Oxford, 2000), pp. 90–2, 185–91.

7. Matthews, 'Building the Body Beautiful'.

8. G. Browne (Hulton Press), *Patterns of British Life* (London, 1950), pp. 60–2, 133–4; I. Zweiniger-Bargielowska, 'Women under Austerity: Fashion in Britain During the 1940s', in M. Donald and L. Hurcombe (eds), *Gender and Material Culture: Historical Perspectives* (Basingstoke, 2000), pp. 218–37; R. Scott, *The Female Consumer* (London, 1976).

9. Wolf, *The Beauty Myth*, p. 191; S. Orbach, *Fat Is A Feminist Issue and Its Sequel*, new edn (London, 1998); T. Sanders and P. Bazalgette, *You Don't Have to Diet* (London, 1994). See also references in note 3 above.

10. *Health Survey for England. The Health of Young People '95–97: Summary of Key Findings* (Stationery Office, 1999), pp. 8–9; *Health Survey for England '96* (Stationery Office, 1998), p. 285; see also Offer, 'Epidemics of Abundance'.

11. J. Fonda, *Jane Fonda's Workout Book* (New York, 1981); *General Household Survey, 1977–* [*Living in Britain* after 1995]; K. Marks, 'Gym Industry Now Worth Healthy £1bn', *Independent* 21 August 1998, p. 8.

12. A. Gordon, *Anorexia and Bulimia: Anatomy of a Social Epidemic* (Oxford, 1990); S. Orbach, *Hunger Strike: The Anorectic's Struggle as a Metaphor For Our Age*, second edn (Harmondsworth, 1993). This section is based on these sources, relevant references in the bibliographical note and M. Lawrence and M. Dana, *Fighting Food: Coping with Eating Disorders* (London, 1990); S. Abraham and D. Llewellyn-Jones, *Eating Disorders: The Facts*, third edn, (Oxford, 1992); and H. Steiner and J. Lock, 'Anorexia Nervosa and Bulimia Nervosa in Children and Adolescents: A Review of the Past 10 Years', *Journal of the American Academy of Child and Adolescent Psychiatry* 37, 4 (1998), pp. 352–9.

13. A. Morton, *Diana Her True Story – In Her Own Words*, revised edn (London, 1997), pp. 41–2, 50–1, 54–7, 61–2, 161–2.

14. H. Fielding, *Bridget Jones's Diary: A Novel* (London, 1996), pp. 3, 310.

13

CRIME

Shani D'Cruze

The twentieth-century history of women and crime involved women who offended, who were the victims of crime and who have enforced the law, for example as police officers. These three groups were not entirely discrete. Sometimes they have overlapped fortuitously, but more commonly because of how women have been ideologically and structurally positioned. For example, in 1997 nearly half of 234 imprisoned women offenders interviewed reported experience of physical or sexual abuse.[1] In recent decades women police officers have disproportionately complained of sexual harassment and even violence from male colleagues.

The twentieth-century criminal justice and penal systems in England and Wales were substantially Victorian constructions. Although increasingly outmoded and under strain by the 1980s and despite alternating liberal and conservative policies, substantially the same systems were in force in 2000 as in 1900. These systems defined criminality as a chiefly working-class attribute and directed their activities towards the control and regulation of working people. They also deployed reductionist patriarchal ideologies about femininity, sexuality and women's necessary association with the domestic and sought to normalise women to the dominant ideal. Leniency to women in some respects was arguably outweighed by particularly harsh and punitive treatment in others. Disproportionately the rigour of the police, penal and judicial institutions has fallen on women who have been otherwise socially and economically disadvantaged. Nevertheless these institutions were far from a totalising patriarchal system. Ideologies were not identical to formal laws nor to everyday practices and gender ideologies were modified by those concerning race, class or sexuality. It was above all the impact of second-wave feminism that shifted the ground of scholarship and politicised the responses of at least some groups of women as well as producing real if very incomplete changes in policy and practice in some areas of policing and prison regimes by 2000.

Women Offenders

Twentieth-century women committed significantly fewer and less serious crimes than men. In 1997 more than four-fifths of the 508,000 individuals aged ten years or over found guilty or officially cautioned by police for an indictable offence were male. This gender difference has a long history. In 1900, 8,928 men compared to 1,219 women appeared before Assizes and Quarter Sessions (after 1970 crown courts) which tried (on the whole) more serious crime before a jury. In 1950 the equivalent figures were 17,990 men compared to 945 women and in 1980, 66,348 men and 7,482 women were tried.

Criminal statistics show a decline in recorded crime by the later nineteenth century followed by several decades of comparative stability with some rise attributable to the First World War. Crime rose again during the Second World War, never returned to its interwar levels and crime rates accelerated thereafter, particularly from the 1970s. However, statistics never accurately represent crime levels. The non-recognition of particular behaviours as criminal, non-reporting, re-categorisation by the police and the courts, police initiatives in some areas and lack of action in others (such as domestic and sexual violence) all served to leave unrecorded an unknown 'dark figure' of criminal activity. Nevertheless, it does seem clear that committing crime was comparatively 'normal' for men and 'abnormal' for women. Around 1 in 24 men and boys were arrested in 1901 and 1 in 30 in 1951. Comparable figures for women were 1 in 123 and 1 in 299.[2] Gatrell makes this point to illustrate the extent to which the criminal justice system policed men and boys in poorer communities. Of course, this 'policeman state' was also targeting an exceptional minority of women as deviant while simultaneously constructing most women in these communities as non-criminal.

Women's share of felonies (more serious crime) tried at the Old Bailey between 1687 and 1921 declined markedly from up to 45 per cent of indictments at some points early in the eighteenth century to around 10 per cent early in the twentieth century.[3] This decline accelerated as the nineteenth century progressed and as the 'policeman state' developed. These trends might relate to broader social and economic change which strengthened women's association with domesticity, reduced their involvement in paid work and public life and made them more subject to informal social controls, including victimisation. The Islington Crime Survey of 1986 found that women, especially young women, were at particularly high risk of crime, violence and harassment.

The picture from late nineteenth-century magistrates' court records, though extremely partial seems similar. If informal patriarchal disciplines on women by the early twentieth century partly replaced the formal discipline earlier exercised by the criminal justice system, this coincided with the rise of working-class respectability. This development may have reduced crime rates by promoting domesticity and restraint over drink, disorder and interpersonal violence. Nevertheless, such reticence existed chiefly as an ideal and working-class cultures still furnished the courts with most of the criminality and disorder they dealt with. Dominant explanations, influenced by eugenicist and social Darwinist perspectives, associated criminality and disorder with a residuum of social and mental inadequates. Nevertheless occasional criminality seems to have remained a combination of survival tactic, low-level social protest and leisure activity in poorer communities.

Although poverty remained the experience for some throughout the twentieth century and seemed to be increasing for certain groups in the 1980s, overall standards of living improved, certainly from the interwar period. The relationships between access to resources and crime were complex. The very low levels of women's offending indicate that while crime remained one way of combating poverty it was far from an automatic response. Nevertheless there were correspondences between the minor property crime many women offenders committed and the workings of a domestic economy. In some early twentieth-century communities, children's scavenging and stealing put food on the table and fuel in the hearth and was often condoned or encouraged. Theft could augment young women's consumption associated with leisure and courtship. Liverpool's Ship Street (1940s) disapproved of criminal activity that injured community members but tolerated many other rackets. In London's East End in the 1930s and 1950s, peripheral to the world of organised crime, women shared in the criminality which contributed a few extras to their fairly sparse domestic economies.

Under the Betting and Gaming Act of 1908 (repealed 1961) off-course betting was illegal. However, bookies were endemic in working-class communities. Many were men, but women, too, took bets. In 1912 a Manchester man found the police raiding the betting business his wife ran from their front parlour while he was out at work.[4] Women also placed illegal bets, usually for smaller stakes than men, combining a bit of a flutter with managing the housekeeping. Men and women indulged in the incipient low-level property crime which augmented their consumption. Where women nicked things, took bets or received stolen goods as an extension of a domestic economy, however, only comparatively rarely did this lead to arrest and conviction. This behaviour commonly did not offend against public order and, from the perspective of the 'policeman state' was not 'serious', particularly by mid-century, when working-class communities and police forces had reached some sort of accommodation.

Changing retail methods from the 1950s highlighted the problem of shoplifting because of the move to self-service stores. The popular stereotype was of the shoplifter as a middle-aged woman, maybe menopausal and certainly mentally fragile. Though many men and juveniles also shoplifted, in as much as women shoplifters did approach the stereotype it was through their patterns of augmenting household, personal and domestic purchasing. Most women shoplifters were first offenders. It is perhaps possible to understand adult women's shoplifting in the context of cultural pressures towards consumption or to domesticity; inchoate but purposive tactical responses by individuals whose experience did not accord with dominant norms.

Although most female offenders have committed minor property crime, women were convicted across the same range of offences as men. Women broke the law for political purposes, from the militant suffragettes in the 1900s to women anti-nuclear protesters in the 1950s and 1980s, and campaigners against the export of livestock for the continental meat trade in the 1990s. Far more of this group were middle class. Middle-class women and men have been less heavily disciplined by the criminal justice system. White-collar crime, for example, has been less effectively policed. Motoring offences brought the middle classes before the courts in numbers, but even here women were a minority. Middle-class women who have openly defied the law in protest have posed a contradiction to the criminal justice system. They conformed to its class preconceptions of respectability but by their protest transgressed against approved patterns of femininity. Media representations of women protesters vilified them as unfeminine, often lesbian (inevitably used as a pejorative descriptor) and out of control. These offenders were also able and inclined to respond with forceful critiques of the criminal justice system. Its responses have been erratic, from embarrassment and leniency to harsh rigour, such as the forced-feeding of suffragettes on hunger-strike in prison.

A very few women (presented as examples of feminine frailty and/or sexualised depravity) were charged with drugs offences in the scares over opium among West End socialites in the interwar period and cocaine around the time of the Second World War. However, when the drug culture of the 1960s and 1970s developed, women were both users and a minority of dealers. Because drug cultures have since then also (but not exclusively) overlapped with more affluent youth cultures, middle-class women were also a small minority of drug offenders. Foreign women sentenced for drug smuggling offences comprised a significant minority of the female prison population at the end of the century. Drunkenness associated women with the residuum early in the century. Since the 1870s regular female drunks were thought feeble-minded and suitable for incarceration. By the 1960s the explanations favoured individual psychological damage, made perhaps more plausible because of a marked decline in convicted women drunks, though male offences had increased. Women imprisoned for drunkenness in 1960 were marginalised and impoverished. Given their social exclusion and powerlessness, habitual drunkenness seems a reasonable response.

Violent behaviour early in the century was a strategy of dispute resolution by working-class women, who could use physical violence to defend their own, or their household's reputation. Women's public violence was increasingly condemned by respectable opinion. Young women involved in gang violence – an uncommon but not unknown phenomenon – were especially shocking. Overall women's crimes of violence were few by mid-century. However, the 1970s saw renewed anxieties that girls and women's share of violent crime was increasing rapidly. Greater sex equality was thought to encourage convergence between male and female disorder. Despite some growth in women's crimes of violence in recent decades, because base levels were so low even a small increase produced

Plate 13.1. Women peace campaigners decorating the fence with balloons and cards, Greenham Common, December 1983.

a large percentage change. The putative link with 'women's lib' was tenuous. New-wave feminism was a predominantly middle-class movement, and female offenders were mostly working-class. Indeed, modern women offenders often reported a commitment to comparatively traditional models of gender roles and to aspire to a satisfactory home, partner and children rather than to have career or other ambitions. With the perspective of historical distance it can be seen that the 'New Woman Criminal' was largely a myth.

The most shocked reactions have been in response to women who have been the most violent. Ruth Ellis, who shot her lover in 1955, is discussed below. More recently other women who have killed violent partners, like Sara Thornton, have been able to establish a defence of provocation by abusive behaviour over the long term, which was refused to Ellis. Myra Hindley, convicted in 1965 with her partner Ian Brady of the murder of five children and adolescents – actions undertaken to feed his sado-masochistic personality – has spent over 30 years in prison and still makes headline news. Even more than Brady, Hindley (represented by the notorious photograph taken at the time of her arrest, bleached blond and scowling) has born the brunt of media attention, mostly because the close involvement of a young woman in such horrific violence clashed so disturbingly with dominant norms of femininity. Myra Hindley has become in many ways the archetypal late twentieth-century murderess. Even the equally disturbing series of murders of children and young people committed in the 1990s by Fred and Rosemary West have failed to establish Rosemary West (more mature and less glamorous) as such a demonic figure.

IN FOCUS: Ruth Ellis, 1926–55

In 1953 postwar austerity was waning. Ruth Ellis had separated from her husband and was working as the manageress of a bar and gambling club in the West End of London. She lived above the club with her son and daughter. From a working-class background, by her mid-20s she was (precariously) financially independent and moved in rather more affluent social circles than those of her childhood. She was sexually as well as financially autonomous, and used an illegal abortion to end an unwanted pregnancy. In 1953 she met racing driver, David Blakely, several years younger than herself and within weeks they had become lovers. He moved into her flat and she supported him financially. He could be jealous and difficult. During one separation she began another affair with Desmond Cussen but returned to Blakely when he promised marriage. Blakely was violent, a heavy drinker and sexually unfaithful. She was also jealous, once waiting all night for him outside another woman's house. She stayed with Cussen for a while but the affair continued. Blakely's motor-racing friends, particularly Anthony and Carole Findlater, became implicated in the

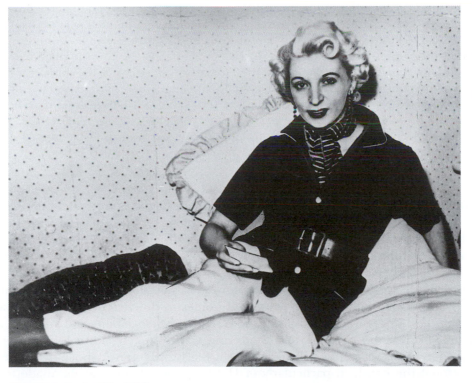

Plate 13.2. Ruth Ellis, 1955.

Ruth Ellis, 1926–55 (continued)

couple's emotional turmoil. In March 1955 Blakely hit her in the stomach and she suffered a miscarriage. On Good Friday 1955, he stood her up and went to the Findlaters for the weekend. Cussen drove her to their house where she made a scene and pushed in the windows of Blakely's car. The police were called. On Easter Sunday evening, Blakely was leaving the Findlaters when Ruth accosted him in the street carrying a gun. Blakely tried to run, but she shot him at close range in the back, firing several more bullets as he lay face down. She was arrested directly.

Her brief trial attracted much public interest. Ruth Ellis was a young, attractive, bleached blonde, smartly dressed and was calm and self-controlled. To hostile observers this demonstrated her callousness. Her counsel attempted to reduce the charge to manslaughter on a plea of provocation. The defence of provocation was then applied to incidents where a sudden event produced an immediate and temporary loss of self-control. Ruth Ellis's counsel argued that different criteria should apply to a woman. A psychiatrist testified that women's rationality was more greatly undermined by their sexuality than men's and that someone of the emotional immaturity that he saw in Ruth Ellis could have been so affected by sexual jealousy as to lose her self-control. The judge refused to allow the plea, making a guilty verdict virtually inevitable. In fact the defence, perhaps unable to counter the construction of Ruth Ellis's transgressive femininity, left many questions unexamined. It was never established how she obtained the gun, nor how she travelled to the Findlaters' to carry out the murder. Some recent assessments have suggested that Cussen may have played a greater role in the murder than the trial revealed. Ruth Ellis insisted that she wanted to die, though she was persuaded to appeal (unsuccessfully) to the Home Secretary for clemency. Ruth Ellis was the last woman to be hanged for a capital crime in Britain. Capital punishment was repealed in 1965.

Although the cases of Ruth Ellis and Myra Hindley are distinct, these were both working-class women whose extreme violence was associated with their relationship with an abusive man. They were both victims and perpetrators of violence. I do not seek to argue that they were 'driven' to kill nor that they were necessarily psychologically dysfunctional. However, aside from the horror of murder, the surviving narratives of both women's relationships with their partners fall substantially into the pattern of domestic violence described by modern studies. These were relationships which included sociability and affection as well as horror and violence, and Brady and David Blakely (Ruth Ellis's lover), like many abusive men, oscillated between the two. However shocking and exceptional the conduct, particularly of Hindley, connections can be made to a far more common experience of twentieth-century women – that of physical and sexual violence from men whom they knew well or intimately.

As discussed in chapter 14, women were the vast majority of those prosecuted for offences associated with prostitution. Women's sexuality and reproduction also positioned them as offenders in other ways. Patriarchal assumptions about female natures produced legislation that mitigated the force of the law of homicide where women killed their babies. Infanticide is the only criminal offence which women alone can commit. In 1922 and again in 1938 Infanticide Acts manipulated contemporary psychological discourse to create a legal view of the parturient female as mentally unstable, thereby justifying shorter sentences for infanticide.

Until the 1967 Abortion Act, measures that many women routinely took to control their reproduction were criminalised. Regulating fertility not by contraception but by 'bringing on' a late period was widespread. Before the introduction of the contraceptive pill women's control over the efficiency of contraception was limited. For any number of reasons both working and middle-class women could find themselves with an unwanted pregnancy. For the more affluent an abortion carried out by sympathetic (or unscrupulous) doctors in a private nursing home was reasonably easily attainable. Working-class women sought out generally female 'amateur' abortionists. Many of these saw themselves as helping other women. By no means all took money for their services. It was an offence not only to carry out but also to procure an abortion whether by chemical or surgical means. Consequently not only the abortionist but also the pregnant woman and sometimes her husband could be prosecuted. After 1967 contraception and abortion were placed firmly in the hands of the medical profession.

Women and Prison

The prison system since the nineteenth century has been based on regimes designed for men, but has categorised prisoners by sex and by age. In 1901 the daily average prison population of sentenced and unsentenced prisoners was 14,459 male and 2,976 female. In 1930, including borstals, there was a daily average of 10,561 males and only 785 females in prison. Prison populations overall have increased considerably since the 1940s; the 1960 totals were 26,198 males and 901 females. Though both the numbers and the proportion of women in the prison population increased, they were still vastly outnumbered by men. In 1997, including young offenders, over 46,400 convicted men were serving prison sentences compared to 2,100 women. Courts have imposed fewer and shorter custodial sentences on women. Around a third of women remanded in custody were subsequently given a non-custodial sentence in the 1970s. Prison has often been seen as inappropriate for women. Nevertheless, some women perceived as transgressing dominant norms of femininity were imprisoned, without being strictly guilty of a criminal offence. Teenage girls were institutionalised for sexual conduct that was not so treated in boys. The first girls' Borstal at Aylesbury opened in 1909. As its woman governor remarked in 1929; 'All their violence and all the things that cause so much trouble are owing to their being oversexed. It has to be got out of them somehow.'[5]

Early in the century treatment of prisoners could be severe, as accounts by imprisoned suffragettes made plain. Prisoners were subjected to compulsory internal examination by male doctors and had their heads shaved. The practice of cutting prisoners' hair persisted until 1932. Harsh and coercive treatment remained a possibility in the 1970s and 1980s. However, the view of female prisoners as 'mad' rather than 'bad' also has a history stretching back into the nineteenth century. Delinquent and criminal behaviour, particularly in women, was explained by 'feeble-mindedness'. The Mental Deficiency Act of 1913, permitted one-year control orders. Feeble-minded women were thought to be highly fertile and the condition hereditary. The associated condition of 'moral insanity' justified the incarceration of women conceiving illegitimate children while in receipt of poor relief. In 1975 it was reported that 'There are very few mentally ill women in Holloway, but, there are many who may be considered "mentally abnormal".'[6]

Regimes in women's prisons have not infrequently adopted re-moralizing or therapeutic measures. The failed plans for a therapeutic regime for the new Holloway prison were introduced in the late 1960s when the penal system as a whole was abandoning policies of rehabilitation. The cultivation of domestic and feminine skills preferably in a rural environment were important techniques of rehabilitation. Women prisoners ceased to wear uniform in the 1960s. Cells were decorated in pastel shades with matching fabrics. Adoption of domestic traits have been indicators of recovery even of the 'dangerous, violent or criminal' women patients in Broadmoor. Askham Grange, the first open prison for women opened in 1947, was envisioned as a rural, semi-agricultural establishment. One of the prisoners was appointed 'Duck Girl', and looked after the flock of Muscovy ducks. 'Women's work' has also marked prisoners' occupations. In 1963 of 632 women prisoners deemed fit to work 55 per cent were employed as cooks, bakers, laundry workers or cleaners compared to 28 per cent (of 21,080) male prisoners. However, heavy work in often poorly equipped laundries served neither to cultivate the skills of bourgeois domesticity that the cheery regime at Askham Grange seemed to be aiming at, nor to develop other more useful skills in prisoners.[7]

Women experienced prison differently from men. Most were in for comparatively short sentences or were on remand and a higher proportion were first-time offenders. Low numbers meant overcrowding and poor facilities because prisons were comparatively small and expensive to run. Women prisoners were moved more frequently than men. Most served much of their sentence far from home, which made visiting difficult. Unlike men, women retained their family responsibilities while inside. Both modern and historical studies remark on women prisoners' anxieties about home, children and family. Consequently imprisonment was a more solitary and alienating experience for women. A compounding problem more recently was the high levels of drug and substance abuse among women prisoners.

Modern women's prison populations demonstrate a range of traits that at the beginning of the century were diagnosed as 'feeble-mindedness': illegitimate

Plate 13.3. Askham Grange, originally a country mansion complete with ballroom, was opened as the first UK open prison for women in 1947. Its prison regime emphasised domesticity, community and country living as a way of resocialising women offenders. Here its original governor, Mary Size, and her staff pose outside its gabled façade.

children, abusive treatment by male partners, poverty and social exclusion. Overall defiance and disruption were not uncommon in early and late twentieth-century women's prisons. Self-harm and suicide attempts remain more frequent in women's prisons than men's. The therapeutic model underpinned more frequent prescription of psychotropic drugs to women prisoners. A 1997 Prison Inspectorate report points out that prison is a particularly stressful and punitive experience for many of the comparatively small and specifically positioned group of women who become subjected to it.

Domestic Violence and Sexual Violence

Domestic violence in the period to 1960 was integral to the negotiation of power relations in (some) working-class households. It was largely caused by disputes over domestic roles, particularly about the control of household resources. Often the emotional content of working-class marriages was not strong, though some couples were very close. Nevertheless, husbands' expectations of sexual access could also fuel violence. (Sexual violence within marriage was not a criminal offence until 1991.) Conflict could be limited and blows were traded for verbal taunts. Some women exchanged punch for punch. Women (and their neighbours) distinguished legitimate from illegitimate violence and interfered only when that boundary was crossed. Frequently wives tolerated occasional aggression and placed more value on other kinds of loyalty. A 'good' husband 'tipped up' a full pay packet. A bad one spent his wages in the pub and returned home only to be irrationally and excessively violent.

The police saw domestic violence as private and interfered only when public order was compromised by noise or a gathering crowd. Numbers of wife assault cases were decreasing by the 1900s (which may have reflected a decline in actual violence or a reluctance to take cases to court). The domestic violence which came to court or to the attention of welfare professionals was understood as part of a complex of behaviours warranting intervention into family life with a prime intention of saving the child rather than ending violence to adult women. Respectability increasingly meant domestic privacy and personal restraint, and arguably domestic violence may have been even more difficult for many women to disclose. The new discourses of sexology raised the stakes of a satisfactory marriage and now sexual fulfilment for both sexes (achieved albeit by a wife's submission) was also necessary. If domestic violence hinged around disputes over the fulfilment of marital roles, arguably those role expectations came to include a more intense emotional element.

Consequently by the mid-twentieth century, domestic violence was often a matter of silence and shame until new-wave feminism drew it to public attention. Because the women's movement in the 1960s and 1970s was mostly a middle-class affair, middle-class women above all had a new forum in which they could articulate the abuse suffered by some of them. If the personal and the private were also political, domestic violence became a problem of power relations by gender and as much an outcome of patriarchy as women's disadvantages in paid work. Feminists demonstrated how serious, widespread and prolonged the violence inflicted by men in the home can be. Violent men arguably sought to impose control over all aspects of a couple's relationship, emotional and sexual as well as domestic.

Modern studies show that women can find it difficult to leave abusive relationships. The bad times tend to alternate with very good ones. As one woman in interwar Southampton told her daughter, 'You can't just stop loving someone, like turning off a tap.'[8] Even with women's increased access to the job market since the Second World War they were likely to have financial problems providing for themselves and often their children. Abusive men also tend to become more violent against a woman who leaves. A court injunction alone is little protection against a man determined to seek out and do harm to a woman. Erin Pizzey set up the first women's refuge in Chiswick in 1971 and publicised the problem in her book *Scream Quietly or the Neighbours will Hear* (1974). Despite difficulties, chronic underfunding and disputes the refuge movement has provided a lifeline for many thousands of women since then and exposed the lamentable ways in which the police were dealing with domestic violence. In the 1970s as in the 1900s, domestic violence was treated as a private matter between husband and wife. Despite the persistence of these attitudes in some quarters, police policy and practice on domestic violence has changed markedly elsewhere.

Late nineteenth-century court records reveal sexual violence within courtship, social and leisure relationships as well as the stereotypical model of an attack outdoors by a stranger. This latter model, however, certainly informed many courts' understandings of sexual violence throughout the twentieth century. Patriarchal notions of female sexuality as activated by male 'persuasion', even including violence, were written into legal doctrines on consent. Courts acknowledged that male importunate sexuality represented a problem for some women, but, unless substantial physical violence occurred or the woman was of a significantly higher social class than the man, treated the harm done to women by sexual assault as not particularly serious. Male sexuality was considered to be at times an irresistible force, overcoming even the most manly restraint. A judge commented in 1923 in a case of child rape 'Gentlemen, we are all liable to fall'. Courts acted to protect the characters of men accused of sexual violence at the expense of the women involved. The Law Lords ruled in 1975 that a man who *believed* a woman had consented to sex, no matter how unreasonably, was not guilty of rape.[9]

The amount of sexual assault (rapes and indecent assault on women and girls short of homicide) listed in the British Criminal Statistics has increased markedly from 958 in 1900, to 1,960 in 1930, to 6,992 in 1960 and 12,723 in 1980. The rise accelerated from the Second World War though under-reporting and a refusal by the criminal justice system to take much sexual violence seriously continued into the 1990s. Police assumed that false accusations of rape were common. As new-wave feminists complained so vociferously, the treatment of women bringing complaints of sexual assault by both the police and the courts was so oppressive that many women withdrew charges or found their attackers acquitted or given mild sentences, while they had been forced to endure a protracted ordeal.

Two incidents in January 1982 focused these complaints. Firstly, John Allen, convicted for raping a young women (a stranger) who had accepted a lift when she had been left without transport after an evening out, was only fined £2,000. The judge considered her hitch-hiking at night and her tight trousers to constitute 'contributory negligence' and held Allen to be a 'respectable' family man. There was public outcry and the judge was censured. A tv documentary ten days later ('Police', 18 January 1982) showed a Thames Valley Police interrogation of a woman bringing a complaint of rape. The viewing public was shocked by the bullying and oppressive treatment the film revealed. In the subsequent 20 years, police practices changes in some areas, though this improvement remained patchy and elsewhere the older prejudices remained, firmly entrenched in the assumptions of masculinist police culture.

Despite individual injustices, the increased attention to the seriousness of rape from the 1970s certainly encouraged greater numbers of women to report the crime. Home Office figures indicate that 1,842 rapes were recorded in 1985 compared to 5,930 in 1996. More reported cases fell outside the 'outdoor' 'stranger-rape' stereotype and by the mid-1980s there was an apparently greater willingness to convict rapists who were known to their victims. However, conviction rates declined subsequently. Gregory and Lees argue that since the Crown Prosecution Service (CPS) took over the role of prosecutor from the police in 1986, the 'stranger' model had re-asserted itself and the CPS, under pressure of an ever-increasing case-load, tended to drop cases of acquaintance or 'date' rape. While 24 per cent of reported rapes resulted in conviction in 1985, fewer than 10 per cent did in 1996.[10]

Women and Law Enforcement

Women who were part of the criminal justice system as professionals negotiated comparable attitudes to femininity and women's capacity as were applied to women offenders and victims. This is particularly clear in the case of women police officers. Women police originated partly in feminist concerns about the treatment of women and girls by the all-male police force, especially in cases of sexual assault and partly emerged from nineteenth-century moral rescue philanthropy.

Volunteer women police units, formed in 1914, were used to police the perceived sexual licence of wartime. Attested women officers were employed at the discretion of police authorities, in separate women's departments. They enforced wartime curfews in garrison towns. In Grantham, PC Edith Smith drew up a blacklist of disorderly girls who were to be refused permission to enter theatres and cinemas. As a result, 'the frivolous girls . . . bowed down'. Despite much skilled work interviewing victims of abuse, the interwar women police frequently saw themselves as professionals of a superior class to the women and children they dealt with and continued to police women's leisure activities and occupation of public space. The postwar retrenchment in government expenditure of 1922 fell heavily on the women police whose numbers in the Metropolitan force were reduced from 114 to 20. Because their duties were seen as welfare and moral regulation they were marginalised from the core project of policing, that of reducing crime. However, a Royal Commission on Police Powers and Procedures in 1929 endorsed their work with women and children and argued that their 'feminine qualities of quickness and intuition' could be useful in detective work.[11] Regulations specifying uniform conditions of service for all policewomen were secured in 1931, but their numbers, promotion prospects and scope of duties increased only from the Second World War onwards. Women comprised a mere 4 per cent of police strength as late as 1971.

In 1975 the Equal Pay Act (enacted 1970) and the Sex Discrimination Act came into force. The Metropolitan Police had disbanded separate policewomen's departments in 1972. From 1975 women and men officers undertook the same duties as a single organisation. Women gained equal pay, but had fewer possibilities for career progression and less autonomy in their work with women and children. They were also required to accept equal working conditions, including shift work. Police forces also continued to employ (illegal) discriminatory practices. 'Operational' concerns were cited as reasons for prohibiting women from particular areas of police work and there were quotas for recruitment and promotion. Women officers comprised around 14 per cent of the police in the 1990s and a few women reached high rank. The first woman Chief Constable was Pauline Clare, appointed in Lancashire in 1996.

Women officers in the integrated police forces were confronted with a very masculine, racist and sexist 'cop culture'. Women who developed the normative 'masculine' skills achieved some grudging acceptance but could be denigrated for their lack of femininity. A number of women police officers in the 1980s and 1990s brought high-profile cases of sexual discrimination which revealed severe sexual harassment and bullying. Even more disturbingly, other women police officers have experienced sexual assault from male colleagues. Investigations by Her Majesty's Inspectorate of Constabulary in 1992 and 1996 revealed evidence of widespread and uncontrolled harassment. Some good practice was set alongside 'scepticism, tokenism and indifference'.[12] Nevertheless, by 1999 there was more mobilisation by trades unions and other organisations to tackle these cultures of harassment and discrimination and to compel forces to implement effectively the equal opportunities policies adopted since the 1970s by fundamentally changing the masculine 'cop culture' of the police.

Conclusion

Compared to men, twentieth-century women were significantly under-represented as both criminals and law enforcers. Much victimisation (particularly sexual and domestic violence) was masked by the operation of the criminal justice system itself as well as by wider patriarchal subordination. Historical and criminological research was scant until feminists began to explore the issues and provided interview and survey data from the 1970s. However, important similarities emerge between this feminist work and historical studies whose chronologies reach the First World War. While this brief survey does not provide a comprehensive overview, it does indicate that patterns of female offending and victimisation of women seem not to have changed substantially since 1900, despite a striking rise in crime rates overall. Women's encounters with the criminal justice system, whether as victims, as law enforcers or as offenders have been characterised by the differentiated application of broad ideological constructions which seek to position them as in some way deficient. Perhaps in the twenty-first century the question posed both by researchers and policy makers will not be why women's criminality is so abnormally low, but why men's is so abnormally high.

Bibliographical Note

Although there is little recent historical research published in this area, there are some older relevant studies, for example, B. Brookes, *Abortion in England, 1900–1967* (London, 1988); J. Lock, *The British Policewoman* (London, 1979); and A. Smith, *Women in Prison* (London, 1962). L. Zedner, *Women, Crime and Custody in Victorian England* (Oxford, 1991) also considers the early twentieth century, as do the items by Feeley and Little on the incidence of crime, Forsythe on women and prison and Carrier on the early women police, cited in the endnotes. More recent publications with some useful material, particularly for the period to 1950 include A. Davies and G. Pearson (eds), 'Histories of Crime and Modernity', *British Journal of Criminology*, special issue, 39, 1 (1999); and S. D'Cruze (ed), *Everyday Violence: Gender and Class, c. 1850–c. 1950* (London, 2000). There is useful material in M. Kohn, *Dope Girls: The Birth of the British Drug Underground* (London, 1992). There are several popular biographies of Ruth Ellis. More academic approaches can be found in A. Ballinger, 'The Guilt of the Innocent and the Innocence of the Guilty: The Cases of Marie Fahmy and Ruth Ellis', in A. Myers and S. Wright (eds), *No Angels: Women who Commit Violence* (London, 1996); and D.M. Farran, *The Trial of Ruth Ellis: A Descriptive Analysis* (University of Manchester, Sociology Department, 1988). P. Rawlings, *Crime and Power: A History of Criminal Justice, 1688–1998* (London, 1999) is a useful overview which, while it does not specifically consider women, is not gender-blind. An excellent recent survey of the contemporary issues with some historical perspective is F. Heidensohn, *Women and Crime*, 2nd edn (London, 1996). M. MacGuire *et al.*, *Oxford Handbook of Criminology* (Oxford, 1994), has helpful chapters by Heidensohn on 'Gender and crime', and by Zedner, on 'Victims'. Key feminist texts which can help theorise historical enquiry include C. Smart, *Women, Crime and Criminology: A Feminist Critique* (London, 1976); E.A. Stanko, *Intimate Intrusions: Women's Experience of Male Violence* (London, 1985); R.E. Dobash, and R. Dobash, *Violence Against Wives: A Case Against the Patriarchy* (Shepton Mallet, 1980); and L. Kelly, *Surviving Sexual Violence* (Cambridge, 1988). For data covering the last 30 years see H. Birch (ed), *Moving Targets: Women, Murder and Representation* (London, 1993); B. Hutter and G. Williams (eds), *Controlling Women: The Normal and the Deviant* (London, 1981); and P. Carlen and A. Worrall (eds), *Gender, Crime and Justice* (Buckingham, 1987). Recent crime surveys which provide information on women and victimisation, include T. Jones *et al.*, *The Islington Crime Survey* (London, 1986); and P. Mayhew *et al.*, *The 1988 British Crime Survey* (London, 1989).

Notes

1. HM Chief Inspector of Prisons, *Women in Prison: A Thematic Review* (London: HMSO, 1997), p. 14.

2. J. Pullinger (ed), *Social Focus on Women and Men* (London: HMSO, 1998), p. 70; N. Walker, 'Crime and Penal Measures', in A.H. Halsey (ed), *British Social Trends Since 1900*, 2nd edn (London, 1988), pp. 616–43. Unless otherwise referenced all other statistics are drawn from Walker's article. V.A.C. Gatrell, 'Crime, Authority and the Policeman-State', in F.M.L. Thompson (ed), *The Cambridge Social History of Britain, 1750–1950*, vol. 3: *Social Agencies and Institutions* (Cambridge, 1990), pp. 280–1.

3. M. Feeley and D.L. Little, 'The Vanishing Female: The Decline of Women in the Criminal Process, 1687–1912', *Law and Society Review* 25, 4 (1991), p. 722.

4. M. Clapson, *A Bit of a Flutter: Popular Gambling and English Society, c. 1823–1961* (Manchester, 1992), p. 59.

5. Pullinger, *Social Focus*, p. 71; F. Heindensohn, 'Women and the Penal system', in A. Morris (ed), *Women and Crime: Papers Presented to the Cropwood Round Table Conference* (Cambridge, 1981), p. 127; Lilian Barker, quoted by B. Forsythe, 'Women Prisoners and Women Penal Officials, 1840–1921', *British Journal of Criminology* 33, 4 (1993), p. 535.

6. C. Rowett and P.J. Vaughn, 'Women and Broadmoor: Treatment and Control in a Special Hospital', in B. Hutter and G. Williams (eds), *Controlling Women: The Normal and the Deviant* (London, 1981), p. 131.

7. *Ibid.*, p. 133; B. Lewis and H. Crew (eds), *The Story of a House: Askham Grange Women's Open Prison* (Castleford, 1997), pp. 45, 55, 144; R.J. Simon, *Women and Crime* (Lexington, MA, 1975), p. 100.

8. Quoted in J. Bourke, *Working-Class Cultures in Britain, 1890–1960: Gender, Class and Ethnicity* (London, 1994), p. 71.

9. S. Jeffreys and J. Radford, 'Contributory Negligence or Being a Woman?', in P. Scratton and P. Gordon (eds), *Causes for Concern: Questions of Law and Justice* (Harmondsworth, 1984), p. 161.

10. *Ibid.*, pp. 170–4; J. Gregory and S. Lees, *Policing Sexual Assault* (London, 1999), pp. 100–1.

11. A. Woodeson, 'The First Women Police: A Force for Equality or Infringement?', *Women's History Review* 2, 1 (1993), pp. 228; quoted in J. Carrier, *The Campaign for the Employment of Women as Police Officers* (Aldershot, 1988), p. 212.

12. Quoted in J. Gregory and S. Lees, *Policing Sexual Assault*, p. 35.

14

PROSTITUTION

Paula Bartley and Barbara Gwinnett

Between 1975 and 1981 a lorry driver named Peter Sutcliffe murdered thirteen women and attacked at least seven more mainly in the Leeds/Bradford areas of northern England. Some of these women were prostitutes. Despite six years of police investigations Sutcliffe was arrested by chance when two officers on routine patrol in Sheffield noticed his car had illegal number plates and stopped him for questioning.

Plate 14.1. 'Prostitutes' Dignity'. Protesters led by former Labour minister Maureen Colquhoun gather outside the Old Bailey to protest against the judge's and media's distinction between prostitutes and 'respectable women' during the celebrated Yorkshire Ripper case, May 1982.

One reason why it took the police so long to arrest the killer may have been due to their attitudes towards prostitutes. The police very quickly formed a view that the murderer was a latter-day 'Jack the Ripper' – a killer of prostitutes. There was widespread belief underpinning the police investigations that prostitutes murdered by Sutcliffe (soon dubbed the Yorkshire Ripper) were somehow more deserving of being murdered than other women – often termed by police and press, 'innocent victims'. One officer stated during the investigations: 'He [Sutcliffe] has made it clear that he hates prostitutes. Many people do. We, as a police force, will continue to arrest prostitutes.'[1] In other words, despite the fact that the police believed there was a serial killer operating in their area, they did not extend police protection to women suspected of being likely victims. To their minds, those who had been murdered (i.e. prostitutes), not the murderer, were the real criminals.

These murders raised a number of issues relating to prostitution. They highlighted police attitudes towards prostitutes, they revealed the vulnerability of prostitutes and they engaged the broader women's movement in campaigning to make the streets safe for all women. In effect, the case encouraged feminists to look carefully at the relationship between prostitution and the law. This chapter explores these themes by examining the regulation of prostitution, explanations for its continuation and the relationship between prostitution and other social concerns.

Prostitution and Criminality

The Law

Prostitution itself – the selling of sexual services – has never been illegal in Britain but it has been, and continues to be, a socially stigmatised activity surrounded by so many legal restrictions as to be illegal in all but name. Women remain the objects of scrutiny since prostitution continues to be considered *mainly* a female – not a male – problem. Moreover, there are serious shortcomings in the way the legal system views and treats prostitutes: women remain defined as 'common' prostitute – a label not applied to other categories of offender. It is an adjective resonant with meaning which reveals the underlying attitudes of the law enforcers. Not surprisingly, prostitutes objected to being referred to in this way: 'You go in through a door and everyone's waiting for you. . . . Then they say those awful words: "Being a common prostitute"', complained one in the 1950s.[2]

Throughout most of the twentieth century prostitutes have been arrested, prosecuted and convicted for behaviour which was not an offence if committed by other people. No single law has ever covered prostitution and prostitutes come under a series of miscellaneous provisions contained in local acts dealing with a variety of other offences. For example, the 1847 Town Police Acts, which remained in effect until 1956, fined prostitutes for loitering if they annoyed the local inhabitants or passers-by. It was not an offence for women to be prostitutes, or for prostitutes to loiter; nor was loitering an offence in women who were not prostitutes; loitering was only a crime if committed by known prostitutes and police believed it caused annoyance to others. This law offended one of the fundamental principles of British law: that no previous conviction should be cited in evidence before a trial had taken place in case it prejudiced the court.

At times of national emergencies laws became even more stringent. In both world wars, governments revived a version of the notorious nineteenth-century Contagious Diseases Acts. The government, concerned about the health of its armed forces, passed laws to protect men in the army, navy and air force from venereal disease. In 1918 Regulation 40(d) of the Defence of the Realm Act (DORA) forced any woman to be subjected to medical examination if a member of the Armed Forces stated that she had infected him with venereal disease. During the Second World War the government feared that international relations would be jeopardised if the American troops stationed in Britain caught venereal disease from British prostitutes. In 1942, the Ministry of Health introduced, under DORA, Regulation 33(b) which (once again) compelled women to be examined and treated for venereal disease if two or more infected men named the same individual as the source of their infection. If accused women refused then they could be fined and imprisoned.

Reformers campaigned to give British prostitutes greater legal rights but their endeavours were largely unsuccessful. In 1925 Nancy Astor advocated equality between the sexes and the elimination of the term 'common prostitute' from the legal code. Her efforts, which led to a Department Committee of Inquiry on Street Offences 1927 and several Parliamentary Bills, ultimately failed. The 1948 Criminal Justice Act and the 1951 Criminal Law Amendment Act both gave prostitutes and those associated with them greater human rights but these were short-lived as the next major Acts, the Sexual Offences Act 1956 and the 1959 Street Offences Act marked a return to and consolidation of an already repressive system. In 1985, after almost a century of complaints that the legal system discriminated against women, the Sexual Offences Act was introduced specifically to tackle male kerb crawlers. This Act made it an offence to solicit women for the purposes of prostitution through 'persistent' kerb crawling but it has proved problematic to define 'persistent' and to establish the degree of nuisance caused.

Policing Prostitution

The existence of laws, as Jeffrey Weeks points out, was not 'a guarantee of their punitive usage'[3] since the law, of course, depended largely on the police force and the judicial system to administer it. The police, conscious of the fact that they were accountable to outside bodies, enforced the law differently at various times. In London the Metropolitan police force was under the direct control of the Home Secretary whereas elsewhere police forces were answerable to the local authority. Consequently, the response of the police towards prostitution often depended on the opinions of the ruling national and local political elite. It was also affected by the attitudes of the magistrates, press reaction and the opinions of a more widespread public.

Before the Street Offences Act 1959, police officers were often reluctant to arrest prostitutes for soliciting because of the inconvenience involved:

> Action is attended by much trouble, by very likely a scuffle, by cross-examination by the Station Inspector, by the necessity of making out a written report, by the loss of at least four hours' rest next day at the police court, by risk of blame by the magistrate and of other consequences.[4]

For most of the century the police have felt themselves constrained by the law and its application.

At the beginning of the twentieth century the police remained wary of arresting prostitutes so much so that it was allegedly 'impossible to walk down Piccadilly at that time without molestation'.[5] Understandably, the police felt themselves to be at serious risk of making a mistake, which might involve damage to a rising career in the police service, so that constables would tend not to arrest prostitutes. Metropolitan Police Officers therefore ignored prostitution in case it brought them into conflict with the magistrates, the press, the public and their employers, the Home Office. This was confirmed by the bad publicity received in a number of cases of wrongful arrest in the first half of the century. The public and parliamentary criticism of the police force which ensued made the police very cautious in dealing with prostitutes and prosecution figures dropped dramatically after each public outcry.

By the 1930s police officers, still wary of wrongful arrest, were cautioning women three times before arresting them. In the 1940s the relationship between police and prostitutes was thought to be amicable: the Metropolitan Police allegedly had a rota of arrest, and arrested A on Monday, B on Tuesday, C on Wednesday. Even so, prosecutions remained low. Similarly, the Sexual Offences Act 1956 was not widely enforced by the police due to problems of investigation and gathering evidence.

There was little coherent legal practice since magistrates interpreted the law differently. Some magistrates convicted on the uncorroborated evidence of the police but others refused to pass judgement unless the man solicited gave evidence in Court – an extremely rare occurrence. For example, in places like Brixton, few prostitutes were arrested because magistrates consistently dismissed cases involving soliciting. Other London magistrates were thought to be personally 'erratic in dealing with cases of soliciting and one never knows what attitude he is likely to take in a case coming before him'.[6] Even when a conviction was assured, magistrates often awarded light sentences or small fines.

IN FOCUS: The Wolfenden Report on Homosexual Offences and Prostitution (1954–57)

The Wolfenden Report represents a watershed in twentieth-century sexual legal history and has remained pivotal in policing strategies. It is generally regarded as a liberalising enquiry. This may have been so in respect of homosexuality but this was not the case for prostitution since the resulting legislation (the 1959 Street Offences Act) was more repressive than previous laws. For the first time in British history the 1959 Act allowed women to be convicted for soliciting on the uncorroborated word of a single policeman – the term soliciting covering 'not only spoken words but also various movements of the face, body and limbs such as a smile, a wink, making a gesture and beckoning or wriggling the body in a way that indicates an invitation to prostitution'.

What was it that brought homosexuality and prostitution together into one parliamentary enquiry? By the early 1950s Britain's economy was recovering and expanding in the postwar period. Unprecedented numbers of tourists were visiting London for major public events such as the Festival of Britain in 1951 and the Coronation in 1953. A report commissioned by the British Social Hygiene Council in the late 1940s suggested that public solicitation had increased. Their report was widely circulated in the press and raised prostitution as a matter of public concern. Certainly, police prosecutions increased. All of this provoked a public debate about moral standards which both prostitution and homosexuality allegedly undermined.

We can speculate as to whether prostitution was actually increasing, or just becoming more visible. Indeed, the police may have had more time to patrol the streets and there is no doubt that prosecutions increased in the 1940s and 1950s.[7] Weeks suggests that three key figures – the Director of Public Prosecutions (DPP), the Metropolitan Police Commissioner and the Home Secretary were all fervent moralists who took the opportunity to press for changes in the law.

The Wolfenden Committee, which was composed of three women and twelve men, took evidence from witnesses ranging from chief police officers, psychiatric doctors, social workers, church groups, moral improvement societies to women's organisations, the military and private individuals. Significantly, they also took evidence from the Paddington Moral Reform Council and the Mayfair Association. From a survey of the Wolfenden Papers, there is no doubt that residents from Paddington and Mayfair, areas of London notorious for street prostitution, exerted a great deal of pressure both directly and indirectly on the Wolfenden Committee. The representatives of these local organisations raised a number of issues, including annoyance, disturbance and embarrassment; complaints from foreign embassies and visitors, increased traffic, respectable men and women being accosted; the danger of sub-letting rooms for prostitution and an

The Wolfenden Report on Homosexual Offences and Prostitution (1954–57)
(continued)

increase in drinking clubs. Indeed, one of the key issues for the
committee was how to clear up the streets, the likely consequences of
driving prostitution off the streets and a concern with 'innocent' women.

The Wolfenden Inquiry is generally regarded as a liberalising moment in
the postwar years but it was reluctant to hear evidence from women's groups
with a radical agenda. For example, the National Council of Women of
Great Britain, which was an eminently respectable pressure group, was only
one of two women's groups invited to give evidence. This group argued for
a single, uniform law for men as well as women. They suggested that the
law target the estimated quarter of a million men who visited prostitutes
each week in London rather than the lower numbers of women engaged in
prostitution. The Public Morality Council (an interdenominational church
group) also argued strongly that no one should be convicted of an offence
relating to prostitution unless the 'aggrieved party' gave evidence. They
recognised the demand side of prostitution by calling for a single moral
standard for both parties involved in public soliciting. Changes in the law
based on this premise would indeed have been radical.

Overall, Wolfenden advocated that the law should not intervene in moral
issues; suggested that prostitution be controlled through tighter legislation;
and recommended better policing of the streets to remove public forms
of prostitution. In a prophetic statement, Wolfenden questioned whether
clearing the streets of prostitutes would lead to other, equally problematic,
consequences in ten to fifteen years' time.

The 1959 Street Offences Act eliminated most of the difficulties faced by the
police in curbing prostitution by allowing women to be arrested, prosecuted
and sentenced on the evidence of police officers alone. After two cautions
for soliciting, women could be charged as 'common prostitutes' and, if convicted,
were liable to imprisonment. As a result of this legislation, prostitution moved
off the streets during the 1960s. In London, prostitutes moved to indoor locations: strip clubs; sex shops in Soho; escort agencies; or became call girls. This
inadvertently led to the increased commercialisation of prostitution and brought
it within the orbit of organised crime. In 1982, the Act was amended and fines
were substituted for imprisonment but of course women were imprisoned for
non-payment of fines. Ironically, it had the unintended consequence of keeping
women on the streets since they needed to work to pay off their fines.

In the late twentieth century, police response to prostitution varied. In some
areas prostitutes who broke the law daily by soliciting for business on the streets
of red light areas have been criminalised and harassed by police and local
residents. The actions of pickets in the 1990s in Balsall Heath, Birmingham

drove them from the streets, which not only reinforced their status as an underclass but also sometimes forced them to work in more dangerous locations. However, an initiative in the late 1990s piloted in Nottingham and Wolverhampton considered young prostitutes to be 'victims of abuse and coercion',[8] and referred them to social workers rather than the courts, prosecuting clients and pimps under the Children Act.

Nonetheless, Home Office statistics show that prosecutions of women for soliciting continue to far outweigh the numbers of men prosecuted for kerb crawling which indicates that the police – whatever the legal changes – continue to view women, rather than men, as criminals. This has been confirmed by the 1996 Report of the Parliamentary Group on Prostitution which maintained that men and women were still not considered equal citizens in legal practice since the current laws continued to criminalise women working as prostitutes rather than the men who were involved.

Causes of Prostitution

The reasons why women, even when persecuted, punished and imprisoned, have continued to offer sexual services to men who wish to purchase them are complex. Prostitution was thought to occur from a combination of personal moral weakness, family dysfunction, social injustice and economic inequality. More recently, feminists have moved away from causes within the personality or psychological make-up of individual women, to emphasise social and economic causes and the gendered differences embedded in society. In seeking to identify causes, it is important to bear in mind that 'prostitution' encompasses a range of activities in different locations. Furthermore, any woman has the potential to be a prostitute. There is not space in this chapter to try and single out specific causes for particular forms of prostitution, only to discuss them in the most general terms.

Personal Failure

Rescue workers in the early part of the twentieth century maintained that prostitutes had a wild impulsive nature and a need for independence, which drove them onto the streets. Delegates at the British National Committee for the Suppression of Traffic in Women and Children maintained that some prostitutes 'are constitutionally lazy and have taken to the life in the first instance as an easy way of earning money'.[9] Others, they supposed, were oversexed. The latter point has been challenged by more recent ethnographic research among prostitutes. This latest research shows that, rather than enjoying sex, prostitutes deploy a range of strategies to distance themselves from their clients physically and psychologically.

Drink and/or drugs have long been associated with prostitution. Alcohol was thought to stimulate the 'animal passions' while lowering moral sensibilities thus making sexual promiscuity, if not prostitution, highly likely. The sober prostitute was rarely encountered. By the end of the twentieth century, both drugs and drink are commonly used before working. The issue here is the extent to which drug dependency is a cause of prostitution. Certainly research shows that, once women work as prostitutes and become drug users, they are more likely to work longer hours and take more risks in order to support their own, or their partner's, habit.

Men, Sexism and Patriarchy

Some people blamed men. Male sexual desire was considered to be the root cause of prostitution. Prostitution was thought to be a social necessity since it preserved the virtue of young women and the sanctity of marriage. Sexual desire in men was allegedly overpowering – in the 1930s, George Ryley Scott believed that the sexual appetite of the naturally polygamous male was the real cause of prostitution because 'its existence is due to . . . the selfsame urge as that which actuated the dog hanging around the bitch which is in heat'.[10] Married men and bachelors, who were willing to pay for the means of satisfying their sexual needs, therefore needed prostitutes to avoid pestering their wives too much or their girlfriends at all. The ideology of the male sex drive has remained an important legitimisation for the continuation of prostitution throughout the twentieth century. Indeed, prostitutes were thought to perform a social service for male inadequates who otherwise would not have their needs met: sado-masochists; the impotent; the malformed; and the diseased among them. Functionalist arguments used to justify prostitution, for example that prostitution stops rape, do not hold up under close scrutiny. For instance, the incidence of rape has not declined as prostitution has proliferated. Moreover, such arguments ignore the fact that prostitutes themselves can be (and are) raped by clients.

Both first and second-wave feminists rejected the idea that the allegedly biological masculine sexual drive should be satisfied. The suffragettes who called for male sexual chastity maintained that prostitution was a by-product of the double standard of morality whereby certain designated women sexually serviced men who wished to keep their own sisters, daughters and other female relatives pure. Towards the end of the century a number of modern feminists similarly believed that prostitution epitomised and reinforced men's oppression of women. Radical feminists locate prostitution in the patriarchal structure of society arguing that men pay for sexual services, men control related aspects – as pimps, landlords, drug dealers and organisers of crimes associated with prostitution. And male police officers regulate them all. For feminists such as Carol Pateman prostitution represents another example of men's sexual access to women.[11] Prostitution, along with other forms of the sex industry (pornography, sex shows, etc.), arises out of men's ability to commodify and exploit women's bodies.

Plate 14.2. Two prostitutes leaning out of the window of a brothel in Soho, London, 1956.

Economic Reasons for Prostitution

There is no doubt that prostitution is founded on the poverty of working-class women since there is a direct causal relationship between the low level of women's wages and the recruitment of prostitutes. Even in prosperous times, it was difficult for working-class women to live on their meagre wages, let alone save towards leaner times, so that prostitution remained an attractive possibility. Of course, the inability of women to *find* work was a contributory factor. The interwar years may have given some women new employment opportunities but it closed them down for others as traditional industries, such as the textile trade, declined. If unemployed women turned to prostitution once their savings had been spent, but before they had pawned all their clothes, they could maintain themselves and their home and return to respectability when work became available. By the 1950s it was assumed that the increasing economic prosperity made prostitution unnecessary for women. However the shift from street work-ing to clubs and bars glamorised prostitution and may have inadvertently made it more attractive as illustrated by the Profumo scandal in 1963.

The 1980s saw a rise in women working on the streets again. In this period, general levels of poverty rose with unprecedented rates of unemployment, cuts in welfare benefits and an increase in the number of single-parent families. Employed women were frequently subjected to low pay, part-time and insecure jobs in the service sector. All these factors have led to many groups of women experiencing poverty despite the welfare state.

At the end of the twentieth century, when British women were in a stronger economic position compared to women in the past, prostitution continued. This was because it was based on the inequitable distribution of wealth. It still needed one section of the community, namely men, to have enough surplus money to be able to afford to pay for the sexual services of another section of the community, namely women, who were financially less well off.

Social Reasons for Prostitution

Poverty may have been, and continues to be, the overwhelming reason for prostitution but inadequate wages did not necessarily drive women onto the streets. For the very impoverished, prostitution was never an alternative. Elderly working-class women, desperately poor throughout the twentieth century, rarely became prostitutes however low their incomes might sink. Other very poorly paid women, who may have had the 'opportunity' to become prostitutes, accepted low wages as their lot and acquiesced in their pauperism. Very poor women were generally not driven to prostitution unless they were homeless and without family or friends. In the absence of a welfare state women had to rely upon their families to support them in times of crises. Families could, and did, provide invaluable moral and economic support, as girls who lived at home with caring parents rarely became prostitutes.

Poor biological parenting was certainly blamed for prostitution. Prostitution, it was supposed, resulted from the endemic indecency, which existed among the working class: young girls, brought up by disreputable parents, naturally became sexually promiscuous. In 1934, the British National Committee for the Suppression of Traffic in Women and Children held that 'many of those practising prostitution are from poor and wretched surroundings, in which a low type of morality abounds and poverty prohibits reasonable standards of cleanliness, nourishment and recreation. . . . Some, indeed many more than have been early accustomed to knowledge of vice.'[12] Today, social workers have traced a connection between prostitution and child sexual abuse.

Unsatisfactory home conditions often led to homelessness. Before the First World War, common lodging houses were seen as potential recruiting grounds for prostitutes since men, women and children slept the night, huddled together, often in one bed in these wretched hovels. In the late twentieth century unprecedented levels of homelessness, particularly among young people, have been cited as a potential cause of prostitution. Campaigning groups like Shelter and charities such as Barnardo's have studied the links between child abuse, local authority care, homelessness and prostitution.[13] Residential care homes can be recruiting grounds for pimps to find young girls who can be 'groomed' for prostitution. The removal of 16 and 17 year olds from benefits entitlement in 1988 undoubtedly had an impact on youth homelessness, increasing the number of young people vulnerable to prostitution.

Pornography and Prostitution

In the early part of the twentieth century, pornography was, if not inextricably linked, certainly intimately connected with prostitution. Pornography was thought to foster prostitution and, in turn, was fostered by it. Words, as well as deeds, were thought to undermine morality. Obscene literature, indecent advertising and immoral plays as much as pictorial representations were linked with moral turpitude. Exposure to such literature, it was believed, encouraged sexual incontinence and augmented the pervasive corruption of the day because it created the climate in which immorality thrived. Indecent advertisements, for example, were blamed for inciting immoral thoughts in the minds of impressionable young people which in turn led to immoral actions. For social reformers, there was a definite link between language and action: indecent literature fostered indecent behaviour. The claim that pornography was merely fantasy was rejected since obscene literature was sold in brothels and illustrations of sexual perversity were seen to be part of the stock in trade of prostitutes.

As the century progressed, with the expansion of the sex industry more generally, some feminists questioned the links between prostitution and pornography. Indeed, pornography was seen to empower, rather than degrade, women since it challenged the very sexual conservatism that oppressed them by allowing them to express their own desires. In contrast, other feminists alleged that women involved in pornography were little more than sexual chattels. Pornography, they believed, should not be separated from prostitution as it was part of the same continuum of sexual commodification and exploitation whereby women were objectified to satisfy masculine sexual urges. Prostitution and pornography, Sheila Jeffreys argues, was indivisible: pornography inducted new prostitutes into sexual work whereas women used in pornography were paid, like prostitutes, to have sex with strangers. The sex industry, seen to represent male rather than female sexual values, reflected and consolidated women's subordinate position within society.

Whatever the merits of each of these arguments, it is safe to assume that the sheer magnitude of the pornography trade, with its vast amounts of profit, makes it difficult for governments and legal authorities to keep it in check. The Obscene Publications Act of 1959, anticipating the permissive society of the 1960s, relaxed the publishing laws. As a consequence, government intervention in matters of sexual morality significantly diminished while at the same time there was greater public toleration of what had once been taboo areas. Increasingly violent, and 'hard-core', pornography has superseded the so-called 'soft' pornography of *Playboy* and other magazines. Certainly, what is defined as pornography has changed over the last hundred years as more and more sexually explicit material is thought acceptable. The cultural representation of women in newspapers like the *Sun* would have shocked early twentieth-century society who witnessed the censorship of books by authors (such as D.H. Lawrence) now on secondary school reading lists. Images of women in advertisements, film, the national press and even the *Sunday Times* owe much to what Marcus Collins calls the 'seepage of sex' into all aspects of society, and with it, the increasing sexualisation of misogyny. Pornography, like prostitution, is therefore considered a symptom, rather than a cause, of the objectification of women and their bodies.

Prostitution, 'White Slavery' and Immigration Control

Prostitution has often been blamed on an international trade and in some instances the 'foreign' male. It was maintained that 'foreign' men decoyed young British girls with bribes of money or else procured them for brothels by pretending to recruit them for respectable jobs. The nature of the 'foreigner' interestingly changed over time. At the beginning of the twentieth century, Jewish men were accused of managing prostitution, in the 1940s and 1950s the Maltese were believed to be the main offenders whereas in the 1980s and 1990s Afro-Caribbean men were associated with prostitution. Of course, evidence of these links was often dubious and based on racialised stereotypes.

Not surprisingly, prostitution has been allied to immigration control. One of the most important pieces of legislation to be passed as a result of social purity, and indeed eugenic, pressure was the Aliens Act of 1905. This was passed to limit the number of Jewish immigrants fleeing from the pogroms of Russia entering Britain, and included a clause which allowed the expulsion of 'improper and scandalous foreigners'. Immigration officials could refuse entry to any person judged (by them) to be immoral and gave magistrates the right to expel those convicted of soliciting, living upon the results of prostitution or of keeping immoral houses.

As well as targeting 'foreign' men, several international conferences to combat 'white slavery' were organised. In 1902, sixteen countries ratified an International Convention for the Suppression of the White Slave Trade Traffic. This aimed to appoint specially trained officials to keep a watchful eye at railway stations and ports; to question known prostitutes of foreign origin about the ways in which they were recruited; and to keep a surveillance over employment agencies professing to find work for women. The League of Nations, formed after the First World War, and the United Nations, formed after the Second World War, both took up the question of international prostitution and set up various agencies to help combat it.

In the period following the Second World War, the links between prostitution, immigration and crime continued to be made explicit. Caught up in the notorious case of the Messina brothers,[14] Maltese settlers in Britain were closely identified with organised prostitution, particularly in London. From 1955 to 1964 prosecutions of Maltese for living on immoral earnings in London were disproportionately high compared to other migrant groups or their British counterparts.

In the late 1950s the public and political discourse increasingly framed immigration control in the context of the alleged involvement of migrants and immigrants in prostitution. Pimping, in particular, served as a legitimisation for racist discourse and arguments for tighter immigration control. Apart from the involvement of Maltese, there is little evidence of systematic, organised prostitution rackets involving immigrants. A study of policing and race relations in Birmingham's red light district, found little evidence that newly arrived immigrants – whether Afro-Caribbean or South Asian – were disproportionately involved in prostitution. Thus the public discourses reflect the growing politicisation of immigration control and prostitution served as another moral panic around which such debates could be constructed. Indeed, by the time of the 1965 White Paper on immigration control, the government's own research found that immigrants had a lower crime rate than their white counterparts and there were no grounds for specifically connecting them to prostitution.

In the 1980s concern about trafficking in women was renewed in both the European Union and the United Nations. The growing international sex industry and sex tourism caused widespread alarm. In 1989 the European Parliament issued a resolution on the exploitation of prostitutes and the traffic in people. In 1991 the Council of Europe held a seminar on 'forced prostitution and trafficking'.[15] European concern has also been raised in relation to women moving from former Eastern European countries into the European Union to work in prostitution following political instability in their home countries. This movement of women is further complicated by immigration controls in European Union countries so that, with the increasingly restrictive immigration policies of richer countries, the traffic in women tends to become more and more an issue of illegal or 'unorderly' migration. The point is that women who enter a country illegally, with the promise of work, are vulnerable to threats that their illegal status will be reported if they do not enter prostitution. Indeed the report emphasised the problem of defining coercion and the extent to which entry into prostitution is forced.

Conclusion

Unquestionably, there have been important shifts in sexual morality over the twentieth century. Women were no longer condemned for being sexually active and more and more couples preferred to live together rather than cement their relationship in marriage. One might imagine that with the advent of the birth control pill, combined with the 'sexual revolution' of the 1960s, prostitution would have diminished. This has not been the case and prostitution continued to flourish in Britain. Of course, the sexual revolution was swiftly followed by women's liberation which, because it encouraged women to demand their own sexual satisfaction, may have undermined male hopes of free unconditional sex. Paying for sex allows men to avoid worrying about their own sexual performance since the only demand that is made on them is a financial one.

This 'sexual revolution' did not significantly affect attitudes towards the prostitute population. Parallels can certainly be drawn between prostitution at the beginning of the century and at the end. For prostitutes, the twentieth century has been a century of persecution either in the name of public health, morality, public order or national expediency. Thousands of women and girls have been arrested, prosecuted, fined, imprisoned and accused of spreading venereal disease or AIDS. The men who use them or who benefit from their work in other ways continued, for the most part, to be free to do so.

The new millennium, however, may augur significant changes since there has been a discernible shift in police attitudes towards younger prostitutes in particular. Police officers prosecuted the men who attempted to buy the sexual services of younger prostitutes. This not only benefited the young prostitute who was 'looked after' by social welfare workers but it also produced tangible social and economic benefits that far outweighed the policing costs involved. Certainly, the cost of policing prostitution was repaid by savings in the costs of policing other criminal activities, notably drug dealing and theft as well as improving social order more generally. Eventually the British law may begin to reflect these changes in policing strategies and maybe not just tackle prostitution but tackle what feminists believe to be the fundamental cause of prostitution – men's desire to buy sex. A punitive approach towards prostitutes has, historically, not diminished the supply of prostitutes: stopping the demand might.

Not everyone believes prostitution is a problem. On the contrary, a number of feminists and others prefer to use the term 'sex-worker' for women who service men's sexual needs. Those who regard prostitutes as sex-workers consider prostitution to be legitimate work and believe that prostitutes have made some sort of choice to work in the 'sex industry'. As a consequence, rather than call for the elimination of prostitution, these groups campaign for better working conditions for women working as prostitutes.

Finally, it is interesting to compare prostitution to other aspects of women's experiences in the twentieth century. For the most part, there have been some significant improvements in women's economic, social and cultural status. However, set against the gains achieved by women in general, prostitution remained resolutely imbued with most of the negative connotations which existed at the start of the century.

Bibliographical Note

Although there has been little academic research published about the early twentieth-century history of prostitution both J. Weeks, *Sex, Politics and Society: The Regulation of Sexuality since 1800* (London, 1989); and S. Jeffries, *The Idea of Prostitution* (Melbourne, 1997) place their work in historical context. C. Haste, *Rules of Desire* (London, 1992) which details the major sexual trends in Britain from 1914 until the early 1990s is not only a good read but makes some interesting points. M. Collins, 'The Pornography of Permissiveness', *History Workshop Journal* 47 (Spring 1999) is very useful. The later twentieth century has been well documented. Two classic ethnographic studies of prostitution are E. McLeod, *Women Working: Prostitution Now* (London, 1982); and N. McKeganey and M. Barnard, *Sex Work on the Streets* (Buckingham, 1996).

Notes

1. J. Smith, *Misogynies* (London, 1989), p. 127.

2. *Empire News*, 21 January 1955.

3. J. Weeks, *Sex, Politics and Society: The Regulation of Sexuality since 1800* (London, 1989), p. 219.

4. Public Record Office, Kew (hereafter PRO), MEPO 2/8835, *Confidential Memorandum on Prostitution and Solicitation*, 1906.

5. House of Commons, 13 July 1900, p. 1539.

6. PRO, MEPO 2/2290, *Vine Street Station Memorandum*, 12 August 1924.

7. *Guardian*, 29 December 1998, p. 5.

8. PRO, HO 345/6, Evidence to the Wolfenden Enquiry.

9. British National Committee for the Suppression of Traffic in Women and Children, Westminster, London, 1934.

10. George Ryley Scott, *A History of Prostitution* (London, 1936), p. 17.

11. C. Pateman, *The Sexual Contract* (Cambridge, 1988).

12. British National Committee for the Suppression of Traffic in Women and Children, Westminster, London, 1934.

13. For example see reports such as *The Game's Up* (the Children's Society), 1996; Barnardo's report into child sex abuse in Bradford, *Guardian*, 21 August 1996.

14. The Messina Brothers were prosecuted between 1945 and 1951 for living on immoral earnings. They were reputed to run organised prostitution in London's West End. Although of Italian/Maltese origin, and having come to Britain from Egypt, the Messina Brothers were identified by the press as being Maltese. This undoubtedly added to the already growing reputation of Maltese settlers as involved in prostitution through cafés in the East End. See PRO, HO 345/12, Evidence to Wolfenden Inquiry papers.

15. Internet site: http://home.pi.net/-notraf/backgr/preface.htm.

15

LEISURE AND POPULAR CULTURE

Martin Francis

The twentieth century has seen significant increases in the leisure time available to both sexes, but this development has benefited men far more than women. While men were rewarded for higher productivity in the workplace by a shorter working week and longer holiday entitlements, household responsibilities limited women's scope for leisure and recreation. In working-class communities in the first half of the century men had spending money which could be freely devoted to leisure, but women were forced to take money for entertainment out of the housekeeping budget. Spending money on going to the cinema seemed self-indulgent to women who were responsible for feeding, housing and clothing their families.

In a 1930s survey of working-class wives, Margery Spring Rice found that women with large families were effectively prisoners in their own homes. Some mothers did receive support from elder daughters, and some men were willing to look after the household while their wife went out in the evening. However the oral testimony of Lancashire women in the interwar period, collected by Elizabeth Roberts and Andrew Davies, reveals that there were strong levels of disapproval directed at women who put personal pleasure before the welfare of their families. In Manchester and Salford in the 1920s and 1930s this outlook was institutionalised through the custom of 'bucket night', during which even young women were expected to stay home and clean hearths and pavements.[1]

After the Second World War rising living standards and the proliferation of new labour-saving devices seemed to offer the possibility of increased female leisure time. Indeed it has been estimated that both employed women and housewives saw their leisure time increase by half an hour a day or more between 1961 and 1984. However in the same period, while employed working men's hours fell by 10 per cent, the fall for employed women was only 4 per cent, and there was no decrease at all for women in part-time jobs. This data is highly significant, given the increased participation of women in the labour force since the 1950s. And of course, for women in paid employment, time after work was rarely free, since they usually had to prepare meals and put children to bed. Even when poverty was not acting as a major constraint on women's leisure, time (or, more accurately, the lack of it) remained a limiting factor.

Leisure in the Home: Reading

Given that women's lives were restricted by time, money and contemporary conventions about a 'woman's place', it is not surprising that what little leisure time women were able to secure was spent in the home and directly tied to their domestic responsibilities. Spring Rice noted that women were likely to name sewing, knitting or darning as their most common leisure pursuits. Such activities have remained an important feature of female leisure throughout the century, for the 1999 issue of *Social Trends* found 37 per cent of women claimed to sew or knit. While men were much more likely than women to dedicate time to home improvement and household repairs, women's and men's home-based leisure activities in general have not been markedly different. In 1997, 99 per cent of both women and men said they watched tv, 87 per cent of women and 90 per cent of men listened to the radio, while 71 per cent of women and 58 per cent of men read books.[2] Gardening was also popular with both men and women. This is not surprising given the legacy of Edwardian female garden designers Gertrude Jekyll and Vita Sackville-West or the popularity of tv gardener Charlie Dimmock in the 1990s. This evidence confirms the notion of a domesticated and companionate male, happy to spend his free time in the home relaxing with his wife and children, but it obscures the different contexts in which male and female leisure operated. Housewives were much more likely to have to abandon reading or watching television to deal with household responsibilities than their husbands. Employed men's domestic labour only increased from 74 minutes per day in 1961 to 98 minutes per day in 1984, which suggested their household leisure was only rarely interrupted by cooking, cleaning or baby feeding. In her 1907 survey of the reading habits of Middlesbrough workers, Lady Bell noted that 'the workman reads, as a rule, more than his wife . . . because he has more definite times of leisure in which he feels he is amply justified in "sitting down with a book"'.[3]

Moreover, even if men and women both read, it was likely they read different types of literature. The exception was newspaper reading, where class was more likely to be the major determinant of choice than gender, the Hulton Readership survey of 1947 revealing negligible differences in the newspapers read by husbands and wives. However, when it came to books or journals, there were of course certain literary genres – the 'woman's novel' or 'romance novel' and the woman's magazine – whose target audience was gender-specific (although it has often been observed that substantial numbers of men read their partners' magazines).

Women's popular reading has received extensive attention from feminist scholars and cultural theorists in recent decades. Initially most of these studies were highly critical, particularly of the romance, which appeared to promote masterful masculinity and submissive femininity. Left-wing critics condemned the way such novels presented a cosy and escapist vision of the world in which love was a substitute for class conflict and the redistribution of economic power. However in recent years a new generation of scholars has argued for a more nuanced understanding of the romance, suggesting that romantic plots were more complicated than might first appear and that left-wing criticism reflected both elitism and a puritanical fear of pleasure. Others have used psychological methodologies to argue that the reader's relationship with a text is not simply one of compliant passivity. Elizabeth Frazer's survey of female readers in the late 1980s revealed how women, when talking about magazines, parody and mimic them, fully aware of their status as fantasy rather than social realism.[4]

The complex relationship between reader and text was further elaborated by the dialogue between different women readers. Popular romances and magazines were often shared between women, and their plots interrogated and judged. During the Second World War, female factory workers were to be found debating the merits of Margaret Mitchell's best-seller *Gone With the Wind*, and bemoaning its ambiguous concluding scene. Far from legitimising the status quo, popular romance could potentially challenge it. In the austerity years of the 1940s, popular romance celebrated escapism and self-expression of the libido at a time when the government was keen to promote the self-discipline necessary for a successful prosecution of the war effort and postwar reconstruction. Historians have attempted to build on these developments in cultural studies and literary criticism, and are beginning to demonstrate that not merely are the messages of women's magazines and novels multi-dimensional, but that they are also historically contingent, and reflect changing representations of femininity and masculinity throughout the century.

Having said this, some commentators have been quick to point out that the main ingredients of twentieth-century women's magazines were already in place in 1900. A cursory glance through copies of the top-selling women's magazines of that year (*Home Chat*, *Woman At Home* and *The Gentlewoman*) would reveal short stories and romantic serials, articles on housewifery, family relationships and childcare, recipes, fashion tips, the letters pages dealing with 'personal problems', gossip columns, illustrated articles on royalty and celebrities, advertisements for beauty products, home furnishings and domestic utility goods. However such continuity was interwoven with change. While the convention of the letters page remains unaltered, with an expert offering advice to individual readers, the subjects discussed have shifted from being largely concerned with etiquette in the Edwardian era to marital relationships in the 1950s and sexual technique in the 1980s and 1990s. The tone of the 'aunts' has also become less authoritarian and judgemental, and more democratic and permissive. Leonora Eyles, despite being one of the most progressive agony aunts during her time on *Woman's Own* in the 1940s, was still very rigid in her views on what constituted wifely duty, testily admonishing wives who dared complain about their domestic burdens, suggesting women forgive unfaithful husbands, but unequivocally condemning female sexual incontinence. By contrast in the 1980s, Irma Kurtz of *Cosmopolitan* advised women to be unapologetic in their search for sexual pleasure and compatible relationships.

In the first three decades of the century the market for women's magazines was highly fragmented, publishers believing that Britain's class structure precluded the market uniformity necessary for a mass-market magazine. The arrival of *Woman* in 1937 marked a significant departure, aimed as it was at a cross-section of women, and with a circulation of 3.5 million copies by the 1950s. From the late 1940s women's magazine publishing became a giant economic enterprise, especially after the monopolistic takeover of much of the industry by the International Publishing Corporation (IPC). The bubble burst in the late 1950s, and total circulation of women's magazines fell from 50 million in the early 1960s to 24 million in 1984. In this dramatically reduced market, publishers in the 1960s attempted to modernise their products, *Good Housekeeping*, for example, emphasising home furnishing and haute cuisine rather than embroidery and knitting. How far this modernisation was accompanied by an increased salience of feminist perspectives is not entirely clear. *Good Housekeeping* and *Everywoman* had in the interwar period carried serious articles of interest to women as citizens, some of them written by feminists like Rebecca West and Lady Rhondda, but in the postwar decades commercial considerations meant these were replaced by an almost exclusively consumerist content. As a result, when *Nova* appeared in 1965, with its appeal to educated and lively-minded women, it was able to convince itself that it was a breakthrough in women's publishing. Post-1960s magazines such as *Cosmopolitan* (1972) celebrated the liberated woman, but their progressive and feminist credentials were rather thin. *Cosmopolitan* still presented women as objects of male desire (not surprisingly since it incorporated the discourse of male-authored 1960s sex manuals) and emphasised sexual difference rather than sexual inequality.

The romantic novel had been a feature of female reading since the eighteenth century, but its success in the twentieth century was assured by the rationalisation and commodification of publishing. The appearance of the paperback, pioneered by Allen Lane in the 1930s, was a critical, but not the sole, factor here. In fact the most well-known publisher of romance fiction since the 1920s, Mills and Boon, was an exclusively hardcover imprint until the 1960s. Mills and Boon exploited the growth between the wars of 'tuppenny' lending libraries, which catered to lower middle-class and working-class women who had felt uncomfortable going to public libraries, with their preference for 'highbrow' and 'improving' literature. This is not to say that romances were only read by the poor or uneducated: Mills and Boon titles were a staple of Harrod's circulating library in the 1930s and 1940s. The decline in library users since the 1960s has been offset by the growth of paperback publishing, and in 1985 Mills and Boon sold 20 million books in Britain.

Popular romance is inevitably highly formulaic – largely concerned with finding a potential husband – but emphases did change during the century. In the period immediately after the First World War the popularity of the so-called 'sex novel' agitated sections of the press into a moral panic. Best-selling novels such as Michael Arlen's *The Green Hat* (1924) and Margaret Kennedy's *The Constant Nymph* (1924) all had contemporary young women as their heroines and concerned themselves with issues of modern sexual morality. The violent plot of E.M. Hull's *The Sheik* (1919), in which a young Englishwoman is abducted by a Bedouin prince, whom she comes to love, but only after he has raped her, might appear to offer sado-masochism as a substitute for eroticism. However, as Billie Melman has argued, *The Sheik* does recognise and legitimise female sexuality, and 'the Englishwoman who is ravished in the Sahara does not virtuously die but lives to enjoy a blissful state of concubinage'.[5]

Nevertheless this exploration of female sensuality still satisfied the requirements of propriety by having sexual bliss take place in a faraway exotic location. Mills and Boon were keen to avoid accusations of immorality and editors rigorously enforced their wholesome formula, in which women remained virgins until marriage. However purity did not imply prudishness. Barbara Cartland, who published her first romance in 1923 and went on to produce over 500 titles, used her texts to condemn modern morals and celebrate passive femininity. When a changing world made her plots appear outdated, she abandoned contemporary romance for historical narratives, and all her novels after 1948 were set in the period 1790–1914.

Mills and Boon, by contrast, prided itself in being more contemporary, and indeed in the 1930s most of its authors were women in their early 30s who were in touch with the sensibilities of their readers and sympathetic to the single working life. The typical heroine's ambition was homebuilding, but through a companionate marriage. Mills and Boon offered escapism, but within a relatively familiar environment. Their heroines were to be found working in a suburban office or shop rather than partying in Mayfair or travelling in the desert and, as George Orwell quipped, were more likely to marry a bank manager than an earl. In the 1930s a belated revulsion against the slaughter of the First World War made the brutality of *The Sheik* less appealing, and exotic settings were less popular in a period when national identity had become less imperial and more domestic (in all senses of the term). This 'suburbanisation' of the romance from the 1930s could be presented as the triumph of bourgeois values.

The romance novel has promoted a variety of social perspectives. The works of Catherine Cookson, one of Britain's most popular romantic novelists between the 1950s and the 1980s, were set amid the Durham coalfields of the nineteenth century, and had strongly drawn working-class heroines. Daphne Du Maurier's *Rebecca* (1938), the classic middlebrow version of the genre, has the bourgeois values of its narrator challenged by the attractions of an alternative, aristocratic (and sexually uninhibited) conception of femininity, in the form of the (deceased) first Mrs de Winter. Since the 1960s romances have become more sexually explicit and have tried to present a less passive vision of women. One of the leading best-sellers of the 1980s, Barbara Taylor Bradford's *A Woman of Substance* told the story of an assertive and ambitious female entrepreneur, whose rugged individualism and conspicuous consumption accorded with the Thatcherite values of that decade. The popular romance therefore suggests

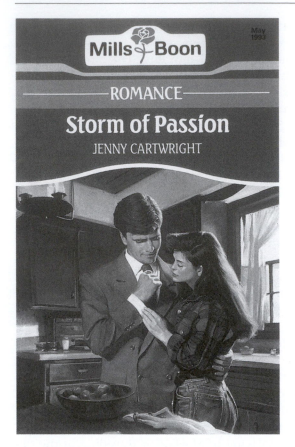

Plate 15.1. A Mills and Boon cover from 1993. Note the everyday and familiar setting, which is typical of the Mills and Boon romance.

both the continuities and the transformations in female lives and their representation since 1900.

Radio and Television

The status of reading as one of the dominant leisure activities for women in the home was challenged by the arrival of radio in the 1920s and television from the 1950s. Given the domestic focus of women's lives, these new home-based media were often shaped to appeal specifically to women. In the 1920s radio was largely a male hobby, weak signals and low-quality valves requiring an emphasis on tinkering with the equipment rather than the pleasure of listening. This situation changed in the 1930s as reception improved and the radio became a new focus for family entertainment. Housewives found listening to the radio could be combined with domestic labour, and producers of daytime radio conceptualised their normative audience as female and housebound.

Interviewed in 1973 the BBC daytime disk jockey David Hamilton patronisingly visualised his typical listener as 'a young woman, a housewife.... She's probably on her own virtually all day. She's bored with the routine of house-work and with her own company and for her I'm the slightly cheeky romantic visitor.'[6] In fact BBC audience research figures in the 1970s found that, while housewives constituted the largest single category of listeners, they were by no means a majority, and that daytime radio was also popular with students and men in the workplace. Despite the serious under-representation of women as producers in the BBC and commercial radio, radio as a medium has offered some space for the expression and serious discussion of women's issues. *Woman's Hour*, first broadcast by the BBC in 1946, had an all-woman team of presenters and producers, although it tended to neutralise contentious issues by surrounding them with traditional topics such as fashion or cooking. Radio drama has attracted a large number of women writers, possibly because of the personal, private voice which the medium offers. However feminist critics have suggested that phone-in and medical advice programmes, which mushroomed in the 1970s and 1980s, often reinforced images of helpless women requiring guidance from male experts.

Television was for much of the postwar period watched by families together, not least because it was rare before the 1980s for a household to possess more than one set. Until the 1970s programming was confined to the evenings and the number of channels available was limited, even after the arrival of ITV in 1955. Whether men or women exercised ultimate control over what was watched is impossible to establish conclusively, but it would be difficult to argue that women's specific preferences were ignored. Given the genre's preference for private and familial concerns over the male-dominated world of public affairs, it is not surprising that the persistent presence of the television soap opera in audience figures since the 1950s has frequently been attributed to its popularity with female viewers.

The longest-running British television soap opera, the Salford-set *Coronation Street* (first broadcast on ITV in 1959), celebrated proud and resilient working-class women, while ridiculing the men in their lives as slow-witted fools. Else-where however women were frequently stereotyped as passive housewives or sex objects, and some of the most lauded and innovative television programming – *Monty Python* in the early 1970s and Denis Potter's dramas in the 1980s – were sexist, if not openly misogynist. The explosive growth in satellite and cable channels since the early 1990s makes it even more difficult to generalise about televisual representations of women in the last decade, but the precarious status of women in these media appears to have been confirmed by the mushrooming of the coverage of male sports and by accusations of 'laddism' directed at novelty-based quiz shows such as *Have I Got News for You* and *They Think It's All Over*.

Leisure Outside the Home: Drinking and Sport

The uneven and complex impact of the commercialisation of leisure on women is also evident in regard to activities outside the home. Gender divisions were highly significant, but were not always universal. Recent studies of male leisure have emphasised the resilience, especially in poorer areas, of traditional, informal and communal forms of leisure (particularly those associated with drinking) throughout the years up to the Second World War. This claim can be applied with equal justification to women, although their participation in the world of the pub was much more qualified and circumscribed than it was for men. However the image of male indulgence and female exclusion is a stereotype which obscures a variety of experiences.

Rowntree estimated in the late 1930s that 26 per cent of the pub customers in the poorer parts of York were women, and he was convinced (and horrified) that the levels of female drinking had actually increased since 1900. Some women only drank if they were taken to the pub as a 'treat' by their husbands, but on entering the pub it was not uncommon for them to split up, the wife choosing the lounge bar, her husband the taproom or vault. This gender segregation in bars was relatively common until the 1970s, when it was undermined by the transformation of many pubs into what might be more accurately labelled informal licensed restaurants. However even in the interwar years some women drank independently, albeit usually in moderation and sometimes only on special occasions such as holidays or birthdays.

Like the pub, organised sport was a highly masculine environment, but again one in which female marginalisation did not necessarily imply absolute exclusion. This is not to deny that, in the words of Richard Holt, 'in modern Britain sport has been one of the ways that men have kept themselves apart',[7] and (both in terms of participation and spectatorship) sport has been an important mechanism in male sociability and the maintenance of masculine identity (whether of the 'gentlemanly' or the 'popular' variety). Sport's identification with masculine exclusivity explains why Edwardian suffragettes directed many of their actions against the sporting establishment. In 1913 one suffragette was charged with attempted arson after being apprehended at night on Wimbledon's centre court, and in the same year Emily Wilding Davison was killed after throwing herself under the king's horse during the Derby. However the increasing prevalence of Darwinian ideas and fears of racial and national degeneration in the late Victorian and Edwardian eras led to a growing acceptance that sport should be accessible to both sexes. Team games were an important part of the education offered to upper middle-class women in the newly founded women's colleges at the universities of London, Cambridge and Oxford.

Outside such privileged social enclaves, women's participation in sport was more difficult, but by the Edwardian period women were already making progress, especially in those sports which were less associated with male physicality: archery and croquet initially, then tennis and golf, followed eventually by cycling and hockey. Women's participation in these sports exploded myths of female frailty and fears that physical activity would 'masculinise' women. Sport gave middle-class women a greater sense of freedom and autonomy, and activities such as cycling allowed women to circumvent surveillance away from the confining atmosphere of the drawing room. Indeed sport was an important motif in representations of the 'new woman' of the 1890s and 1900s, with her emphasis on energy and activity rather than the mid-Victorian ideal of delicacy and lassitude.

The role of sport in the emancipation of women should not be exaggerated. Team games were acceptable at school or college, but less so for adult women. Hockey was for most of the century the only credible women's team sport, and women's attempts to enter the worlds of soccer and cricket were scorned out of existence. For example the Women's Cricket Association, founded in 1926, failed to attract interest outside the products of a few elite private schools, and the lack of support given to women's soccer by the Football Association was reflected in the failure of England to qualify for the 1999 Women's World Cup. Early women athletes accepted that they would be judged on their appearance rather than their performance, and found that acceptability was conditional on maintaining the requisites of femininity, hence the persistence of cumbersome costumes which inhibited prowess and skill, but which safeguarded modesty.

Female sports subtly reinforced orthodox views on a woman's place. Women's post-college sports were rooted in a new suburban culture centred around the family gardens of tree-lined avenues or the private golf club. Tennis was particularly popular among the interwar middle classes, but it was identified much more with sociability and courtship than with competition: women were encouraged to play, but were discouraged from being too good at it! The association between tennis and traditional femininity was also obvious in the press coverage in the 1920s of such female stars as Joan Austin, Evelyn Colyer and Kitty Godfree, whose photographs were as likely to be found in the social and fashion pages as they were in the sports section. Tennis was unusual in being played by women and men together, and those who advocated female physical recreation usually found it expedient to accept, and encourage, gender segregation: hence the emergence by the 1920s of the archetypal 'games mistress' in schools.

Athletics was initially seen as inappropriate for women and female participation in the Olympics was restricted to figure skating and swimming before 1914. Women began to undertake a broader range of athletic events after the First World War, but as late as 1960 only 18 per cent of Britain's Olympic competitors were women, a figure which was still as low as 36 per cent in 1988. Surveys completed in the 1980s reveal that Britain had one of the lowest female sports participation rates in the Western world (about a third of all women, as opposed to a half of all men). This is perhaps not surprising given the continued undervaluation of women's sports and the exclusion of sport from the 1975 Sex Discrimination Act. Similarly women failed to benefit from the increase in government funding for sport in the 1980s, which was intended to ameliorate unemployment and crime, and was therefore largely targeted at young males.

Cinema and Youth Culture

For much of the century female sport was largely a middle-class activity, demanding resources and time which working-class women rarely possessed. Going to the cinema, by contrast, was a form of recreation available to most women. In the interwar years the majority of those adults (in some towns as many as 75 per cent) who went to 'the pictures' were female, not merely young women but also married housewives, fitting in a matinée between shopping and collecting the children. The Mass-Observation survey of Bolton cinema-goers in 1938 found that, while crime films were more popular with men, and history or love stories with women, the preferences of male and female audiences generally coincided. Both men and women listed musical romance and drama as their first choice. And both sexes also showed a marked preference for Hollywood over British films.[8]

Cinema was closely related to other aspects of women's lives, especially fashion and beautification, as J.B. Priestley's oft-quoted lament about 'factory girls looking like actresses' in the 1930s testified.[9] However, while female cinema audiences responded eagerly to the escapism and glamour of the Hollywood heroine, it was also true that American films were popular because in them viewers saw their own reality, albeit in an exotic form. British films, by contrast, were frequently derided for their social conservatism and drawing-room settings. Significantly, the only two British women who attained 'star' status before the Second World War were Betty Balfour and Gracie Fields, actresses who played working-class heroines.

Feminists, utilising psychological methodologies, have drawn attention to the complexity of women's relationship to cinema as a cultural artefact. Cultural theorists have long discussed women in terms of their status as 'objects' of the male gaze, but cinema obviously offers women the possibility to act as a 'subject' as well, through their participation in the act of watching a movie. The normative dichotomy between male voyeurism and female exhibition is therefore dislocated by the presence of this 'female gaze'. Historians have begun to make use of these theoretical techniques to show that the images of women presented on screen were highly ambiguous, and open to a variety of different readings, as illustrated by the case study on women in Second World War cinema. The possibility of a specifically female reading of the cinematic text appears even more intriguing when it is remembered that most of those involved in the production, as opposed to the content and consumption, of film, were male. There were prominent women producers in the early days of British cinema, notably the former stage actress Ruby Miller, and in the 1940s and 1950s Muriel Box directed a number of acclaimed motion pictures. However female producers and directors were rare, Box appropriately calling her autobiography *Odd Woman Out*, and even the classic women's melodramas of the Gainsborough studios were created by a largely male team of Maurice Ostrer, Arthur Crabtree and Leslie Arliss.

IN FOCUS: Representations of Women in Second World War Cinema

Social historians have in the last decade been sceptical about the degree of change in women's lives brought about by the Second World War. The mobilisation of women into industry and the armed services failed to break down sexual segregation in the workplace, and the failure to secure equal pay reflected the extent to which the citadels of male privilege remained intact. The war reinforced rather than challenged the dominant codes of femininity, domesticity and pronatalism, and women (either through official pressure or personal choice) generally conformed to the traditional ideal of the domestic wife and mother.

British wartime cinema reveals the ambiguities which characterise visual representations of women in the 1940s. While officially sponsored film about women's war work deliberately encouraged female mobilisation, at the same time they were obliged to reassure male audiences that gender roles would not be substantially changed by women's participation in the workforce. The female anti-aircraft crew in *The Gentle Sex* (1943) and the female munitions workers in *Millions Like Us* (1943) retained the signifiers of conventional femininity: they were still concerned about clothes, beautification and the need to find a man to love and support them. Films aimed at middle-class audiences such as *Brief Encounter* (1945) broached the subject of marital infidelity, which had been rendered topical by the social and psychological upheavals of war. However such films also tried to enforce an aesthetic of restraint, in which American-style glamour and artificiality was renounced in favour of simplicity and realism. *Brief Encounter*'s emphasis on 'ordinary lives' and its deglamorised female leading character – Laura Jesson – repudiated spectacle and display, thereby stigmatising the extravagant appearance of Hollywood heroines. Moreover Laura and her lover Alec decide not to consummate their relationship, the latter choosing instead to start a new life with his wife and family in South Africa, while asserting 'The feeling of guilt, of doing wrong, is too strong, isn't it?'

By contrast the costume melodramas produced by the Gainsborough studios – *The Man In Grey* (1943), *Madonna of the Seven Moons* (1944) and *The Wicked Lady* (1945) – were far from restrained, with their independent-minded, sexually adventurous heroines, flamboyant costumes and revealing *décolletage*. However even within this genre the ambiguities surrounding female representation were still present. While women audiences were in theory free to identify with Lady Barbara in *The Wicked Lady* as she eschewed domesticity for the life of a female highwayman, the film ultimately reminded them that such 'deviancy' would not go unpunished, for Barbara ends up being killed. The same fate awaits Maddalena, the heroine of *Madonna of the Seven Moons*, who leaves her comfortable Italian aristocratic family for a life of crime and adultery among a group of gypsy cut-throats.

Representations of Women in Second World War Cinema (continued)

Plate 15.2. Margaret Lockwood as Lady Barbara in *The Wicked Lady* (1945). The extravagant costume and hairstyles of the film were a welcome antidote to the austerity of the 1940s.

Moreover Maddalena's behaviour is attributed (significantly by male authority figures – her husband and her doctor) to her suffering from schizophrenia. In other words her exhibition of independence, far from being condoned, is, in fact, pathologised.

Sue Harper suggests that the Gainsborough melodramas could be read by their female viewers as radical texts, presenting the past as a site of female sexual pleasure.[10] The gorgeous costumes of *The Wicked Lady*, for example, were not intended to arouse and satisfy male desire, but were an expression of female erotic power and fulfilment. Certainly it is not difficult to imagine the appeal of such lavish apparel and scandalous story lines to women who, faced with rationing, shortages and austerity, found little glamour and excitement in the world around them. In the postwar years this potential conflict between the self-discipline required for the building of the 'New Jerusalem' and the expressive libido celebrated in the melodrama became even more acute. By 1949 the genre had virtually disappeared, and subsequently there were few British films with strong-willed and sexually adventurous heroines. In the 1950s the paradigmatic British movie was the war film which celebrated the emotional inexpressivity and homosocial world of the male officer class.

The history of leisure has frequently been yoked to the development of a distinct 'youth culture', which was already present in embryonic form in the street gangs of Edwardian Britain, but which first came to prominence in the lifestyles of young wage-earners in the 1930s. In the postwar years, youth culture was given a more heightened sense of identity by the emergence of rock and roll music, and from the 1960s by the expansion of further and higher education. Unfortunately, while cultural anthropologists and historians have examined youth sub-cultures in some depth, many of these studies have been effectively gender-blind. Assertions about women's status in youth culture are often based on impressionistic or anecdotal evidence. It is certainly true that, while concerns about juvenile delinquency were largely focused on the male adolescent, anxiety about the 'Americanization' of Britain and the decline of authentic working-class culture was also likely to be focused on young women – the hard-drinking, smoking and sexually promiscuous 'good time girls' of the late 1940s or the 'girl gangs' of the 1950s.

The countercultural possibilities of youth culture, and pop music in particular, were usually not extended to challenge traditional gender roles. Rock music from the late 1960s celebrated a masculine variety of heroism, in which misogyny was seen as an acceptable ingredient in the artist's confrontation with the bourgeois world, and even the 'glam rock' of the early 1970s, while it parodied the exaggerated masculinity of the rock star, was still an exclusively male movement. While there were female rock stars (such as Dusty Springfield in the 1960s and Chrissie Hynde in the 1970s), feminist critics such as Angela McRobbie have stressed how the vocabulary of rock (in contrast to other musical genres, particularly folk) leaves little space for female perspectives.[11]

The Punk movement of the late 1970s, with its intention to renew pop culture for everybody, was seen by many as a lost opportunity. The prominence of the female punk with safety-pin and mohican hair cut in the visual discourses of the movement suggested that Punk's promise to give expression to the frustration of the marginalised was a cultural project which would include women. However feminists soon found themselves alienated by Punk's emphasis on the language of 'street fighting' and 'combat rock', 'male experiences of unsupervised adventure' from which women were excluded.[12] Since the 1980s there have been substantial changes in the culture of popular music, with the rise of the female singer–songwriter and the Madonna phenomenon providing a model of independent female sexuality for many young women, but the music industry remains male-dominated.

Conclusion

The commercialisation of leisure in the twentieth century was frequently experienced very differently by women than it was by men. Women's leisure time increased during the century, but not as much as it did for men. True, gender differences in leisure were certainly less acute in 2000 than they were in 1900, and the patterns of male and female leisure have become more similar, especially in the last two decades. The most recent *Social Survey* revealed that women were more likely to do DIY and less likely to knit or sew in 1997 than in 1977. Likewise, while men were more likely to take part in sport than women, the gap has narrowed: from 70 per cent of men and 52 per cent of women in 1987, to 71 per cent and 58 per cent respectively in 1997. However it is also evident that women and men pursued very different types of sporting activity, women preferring keep fit and yoga to snooker or pool, and competitive women's sports remained institutionally and culturally marginalised. Moreover, while only 37 per cent of women engaged in needlework or knitting in 1997 (compared to 51 per cent in 1977), this still needs to be compared with the 3 per cent of men who did so, which amounted to only a 1 per cent increase from 20 years previous. The co-existence of continuity and change is also evident in the products of popular culture on which the leisure industry is founded. Throughout the century women were represented in popular literature, music, television, radio and cinema in complex and polyphonic forms – as both passive housewives and as sexually emancipated heroines – suggesting that conventional gender roles have always been simultaneously contested and reinforced in the media of mass culture.

Bibliographical Note

Patterns of working-class women's leisure before the Second World War are detailed using oral evidence by A. Davies, *Leisure, Gender and Poverty: Working-Class Culture in Salford and Manchester, 1900–1939* (Milton Keynes, 1992); and E. Roberts, *A Woman's Place: An Oral History of Working-Class Women, 1890–1940* (Oxford, 1984). The most significant changes since 1945 are outlined in C. Brackenridge and D. Woodward, 'Gender Inequalities in Leisure and Sport in Post-War Britain', in J. Obelkevich and P. Catterall (eds), *Understanding Postwar British Society* (London, 1994). Lady Bell, *At the Works* (London, 1907) and B. Seebohm Rowntree and G.R. Lavers, *English Life and Leisure: A Social Study* (London, 1951), provide interesting, if frequently judgemental, insights into popular reading patterns. A theoretical approach to the 'woman reader' is offered by J. Radway, *Reading the Romance: Women, Patriarchy and Popular Literature* (London, 1987). On women's magazines see R. Ballaster *et al.*, *Women's Worlds: Ideology, Femininity and the Woman's Magazine* (Basingstoke, 1991); and C. White, *Women's Magazines, 1693–1968* (London, 1970). Historical studies of the women's novel are B. Melman, *Flappers and Nymphs: Women and the Popular Imagination in the Twenties* (Basingstoke, 1988); and J. McAleer, *Popular Reading and Publishing in Britain, 1914–50* (Oxford, 1992). Historians of radio have been surprisingly uninterested in gender issues, but see A. Karpf, 'Women and Radio', in H. Baehr (ed), *Women and Media* (Oxford, 1980). R. Holt, *Sport and the British: A Modern History* (Oxford, 1989) provides a subtle commentary on women's sports up to the 1930s. On women's sport and emancipation see K. McCrone, *Playing the Game: Sport and the Physical Emancipation of English Women, 1870–1914* (Lexington, KY, 1988). The leading discussions of representations of women in British film are A. Lant, *Blackout: Reinventing Women for Wartime British Cinema* (Princeton, NJ, 1991); and S. Harper, 'Historical Pleasures: Gainsborough Costume Melodrama', in C. Gledhill (ed), *Home Is Where the Heart Is: Studies in Melodrama and the Women's Film* (London, 1987). On youth culture and pop music see A. McRobbie, *Feminism and Youth Culture: From Jackie to Just Seventeen* (Basingstoke, 1991).

Notes

1. M. Spring Rice, *Working-Class Wives: Their Health and Conditions* (London, 1939); A. Davies, *Leisure, Gender and Poverty: Working-Class Culture in Salford and Manchester, 1900–1939* (Milton Keynes, 1992); and E. Roberts, *A Woman's Place: An Oral History of Working-Class Women, 1890–1940* (Oxford, 1984).

2. *Social Trends* 29 (1999), p. 210.

3. Lady Bell, *At The Works* (London, 1907), p. 145.

4. Frazer's survey forms the basis for chapter 4 of R. Ballaster *et al.*, *Women's Worlds: Ideology, Femininity and the Woman's Magazine* (Basingstoke, 1991).

5. B. Melman, *Flappers and Nymphs: Women and the Popular Imagination in the Twenties* (Basingstoke, 1988), p. 93.

6. Quoted in A. Karpf, 'Women and Radio', in H. Baehr (ed), *Women and Media* (Oxford, 1980), p. 46.

7. R. Holt, *Sport and the British: A Modern History* (Oxford, 1989), p. 348.

8. J. Richards and D. Sheridan (eds), *Mass-Observation at the Movies* (London, 1987), pp. 32–41.

9. J.B. Priestley, *English Journey* (London, 1934), pp. 376, 401–2.

10. S. Harper, 'Historical Pleasures: Gainsborough Costume Melodrama', in C. Gledhill (ed), *Home Is Where the Heart Is: Studies in Melodrama and the Women's Film* (London, 1987).

11. A. McRobbie, *Feminism and Youth Culture: From Jackie to Just Seventeen* (Basingstoke, 1991).

12. This phrase is from G. Rumsey and H. Little, 'Women and Pop: A Series of Lost Encounters', in A. McRobbie, *Zoot Suits and Second-Hand Dresses* (Basingstoke, 1989), p. 242.

Part Four

THE STATE AND CITIZENSHIP

16

THE WOMEN'S MOVEMENT, POLITICS AND CITIZENSHIP FROM THE LATE NINETEENTH CENTURY UNTIL 1918

Sandra Stanley Holton

This chapter examines the path of women to the parliamentary franchise, and its relation to the pursuit of citizenship. It indicates some of the ways that women found to enact their aspirations to citizenship, long before the right for some women to vote for parliament was gained in 1918. It is impossible to understand women's entry into the political arena without recognising the many other civil disabilities they had to address along the way. In this sense, establishing women's rights over their own persons was central to the project of achieving full citizenship. For this reason, it is necessary to look backwards to the late nineteenth century, when the first longstanding societies for women's suffrage were established, and when suffragists simultaneously campaigned to regain for women inalienable rights over their own persons.

The 'Women's Question' and Citizenship

The women's suffrage campaigns of the early twentieth century were in a sense 'unfinished business' from the radical politics of the preceding century. Women's capacity for citizenship had long been a subject of debate. In the nineteenth century this issue became part of the controversy over the 'women's question', concerning the proper place of women within society: should women's responsibilities most properly be restricted to the private world of the domestic sphere? Was a true femininity compatible with the rough and tumble of public life? Did women have the temperament and capacities to deal with affairs of state and the government of empire? The civil disabilities of women were extensive and

Plate 16.1. 'The Modern Inquisition', designed by A. Patriot (Alfred Pearse) and published by the Women's Social and Political Union (WSPU) for the January 1910 General Election. Force-feeding of suffragettes on hunger strike is a good example of an excessively harsh response by the state to women who transgressed conventional gender boundaries.

still growing in the early nineteenth century, while the same period saw the beginnings of a modern political system, most notably in the gradual extension of the franchise to large numbers of men. The 1832 Reform Act, for example, extended the suffrage to many middle-class men, while for the first time expressly excluding women from the parliamentary franchise. The 1835 Municipal Corporation Act brought the same exclusion at the level of local government. In the area of family law, 1833 saw the ending of dower right (the automatic right of widows to some portion of their husband's estate).

Equally significantly, under Common Law the legal standing of a woman was severely curtailed after marriage. As a 'feme covert' her legal personality was subsumed under that of her husband, and she lost her rights in any real property that she brought to the marriage, and to any subsequent earnings, while also becoming legally incapable of making a contract. Nor did she have rights of custody over her children. Coverture also denied married women ownership over their own persons, something that might, like their lack of property, serve to undermine their claims to full citizenship, which in radical thought in Britain remained based on notions of 'independence'. The reform of marriage laws became the focus of the first organised campaign on behalf of women's rights in the 1850s among a group of middle-class women, many with links to the radical intelligentsia and radical politics.[1]

Becoming Citizens

Women were not entirely excluded, however, from all participation in public life or political activism. In the nineteenth century church-based activities, for example, and philanthropic work provided upper and middle-class women with a range of roles in civil society. Others became writers and thinkers among the radical intelligentsia, especially in Unitarian circles. Many also became active in reform campaigns, for example, to abolish slavery. Another notable departure was their involvement in political campaigning, fund-raising, canvassing, and attending public meetings, for example, on behalf of the Anti-Corn Law League of the 1830s and 1840s. Similarly, working-class women might find a public voice in the temperance campaigns, or as preachers among churches like the Primitive Methodists. They were also evident in the Owenite and Chartist movements of the 1820s–1840s, and took a prominent part in building the Independent Labour Party from 1894. In such ways, therefore, women established a place in the world outside the domestic sphere, helped to shape social and political movements, learned some of the skills needed for public life and in some instances became acknowledged experts in matters of public concern.[2]

Extending Political Rights to Women

Radical claims to the vote in Britain had long been based on notions of 'independence', a standing usually linked to the ownership of property, and to the ability to bear arms. These capacities supposedly ensured that the male citizen was in a position to exercise his own best judgement for the common good, and free from coercion. Women were implicitly excluded from such a conception of the right to the vote – few could expect to become or remain property-holders in their own right, and there was no place for women in the armed forces. So when parliamentary reform once again came onto the political agenda in the mid-1860s, women were not included in the claim made for further extensions to the franchise.

Some of those women's rights activists who had been working for a decade on reform of the marriage laws, and on expanding women's access to higher education and professional careers, helped organise the first sustained campaign for women's suffrage in the mid-1860s. Their efforts met without success, however. Women remained disfranchised under both the 1867 and 1884 Reform Acts by virtue of their sex. The embodied and gendered nature of citizenship was equally plain in the further entrenchment of the civil disabilities of women.

The 1870 Married Women's Property Act, for example, gave married women rights over their earnings, but the measure was amended by the all-male parliament so as to keep in place a husband's rights over his wife's person. Such disabilities continued to undermine the claims of married women to be included in the demand for the vote, and this issue became a divisive one among suffragists, some of whom sought to limit the demand to single women.

Patricia Hollis has recently reminded us that the first breakthrough for suffragists occurred in the area of local government.[3] In 1870, women ratepayers were enfranchised under the Municipal Corporations Act, and allowed to vote for, and stand for election to, the new school boards established by the Education Act of the same year. Subsequently, they were included in the franchise for the Poor Law Boards, and might qualify to stand for election. In this way, women began to hold public office before they gained the right to vote in parliament. They also played an increasing role in political life as methods of election campaigning were more tightly controlled, so as to end longstanding corrupt practices. The major parties looked to party-political associations formed in the 1880s, such as the Women's Liberal Federation, to supply essential electoral support in terms, for example, of canvassing. Conservative women made a similar contribution through the Primrose League. Women were also finding a more prominent role as speakers and organisers in the newly emerging socialist movement. Equally, coverture was whittled away in the 1880s and 1890s.

The Twentieth-Century Campaigns for the Vote

By the turn of the twentieth century, the hopes of many suffragists went beyond simply joining the political sphere of men. Rather, they sought 'the feminisation of democracy' not simply to expand the rights of their sex, but to further the project of progressive politics, and to create a state able more adequately to respond to problems that had long been women's responsibility – the care of the poor, sick and needy. Suffragists also increasingly appealed to women as members of a sex-class, fostering a sense of sexual solidarity that might cut across economic-class consciousness and unite women in their shared interests as a subject group. Equally, even the most radical might articulate an imperial feminism that saw it as the historical role of British women to defend the rights of their subject sisters, rarely acknowledging the political and social subordination, and the differing religious and cultural values, that separated them from each other.[4]

By 1903 it appeared that the Liberal Party was most likely to form the next government, and go to the electorate on a programme of extensive domestic reform. The suffrage movement was now well-placed to mount a new campaign. It comprised a range of suffrage organisations that reflected the growing social and political diversity within the movement. These new bodies brought with them fresh perspectives, campaigning methods and tactics, borrowing variously from the socialist and labour movements, and Irish Nationalists. Around a third of adult men remained without the vote, however – and at a time when the Labour Party began increasingly to challenge the Liberal Party in working-class constituencies. Hence, the demand for women's suffrage took on greater urgency as pressure began to mount from within the socialist and labour movements for adult suffrage. It was feared that this demand might well be satisfied by a measure limited to manhood suffrage – many labour and socialist men remained indifferent to the cause of sexual equality, while a few were positively antagonistic to women's suffrage.[5]

The National Union of Women's Suffrage Societies was formed in 1897 from a number of pre-existing societies. Liberal women were prominent among its leadership, but it was headed by Millicent Garrett Fawcett, a Liberal Unionist, and Labour and Conservative women were to be found among her closest friends and colleagues. The National Union framed its demand in terms of equal votes for women. Though this formulation would have established the principle of sexual equality in the franchise, it would also only have secured the vote for property-holding women, given the existing qualifications for the suffrage. Shortly, the National Union's influential Manchester Society began a systematic campaign among the women textile workers of that region, already well-organised through the trade union movement and the Independent Labour Party. Petitions from this new presence within the suffrage movement caused something of a stir and marked a major turn in the character and methods of campaigning of the suffrage movement in Britain.[6]

In 1903 a new suffrage organisation was formed by Esther Roper, previously secretary of the Manchester Society of the National Union. Together with her lifetime companion, Eva Gore Booth, she established the Lancashire and Cheshire Textile and Other Workers Committee (LCTOWRC). This society formulated its demand in terms of 'womanhood suffrage', the vote for all adult women, a radical demand when around a third of men remained without the vote. It signalled that the demand of the National Union appeared too narrow to many working-class women, who also found increasingly uncertain, however, the support for women's suffrage within the labour and socialist movement. This separate, autonomous group of those termed 'radical suffragists' by their historians, Jill Liddington and Jill Norris, sought to reflect the particular perspective of working-class suffragists.[7]

A second new suffrage society, the Women's Social and Political Union (WSPU) was also formed in Manchester in 1903. Its founder, Emmeline Pankhurst, was among the first members of the Independent Labour Party in 1894, and a campaigner for women's suffrage for many years. Initially, the principal aim of the WSPU was to act as a ginger group within the labour and socialist movements, to maintain and strengthen support for sexual equality. Thus the WSPU, like the National Union, formulated its goal in terms of equal votes for women. The two bodies differed, however, in a number of other respects: the National Union aimed to be a national umbrella organisation, while the WSPU began as a locally based society in the North-West. The former pursued an election policy of supporting the candidate who established himself as the 'best friend' to the cause of women's suffrage, aiming to build cross-party support for a bill to be introduced as a private member's measure, while the latter sought to put pressure on the Liberal Party, as the soon-to-be governing party, to take up the demand and bring in a government bill. The National Union was still a largely middle-class organisation in which women Liberals were a large and influential presence, while the WSPU initially sought to build support from the mainly working-class rank-and-file of the labour and socialist movements.

As a consequence their styles of campaigning and form of organisation also differed – the National Union continued to use the well-established methods of pressure-group politics, for example, in the organisation of petitions, and the holding of occasional large-scale public meetings in the town halls of major cities, together with drawing-room meetings at the homes of local notables, to educate opinion and build support. It sought to establish a permanent and widespread network of branches to organise pressure from the constituencies, and over time established a democratic constitution which gave considerable autonomy to federations of branches at a regional level, and required regular national meetings where the leadership might consult with the rank-and-file membership.

The WSPU, in contrast, took the issue to local trade union and socialist branch meetings, holding open-air meetings at the factory gate or on the street corner, in search of popular support. Both the LCTOWRC and the WSPU were women-only bodies. In contrast, the National Union remained open to men and women, though men were increasingly eased out of its leadership in the early years of the twentieth century. Equally, a few men played important support and advisory roles within the WSPU, until the split between Emmeline and Christabel Pankhurst and Emmeline and Frederick Pethick Lawrence late in 1912. Decision-making was at once highly centralised and dispersed in the WSPU: a small, self-appointed leadership decided matters of national policy and kept a firm grip on its purse strings, while local branches enjoyed considerable autonomy in matters of day-to-day organisation, and the development of tactics often followed from individual initiatives over which the leadership sometimes had difficulty in exerting its control.

What soon came to distinguish the WSPU from other suffrage bodies, however, was the adoption of 'militancy'. Initially, this entailed a more confrontational approach toward leading Liberal politicians at public meetings, one which led to the arrest in October 1905 of Christabel Pankhurst, eldest daughter of Emmeline, and Annie Kenney, a mill worker. They had been ejected from a Liberal party meeting after persistent heckling, and Christabel Pankhurst had then committed a technical assault on a police officer. The two were fined, and on refusing to pay, were committed to prison. This protest succeeded in its primary goal, to break the press boycott on the women's suffrage issue. The WSPU was now in the national eye, though in a way that many suffragists found personally offensive and potentially harmful to their cause. There was now a tension between the supporters of suffrage militancy and those who held to the 'constitutionalist' approach of the National Union. The press designated the former 'suffragettes', a label that the WSPU took up and made its own so as to distinguish its members as a new type of suffragist.[8]

From Symbiosis to Divergence: Militancy versus Constitutionalism

In 1906, the WSPU moved its headquarters to London, beginning to broaden its support base which in time came to include members of social and intellectual elites, and further challenging the constitutionalists for national leadership of the movement. Initially, Millicent Garrett Fawcett sought to avoid an open split between militants and constitutionalists. While she herself doubted the wisdom of militancy, she applauded the courage demonstrated by its adherents, and acknowledged the large influx of members that it began to bring to both the National Union and the WSPU. The National Union also expanded its methods of campaigning. In 1907 it organised the first suffrage procession through London, dubbed the 'Mud March' because of the poor weather. It also established an effective press department. At a local level, it was not uncommon for an individual suffragist to be active in both constitutionalist and militant branches. The two bodies acted in many ways in symbiosis – while the National Union undertook the time-consuming work of constituency organisation and public education, the WSPU gave the issue a fresh immediacy and glamour.

The National Union and the WSPU remained practically separated by their differing political policies: the National Union continued to work toward a private member's suffrage bill, while the WSPU sought to pressure the Liberal government to take up the issue. Hence, the National Union remained non-party in its policies, while the WSPU offered active opposition to Liberal Party candidates, and also increasingly distanced itself from the socialist and labour movements, disenchanted by the performance of Labour MPs on the issue of women's suffrage. The political situation worsened from 1908, when Herbert Asquith, the anti-suffragist Liberal prime minister, indicated his government's support for *manhood* suffrage. All plans for franchise reform went on hold, however, with the constitutional crisis of 1909, that followed the House of Lords' rejection of Lloyd George's 'People's Budget', a crisis that was not resolved in the government's favour until 1911.

Militant tactics shifted in these years from the peaceful demonstration of popular support for women's suffrage to deliberate threats to public order. Individual militants began to break the windows of government buildings in 1908, both as a form of protest and to ensure a quick arrest and safety from growing crowd hostility, and the WSPU leadership quickly endorsed the practice. The government retaliated by refusing to allow militants to serve their sentences in the first division of the prison system. This was usual procedure for political prisoners, and permitted a range of privileges including the right to wear one's own clothes, arrange for one's own food to be delivered to the prison and to have books and writing materials. When Marion Wallace Dunlop was denied this status, she introduced the tactic of the hunger strike in protest and was quickly released from gaol. The WSPU leadership endorsed her action, and the hunger strike became a common resort of suffrage prisoners. The government responded with the introduction of the barely disguised torture of forcible feeding. The degree of violence attending the militant–government confrontation now escalated. Subsequently, the government extended the possible punishment of militant prisoners through the 'Cat and Mouse Act'. This measure provided for the release of hunger-striking prisoners on licence, and their subsequent repeated rearrest (and possible repeated forcible feeding) until their sentences were completed. WSPU demonstrations began to be more harshly policed, most notoriously on 'Black Friday' in 1910, when some demonstrators claimed to have been sexually abused, while others suffered serious injuries.

In 1912 the government moved against the WSPU leadership itself, forcing Christabel Pankhurst to flee to Paris while the government secured the conviction of Emmeline Pankhurst and the Pethick Lawrences for conspiracy, a serious charge that brought long prison sentences. The WSPU's financial resources were also threatened, while its paper, *Votes for Women*, became subject to censorship. Militant protests in consequence became increasingly clandestine and more violent, entailing attacks on private as well as public property, and extending now to arson and bombing, as well as incidences of personal violence against members of the government. These developments were defended by the WSPU leadership as provoked by government repression, and as limited only to 'symbolic' acts of violence. The National Union, while also highly critical of the government's response to militancy, believed it was now necessary to disassociate itself from such lawlessness.

Perhaps not surprisingly, under such pressures the WSPU underwent a series of splits: in 1907 a breakaway militant organisation, the Women's Freedom League was formed by some leading socialist suffragists among the militant leadership; in November 1912 Emmeline and Frederick Pethick Lawrence were expelled from the leadership, and subsequently helped establish a mixed suffrage body, the United Suffragists; early in 1914, Sylvia Pankhurst was similarly expelled, because of the links she continued to build between the East London Federation of Suffragettes, which she had helped establish, and the local labour and socialist movements. At the centre of such divisions were several issues: the lack of any internal democracy within the WSPU; the abandonment of popular campaigning in favour of increasingly violent protest; and the deepening hostility of Emmeline and Christabel Pankhurst toward the labour and socialist movements, and to male political advisers.

IN FOCUS: Mary Gawthorpe: Socialist, Militant and 'Freewoman'

Mary Gawthorpe (1881–1973) came from a working-class district of Leeds. Family circumstances made it impossible for her to take up a scholarship, and so she pursued her ambitions to become a professional woman through

Mary Gawthorpe: Socialist, Militant and 'Freewoman' (continued)

Plate 16.2. Mary Gawthorpe, *c.* 1909.

the pupil teacher system. By the time the twentieth-century campaign for women's suffrage was underway, she was a fully certificated teacher, and had established an independent household of her own in order to rescue her mother and brother from her unreliable and abusive father. Now a ratepayer she also gained a vote in local government elections. She was, too, by this time a prominent figure in the local socialist movement, and this connection brought her into contact with the suffrage movement.

Initially, around 1904, she joined the Leeds Society of the National Union, led at this time by the well-to-do Isabella O. Ford, one of the founding members of the Independent Labour Party. But she was soon attracted to the more colourful tactics of the Women's Social and Political Union. A lively, personable, fearless speaker she was increasingly in demand, and gave up teaching to work as a socialist organiser in 1906. In this capacity, she spoke in support of the miners' leader, Robert Smillie, in the 1906 Cockermouth by-election. It was here that a shift in militant policy first became evident, as the WSPU sought to distance itself from its socialist origins. Militant campaigners in the election opposed Robert Smillie and the Liberal government's candidate equally. Mary Gawthorpe found herself

Mary Gawthorpe: Socialist, Militant and 'Freewoman' (continued)

increasingly torn between her loyalty to the socialist movement and her commitment to women's suffrage.

Shortly, she was recruited by the WSPU, and became one of its most popular and effective organisers. In 1907 the socialist suffragists Charlotte Despard and Teresa Billington Greig split away from the WSPU to form another militant society, the Women's Freedom League. Mary Gawthorpe's personal loyalty to the Pankhursts was evident in her joining the small national executive now established to legitimate the remaining leadership of the WSPU. Over the next few years Mary Gawthorpe campaigned tirelessly and underwent several imprisonments and the hunger strike, but was fortunate in never being forcibly fed. Both her personal life and her health were undermined by a relentless commitment to the suffrage cause, however. Her health broke down again in 1910, after a violent assault by a Liberal Party supporter when she and a companion disrupted an electioneering meeting for Winston Churchill.

Her convalescence was prolonged and she found herself increasingly alienated from the WSPU leadership. By this time, a few prominent suffragists, including Teresa Billington Greig, were questioning the single-minded concentration on the vote and the effectiveness of militant methods. A close colleague of Mary Gawthorpe, Dora Marsden, was also by now at odds with the WSPU leadership. She, too, questioned the adequacy of the suffrage demand to achieving full emancipation for women. Together, Mary Gawthorpe and Dora Marsden established a new journal in 1912, *The Freewoman.*

This paper insisted that sexual and economic liberation were central to the goal of women's emancipation. It spoke on behalf of those who began from this time to identify themselves as 'feminists', advocating a much broader and even more controversial approach to advancing the social position of women, and identifying the institution of marriage as at the root of women's subjection. Dora Marsden also used *The Freewoman* to launch personalised attacks on the Pankhursts. It was on this issue, and in continuing poor health, that Mary Gawthorpe withdrew from any association with the journal.

In 1916, she realised a longstanding hope to visit family and friends in the United States. It was here that she returned to suffrage campaigning, and to working once again as an organiser for the labour movement, and on behalf of radical causes. In 1922 she married and settled for good in the United States. She stayed in touch, however, with former colleagues from the suffrage movement in Britain, and was prompted in the 1930s to begin her memoirs by the establishment of the Suffragette Fellowship. Eventually, she published privately a full-length account of how she became a militant, entitled *Up Hill to Holloway.*[9]

'Democratic Suffragists' and the National Union

The National Union, for its part, was pushed toward more forceful strategies by the difficult political situation confronting the suffrage movement from 1908. In this period those I have elsewhere termed 'democratic suffragists' emerged among its leadership. They were part of a current that was to be found through-out the suffrage movement, one strongly sympathetic to the ultimate goal of universal suffrage, and increasingly ready to cooperate with the labour and soci-alist movements to achieve such an end. At a local level, a number of National Union societies began from 1908 to offer support to Labour candidates as the 'best friend' to the cause, while at a national level the leadership began to move into closer cooperation with a new adult-suffrage body, the People's Suffrage Federation.

The aim of such tactics was to ensure that, if adult suffrage were to be granted, women would not be excluded from that advance. While the Liberal govern-ment had become less sympathetic to women's suffrage under Asquith's leader-ship, some prominent Labour MPs had begun to insist that women's suffrage must form part of any adult suffrage measure. Their position was endorsed at the Labour Party annual conference in 1912. To consolidate this advance, the National Union instituted through its Election Fighting Fund a policy that sought cooperation with the Labour Party during elections. By this means it hoped both to pressure the Liberal government by encouraging more three-cornered elections, and to strengthen the commitment of the labour and socialist move-ments to women's suffrage.

In 1914, the Liberal government began to prepare for the general election due within the next year or so. Its own Reform Bill had foundered the previous year on the issue of the exclusion of women. So franchise reform became an important part of its next election programme, and some accommodation now had to be sought with women's suffragists. The government opened nego-tiations with various parts of the movement, and in the months before war broke out, appears to have found a solution acceptable to all but the WSPU leadership: a government adult suffrage measure, capable of women's suffrage amendments, to which leading government ministers, including Lloyd George, would be free to give their unequivocal support. It seems likely, then, that if the Liberals had been returned to power in the general election anticipated in 1915, the next parliament would have seen the enactment of some measure of women's suffrage. The outbreak of war intervened, however.

All the main suffrage bodies announced the suspension of suffrage cam-paigning for the time being, but most nonetheless succeeded remarkably in maintaining their organisational base. The National Union deployed its resources to relieve some of the immediate distress occasioned by the outbreak of war, setting up workshops for the unemployed at home, and ambulance units for the wounded in the war zones. The WSPU leadership threw itself into the war effort, and helped in the drive to recruit men into the armed forces. Subsequently, groups of internationalist and pacifist militants broke away, unhappy with the suspension of suffrage campaigning and the jingoism of its leaders, among them the Independent Suffragettes of the WSPU. There were also many socialists among the dissident militant groups, many of whom were internationalists and pacifists, and these chose a very different path. The Women's Freedom League, for example, concentrated its efforts on the relief of distress occasioned by the war, while upholding the cause of peace. The East London Federation of Suffragettes focused on the problems confronting women and children in that part of London, and moved further to the left. Subsequently, as the Workers' Suffrage Federation, it broadened its demand and called for universal suffrage.

The democratic suffragists among the leadership of the National Union also shared views that were internationalist and anti-war. Millicent Garrett Fawcett, however, had no problem with the war, believing it to be fought on behalf of the same democratic values that the suffrage movement had stood for, against German militarism and autocracy. For many of her closest colleagues, however, the matter was not so black and white. They believed the National Union should use its considerable experience and resources to educate opinion on the causes of war, and sought cooperation with groups opposed to the war, such as the Union for Democratic Control. When an international women's convention was called in the Hague in 1915 to discuss ways of ending the conflict, Millicent Garrett Fawcett successfully resisted efforts to send delegates from the National Union. The democratic suffragists who formed the majority of its executive committee resigned at this point, while some branch societies defiantly announced they would send delegates despite this reversal, and a number of leading constitutionalists took part in the convention. Subsequently, internationalist and pacifist suffragists from all parts of the movement helped form the Women's International League for Peace and Freedom.

When a Speaker's conference was established to consider the franchise laws and how to reform them in 1916, the suffrage movement was able to make an effective intervention in support of the inclusion of women in any future legislation. Only the WSPU refused to resume the suffrage demand. A consultative committee was established to maintain an informal forum for exchange of views with members of the conference, like Sir John Simon, one of the government ministers with whom suffragists had been able to deal prior to the outbreak of war. Through this channel suffragists were kept informed of debates within the convention. Many leading suffragists were by now convinced that a universal franchise was both desirable and attainable. But a major concern for many male politicians was that women should not form a majority in any new electorate, as would have happened under any measure of complete adult suffrage. Some compromise was sought that might meet acceptance by the convention and by most of the suffrage movement. The Representation of the People Act of 1918 enfranchised all women over 30 who were on the local government registers, or who were wives of men on those registers, together with women university graduates. Shortly, women also gained the right to stand for parliament. The sexual disqualification established in the 1832 Reform Act had at last been ended, and full sexual equality in the franchise laws was finally achieved in 1928.

Interpretations

In a range of contrasting accounts the suffrage movement has been variously presented as quite distinct and separate from other political developments, as merely a symptom of some broader political malaise, or as a significant aspect of the broader political development of British society.[10] Earlier writers like Roger Fulford treated the demand simply as a single-issue campaign, while a more recent generation of historians, including Lisa Tickner and myself, have seen it as involving a profound challenge to gender stereotypes and the gender hierarchy, with a symbolic significance beyond any immediate practical outcomes. Similarly, George Dangerfield's early influential interpretation focused on the twentieth-century campaigns as a quite new phenomenon, while my own recent research has established significant continuities with the nineteenth century, not least in militant tactics and outlook.

Another influential early account, Sylvia Pankhurst's *The Suffragette Movement*, presented militancy as the critical development which finally brought 60 years of campaigning to a successful conclusion. In contrast, present-day historians, including Jill Liddington and Jill Norris, Lesley Parker Hume, Liz Stanley and Ann Morley, and myself, have argued that such a narrow focus ignores the complexity of the internal politics of the movement, and of constitutionalist-militant relations. It also neglects the significant contributions of other groups like the LCTOWRC and the National Union, and of dissidents within the WSPU.

Some early twentieth-century suffragists came to see the demand as in itself inadequate to the goal of women's emancipation. In their view it deflected attention from more pressing issues, such as sexual freedom, economic equality and women's control of their own fertility. Any sense of sexual solidarity was also fragile, masking the very real diversity of needs among women that emerged even more clearly after the vote was won. The interwar period may appear, in consequence, one of fragmentation, division and dispersal of energies within the women's movement. Alternatively, it might be argued that if women's politics became more diffuse and less noisy after the war, this reflected the importance of the gain that had been made. Moreover, experienced organisations and extensive networks remained in place to pursue a broader agenda for change, with women activists adopting a pragmatic division of labour among themselves so as to achieve a still fuller realisation of their claims to citizenship.

Bibliographical Note

For examples of women's involvement in the public and political life of the last two centuries see J. Rendall (ed), *Equal or Different: Women's Politics, 1800–1914* (Oxford, 1987); and H.L. Smith, *British Feminism in the Twentieth Century* (Aldershot, 1990).

R. Strachey, *The Cause: A Short History of the Women's Movement in Great Britain* (London, 1978 reprint [1928]) provides a comprehensive history of the women's movement, while B. Caine, *English Feminism 1780–1980* (Oxford, 1997) brings the story up to date. O. Banks, *Faces of Feminism* (Oxford, 1979) is a comparative analysis of some of the political, social and intellectual origins of the women's movement. P. Levine, *Victorian Feminism 1850–1900* (London, 1987) provides a concise overview of the nineteenth-century campaigns for women's rights.

On the first breakthrough, in local government, see P. Hollis, *Ladies Elect: Women in English Local Government 1865–1914* (Oxford, 1987). A concise recent history of the suffrage movement is S.S. Holton, 'Women and the Vote', in J. Purvis (ed), *Women's History: Britain 1850–1945* (London, 1995). S.S. Holton, *Suffrage Days: Stories from the Women's Suffrage Movement* (London, 1996) explores suffrage history from the 1860s to 1918, and contains a chapter on further reading. An invaluable survey of local studies of the suffrage movement is to be found in L. Leneman, 'A Truly National Movement: The View from Outside London', in M. Joannou and J. Purvis (eds), *The Women's Suffrage Movement: New Feminist Perspectives* (Manchester, 1998). H.L. Smith, *The British Women's Suffrage Campaign, 1866–1928* (London, 1998) is an indispensable and wide-ranging discussion of changing interpretations of the suffrage movement, and of debates among suffrage historians, together with a selection of documents and extensive bibliography.

Some important and influential early histories include E.S. Pankhurst, *The Suffragette Movement: An Intimate Account of Persons and Ideals* (London, 1977 reprint [1931]); G. Dangerfield, *The Strange Death of Liberal England* (London, 1970 reprint [1935]); and R. Fulford, *Votes for Women* (London, 1957). A major challenge to such accounts are J. Liddington and J. Norris, *One Hand Tied Behind Us: The Rise of the Women's Suffrage Movement* (London, 1978); L.P. Hume, *The National Union of Women's Suffrage Societies, 1897–1914* (New York, 1982); and S.S. Holton, *Feminism and Democracy: Women's Suffrage and Reform Politics, 1897–1918* (Cambridge, 1986).

A. Rosen, *Rise Up Women: The Militant Campaigns of the Women's Social and Political Union, 1903–14* (London, 1974) remains the most comprehensive account of the WSPU but is focused on the national leadership. L. Stanley and A. Morley, *The Life and Death of Emily Wilding Davison* (London, 1988), in contrast, looks at a circle of rank-and-file WSPU supporters to suggest the complex meaning of 'militancy', and the role of dissidents within the WSPU in the development of fresh militant tactics. Militant breakaways are also receiving increasing attention, for example, C. McPhee and A. Fitzgerald, *The Non-Violent Militant: Selected Writings of Teresa Billington Greig* (London, 1987). For a superbly illustrated analysis of the iconography, and cultural and symbolic significance of the twentieth-century suffrage campaigns see L. Tickner, *The Spectacle of Women: Imagery in the Suffrage Campaign, 1907–14* (London, 1987). C. Walker, *Suffrage and Power: The Women's Movement, 1918–28* (London, 1997) looks at the continuing campaigns for sexual equality after 1918.

Notes

1. On the nineteenth-century women's rights movement, see P. Levine, *Victorian Feminism 1850–1900* (London, 1987). S.S. Holton, *Suffrage Days: Stories from the Women's Suffrage Movement* (London, 1996) examines the role of suffragists in the campaign for the end of coverture. B. Harrison, *Separate Spheres: The Opposition to Women's Suffrage in Britain* (London, 1978), analyses the arguments used against women's suffrage.

2. For a helpful survey, see J. Hannam, 'Women and Politics', in J. Purvis (ed), *Women's History: Britain, 1850–1945* (London, 1995).

3. P. Hollis, *Ladies Elect: Women in English Local Government 1865–1914* (Oxford, 1987).

4. On the ideology of the women's suffrage movement, see S.S. Holton, *Feminism and Democracy: Women's Suffrage and Reform Politics, 1897–1918* (Cambridge, 1986), esp. ch. 1. For a survey of the literature on imperial feminism, see C. Midgley, 'Gender and

Imperialism: Mapping the Connections', in C. Midgley (ed), *Gender and Imperialism* (Manchester, 1998).

5. On the tensions between adult suffragists and women's suffragists, see Holton, *Feminism and Democracy*, esp. ch. 3.

6. On the National Union, see L.P. Hume, *The National Union of Women's Suffrage Societies, 1897–1914* (New York, 1982); and Holton, *Feminism and Democracy*.

7. J. Liddington and J. Norris, *One Hand Tied Behind Us: The Rise of the Women's Suffrage Movement* (London, 1978).

8. Holton, *Feminism and Democracy*, ch. 2, provides an extended comparison of militants and constitutionalists.

9. M. Gawthorpe, *Up Hill to Holloway* (Penobscot, ME, 1962), which tells her story up to her first imprisonment in 1906. For her subsequent career, see Holton, *Suffrage Days*.

10. For full references to works cited in this section, see the bibliographical note, and for a more extended discussion of differing interpretations, see H.L. Smith, *The British Women's Suffrage Campaigns* (London, 1998).

17

THE WOMEN'S MOVEMENT, POLITICS AND CITIZENSHIP, 1918–1950s

Caitriona Beaumont

'No doubt some of us exaggerated [the power of the vote].'[1] This was the view expressed by the feminist campaigner Eleanor Rathbone in 1936 eighteen years after the enactment of the 1918 Representation of the People Act. Despite this great victory for the suffrage movement, the campaign for the right of all women to full political, social and economic equality within British society was far from over. This chapter explores the ongoing campaign for women's rights in Britain in the four decades following the extension of the parliamentary franchise to women over thirty. The aims and achievements of the women's movement during these years and the involvement of women in public life will be considered. Here the term women's movement is defined in its broadest context to include feminist, political and mainstream women's organisations all of whom, in different ways, campaigned to enhance the role and status of women in British society. From this perspective, the chapter argues that there was an active and vibrant women's movement in Britain throughout the middle decades of the twentieth century.

After the Vote 1918–28: Equal Rights Versus New Feminism and the Continuing Campaign for Women's Rights

The passing of the 1918 Representation of the People Act marked an important and symbolic victory for the suffrage movement. After years of campaigning, women over thirty who were local government electors or who were married to local government electors had finally been awarded the right to full political citizenship. Many suffrage campaigners, including the Pankhursts, perceived that the fight for the vote was now over and moved on to pursue other interests. The greatest challenge for those who remained active in the women's movement was

Plate 17.1. 'A perfect woman', designed by John Hassall for the National League for Opposing Woman Suffrage, 1912.

how best to continue campaigning for women's rights now that women were included, at least in principle, in the political process of the nation. The fact that one of the leading suffrage societies, the National Union of Women's Suffrage Societies (NUWSS), changed its name to the National Union of Societies for Equal Citizenship (NUSEC) in 1918 suggests that the Union clearly recognised the need to extend its campaigning activities beyond the vote to encompass a wide range of political, social and economic rights for women citizens.

Under the leadership of Eleanor Rathbone, elected President of the NUSEC in 1919, the organisation searched for a new identity in the wake of the women's franchise. What emerged from this process was a division within the organisation over the question of priorities. At the heart of this debate, which lasted throughout the 1920s and beyond, was whether or not the Union should give precedence to the campaign for 'dead level' equality between men and women or to issues which specifically addressed women's traditional role in society, that of wife and mother. Those within the NUSEC who wished to place equal rights at the top of the agenda became known as equal rights or egalitarian feminists and included prominent suffrage campaigners, for example Millicent Fawcett and Monica Whately.

While accepting the importance of egalitarian demands Eleanor Rathbone and her supporters argued that it was time to concentrate on reforms which would enhance the lives of the majority of women in Britain, who at this time were wives and mothers working within the home. The payment of family allowances to married mothers, the provision of birth control information and improved housing conditions were among the demands which Rathbone and her followers within the NUSEC believed should be given priority now that the vote had been won. The belief that the specific needs of women as wives and mothers should become the central focus of the feminist movement was known as new feminism. Having debated the merits of new versus egalitarian feminism for a number of years the NUSEC split in 1927 when the union voted to add a number of new feminist demands to its national agenda.

Much has been made of this division within the feminist movement during the 1920s. It would be wrong to suggest however that the ideological differences between new and egalitarian feminists created two diametrically opposed factions within the women's movement during the interwar period. In reality new and egalitarian feminists continued to share many common aims and were united in their desire to improve the lives and status of women. Despite its affirmation of new feminism after 1927 the NUSEC continued to support egalitarian reforms such as the equal franchise, the right of women to a high standard of education and the right of married women to employment. Similarly egalitarian feminists who were represented by societies such as the Women's Freedom League (1907), the Six Point Group (1921) and the Open Door Council (1926) were not averse to lending their support to demands for better housing and improved child care while at the same time focusing their attention on traditional egalitarian reforms. It could be argued that new and egalitarian feminist societies, rather than being in conflict with one another were in fact able to work side by side representing different, but equally valid, interpretations of how best to campaign for women's rights during the interwar period.

Despite these divisions over the nature of feminism, the need to continue fighting for women's rights united all women's organisations at this time. A number of important legislative reforms were introduced during the early 1920s which did improve the position of women, for example the 1923 Matrimonial Causes Act and the 1925 Guardianship of Infants Act. Although significant, these reforms along with the extension of the franchise, did not signify an end to women's social and economic inequality. The 1919 Sex Disqualification (Removal) Act did not protect women from the marriage bar and many women working in both the public and private sectors were forced to leave their jobs on marriage. Women continued to be regarded as dependants of men, a fact reflected in the low levels of pay for women workers and the exclusion of housewives from free health care under the 1911 National Health Insurance Scheme. Women were also under-represented in local and national politics with only 38 women elected to the House of Commons during the years 1919 to 1945.

Perhaps the most symbolic inequality of all was the fact that women continued to be deprived of the right to vote in national elections on equal terms with men.

The NUSEC led the campaign to extend the franchise to women over twenty-one and single women throughout the 1920s. The delay in granting all women the parliamentary vote has been attributed to a number of factors. They include the uncertainty among politicians about how younger women would vote in general elections, a belief that twenty-one was too young an age for either men or women to vote and the succession of general elections during the 1920s which interrupted proposed legislation on this matter. The NUSEC along with other women's societies, most notably the Women's Freedom League, played a major role in maintaining pressure on consecutive governments to introduce this crucial egalitarian reform. Support for equal franchise was also forthcoming from a number of women MPs namely the Conservative Nancy Astor, the Liberal Margaret Wintringham and Labour's Dorothy Jewson and Susan Lawrence. Following the failure of the 1924 Labour Government to introduce the necessary reform, the campaign for the equal suffrage was intensified, culminating in a mass meeting of some 3,500 women from all over Britain in Hyde Park in July 1926 which received considerable press coverage.

A new body, the Equal Political Rights Campaign Committee (EPRCC) was set up by members of the Six Point Group to build on the publicity generated by this meeting. Together with the NUSEC this new committee organised numerous protest meetings and parades calling for the equal franchise throughout the remainder of 1926 and 1927.[2] This escalation in the suffrage campaign, along with a realisation by the Conservative Prime Minister Stanley Baldwin that five million new women voters would not necessarily disadvantage the Conservative Party, led to the enactment of the Representation of the People (Equal Franchise) Act in 1928.

The Wider Women's Movement: Domesticity and the Campaign for Equal Citizenship 1929–39

The passing of the 1928 Equal Franchise Act marked an end to the suffrage campaign in Britain. Equally significant was the fact that with the removal of this last symbol of political inequality for women the feminist movement went into decline. The NUSEC, the most influential feminist society at this time experienced a rapid fall in branch membership from 220 in 1920 to just 48 in 1935. Similarly egalitarian feminist societies such as the Six Point Group, the Open Door Council and the Women's Freedom League remained small and somewhat ineffectual pressure groups during the 1930s (see Table 17.1). There are a number of reasons why feminist societies were unable to capitalise on the success of the suffrage campaign in the two decades following enfranchisement.

With the vote won a number of former suffragists believed that the need for women-only pressure groups had passed. As a result these women turned their attention to new ways of expressing their interest in public affairs either by

Table 17.1. **Membership of Women's Organisations, 1930–60**

	1930s	1950s
Labour Party Women's Sections (est. 1918)	250,000	364,000
Mothers' Union (est. 1885)	538,000	500,000
National Council for Equal Citizenship (est. 1928)	48 branches	3,000
National Union of Townswomen's Guilds (est. 1928)	54,000	250,000
National Federation of Women's Institutes (est. 1915)	238,000	500,000
Six Point Group (est. 1921)	NA	200
Women's Co-operative Guild (est. 1883)	90,000	48,000
Women's Freedom League (est. 1907)	26 branches	NA
Women's National Liberal Federation (est. 1918)	88,000	400 branches
Women's Unionist Association (est. 1918)	940,000	2.8 million

Note: Figures approximate only.

Sources: M. Pugh, *Women and the Women's Movement in Britain 1914–1959* (London, 1992); and I. Zweiniger-Bargielowska, 'Explaining the Gender Gap: the Conservative Party and the Women's Vote, 1945–64', in M. Francis and I. Zweiniger-Bargielowska (eds), *The Conservatives and British Society 1880–1990* (Cardiff, 1996).

joining mainstream women's organisations, the established political parties or becoming involved in single-issue campaigns such as the interwar peace campaign. In addition feminist societies experienced difficulty in recruiting new members particularly among younger women during the interwar period. One of the reasons why the majority of women were not attracted to feminist societies was the negative public perception of feminism and feminists which existed at this time. Feminist societies were often portrayed as radical, even revolutionary groups of women who wished to transform society and break up the family. This was in spite of the fact that feminist societies during this period never challenged traditional gender roles within the family and accepted that most women would choose to work at home as wives and mothers. Individual feminists were also often viewed with disdain verging on contempt. Vera Brittain, the well-known women's rights campaigner, remarked in 1928 that feminists were portrayed as 'spectacled, embittered women, disappointed, childless, dowdy and generally unloved'.[3]

This stereotypical representation of a feminist, a legacy from the suffrage campaign, contrasted sharply with the more popular image of contented and happy wives and mothers. Women's magazines and journals of this period, such as *Woman* and *Woman's Own*, reflected the prevailing ideology of domesticity which dominated during the interwar period. Following the social upheaval of the First World War, where women had temporarily taken on 'men's roles', the desire to return to normality, among both men and women, was reflected in the ideology of domesticity. Women were encouraged to marry and where possible devote themselves to their traditional domestic role as wives and mothers. The marriage bar, low pay for women workers and inadequate childcare facilities acted as further incentives for married women to conform to the domestic ideal.

Nevertheless it would be wrong to suggest that the unpopularity of feminist societies and the prevailing ideology of domesticity signified an end to the women's movement during the interwar years. The fact that the majority of women were not attracted to feminist pressure groups, and once married worked within the home, did not mean that women withdrew from public life during the 1930s. Indeed it was during this period that female membership of main-stream women's societies and political organisations expanded and a significant number of women became outspoken on the newly won right of all women to the benefits of equal citizenship. Among the demands made by these groups were social welfare reforms, such as the provision of family allowances, free health care for housewives and improved maternity services along with more traditional egalitarian rights.

The most popular voluntary organisations for women at this time were soci-eties representing the interests of wives and mothers working within the home. The largest and most successful voluntary women's organisations during the interwar period were the Women's Co-operative Guild (1883), the National Federation of Women's Institutes (1915), the National Union of Townswomen's Guilds (1928) and the Mothers' Union (1885) (see Table 17.1). The Women's Co-operative Guild, closely allied to but independent of the Labour Party, was an organisation for working-class housewives and mothers. The other three voluntary societies were not associated with any political party and recruited both working-class and middle-class women. It should be noted however that these three organisations maintained a steadfastly middle-class perspective throughout the interwar period.

While the Women's Co-operative Guild concentrated on the interests and needs of working-class wives and mothers, the Women's Institute Movement represented women living in rural areas, the Townswomen's Guild was a society for women living in towns and cities and the Mothers' Union an organisation for Anglican mothers. Of these four women's groups, the Women's Co-operative Guild was the most radical, socialist and overtly feminist society leading the campaign for a number of key reforms including the provision of birth control information and improved health care for married women. Conversely the Mothers' Union was the most conservative women's organisation during this period, being a fervent opponent, on religious grounds, of divorce, birth con-trol and abortion. In spite of their obvious differences, all of these organisations were united in their desire to enhance the status of housewives and mothers and willing to campaign for what they believed to be the citizenship rights of all women. In return for fulfilling their domestic role each organisation argued that women as equal citizens were entitled to economic and social welfare support from the state. Family allowances, free health care for housewives and

Plate 17.2. 'Mother's Place Is in the Home', *Woman*, July 1937.

improved maternity services were reforms demanded by all of these societies during the interwar period.

Membership of a political party was another way for women to become involved in public life and voice concern about the status and welfare of women. Following the extension of the franchise to women in 1918 the established political parties accepted women as full members and female supporters joined in their thousands (see Table 17.1). In the past it has been suggested that women within the three main political parties were willing to put party loyalty before issues such as women's welfare and equal rights. However more recent research has shown that a significant number of women were vocal within their respective parties, albeit with varying degrees of success, in an attempt to keep the question of women's rights to the forefront of the political agenda.

During the 1930s women in the Labour Party's Women's Sections acknowledged the work done by housewives and mothers and advocated reforms which would improve the lives of women working at home. In common with many feminist and mainstream women's societies, Labour women argued that women as citizens had a right to social welfare services such as the introduction of day nurseries, and improved maternity and health services for women. Labour women also supported family allowances and the provision of birth control information to married women throughout the 1930s despite the unwillingness of the Party leadership to adopt such measures. Conversely women active within the Women's

Unionist Association, in line with Conservative Party policy, rejected calls for the provision of family allowances and birth control information. Nevertheless the Association did support less controversial and less expensive reforms such as low food prices and lower-cost housing. Reflecting the inexorable decline of the Liberal Party during the interwar period the Women's National Liberal Federation (WNLF) was unable to match the popularity of either the Conservative or Labour Party among women. Nevertheless the WNLF did support a mixture of new feminist and equalitarian reforms throughout the 1920s and 1930s including equal pay, divorce law reform and the payment of family allowances.

It is now clear that, despite the narrow appeal of overtly feminist groups during the 1930s, hundreds of thousands of women were active in a wide and diverse range of women's organisations which continued to campaign for the social and economic rights of women citizens. Improvements were made in a number of areas, most notably in maternity services, the limited provision of birth control information at local authority clinics from 1931 and liberalisation of the divorce law in 1937. However long-standing demands for family allowances, equal pay and free health care for housewives remained unfulfilled with both Labour and Conservative administrations unwilling to introduce such costly initiatives during a period of worldwide economic depression.

The Women's Movement and Second World War: The Home Front, Equal Pay and Equal Rights

The outbreak of war with Germany in September 1939 marked an important revival in the fortunes of the women's movement in Britain. War provided women citizens with an opportunity to demonstrate that like men they were capable of making an important contribution to the national war effort. By 1943 an estimated 7,750,000 women between the ages of 18 and 50, 43 per cent of whom were married, had been conscripted into the wartime workforce to replace male workers. Women with domestic duties, in particular mothers with children under fourteen, were not required to undertake war work, reflecting the accepted opinion that women with young children had a duty to care for them at home. Nevertheless ongoing labour problems forced the government to encourage mothers with domestic duties to take up part-time work where possible.

This influx of women into the paid workforce had, at least in the short term, a major impact on the lives of women workers, wives and mothers. Although the majority of women conscripted into the wartime workforce had worked before the war, the additional demands of war work brought with it new challenges for women. Women recruited into heavy industry such as munitions and engineering had to learn new skills previously the preserve of male workers, but were still often paid less than men. Women were expected to work long hours, sometimes up to 12 hours a day including Saturdays. Many women also had to cope with the double burden of paid work and housework which meant queuing for food, cooking and cleaning after a long day at work.

Awareness of the wartime demands made on women and the opportunity that women's continued cooperation during wartime afforded, led women's organisations and a number of women MPs to galvanise support for economic and social reforms. Greatest priority was given to demands for equal pay, improved health and maternity services and family allowances. The introduction of equal pay had been on the agenda of a number of women's societies throughout the interwar years. They included the NUSEC, the Women's Freedom League, the Open Door Council, the Women's Sections of the Labour Party and the Women's Co-operative Guild. The cost of equal-pay legislation had been a major factor in blocking the introduction of this egalitarian measure. However the dramatic increase in the number of women workers following the outbreak of war brought the whole question of equal pay to new-found prominence.

A crucial boost for the equal-pay campaign was the success of the Equal Compensation Campaign Committee (ECCC), in amending the 1939 Personal Injuries (Emergency Provisions) Act in April 1943. The ECCC was set up by over forty women's groups in 1941 to reverse the government's decision to pay women less compensation for war injuries than that paid to men. This was one of the most significant victories of the women's movement during the war and had implications for the equal-pay debate. Men and women were now entitled to the same rate of compensation when forced out of work due to war injuries. Consequently supporters of equal pay were optimistic that the government would have to review the policy of paying men and women differential rates when in work. Such optimism, however, proved short-lived.

Although the contribution of women workers to the war effort was praised by the Minister for Labour and National Service Ernest Bevin in September 1943, it was made clear that the wartime coalition government had no intention of introducing equal pay for women at that time. In response the Equal Pay Campaign Committee (EPCC) was set up in January 1944 to co-ordinate the work of women's societies campaigning for equal pay. This new body focused its campaign on the common grades of the civil service where men and women performed the same work but received differential pay rates. By 1946 seventy-two women's societies had affiliated to the EPCC including the National Council for Equal Citizenship (formally the NUSEC), the Women's Co-operative Guild, the Open Door Council, the Women's Liberal Federation and the National Federation of Women's Institutes. By March 1944 the EPCC, under the chairmanship of the Conservative MP Mavis Tate, had collected 160 signatures from MPs calling for a parliamentary debate on equal pay in the civil service.

The campaign received valuable support from women MPs of all parties, for example Nancy Astor (Conservative), Edith Summerskill (Labour), Megan Lloyd-George (Liberal) and the Independent MP Eleanor Rathbone. Support was also forthcoming from the Woman Power Committee, a cross-party group of women MPs set up to represent the interests of women and especially women workers during wartime. Growing support for the principle of equal pay led to an amendment to the 1944 Education Bill which proposed to abolish differential pay rates between male and female teachers. The amendment was passed in the House of Commons but was quickly overturned by a vote of confidence in the government called by the Prime Minister Winston Churchill.

The government, having blocked the introduction of equal pay, became increasingly alarmed by the upsurge of support in the House of Commons for equal pay. In a deliberate effort to block further progress towards equal pay, the government announced that a Royal Commission on Equal Pay would be set up to investigate and report on the implications of equal pay legislation. The Royal Commission was rightly regarded by women's groups as a stalling tactic intended to abate support within the Commons for equal pay. Nevertheless the EPCC agreed to suspend its campaign until the Commission concluded its investigation. As a result the question of equal pay was put on hold for the remainder of the war years only to re-emerge in October 1946 with the publication of the report.

Low pay rates were not the only difficulties encountered by women during wartime. Evacuation, food shortages, childcare for working women and the disruption of normal services all had an impact on women's lives during this period. In 1939 the Women's Group on Public Welfare (WGPW) was set up to co-ordinate the work of women's societies representing the needs of wives and mothers. Membership of this new body included the Townswomen's Guilds, the Women's Institute Movement, the Mothers' Union, the Women's Co-operative Guild and the Labour Party's Women's Sections. Throughout the war years the WGPW highlighted the public welfare needs of women and children and expressed particular concern about urban working-class women and children whose poverty was laid bare by evacuation during the first year of the war.

William Beveridge's Inter-Departmental Committee on Social Insurance and Allied Services (1941) and the Royal Commission on Population (1944) provided women's organisations with an ideal opportunity to voice their opinion that women citizens were entitled to adequate state-funded welfare services. Familiar demands were made ranging from free health care for housewives to the payment of family allowances. Organisations such as the Townswomen's Guilds and the Women's Institutes welcomed the publication of the Beveridge Report in 1942 which acknowledged the unpaid work of housewives and recommended the introduction of wide-ranging social welfare reforms.

IN FOCUS: The Women's Movement and the Campaign for Family Allowances

---

One of the most high-profile and controversial campaigns fought by women during the period 1918–45 was for the payment of family allowances to married mothers. Eleanor Rathbone, who spearheaded the campaign for family allowances, was determined to see an end to the financial dependency of women in marriage. In *The Disinherited Family* (1924) she warned of the dangers of economic dependency which placed wives at their husband's mercy. The issue of family allowances also touched on the question of child poverty, the equal-pay debate and the survival of the

The Women's Movement and the Campaign for Family Allowances (continued)

'family wage'. In addition concern about the falling birth rate during the 1920s and 1930s led some campaigners to argue that the payment of family allowances was a good way to encourage women to have more children. Eleanor Rathbone and the Family Endowment Society (1925) recognised that to focus narrowly on the right of mothers to economic independence would not receive widespread support at a time of high male unemployment and so highlighted all of the benefits of family allowances.

Egalitarian feminist societies did not back the family allowance campaign on the grounds that it placed too much emphasis on the role of women as wives and mothers. In contrast the Women's Co-operative Guild and the Women's Sections of the Labour Party had been among the earliest advocates of state-funded family allowances which they believed would benefit working-class families in particular. As the campaign for family allowances continued throughout the 1920s and 1930s, middle-class organisations offered their support. Along with the NUSEC, the Women's Institute Movement, the Townswomen's Guilds and the Mothers' Union argued that family allowances would not only help eliminate child poverty but would also acknowledge the work performed by women within the home. Neither the Conservative nor Labour administrations were willing to introduce family allowances during the interwar period. With the outbreak of war in 1939 this situation altered dramatically. The evacuation of children from inner-city areas increased public awareness about the extent of child poverty. Anxiety about the health of children, compounded by fears concerning population levels when young men were being sent into battle, did much to persuade the government to introduce family allowances. When William Beveridge recommended allowances for children in the Beveridge Report he was more concerned about the population question and child poverty than about implementing a radical scheme of 'wages for mothers'.

In June 1944 the wartime coalition government set out its proposals for family allowances with the publication of the Family Allowances Bill. The principal reason for introducing the Bill at this time was to curb inflationary wage claims with cash benefits for children. Family allowances were seen as a way of achieving this goal while at the same time addressing the problem of child poverty and the low birth rate. Much to the consternation of stalwart campaigner Eleanor Rathbone and numerous women's groups, the government announced its intention to pay the allowance to the father. Faced with an onslaught of criticism from respected and influential women's organisations, the government was forced to capitulate and an allowance of five shillings a week for all children after the first was paid to mothers from 1946. The government did not regard family allowances as a 'wage for mothers' or a means of giving housewives more economic independence. Nevertheless, the payment of a state allowance to mothers, however meagre, was an important measure and went some way to enhance the lives of wives and mothers.

The Women's Movement in the Postwar World 1945–59: Housewives, Workers and Citizens

The involvement of women in the war effort, whether in voluntary or paid work, heightened expectations among women's groups that the status of women in British society would be enhanced in the postwar period. The Family Allowances Act of 1945 and the welfare reforms of the postwar Labour Government were welcomed by women's societies. Under the terms of the 1946 National Insurance Act women workers were entitled to 13 weeks' paid maternity leave. From 1948 the new National Health Service ensured that all citizens, including housewives, had access to free health care. These were important reforms which did much to improve the general health of all women during the postwar years and beyond.

Just as the winning of the suffrage in 1918 had led suffragists to reflect on their future role, the improvements in social welfare provision for women with the coming of the welfare state marked a new phase in the history of the women's movement in Britain. At the end of the war thousands of young women left their wartime jobs and married resulting in a dramatic rise in the number of marriages and a 'baby-boom' during the late 1940s. The total percentage of women workers fell from 51 per cent in 1943 to 40 per cent in 1947. Although wartime work had offered new experiences for women, long working hours for low pay coupled with domestic responsibilities and inadequate childcare facilities meant that a return to full-time housework was a relief for many. Popular women's magazines such as *Woman* and *Woman's Own* encouraged readers to devote themselves to home and family, portraying marriage as the ultimate career choice for women throughout the late 1940s and 1950s. At the same time the views of childcare experts became increasingly popular advising mothers that they must care for young children within the home.[4]

The war did however have an impact on work patterns for women with the number of older married women going out to work increasing gradually during the late 1940s and 1950s. In response to the postwar labour crisis the Labour Government urged women to take up paid employment but focused their campaign on single women and older married women whose children had grown up. Job opportunities for women expanded in light industries such as electrical engineering, where women were engaged in low-paid, unskilled and repetitive work. The postwar labour shortage led to the removal of marriage bars thereby increasing the number of women working in teaching, clerical and administrative jobs. Part-time work for women became increasingly available during the 1950s allowing women to combine paid work with domestic duties. The fact that women workers, both single and married, continued to receive less pay than men was an outstanding grievance for many women's organisations. In 1946 the Royal Commission on Equal Pay reported that there was no logical reason why equal pay for equal work should not be introduced in the civil service. The EPCC resumed its activities in November 1946 and in January 1947 called a mass meeting at Westminster attended by 2,000 women representing 77 women's societies and 9 trade unions. Although the Labour Party agreed to the principle of equal pay for equal work, the post-war Labour Government announced in June 1947 that it would not introduce equal pay in the public sector on the grounds that higher wages would lead to inflation. This remained Labour policy until the party lost the 1951 general election.

The EPCC continued to campaign for equal pay throughout the late 1940s and early 1950s. Although women within the Labour Party supported equal pay, there was a tendency to follow the party line and accept that equal-pay legislation was not possible during a period of economic austerity. Conversely women in the Conservative Party became increasingly outspoken on the issue of equal pay.[5] Recognising the importance of the women's vote, the Conservative Party's Central Women's Advisory Committee focused on the rights of women citizens and identified equal pay, better housing and an end to austerity as key issues of concern for female voters. Continuing efforts by women within the Conservative Party along with the well-publicised activities of the EPCC, contributed to the introduction of equal pay in the public sector by the Conservative Government in 1955. Following this landmark victory the EPCC disbanded, signifying a lull in the campaigning activities of women's societies for the remainder of the 1950s.

Feminist societies continued to press for egalitarian reforms such as equal pay and opportunities for women in the private sector but with limited support and resources they failed to make any significant impact. The Women's Co-operative Guild remained an important outlet for the views of working-class women but experienced a gradual decline in membership during the 1950s (see Table 17.1, p. 266). Mainstream middle-class women's organisations such as the Mothers' Union, the Townswomen's Guilds and the Women's Institute Movement fared better in terms of membership although they too had difficulty attracting young women as members. Like the leading women's magazines, these organisations welcomed and endorsed the postwar emphasis on traditional family life with the mother at its centre. However it is important to note that all three societies acknowledged that married women had a right to work outside the home and urged women to involve themselves in public life. Having welcomed the introduction of social welfare reforms for women in the late 1940s, during the 1950s organisations such as the Mothers' Union and the Townswomen's Guilds focused on providing practical support and recreational activities for women many of whom were adapting to the double burden of paid employment and domestic life.

During the period 1945 to 1959 twenty-nine Labour women candidates, fifteen Conservative women and one Liberal were elected to the House of Commons. Although a small number of women MPs, for example Edith Summerskill (Labour) and Joan Vickers (Conservative) continued to highlight 'women's issues' such as equal pay and divorce law reform, the majority of women MPs preferred to concentrate on party political questions. One reason for this was a belief that to focus too narrowly on gender issues would limit their influence within their respective parties. At party level Conservative women proved to be the most vocal in promoting women's interests during the 1950s thereby contributing to a swing in support among women voters to the Conservative Party in the 1951 and 1955 general elections. In contrast the Labour Party failed to exploit the women's vote during the 1950s and it was only in the 1960s that the Labour Party Women's Sections focused once again on promoting equal rights for women citizens.[6]

Historical Interpretations: Was there Always a Women's Movement in Twentieth-Century Britain?

In the past, histories of the women's movement in Britain have tended to focus on periods of greatest feminist activity, namely the suffrage campaign and the emergence of the Women's Liberation Movement in the late 1960s. As a result the 1930s, 1940s and 1950s have often been characterised as a time when the women's movement went into inexorable decline and failed to capitalise on the triumph of the suffrage campaign. More recently historians of the women's movement in Britain have looked beyond the activities of overtly feminist pressure groups and considered the feminist principles of other organisations for women. Pat Thane has argued that the Women's Sections of the Labour Party made a significant contribution to the campaign for women's political and welfare rights during the 1930s and early 1940s.[7] Similarly, Ina Zweiniger-Bargielowska has shown how women within the Conservative Party highlighted the rights of women as citizens during the 1950s, most notably in their support of equal-pay legislation. Gillian Scott has considered the role of the Women's Co-operative Guild in demanding egalitarian and social reforms on behalf of working-class wives and mothers.

The result is a broader and more accurate picture of the political and social activities of women during the 1930s, 1940s and 1950s. However the role of middle-class, mainstream and non-political organisations for women in local and national affairs is still frequently underestimated, and often ignored. Margaret Andrews's study of the Women's Institute Movement and Caroline Merz's history of the Townswomen's Guilds are two notable exceptions. This chapter has shown that despite the decline in popularity of feminist societies in the four decades after 1918, hundreds of thousands of women remained active in a wide range of women's organisations and consistently highlighted the social and economic rights that women had as equal citizens. It is now clear that there was a vibrant and diverse women's movement in Britain throughout the 1930s, 1940s and 1950s. Considerable progress had been made by the end of the 1950s. The Welfare State did much to improve the health and welfare of women working in the home, women had greater opportunities in the labour force and the principle of equal pay for equal work had been established in the public sector. Nonetheless many gender inequalities remained and no women's organisation, feminist, political or mainstream, had yet challenged the traditional assumption that women had a primary duty to care for their husbands and young children at home. Such a challenge would come with the emergence of the Women's Liberation Movement in the late 1960s.

Bibliographical Note

The best introduction to the history of the women's movement in Britain is M. Pugh, *Women and the Women's Movement in Britain 1914–1999*, 2nd edn (London, 2000). Other good surveys are S. Bruley, *Women in Britain since 1900* (London, 1999); J. Lewis, *Women in England 1870–1950: Sexual Divisions and Social Change* (Brighton, 1984); and J. Alberti, *Beyond Suffrage: Feminists in War and Peace 1914–1959* (London, 1989). For more in-depth accounts of the equal suffrage campaign and the feminist movement during the 1920s and 1930s see: C. Law, *Suffrage and Power: The Women's Movement 1918–1928* (London, 1997); H.L. Smith, 'British Feminism in the 1920s', and M. Pugh, 'Domesticity and the Decline of Feminism 1930–1950', both in H.L. Smith (ed), *British Feminism in the Twentieth Century* (London, 1990). P. Summerfield, 'Women, War and Social Change: Women in Britain in World War II', in A. Marwick (ed), *Total War and Social Change* (London, 1988) provides a fascinating account of the impact of war on women's lives. Also see H.L. Smith, 'The effect of the war on the status of women', in H.L. Smith (ed), *War and Social Change: British Society in the Second World War* (Manchester, 1986).

More research is needed on the 1950s, but interesting and informative accounts are J. Lewis, *Women in Britain since 1945* (London, 1992); and P. Thane, 'Towards Equal Opportunities? Women in Britain since 1945', in T. Gourvish and A. O'Day (eds), *Britain since 1945* (London, 1991); and idem., 'Women since 1945', in P. Johnson (ed), *Twentieth Century Britain: Economic, Social and Cultural Change* (London, 1994). For an account of women in party politics see P. Graves, *Labour Women: Women in British Working-class Politics 1918–1939* (Cambridge, 1994); P. Thane 'The Women of the British Labour Party and Feminism 1906–1945', in H.L. Smith (ed), *British Feminism in the Twentieth Century* (London, 1990); B. Campbell, *The Iron Ladies: Why do Women Vote Tory?* (London, 1987); and I. Zweiniger-Bargielowska, 'Explaining the Gender Gap: The Conservative Party and the Women's Vote 1945–1964', in M. Francis and I. Zweiniger-Bargielowska (eds), *The Conservatives and British Society 1880–1990* (Cardiff, 1996).

For specific campaigns see H.L. Smith, 'British Feminism and the Equal Pay Issue in the 1930s', *Women's History Review* 5, 1 (1996); H. Land, 'Eleanor Rathbone and the Economy of the Family', in H.L. Smith (ed), *British Feminism in the Twentieth Century* (London, 1990). For individual women's societies see G. Scott, *Feminism and the Politics of Working Women: The Women's Co-operative Guild, 1880s to the Second World War* (Brighton, 1998); C. Merz, *After the Vote: The story of the National Union of Townswomen's Guilds in the Year of its Diamond Jubilee 1929–1989* (Norwich, 1988); and M. Andrews, *The Acceptable Face of Feminism: The Women's Institute as a Social Movement* (London, 1997).

Notes

1. E. Rathbone, 'Changes in Public Life', in R. Strachey (ed), *Our Freedom and its Results* (London, 1936), p. 16.

2. C. Law, *Suffrage and Power: The Women's Movement 1918–1928* (London, 1997), pp. 208–20.

3. *Manchester Guardian*, 13 December 1928.

4. For example see J. Bowlby, *Forty-four Juvenile Thieves* (London, 1946); and D. Winnicott, *Getting to Know Your Baby* (London, 1947). For a critique of this argument see D. Riley, *War in the Nursery: Theories of Child and Mother* (London, 1983).

5. Ina Zweiniger-Bargielowska, 'Explaining the Gender Gap: The Conservative Party and the Women's Vote, 1945–64', in M. Francis and I. Zweiniger-Bargielowska (eds), *The Conservatives and British Society 1880–1990* (Cardiff, 1996), pp. 210–15.

6. Ibid, pp. 215–16.

7. See Bibliographical Note for references.

18

THE WOMEN'S MOVEMENT, POLITICS AND CITIZENSHIP, 1960s–2000

Harold L. Smith

During the 1960s social attitudes toward women changed as women developed a new consciousness of their oppression and this sense of injustice spread through society. This contributed to the most important flowering of the British women's movement since the pre-1914 suffrage campaign. While traditional feminist groups, such as the Fawcett Society, were reinvigorated, it was the Women's Liberation Movement (WLM) which distinguished the new women's movement from that of earlier periods. Instead of seeking equality with men, the WLM wished to change the male-dominated social structures which it considered the source of women's oppression. The result was the unleashing of a powerful, if somewhat diffuse, reform movement that culminated in numerous social experiments and the most important burst of legislation affecting women's legal position since the 1920s.

The Women's Liberation Movement

The belief that the women's movement was moribund from the late 1920s until the WLM revived it in the late 1960s is misleading as demonstrated in the previous chapter. Feminist organisations such as the Fawcett Society (originally the London Society for Women's Suffrage) and the Six Point Group remained active throughout the period, providing a link between the earlier campaigns and those after 1960. Feminist efforts to draw women into politics on behalf of women's interests in the early 1960s were reinforced by a variety of women's groups: the Conservative and Labour Party women's organisations, the trade unions' women's sections, and the Townswomen's Guilds. Many women were also active in mixed single-issue pressure groups such as the Abortion Law Reform Association. Women working through organisations like these helped bring about the mid-1960s' feminist revival that was already underway when the first WLM groups were formed in 1968.

The Fawcett Society was probably the most important of these pre-WLM feminist groups. Although its membership was small and largely London-based, its influence on equality legislation in this period was disproportionate to its size. It was, for example, involved in drafting the anti-sex discrimination bill in the early 1970s, and its lobbying helped ensure the establishment of the Equal Opportunities Commission.

The WLM's emergence in the late 1960s injected new energy and a radical edge into British feminism. Many WLM members were influenced by New Left ideology and had participated in anti-Vietnam War demonstrations; some had been active in the Campaign for Nuclear Disarmament. The 1968 commemoration of the fiftieth anniversary of women's suffrage provided a catalyst for the formation of WLM groups. Some WLM members viewed themselves as descendants of the militant suffragettes and engaged in direct action to achieve their goals.

Although WLM members supported equality legislation, the WLM placed greater importance on personal and sexual issues than traditional feminists. The first national WLM conference, held at Ruskin College, Oxford in 1970, endorsed the following reforms: equal pay, equal opportunities and education, 24-hour nurseries, and free contraception and abortion on demand. During the 1970s the WLM became especially concerned with securing the last two reforms.

Establishing women's reproductive rights has been one of the feminist movement's central objectives since the 1960s. At the beginning of that decade the Family Planning Association provided birth-control assistance at its clinics, but the National Health Service did not. The 1967 National Health (Family Planning) Act removed the legal barrier by allowing local authorities to provide contraceptive assistance. The question of whether free contraceptive supplies should be available from the NHS remained controversial. After being blocked by the Conservative Government in 1973, this was introduced by the Labour Government in the following year.

The struggle to secure and maintain the right to a legal abortion may have been the single most important issue in politicising women since 1960. Feminists who advocated legalised abortion formed the Abortion Law Reform Association in 1936. This pressure group was chiefly responsible for the lobbying which three decades later led to the 1967 Abortion Act. The proposed reform aroused strong opposition. Although some ALRA members believed that the woman involved should decide whether to have an abortion, the ALRA did not insist on this language for fear the bill would be defeated. In order to gain the medical profession's support, physicians were given the power to decide when abortion was appropriate, and maternal health became the primary justification for it. The Act made abortion legal during the first 28 weeks of pregnancy if two doctors agreed that it was necessary to avoid harm to a pregnant woman or if there was a danger that a handicapped child would be born.

Plate 18.1. Fighting for abortion rights, 29 October 1977. Over 5,000 marched through the streets of Birmingham to draw attention to the disgraceful situation that only 10 per cent of abortions were performed on the NHS.

During the 1970s there were repeated attempts to restrict the abortion rights that the Act established. When a private member's bill for this purpose appeared to be gaining a parliamentary majority in 1975, feminists established the National Abortion Campaign to defend abortion rights. It organised a procession by about 20,000 supporters of abortion rights that is believed to have been the largest demonstration on a women's issue since the pre-World War I suffrage campaign.[1] After the 1979 Conservative Government took office there was a further attempt to restrict abortion rights. This time trade union women persuaded the Trades Union Congress (TUC) to help organise a demonstration by about 100,000 persons that contributed to the anti-abortion bill's defeat. The anti-abortion movement's main success came in 1990 when the time limit for a legal abortion was reduced from 28 to 24 weeks after Prime Minister Thatcher expressed support for this change.

The WLM was also deeply involved in campaigns to protect women from domestic violence, sexual harassment and rape. Assisting battered wives became one of the WLM's special concerns. WLM members established refuges where battered women and their children could obtain temporary accommodation. Feminist-generated publicity about the problem helped bring about the 1976

Domestic Violence and Proceedings Act under which a wife could obtain an injunction to prevent her husband from assaulting her. Because discussion of sexual harassment focused on the workplace, trade union women and the Equal Opportunities Commission (EOC) joined with the WLM in drawing public attention to it. In 1986 a Scottish Court ruled that sexual harassment was a form of sex discrimination and illegal under the Sex Discrimination Act. Responding to women's growing fear of rape, feminists organised 'Reclaim the Night' demonstrations in several cities in November 1977 in support of women's right to walk the streets at night. Feminists also helped bring about the 1976 Sexual Offences (Amendment) Act that established the right of a woman bringing rape charges to remain anonymous.

Although the WLM grew rapidly during the early 1970s, the fundamental ideological differences within it became apparent as early as 1973. Many members were socialist feminists who wished to link the WLM with the largely male Labour movement. But many others were radical feminists who considered men responsible for women's oppression, and objected to allying with men, even those who supported the women's movement. The split widened when radical feminists attributed female heterosexuality to false consciousness, and maintained that the WLM should focus on defending women's right to choose lesbianism. The two groups were so bitterly divided at the 1978 WLM convention that no further national conventions were held.

Gender Legislation

During the decade from 1965 to 1975 there was a remarkable surge of legislation on women's issues. The changed climate of opinion concerning women during the 1960s was crucial in bringing this about. With neither party having a solid majority of the electorate, both the Conservative and the Labour parties became increasingly concerned with attracting female voters.

The Conservative Party's women's organisation had been urging the party to sponsor reforms to improve women's status throughout the postwar period, but with the exception of the introduction of equal pay in the public sector they made little headway until the 1960s. Although a Women's Policy Group was established in 1962, party leaders largely ignored its recommendations. The 1964 and 1966 general election defeats shattered this indifference, and stimulated discussion of how the party might attract more female voters. Aware that the women's vote could be decisive in the next election, the Conservatives devoted greater attention to policy concerning women.

In 1968 the party appointed a committee chaired by Anthony Cripps to investigate legal discrimination against women. Its report, 'Fair Share for the Fair Sex', recommended a number of changes in the law designed to bring about a greater degree of gender equality. When the party was unexpectedly returned to office in 1970 these recommendations became the basis for much of the Conservative Government's women's legislation.

Aware of the growing public support for reforms to improve women's status, and of the party's need to attract female voters, the 1970–74 Conservative Government introduced several measures. The 1970 Matrimonial Proceedings and Property Act gave women an increased share of matrimonial property by recognising the wife's non-financial contribution to a marriage. The 1971 Attachment of Earnings Act made it easier for courts to enforce court-ordered maintenance payments against husbands. The 1973 Guardianship Act granted mothers equal guardianship of their children.

But it was the emergence of legislation to ensure equal opportunities that attracted the greatest public interest. Following the introduction of private members' bills to end sex discrimination, the Conservative Government established select committees in both Houses of Parliament to consider legislation. Drawing upon the committees' reports, it announced its intention to introduce a bill making sex discrimination in employment illegal. Feminists considered the government's scheme much more limited than the feminist-backed proposals, and suspected the government of endorsing reform in order to attract female voters in the approaching general election. The government fell before it could introduce legislation, but when the Labour Government's bill was considered the Conservative Party supported the principle underlying it.

The Labour Government's 1975 Sex Discrimination Act differed in important ways from the Conservative Government's scheme. It was expanded to include education, housing and the provision of goods, facilities, and services in addition to employment. While both provided for the establishment of an Equal Opportunities Commission, only the Labour Government's legislation granted it enforcement powers. In the House of Commons the Labour Government's bill was amended to include 'indirect' as well as direct discrimination, and to make 'positive' discrimination legal.

The Labour Government also took steps to establish maternity rights for employed women through the 1975 Employment Protection Act. By 1971 49 per cent of married women were employed, but prior to 1975 they had no legal protection against job dismissal if they interrupted their employment for childbirth. The Act as amended in 1978 protected an employee against dismissal because of pregnancy, and established the right to maternity leave and to maternity pay for six weeks at 90 per cent of the normal week's pay.

Policy toward lone mothers became an increasingly vexed issue after the 1960s. Under the 1945 Family Allowances Act a five-shilling weekly benefit was paid to the mother for each child after the first. Feminists viewed this as recognition that motherhood was socially valued work. When the Conservative Government proposed in 1972 to replace it with a system of tax credits paid to the father, feminists organised local and national demonstrations in support of their claim that the benefit should be paid in cash to the mother. This proved to be one of the most successful 1970s' feminist campaigns. The Labour Government's 1975 Child Benefit Act provided a tax-free, non-means-tested benefit paid directly to the mother, and for lone parents it improved upon the Family Allowances Act by paying benefit for the first as well as subsequent children.

IN FOCUS: The Equal Pay Issue

Women's pay rates have historically been lower than men's, even when they had the same qualifications, experience and did the same work. In the mid-1950s, after a long campaign by feminists and white-collar trade unions, the government conceded equal pay to public employees, such as teachers and civil servants, who did equal work.[2]

During the 1960s the main pressure to extend equal pay to the private sector came from two sources: the European Economic Community (EEC, later European Community or EC) and female trade unionists. The 1957 Treaty of Rome which created the EEC required member states to establish 'equal pay for equal work'. When the Labour Government applied for EEC membership in 1967, it planned to introduce equal pay legislation to comply with this, but dropped the reform after its application was rejected.

Pressure from militant trade union and Labour Party women revived the equal-pay issue. In 1968 female sewing-machinists at Ford's Dagenham plant went on strike for a regrading of their jobs, and for equal pay. In the following months women workers elsewhere initiated equal pay strikes and the National Joint Action Campaign Committee for Women's Equal Rights was established to encourage women to demand equal pay. The perception that this was the beginning of a new surge of militancy to obtain equal pay strengthened Employment Secretary Barbara Castle's hand when she urged the cabinet to forestall labour unrest by introducing an equal pay bill.

The Labour Government's 1970 Equal Pay Act stated that an employee was entitled to equal pay if the work she did was the same or broadly similar ('like work') to that of a man in the same establishment or if a job evaluation rated their work as equivalent.[3] Although it is difficult to distinguish the Act's impact on women's wages from other factors, between 1970 and 1977 women's hourly earnings, excluding overtime, rose from 63.1 to 75.7 per cent of men's earnings. But in the following decade women's earnings, relative to men's, declined slightly as employers found ways to maintain sex-differentiated pay. Most women continued to be employed on jobs considered to be 'women's work' in which there were no male comparators. By reducing the number of female employees doing 'like work', for example, employers could continue to pay women lower rates; the Act thus gave employers additional incentive to sex-segregate jobs.

The Treaty of Rome's equal pay clause was ambiguous as to whether it applied to work of equal value or only when equal work was being done. In 1975 the EEC issued an Equal Pay Directive that the former was required. Several organisations, including the Fawcett Society and the Equal Opportunities Commission, urged that Britain's equal pay law be modified to incorporate this broader application, but the government refused. In 1982 the European Court of Justice found Britain in violation of this Directive and ordered the British Government to revise its equal pay law.

The Equal Pay Issue (continued)

Under EEC pressure, the Conservative Government reluctantly issued the 1983 Equal Pay (Amendment) Regulations stating that an employee was entitled to equal pay if her work was of equal value to that of a male comparator unless the employer could justify the pay differential under one of the defences specified in the Regulations. The Regulations also expanded the defences employers could use. Unequal pay remained legal if the employer demonstrated that the pay differential reflected a material factor other than sex; the Regulations added a new defence by explicitly including market forces as one of the material factors allowed.

Although the equal value regulations have helped some individuals achieve pay equity, they have not eliminated gendered pay structures. Female employees continued to find the law an insufficient instrument for change. An applicant was unlikely to be successful without legal assistance, but this was too expensive for most employees unless their trade union supported them. The length of time involved was also a deterrent. Some cases have taken more than ten years to resolve, by which time the applicant may have moved on to another job. Part of the delay stemmed from the requirement that a tribunal employ an independent expert to do the job evaluation. The 1996 Sex Discrimination and Equal Pay Regulations accelerated the process somewhat by authorising the tribunal to do the evaluation itself (the experts had taken on average about 11 months to do it). But further changes are needed if the equal pay law is to be an effective tool against pay discrimination. Research from the late 1990s revealed a pay gap between men and women of around 20 per cent, suggesting that women continued to be discriminated against in the labour market.[4]

Women and the Conservative Party

The Conservative Party has been heavily dependent on women for party workers and fundraising since the nineteenth century, but few gained election to Parliament. Party leaders became concerned about this following the 1966 election when more women voted Labour than Conservative for the first time since 1945. Labour women not only seemed to have a much better chance of becoming an MP than those who were Conservative, their chances of gaining office were also much greater. Conservative women MPs benefited from the need to correct this image when Ted Heath became Prime Minister in 1970. In addition to appointing more women to ministerial positions, Heath broke with tradition by placing some of them in areas outside of what was considered women's sphere. Margaret Thatcher was the most important beneficiary of the party's desire to make its top women more visible; she became the second Conservative woman ever to hold a cabinet position when she was appointed Minister of Education.

Although women had played a key role in the Conservative Party for decades, Margaret Thatcher's selection as party leader in 1975 was unexpected. Women did not normally fill party leadership roles, and anti-feminist feeling among some sections of the party was so strong that Thatcher's candidacy was not taken seriously at first. She was not the party's women's candidate; the women's sections supported Heath.[5] Thatcher's selection as the first woman to head a British political party was less an indication of widening opportunities for women within the party than a personal triumph.

Thatcher became Britain's first female Prime Minister in 1979 and held that office until 1990. Ironically, female Conservative voting declined during this period. Whereas women were more likely to vote Conservative than men in almost every postwar general election up to 1979, during Thatcher's term as Prime Minister the pro-Conservative electoral gender gap disappeared. Thatcher bore some responsibility for this. She displayed little interest in helping other women advance, made anti-feminist statements and distanced herself from the women's movement.

Thatcher's administrations were committed to reducing public expenditure; this often resulted in cutting programmes benefiting women. Schemes involving universal coverage, such as child benefit, were considered wasteful, since the government wished to restrict benefits to low-income groups. The threat to child benefit stimulated an alliance of women's organisations ranging from the National Federation of Women's Institutes to the Fawcett Society. Under pressure from them, the Conservative Government agreed to continue child benefit but froze the benefit level during a period of rising prices. By the early 1990s its real value was only 77 per cent of what it had been in 1979.

Female voters may also have been alienated by the anti-statist ideology of the Conservative Governments between 1979 and 1990. Even when the Conservative Government introduced measures that should have appealed to women, such as the 1983 requirement that equal pay for work of equal value be granted, it did so in a way that minimised its potential benefits for them. Party leaders made sexist remarks in introducing equal pay, for example, and the legislation was written in unnecessarily complex language that seemed designed to ensure failure.

Conservative Governments under Thatcher also weakened women's employment rights. The Labour Government's 1975 Employment Protection Act had established a woman's legal right to combine paid employment and motherhood by making it illegal to dismiss her because of pregnancy if she had worked for the same employer for at least six months. But in 1980 the Conservative Government revised the law so that a woman must have worked for at least 16 hours per week for the same employer for two years to be covered. Since most working-class women changed jobs frequently or worked less than the weekly hour requirement, those who remained protected were largely female white-collar workers.[6]

The Equal Opportunities Commission became one of the most important forces for gender reform while the Conservatives were in office. Feminists had anticipated it would perform this function when it was established in 1976. But during its first decade the EOC's achievements were modest as it chose to play primarily an educational role. This was partially because neither the Labour nor the Conservative Governments in this period wanted an activist EOC. Those appointed to the EOC's Board of Commissioners represented established interest groups, such as the Confederation of British Industry (CBI) and the TUC; none were selected from feminist organisations.

During the 1980s the EOC gradually emerged as an important pressure group for gender equality. This was partially a matter of securing commissioners and staff who looked at issues from a feminist point of view; it was not until Joanna Foster's appointment in 1988 that the EOC was led by someone with a background in the women's movement. During the decade the EOC changed from being primarily an information agency to taking an active role in strengthening sex-equality law. With EOC support, cases were brought before the European Court of Justice which led to rulings requiring Britain to make revisions in its sex-equality law. This led directly to the 1983 Equal Pay (Amendment) Regulations and the 1986 Sex Discrimination Act.

As the 1975 Sex Discrimination Act's limitations became more apparent, feminists campaigned for stronger enforcement provisions and for its extension to areas which had been excluded. Under pressure from the EC the Conservative Government introduced legislation that became the 1986 Sex Discrimination Act. It made collective bargaining agreements involving discrimination based on sex or marital status illegal, and extended the anti-discrimination law to small businesses that had been exempt. While it widened the law's scope, it avoided the pressure for stronger enforcement and introduced some changes that seemed disadvantageous to women. In a controversial clause welcomed by many employers, protective legislation for women was outlawed. It also declared that sex-differentiated retirement ages were illegal, implying that women's earlier retirement age would be eliminated.

By the 1990s the ambiguities in the concept of equality had become increasingly apparent. This was especially evident during the debate on pensionable age. The 1940 Old Age and Widows' Pensions Act had lowered women's pensionable age to 60 while maintaining men's at 65.[7] Under EC pressure to introduce equality, the Conservative Government chose to achieve it by raising the women's pensionable age to 65. While well-paid women benefited, and the government's financial obligations were reduced, the change is believed to have adversely affected most working-class women.

Women and the Labour Party

Women's position within the Labour Party has undergone a significant transformation since the 1970s. Although women comprised about 40 per cent of the party membership and have always done much of the party's grass-roots election work, they have been under-represented at the party's higher levels. This disparity grew during the postwar period: the number of female Labour MPs fell from 14 in 1950 to 10 in 1970 partially because the number of women candidates declined from 42 to 29. The party constitution specified that women hold at least five of the National Executive Committee's (NEC) 26 seats, but these were rarely an independent voice for women's interests because they were elected by the party conference, which tended to be dominated by trade union block votes. At the 1970 party conference only 143 of the 1,352 delegates were female. While the annual women's conference could discuss issues, its resolutions did not become party policy unless adopted by the party conference, which was not obligated even to consider them.

The women's movement in the 1960s and 1970s had little impact on the status of women within the Labour Party.[8] Although a party report, *Discrimination Against Women* (1972), drew attention to the under-representation of women on the NEC and at the party conference, it led to an attempt to abolish the seats reserved for women on the NEC. The Women's Advisory Committee resisted. It maintained that these seats should continue to be reserved for women until they had parity in party leadership positions, and urged the party to adopt this as its objective. Although the NEC retained the women's reserved seats, it postponed consideration of the proposal for parity by requesting a study of the special problems women encountered in politics. This deflected the pressure for reform and by the end of the 1970s there had been little change in women's position within the party.

Dissatisfied with the party's reluctance to alter its gender structure, Labour feminists established the Labour Women's Action Committee in 1980. It urged that the women's conference elect the women on the NEC so that they would be responsible to the party's women rather than to the male-dominated party conference. It also proposed that the women's conference have the right to send five resolutions to the party conference each year which the latter would be required to debate, and the inclusion of at least one woman on all shortlists from which parliamentary candidates were selected. Although the party did not adopt these reforms, it did agree to create a Ministry of Women which would be the sole responsibility of a cabinet minister. Jo Richardson, who had been an active spokesperson for women's rights, became the party's Shadow Minister for Women.

Labour women did not constitute a united gender bloc in the 1970s and did not become an effective pressure group until they developed a stronger sense of gender identity. Women as well as men were divided by the deep fissure that separated the party's Right and Left wings during the 1980s. Also, there were tensions between older working-class women whose class-based ideology encouraged them to view matters differently than younger feminist women who were often middle-class or better educated.[9] Specific issues, such as the basis for selecting parliamentary candidates, were also divisive. Should Labour feminists, for example, support all women or only those who were feminists? Should they support a female anti-feminist running against a male feminist?

The Social Democratic Party's formation in 1981 contributed to the pressure on the Labour Party to reform itself. The SDP established gender quotas when parliamentary candidates were being short-listed in order to increase the number of female candidates and appeal to women voters. Labour leaders recognised that this might shift female Labour voters to the new party and became more concerned with women's opportunities within the Labour Party.

Ultimately, it was the series of general election defeats between 1979 and 1992 that drove the Labour Party to reform its gender structure. After the 1987 defeat the party's own research indicated that it had a male image, and that this was contributing to the pattern of Conservative voting among women. In the 1992 election Conservative voting by females increased to such an extent that the gender gap became the widest it had been in any of the four elections since 1979. Labour would have won the election if women had voted Labour in the same proportion as men.

Once it accepted that winning the female vote was critical to improving its electoral prospects, the Labour Party introduced significant gender reforms. The 1990 party conference voted to introduce a quota system to increase female representation to at least 40 per cent of all committees and policy-making bodies. After it was required that Shadow Cabinet election ballots include at least three women, four women were elected to the Shadow Cabinet. The number of women on the NEC was increased from 5 to 12 (with 18 men). Some of the senior committees connected with the party leader's office were not affected because they were not under party rules, but with this exception the change was dramatic.

How to increase the number of women MPs proved to be the most difficult part of the scheme. The 1990 party conference voted to raise the proportion of women in the Parliamentary Labour Party (PLP) to 50 per cent within ten years or after the next three general elections, whichever came first. But, while the party supported the principle, there was considerable resistance to granting the NEC the power to implement the change. Constituencies were accustomed to selecting candidates without interference from the NEC, and attempts to pressure them to adopt women candidates were opposed as a step towards party centralisation. The number of women MPs rose from 21 to 37 in the 1992 general election, but as this represented only 14 per cent of the PLP it fell considerably short of the target.

The lack of progress resulted in the adoption of compulsory quotas. The 1993 party conference determined that women candidates should be selected in half the seats in which Labour MPs were retiring and in half of the most winnable seats. This would be accomplished through all-women shortlists – i.e., in selected constituencies only female applicants could be considered. The NEC was given the power to impose a list of female candidates from which the constituency must choose if it would not do so voluntarily.

The quota scheme was supported by John Smith, the new party leader, and by Labour feminist groups such as the Labour Women's Action Committee. But there was strong resistance within the party to the compulsory all-female short-

Plate 18.2. Prime Minister Tony Blair surrounded by (some of) Labour's 101 women MPs at Westminster, May 1997.

lists. After 38 women had been chosen by this method, two men who had been denied consideration because of the new policy claimed it violated the 1975 Sex Discrimination Act. In *Jepson v. The Labour Party* an industrial tribunal accepted their claim, and the party abandoned the policy. This may have important implications for the future, since few women were adopted as candidates for winnable seats after the compulsory short-lists were dropped.

The Labour Party's 1997 victory transformed the PLP's gender mix. The number of female Labour MPs increased from 37 to 101, which raised their proportion in the PLP to 25 per cent. Although there were more women candidates than in the 1992 election (159 to 138), the key to the change was the much greater number who were contesting winnable seats. Traditionally Labour (and the Conservatives) had chosen women to contest marginal seats in which the party's candidate, male or female, had little chance of winning, but the all-female short-lists placed many women candidates in seats that normally voted Labour.

As Labour leaders had anticipated, the greater number of women candidates led to increased female Labour voting. Although the proportion of both men and women voting Labour increased in 1997 compared to the 1992 election, the shift was greater among female voters: 16 per cent compared to 11 per cent by men. The 1992 election gender gap in favour of the Conservatives was eradicated as women and men voted in almost identical proportions for Labour.

The new Labour Government initiated several reforms aimed to appeal to female voters. Five women were appointed to the cabinet – a record high – and the position of a Minister for Women was established.[10] A women's unit was established inside the Cabinet Office. The latter developed new policies to assist lone parents, to encourage family-friendly employment, to reduce violence against women and to implement the principle that 50 per cent of public appointments should be filled by women. Since the implementation of these reforms requires broad support across departmental lines, the creation of a cabinet subcommittee on women, bringing together ministers from all major government departments, increased the likelihood of meaningful reform.

It is unclear whether the increased number of women MPs will be a permanent change. The gains made by women are precarious and could easily be reversed. The suspension of the use of all-women short-lists could have serious consequences, since they contributed significantly to the increased number of female candidates in winnable constituencies. Many of the new women MPs benefited from an unusually large voting shift to Labour in 1997; in a normal election their seats may return to the Conservative Party. Finally, the changes in the party's gender structure were driven by the need to win elections and did not necessarily imply a party consensus that the gender reforms were intrinsically desirable. The election of a large Labour parliamentary majority in 1997 removed some of the pressure for gender reform; it remains to be seen whether the party will continue to reform itself now that the electorally driven sense of urgency has been reduced.

Conclusion

Between 1960 and 2000 the women's movement's revival contributed to fundamental changes in the law relating to women. Female employees have a stronger legal position than in 1960 even though defects have limited the impact of equal pay and equal opportunities legislation. These legal changes have not eradicated gender inequality. Most workers in low-paid, low-status jobs continue to be women. Unexpectedly, the equality legislation has increased class differences between women; educated middle-class women have benefited the most, thus widening the gulf between them and working-class women. Furthermore, the changes in welfare legislation since 1976 have tended to reduce support for women needing assistance, especially lone mothers.[11] The steps taken toward gender justice in this period reflect the success of the women's movement in changing social attitudes, the increased importance of female voters, and the strengthened role of women within the major parties. Further progress toward gender justice is likely to be contingent upon a continuation of these trends.

Bibliographical Note

The developments covered by this chapter are so recent that a survey of the entire period remains to be written. A. Carter, *The Politics of Women's Rights* (London, 1992) provides a good synthesis up to the late 1980s. B. Caine, *English Feminism 1780–1980* (Oxford, 1997) is especially useful on feminist ideology. J. Lovenduski and V. Randall examine feminist involvement in politics in *Contemporary Feminist Politics: Women and Power in Britain* (Oxford, 1993). Elizabeth Meehan provides an overview of the relationship between feminist campaigns and gender legislation in 'British Feminism from the 1960s to the 1980s', in H.L. Smith (ed), *British Feminism in the Twentieth Century* (Aldershot, 1990) and in *Women's Rights at Work: Campaigns and Policy in Britain and the United States* (London, 1985). S. Fredman, *Women and the Law* (Oxford, 1997) reviews the changes in the law since 1960 that affect women. G.E. Maguire's concluding chapters in *Conservative Women: A History of Women and the Conservative Party, 1874–1997* (London, 1998) are helpful on Conservative Party women. The chapters by S. Perrigo, 'Women and Change in the Labour Party, 1979–1995', and C. Short, 'Women and the Labour Party' in J. Lovenduski and P. Norris (eds), *Women in Politics* (Oxford, 1996) are useful guides to the gender changes in the Labour Party.

Notes

1. D. Marsh and J. Chambers, *Abortion Politics* (London, 1981), p. 47.

2. H.L. Smith, 'The Politics of Conservative Reform: The Equal Pay for Equal Work Issue, 1945–1955', *Historical Journal* 35 (1992), pp. 401–15.

3. British sex equality legislation applies equally to men and women although it was assumed that in most instances it would be women who would need legal assistance to obtain equality.

4. Published in the *Guardian*, G2, 22 February 2000.

5. G.E. Maguire, *Conservative Women: A History of Women and the Conservative Party, 1874–1997* (London, 1998), p. 181.

6. In 1992 the EC issued a Directive that forced the Conservative Government to drop the requirements concerning length of service and the number of hours worked per week.

7. H.L. Smith, 'Gender and the Welfare State: The 1940 Old Age and Widows' Pensions Act', *History* 80 (1995), pp. 382–99.

8. S. Perrigo, 'Women, Gender and New Labour', in G.R. Taylor (ed), *The Impact of New Labour* (London, 1999), p. 164.

9. S. Perrigo, 'Women and Change in the Labour Party, 1979–1995', *Parliamentary Affairs* 49 (1996), p. 122.

10. Harriet Harman was originally appointed Minister for Women; in July 1998 she was replaced by Baroness Jay.

11. K. Kiernan, H. Land and J. Lewis, *Lone Motherhood in Twentieth-Century Britain* (Oxford, 1998), p. 292.

19

'RACE', ETHNICITY AND NATIONAL IDENTITY

Wendy Webster

'Where do you come from?'
'I'm from Glasgow.'
'Glasgow?'
'Uh huh. Glasgow.'
The white face hesitates
the eyebrows raise
the mouth opens
then snaps shut
incredulous
yet too polite to say outright
liar[1]

The opening of Jackie Kay's poem, 'So You Think I'm a Mule?', brings into sharp focus white perceptions of race in the late twentieth century from the perspective of a black woman. The opening gambit – 'where do you come from?' – shows the white woman's view that the black woman is not British, let alone Glaswegian, someone who belongs – if at all – elsewhere. In the first half of the twentieth century this 'elsewhere' was generally seen as an empire under British colonial rule, where black people were safely contained and controlled. In the 1950s and 1960s, when the colonial encounter was reversed through black and South Asian migration to Britain, 'coloured immigrants' were seen as a threat to Britishness. The pattern of familial imagery used in an imperial context – where Britain was the 'mother country', and the king was the father of a family which extended throughout the empire – was reversed as 'immigrants' were represented as 'dark strangers'. In twentieth-century mainstream media, the black woman was most likely to be represented as British when she was standing on an Olympic podium, receiving a gold medal.

The voice which dominates Kay's poem is that of the black woman who, in defining herself, resists white racism through self-representation. Relationships between white and black women and black women's resistances to racisms are themes of this chapter, which also traces the history of racisms against white groups. From the Commonwealth Immigration Act of 1962 a series of controls were introduced which were designed to reduce black and South Asian immigration, but controls in the first half of the twentieth century – a series of Aliens Acts from 1905 – were directed primarily at preventing further Jewish immigration to Britain. Anti-alienism continued after 1945, with anti-Jewish riots in many British cities in 1947. Irish migration to Britain was never restricted, but many migrants encountered anti-Irish racism on arrival in Britain, and in the 1950s the sign on private accommodation for rent which announced 'no coloureds' usually also announced 'no Irish'. The terms 'race' and ethnicity which often signal a focus on people who are racially and ethnically marked – as in the common use of 'ethnic minorities' to denote black and Asian people in Britain – are here used to explore white British femininity as a raced category, the ways in which it was defined not only in relation to black, but also to subordinate white ethnicities, and the different roles assigned to women in relation to motherhood, family and paid employment by 'race' and ethnicity.

It is impossible in a survey chapter of this kind to do justice to the complexity of the varied histories of different groups in Britain and differentiation within the groups discussed. 'South Asian women in Britain', for example, is a category which comprises women of different ethnicities, differentiated by religion and language – those who came to Britain from a number of South Asian, African and Caribbean countries and their descendants. Similarly 'white British women' is a category which comprises women of different ethnicities, who practised different religions and spoke different languages. Some of them did not identify as British, and some – notably Irish nationalist women – strongly contested their construction as British. Both categories are also differentiated by – among other factors – class, generation and sexuality. The aim of the chapter is to consider selected aspects of the histories of different groups of women in a British context and to trace some of the connections between these histories.

Motherhood

'By instruction leading to the improvement of the individual we shall aid in preserving women for their supreme purpose, the procreation and preservation of the race, and at the same time promote that race to a better standard, mentally and physically.'[2] In identifying women's national role as motherhood, J.E. Gemmell's message in 1903, in his Presidential Address to the North of England Obstetrical and Gynaecological Society, articulated attitudes which were characteristic of the first half of the twentieth century. At the beginning of the century such an identification was intensified by the Anglo-Boer war of 1899–1902 which produced widespread concern about the 'physical deterioration' of the British population, when more than one-third of volunteers failed to pass the physical exam for the armed forces. In his concerns about the quality as well as the quantity of the population Gemmell also articulated common attitudes. Evidence of declining birth rates, especially among the middle classes, was produced throughout the first half of the century to buttress arguments that the quality of the population was deteriorating due to fertility among the wrong sections of the population – a concern promoted particularly by the eugenics movement. They were also used to show that numbers were declining below replacement level, fuelling fears of 'race suicide'. Pronatalism, albeit qualified by concerns about quality as well as quantity, was pervasive in the first half of the century.

The need to maintain British power and influence in the world was a central concern of those who saw women as 'mothers of the race'. It was assumed that Britain could do the work of an imperial nation only by keeping numbers up, and preferably numbers of sufficient quality. As Herbert Samuel, Liberal President of the Local Government Board, wrote in the preface to the Women's Co-operative Guild's 1916 publication, *Maternity: Letters from Working Women*; 'In the competition and conflict of civilizations it is the mass of the nations that tells. . . . The ideals for which Britain stands can only prevail as long as they are backed by a sufficient mass of numbers.'[3] The 'sufficient mass' was needed not only to staff its industries and armed forces at home, but also to populate the settler territories through emigration, for there were fears that if Britain did not produce sufficient numbers to populate its empire then other European imperial powers would. Women were themselves sometimes encouraged to emigrate, especially to South Africa in the aftermath of the Anglo-Boer war. These concerns were just as apparent by mid-century as they were at its beginning. In 1935 Neville Chamberlain warned that the time would come when 'the British Empire will be crying out for more citizens of the right breed and when we in this country shall not be able to supply the demand'. The Beveridge Report of 1942 stated: 'In the next thirty years housewives as Mothers have vital work to do in ensuring the adequate continuance of the British race and of British ideals in the world.' Winston Churchill, who set up the Royal Commission on Population in 1944, argued in 1943 that for Britain 'to maintain its leadership of the world and survive as a great power that can hold its own against external pressure, our people must be encouraged by every means to have larger families'.[4]

When Gemmell spoke of 'the procreation and preservation of the race', he used a term which was often used interchangeably with 'nation' and usually signalled, either implicitly or explicitly, 'the white race' and sometimes 'the British race' or 'Anglo-Saxon race'. Women were envisaged fulfilling their 'supreme purpose' in an imperial as well as a metropolitan setting, and Welsh and Scottish women were sometimes encouraged to bear children to further not only the cause of empire but also the reproduction of the Welsh and Scottish nations. However, although all females born within the British empire were British subjects, the role of procreating 'the race' was assigned only to white British women. In New Zealand there were fears between the wars of a falling white birth rate in contrast to a rising Maori birth rate. The Royal Commission on the West Indies, reporting in 1945, recommended a reduction in the number of births as an indispensable condition for maintaining the standard of life.

The encouragement offered to some women to reproduce and the discouragement of other women along racial lines applied in a metropolitan as well as a colonial context. Before the 1960s, fears of 'miscegenation' were central to the notion of a 'colour problem' in Britain and meant that it was white women's motherhood of children fathered by black men that was foregrounded, not black women's own motherhood. But in the early 1960s attention shifted from 'miscegenation' towards black women's reproduction, and black and Asian women were seen as over-fecund. Although there were no official policies to control black and Asian reproduction in Britain, long-term contraceptives like Depo Provera were more likely to be prescribed for black and Asian women, as well as white working-class women, and black women were more likely to be encouraged to have abortions and sterilisations.

Family

'Not a day passes but English families are ruthlessly turned out to make room for foreign invaders.'[5] It was in advocating the control of Jewish immigration that William Gordon, Conservative MP for Stepney, imagined English families under threat in a speech in the House of Commons in 1902. The image of an England under siege by foreigners has been common to many advocates of immigration controls directed against particular groups in the twentieth century. Enoch Powell's notorious 'rivers of blood' speech in 1968 used similar imagery in advocating further restrictions on black immigration. In representing Englishness rather than Britishness through reference to the small-scale and familiar – families, home – a particular exclusive and intimate identity was invoked. After 1945 black immigrants were characterised in terms of an incapacity for domestic and familial life, and in such contexts both 'family' and 'home' were constructed as white.

The invasion of England was imagined particularly through the figure of the white woman whose national role as mother involved the policing of internal frontiers, through control of her sexuality and procreation. Concerns about 'miscegenation' surfaced in various contexts in the first half of the century. A newspaper headline in 1906 – 'tainting the race' – referred to the employment of Chinese seamen and resulting settlement of Chinese communities in London and other ports, and spoke of the results of interracial mixing between Chinese men and English women as 'swarms of half-bred children to be seen in the district'.[6] The Chief Constable of Cardiff's proposal of a legal ban on 'miscegenation' in 1929 referred to the employment of African and Indian seamen, and resulting settlement in ports like Cardiff and Liverpool. Although interracial sex was never made illegal, fears of 'tainting the race' were extended during the Second World War as black British and American soldiers served in Britain. In the post-1945 period such fears intensified and were highly gendered, always foregrounding the figures of the black man and the white woman. Characteristic questions were those posed by *Picture Post* in 1954: 'Would you let your daughter marry a negro?', and by the *Daily Express* in 1956; 'Would you let your daughter marry a black man?'[7] Children who were the product of an interracial union, although they might be formally British, were regarded as a threat to Britishness. Black migration to Britain brought a fear of the collapse of boundaries between colonisers and colonised, black and white, and it was particularly through the breaching of this internal frontier that such a collapse was imagined.

The state moved increasingly in the twentieth century to support the white British family. Social policy in the first half of the century, shaped by the emphasis on producing a physically fit population to run the empire, increasingly emphasised women as mothers. After 1945 the expanded postwar welfare state provided a range of benefits to women as mothers, including Family Allowances from 1945, Child Benefit from 1975, and free antenatal care and childbirth through the National Health Service. A concern to support the family through state provision, however, was not as evident for groups who were regarded as non-British or non-white. Some benefits introduced in the early twentieth century – old age pensions and health insurance schemes – made eligibility dependent on residence and nationality qualifications for varying periods of time, excluding many Jewish people in Britain. Some benefits of the expanded post-1945 welfare state also stipulated residence in Britain for a period of time – notably local rules in the allocation of council housing. By the 1980s, as moves were made to exclude 'persons from abroad' from supplementary benefits, black and Asian people increasingly found themselves required to prove their eligibility and benefit agencies sometimes operated as agencies of immigration control. From 1982 onwards free hospital treatment was made dependent on residency tests, and Asian women attending antenatal clinics in Leicester were routinely expected to produce passports since the mid-1970s. Black and Asian people might also be required to produce passports when they made applications for housing or enrolled their children in schools.

It was through immigration controls from the 1960s, that the view of the black and Asian family as one which was not supported by the state became most apparent. Rules designed to limit the entry of dependants meant the enforced separation of many families, particularly through the operation of the 'sole responsibility rule' and the 'primary purpose rule'. The former required that a single parent, seeking to have children join them in Britain, must prove that they had 'sole responsibility' for the child's upbringing. When literally interpreted it was impossible to meet this requirement since the parent was seeking reunion with a child after a period of separation. The 'primary purpose' rule gave immigration officials the power to refuse entry to a foreign spouse if it was judged that the 'primary purpose' of the marriage was to secure residence in Britain, and was directed particularly against Asian women bringing in fiancés or husbands. When the British government was taken to the European court for sex discrimination in 1985, the rule was changed to apply equally to both sexes whose spouses/fiancé(e)s sought entry. Under immigration rules those 'sponsoring' the entry of family members had to show that they could maintain and accommodate them without recourse to public funds.

Paid Employment

In 1955, Basil Henriques, a London magistrate, proposed legislation to regulate the working hours of mothers of school-age children, arguing that 'the strength of the nation is built upon the strength of the home life of the citizens who comprise the nation'.[8] His emphasis on women's home-centred roles as wives and mothers and the opposition between such a role and paid employment was characteristic of the period before 1939, when women's main national role was defined as motherhood, opportunities for paid employment were highly restricted, and a marriage bar operated formally and informally in both the private and public sectors. His proposals indicate a particular response to post-1945 changes, which included the dismantling of the marriage bar. A feminisation of the labour market through increased rates of participation, particularly of married women in part-time work, and the development of the service sector – accelerating in the 1970s – was a main development of the second half of the twentieth century.

Women were differently positioned in relation to these developments by ethnicity which, with other factors, shaped relationships to the labour market, including rates and patterns of participation and concentration in particular sectors. Before 1939, while there were considerable variations in participation rates in different English regions, figures for Wales showed a lower participation rate than for Scotland or for any English region. Irish women, however, were recruited to the labour market in a range of occupations including textiles, nursing and domestic service. Such recruitment provides one example of how migrant women's employment was used to support indigenous women's family and domestic life, and was particularly marked in the period immediately following the war. The acute labour shortages of the late 1940s and the need for female labour conflicted with pervasive pronatalism, and one means of resolving this conflict was through migrant women's labour. Black women were recruited to work in the National Health Service and in hotels and catering, mainly from Africa and the Caribbean, but there was a strong preference for Europeans. Irish women continued to be recruited as nurses and midwives, with 1,176 Irish women starting as nurses in British hospitals in 1947. European Volunteer Workers were recruited particularly into textiles, as were Italian women. Thus, while the role of wife and mother was emphasised for indigenous women, in this period migrant women were regarded primarily as workers.

In the second half of the century, as it became increasingly acceptable for married women to participate in paid employment, the feminisation of the labour market was characterised by an increase in women who worked part-time. This development, however, was particularly marked among indigenous women. Although rates of participation differed between groups, and were higher among African-Caribbean women than indigenous women and lower among Pakistani and Bangladeshi women, a range of groups had higher rates of full-time work than indigenous women including Caribbean, African, Indian, Pakistani, Bangladeshi and Chinese women. While all women's employment was characterised by confinement to a narrow range of occupations throughout the century, most non-indigenous groups were concentrated in an even narrower range of occupations than indigenous women – predominantly in low-paid and low-status work, and in the lower grades of most occupations. There were some changes towards the end of the century, and increasing numbers of women in non-indigenous groups were recruited to sectors like banking, retailing and local government and to managerial positions in the public sector. Class was also an important factor within all groups in shaping relationships to the labour market. It has been argued, for example, that in some contexts, the commonalities between young white and black working-class women were greater than those between all young white women or all young black women.[9] But the broad picture is one in which it was predominantly indigenous women who enjoyed some limited upward mobility in the labour market.

IN FOCUS: Women as European Volunteer Workers in Britain

The term 'European Volunteer Worker' (EVW) merged into one category people of diverse nationalities – chiefly Polish, Ukrainian, Yugoslavian, Estonian, Latvian and Lithuanian – who were recruited to the British labour force in the late 1940s from displaced persons camps in Europe. Some had ended the war in camps as a result of a flight westwards to escape the advance of Russian forces, and others as a result of German occupation of their countries and subsequent deportation to Germany as enforced workers. Although the majority were male, 21,434 women were recruited, mainly to work in the textile industry in Lancashire and West Yorkshire.

EVWs occupied a position on a borderline between all those considered 'undesirable immigrants' – whether Jewish, black or Asian – and dominant white ethnicities in Britain. They were officially seen as 'suitable immigrants' – a term which contrasted with the term 'undesirable immigrants', used in the 1905 Aliens Act. The notion of 'suitable immigrant' was constructed both against Jews and against black migrants. Few Jewish people were recruited as EVWs, and a Foreign Office memorandum instructed that 'the situation in Palestine, and anti semitics [sic], clearly prevent the recruitment of Jews'.[10] The scheme indicated a preference for European migrants over black and Asian migrants from colonies and former colonies who were seen not as 'suitable immigrants' but as a 'colour problem' and a threat to Britishness. Even so EVWs were formally aliens, and as such their labour could be controlled and directed into particular industries and services – predominantly into low-pay and low-status work. Moreover many

Women as European Volunteer Workers in Britain (continued)

encountered hostility on arrival in Britain from neighbours, local communities and fellow-workers.

As questions about who was British, who could become British and who belonged in Britain were addressed after 1945, the notion of EVWs as 'suitable immigrants' signalled the development of a hierarchy of belonging which was not only raced but also gendered. Labour from colonies and former colonies was also recruited in a period of acute labour shortage. But EVW men, although mainly wanted as flexible and mobile workers, were also preferred in part because, unlike black migrants, they were not associated with the notion of 'miscegenation'. The possibility that they might intermarry with white British women and boost the birth rate was even canvassed as a positive aspect of their recruitment. At the same time they were subordinated to dominant white ethnicities in Britain as aliens employed on a contract basis. Thus gendered definitions of EVWs as 'suitable immigrants' were produced both against black migrants and dominant white ethnicities in Britain.

The recruitment of EVW women suggests some of the complexities of the history of gender, 'race' and ethnicity in the twentieth century. At a time when recruitment campaigns were attempting to attract indigenous women into the textile industry, it provided a way of resolving a conflict between pronatalist policies and the need for female labour. As the image of the

Plate 19.1. Young Ukrainian women who came to Britain as European Volunteer Workers. Photo taken by Charles Dak studio, Preston, *c.* 1947.

Women as European Volunteer Workers in Britain (continued)

white British woman war-worker faded quickly after 1945, the EVW woman was represented as an exemplary worker engaged in boosting the export drive, particularly through her efforts in the textile industry. The criteria for suitability in selection procedures in displaced persons camps were able-bodiedness, health and youth, and there was a strong preference for single women who would not bring dependants into Britain. In this context the most important characteristic of indigenous women as defined by a range of pronatalist literatures was their capacity to bear children, while the most important characteristic of EVW women was their capacity to work. EVW women were preferred over black women who were also recruited in the late 1940s and 1950s, but like black women they were defined against indigenous women as workers rather than mothers.

Resistances

In 1996 Farida Khanum acted against Vauxhall car company and in 1997 Amna Mahmood sued Body Shop for racial discrimination. In both cases employers had sacked them for wearing the *hijab*.[11] In this way the *hijab*, which in Western stereotypes of Muslim women signified their oppression was transformed by Muslim women in Britain into a sign of resistance to racism. The image of the passive South Asian woman was also belied by their role in industrial disputes, with women playing leading roles in many strikes including those at Imperial Typewriters in Leicester in 1974, at Grunwick photo-processing in London in 1976, and the much less publicised strike at Burnsall metal finishing plant in Birmingham in 1992–93. Black women ancillary workers also played roles in health service strikes in 1972 and 1982–83.

Much of the work on 'race' and gender in Britain has emphasised the import-ance of familial and community networks as an important source of support for such workplace action, as well as for many campaigns against racism – including the work of the Afro-Asian Caribbean Conference, anti-deportation campaigns and campaigns against Depo-Provera. Women were involved in the develop-ment of community organisations – for example in the foundation of churches and clubs which were common to the histories of many migrants, including Irish, Caribbean, Polish, Cypriot and East African Asian groups. But women also drew on familial and community resources in areas which, through their exist-ence on the boundaries between public and private, do not easily fit a model of community as public. Mary Chamberlain's work on Barbadian migrants has shown how, in a culture of migration, families played an important role in facilitating migration – through loans to pay passages, or provision of childcare – while migrants reciprocated through contributions from their earnings for

Plate 19.2. Asian women in Unison picketing, Hillingdon Hospital, West London, 1996. This strike was one of several labour disputes in which Asian women played a leading role in recent decades.

the support of family back home.[12] This culture, transferred to Britain, enabled the development of support networks as migrants joined friends, neighbours and relatives already in Britain. Caribbean women often played an important role in initiating 'pardners' and 'sou sous' – pooling community resources to fund passages to bring children over to Britain or deposits for buying houses in a context where many experienced great difficulty in establishing family life in Britain as a result of racism in the housing market.

The importance of marshalling familial and community resources to reaffirm ethnic and religious identities in opposition to racisms and to secure emotional as well as physical and economic survival is a well-attested theme in studies of first generation groups. However, communities were heterogeneous, complex and dynamic, and women drew on a range of resources to negotiate identities in Britain in relation to diverse experiences, including racisms. Differences within as well as between groups in the values and meaning assigned to family and community were significant, changing according to context as well as over time. Studies of both Irish and Barbadian migrants to Britain have shown that women's motivations for migration were diverse and included a search for economic independence, and a desire to break away from family ties or restrictions on freedom and autonomy, which could include the need to escape sexual abuse and domestic violence. Bhachu's work on Sikh women has suggested that paid employment in Britain – however low-status and low-pay – allowed for the renegotiation of family roles which was welcome in so far as it allowed a challenge to the authority of older generations.[13] Criticising existing literature for its assumption that ethnic groups enforce ethnicity as fixed rather than fluid and changing structures, Bhachu emphasises Asian women as active negotiators of cultural values that they choose to accept, and originators of new cultural forms, looking at the way Sikh women who participate in the labour market negotiate more dowry than those who do not.[14] However, this is one of the few examples of work which focuses on second-generation women in Britain. Most of the literatures which emphasise the importance of community is on first-generation groups, and work on those born in Britain – who by the late 1980s comprised 57 per cent of Caribbean people in Britain and 50 per cent of Pakistanis – has rarely focused on women or explored issues of gender.

Representations

What was distinctive about white British femininity remained rather ill-defined in the twentieth century. Women had a much more tenuous and indirect relationship to Britishness than men, and were often subsumed into a transnational category particularly through an emphasis on motherhood. Despite this emphasis they could not pass on nationality to children in their own right before 1981. Fears of 'miscegenation' made explicit how far they were regarded as the sexual property of white British men while, before 1948, nationality law meant that on marriage to a man who was legally an alien they lost their nationality. While female figures were often used to symbolise nation, the qualities of Britishness were usually represented through reference to white British masculinity. In stories of the Second World War, for example, which occupied an important place in ideas of British national identity after 1945, men were generally foregrounded, especially as members of the armed forces or prisoners of war. National memorials commemorating the dead did not include one to the largest category in which women died – civilians. While British masculinity was constructed in such stories through contrast with an external 'other' – predominantly German or Japanese – in other narratives the contrast was with internal 'others' which were also defined predominantly in male terms – whether as the Jewish 'Shylock', the black (male) youth as criminal, or the Irish 'Paddy'.

In the second half of the century, however, women were increasingly foregrounded in narratives of nation which told a story of vulnerability and decline. In the 1950s, representations of empire and its legacy – resistance to colonial rule in empire and 'immigrants' in the metropolis – increasingly converged on a common theme: the threat to an Englishness symbolised by the idea of 'home'. In these images the white woman as the guardian of a home was constructed against the black man who violated this domestic sanctuary – as a 'bandit' in Malaya, a Mau Mau in Kenya, or an 'immigrant' in the metropolis. Oppositions between 'immigrants' and Englishness were gendered as well as raced – the former generally represented as a black man and the latter frequently embodied in the figure of a white woman. The black man was often seen as transient and adrift, rarely represented as having family or settled home, and characterised in terms of an incapacity for domestic and familial life. The white woman embodied Englishness as domestic and familial life, and the notions of the rooted and stable – belonging, attachment and settlement – that this suggested.

The black and South Asian woman, invisible in most contexts, was also made visible in reinforcing the association of white British women with civilisation. In the early part of the century the image of the benighted Eastern woman confined to the *harem* or *zenana* was extensively mobilised by white British women, who advanced their claims to the vote through invoking her as a figure who needed them to speak on her behalf, as well as one who showed their racial superiority, and thus their fitness for citizenship. This version of white British femininity as emancipated in contrast to the backwardness of colonised women was sometimes seen as contradicting the emphasis on motherhood. The university woman or suffragist, who might in some contexts be used as a symbol of British civilisation, was castigated in other contexts for her lack of enthusiasm for motherhood and blamed for the declining birth rate. But as the century developed, an emphasis on white British women's active role in the public sphere as a sign of Britain as a modern nation became increasingly dominant.

The signs which denoted primitive/civilised and backward/modern varied, and the opposition was developed in different ways in relation to the black woman and the Eastern woman in colonial and metropolitan contexts at different times in the period to produce competing and contradictory images. The 'other' imagined mainly in a colonial setting before mid-century, was thereafter increasingly likely to be seen as an internal 'other', living in a terraced house in Bradford or wearing the *hijab* at school or work. The white woman was seen as controlled and constrained in contrast to the black African or Caribbean woman who was regarded as more 'body-like', whether her body was seen as dirty, diseased, promiscuous, hypersexual and animalistic or, in ostensibly more favourable images, as instinctive and rhythmic – in dance, sport or childbirth. The white woman was also seen as emancipated through her mobility, ability to travel and access to the public sphere in contrast to the Eastern woman as mysterious and exotic, or passive and submissive to men. These contradictions were compounded by the increasing adoption of sexual freedom as a sign of the modern woman from the 1960s. Vron Ware comments, for example, on the way in which the British Royal Family were often used to reinforce the image of the civilised white woman, marked by her social and sexual freedom, symbolised particularly by her clothes, in media coverage of royal visits to the Middle East, especially by Princess Diana.[15]

Representations of women in empire also drew on these oppositions and frequently showed a doughty and intrepid white British woman participating in a common pioneering adventure with British men whose qualities – singularity, courage, strength – she shared. Colonial nostalgia of the 1980s popularised these representations, often producing romanticised images, and suggested not only the enduring nature of imperial identity in imaginings of the nation, but also the extent to which such an identity could be embodied in the figure of a woman. At the same time pervasive anxieties about white masculinity after 1945, associated with fears of Americanisation, immigration and loss of imperial power were addressed through a misogynistic discourse which showed women emasculating men. The difficulties in articulating national identity as virile and masculine in post-imperial Britain could thus produce a much less flattering portrayal of the white British woman which blamed her for national weakness.

Conclusion

The twentieth century was a period of British national decline, foreshadowed by the Anglo-Boer war and the anxieties about national weakness that this provoked. Developing during the interwar period when colonial rule was contested through the Irish War of Independence and the rise of Indian nationalism, anxieties about decline intensified sharply after 1945 with the loss of imperial power and the rise of the United States and Soviet Union. This context of imperialism and subsequent decolonisation is important to an understanding of the connections between the histories of different groups of women in Britain.

Imperialism was significant in the construction of white British women's national role as mothers in the first half of the century. This was not a role assigned to colonised women, who were represented as backward and benighted particularly through reference to their familial life, in practices like *purdah*. A similar contrast between mothers and 'others' can be traced in the immediate post-1945 period, when labour shortages were filled through the recruitment of migrant female labour, facilitating white British women's role as mothers. As Britain made the transition from colonial power to post-colonial nation after 1945, the emphasis on motherhood was reworked into a more general role assigned to white British women as guardians of the home – a 'home' which sometimes signified domestic and familial life, and sometimes the Englishness of which such life became an increasingly important symbol. A woman in empire guarding such a home against invasion was a common image of colonial wars in the 1950s. By the time of Enoch Powell's 'rivers of blood' speech in 1968, the idea of domestic order guarded by an English woman in a quiet English street had become a common image of a nation under siege by 'immigrants'. State policies developed in the century offering increasing support to the white home and family, while forcibly separating many black and Asian families, show how far the notion of the home and family as white had currency across a range of practices as well as representations.

Resistances to racisms by women in Britain in the twentieth century often developed and marshalled familial and community resources, but in this process a diversity of meanings were assigned to 'family' and 'community' in different contexts. Jackie Kay's poem offers one version of 'community' in a particular context. The white woman's interrogation – 'where do you come from' – is prompted partly by the idea that the black woman belongs nowhere because she is a 'mulatto' – part of the 'mixed race problem'. The black woman's voice identifies 'belonging' with her 'black sisters' and offers black feminism as one version of community in Britain. The poem ends:

> 'I'm going to my Black sisters
> to women who nourish each other
> on belonging
> There's a lot of us
> Black women struggling to define
> just who we are
> where we belong
> and if we know no home
> we know one thing:
> we are Black
> we're at home with that.'
> 'Well, that's all very well, but . . .'
> 'I know it's very well.
> No But. Good bye.'

Bibliographical Note

The literature on white British women and imperialism in the twentieth century does not extend much beyond 1918. See especially A. Davin, 'Imperialism and Motherhood', *History Workshop Journal* 5 (1978); V. Ware, *Beyond the Pale: White Women, Racism and History* (London, 1992); and A. Burton, *Burdens of History: British Feminists, Indian Women, and Imperial Culture, 1865–1915* (London, 1994). For black feminist perspectives on imperialism and the history of black and Asian women in Britain see A. Brah, *Cartographies of Diaspora: Contesting Identities* (London, 1996); B. Bousquet and C. Douglas, *West Indian Women at War: British Racism and World War II* (London, 1991); and two recent collections, D. Jarrett-Macauley (ed), *Reconstructing Womanhood, Reconstructing Feminism: Writings on Black Women* (London, 1996); and H. Mirza (ed), *Black British Feminism: A Reader* (London, 1997). A useful study focusing on employment is R. Bhavnani, *Black Women in the Labour Market: A Research Review* (Manchester, 1994).

Articles on white migrants in Britain which focus on women include B. Gray, ' "The Home of Our Mothers and Our Birthright for Ages"?: Nation, Diaspora and Irish Women', in M. Maynard and J. Purvis (eds), *New Frontiers in Women's Studies: Knowledge, Identity and Nationalism* (London, 1996); W. Webster, 'Defining Boundaries: European Volunteer Worker Women in Britain', *Women's History Review* 9 (2000). There is very little work on second-generation women, but see P. Bhachu, 'Culture, Ethnicity and Class among Punjabi Sikh Women in 1990s Britain', *New Community* 17 (1991). A range of oral histories include A. Wilson, *Finding a Voice: Asian Women in Britain* (London, 1978); B. Bryan, S. Dadzie and S. Scafe, *The Heart of the Race: Black Women's Lives in Britain* (London, 1985); M. Lennon, M. McAdam and J. O'Brien (eds), *Across the Water: Irish Women's Lives in Britain* (London, 1988); Jewish Women in London Group, *Generations of Memories: Voices of Jewish Women* (London, 1989).

A major study of postwar immigration policy is K. Paul, *Whitewashing Britain: Race and Citizenship in the Postwar Era* (Ithaca, NY, 1997). For anti-alienism, see T. Kushner, 'Remembering to Forget: Racism and Anti-Racism in Postwar Britain', in B. Cheyette and L. Marcus (eds), *Modernity, Culture and 'the Jew'* (Cambridge, 1998). There is relatively little written on gendered discourses of Britishness and Englishness in the twentieth century, but see J. Mackay and P. Thane, 'The Englishwoman', in R. Colls and P. Dodd (eds), *Englishness: Politics and Culture 1880–1920* (London, 1986); and W. Webster, *Imagining Home: Gender, 'Race' and National Identity, 1945–64* (London, 1998).

Notes

1. J. Kay, 'So You Think I'm a Mule', in B. Burford, *A Dangerous Knowing: Four Black Women Poets* (London, 1985).

2. Quoted in V. Ware, *Beyond the Pale: White Women, Racism and History* (London, 1992), p. 35.

3. M. Llewellyn Davies, *Maternity: Letters from Working Women* (London, 1916), Preface.

4. Quoted in F. Klug, '"Oh to be in England": The British Case Study', in N. Yuval-Davis and F. Anthias (eds), *Woman–Nation–State* (Basingstoke, 1989), p. 21; E. Wilson, *Women and the Welfare State* (London, 1977), p. 152; B. Brookes, *Abortion in England 1900–1967* (London, 1988), p. 134.

5. Quoted in S. Cohen, 'Anti-semitism, Immigration Controls and the Welfare State', *Critical Social Policy* 13 (1985), p. 74.

6. Quoted in J. Gabriel, *Whitewash: Racialized Politics and the Media* (London, 1998), p. 58.

7. T. Philpott, 'Would You Let Your Daughter Marry a Negro?', *Picture Post*, 30 October 1954; *Daily Express*, 18 July 1956.

8. B. Henriques, *The Home-Menders: The Prevention of Unhappiness in Children* (London, 1955), pp. 33–4.

9. R. Bhavnani, *Black Women in the Labour Market: A Research Review* (Manchester, 1994), p. viii.

10. Quoted in T. Kushner, 'Remembering to Forget: Racism and Anti-Racism in Postwar Britain', in B. Cheyette and L. Marcus (eds), *Modernity, Culture and 'the Jew'* (Cambridge, 1998).

11. Cases reported in *East*, 22 November 1996; *The Observer*, 26 January 1997. I am grateful to Shaheen Safdar for bringing these cases to my attention.

12. M. Chamberlain, 'Gender and Narratives of Migration', *History Workshop Journal* 43 (1997).

13. *Ibid.*; B. Gray, '"The Home of Our Mothers and Our Birthright for Ages"?: Nation, Diaspora and Irish Women', in M. Maynard and J. Purvis (eds), *New Frontiers in Women's Studies: Knowledge, Identity and Nationalism* (London, 1996), pp. 165–6; P. Bhachu, '*Apri Marzi Kardhi*, Home and Work: Sikh Women in Britain', in S. Westwood and P. Bhachu (eds), *Enterprising Women: Ethnicity, Economy and Gender Relations* (London, 1988).

14. P. Bhachu, 'Culture, Ethnicity and Class Among Punjabi Sikh Women in 1990s Britain', *New Community* 17 (1991).

15. V. Ware, *Beyond the Pale: White Women, Racism and History* (London, 1992), p. 15.

20

WAR AND PEACE

Lucy Noakes

The periods that we know as wartime form a large and important part of both written and unwritten histories. War often acts as a springboard for personal memories and testimonies, providing the individual with memories of a time when he or she was active in the public sphere, taking part in events widely recognised as important. Historians have often focused on warfare and wartime, discussing the causes, patterns and effects of warfare for nations, governments and social groups. This chapter focuses upon the relationship of women to war, examining two, opposing, groups of women: those in the military and those active in the peace movement.

Women in the Armed Forces

The most visible way in which total war affected women's lives was the appearance of women in uniform; 80–90,000 women joined the Women's Army Auxiliary Corps (WAAC), the Women's Royal Naval Service (WRNS) and the Women's Royal Air Force (WRAF) in the last two years of the First World War. The numbers of women in the auxiliary services were even greater in the Second World War, reaching 494,000 by 1944. Women in the services undertook a wide range of tasks, ranging from laundry woman to linguist, from hairdresser to height-finder on anti-aircraft sites. However, although it was recognised that women in uniform were performing tasks necessary to the successful conclusion of both wars, their presence remained a problematic one. Femininity and militarism were widely seen as inimical.

Prior to the First World War the female combatant had been an unusual and isolated figure. Women such as Phoebe Hessel (1713–1821) and Mary Anne Talbot (1778–1808) disguised themselves as men in order to serve as soldiers. Because women such as these *were* so unusual their presence did little to challenge and undermine existing gender roles. The First Aid Nursing Yeomanry (FANY) founded in 1907, was the first quasi-military organisation to recruit women. Edward Baker, the Corps founder, envisaged the women serving on the battlefield, riding out to rescue injured soldiers before nursing them. FANY attracted independent-minded women from the upper classes and, although membership of the corps always remained small and socially limited, it provided a model for the sort of voluntary work that women could undertake in wartime.

When war broke out in 1914 FANY was joined by a large number of other voluntary organisations, including the Women's Defence Relief Corps, the Women's Auxiliary Force, the Women's Emergency Corps and the Women's Volunteer Reserve. The initial offers of help from these organisations were rejected by the War Office and the women of FANY spent the war serving with the French army. It was only when the army began to experience manpower shortages that the work of the women's voluntary organisations was recognised. In 1916 the Director General of National Service declared that he would be unable to find the necessary numbers of men for the front line unless more women took up war work. The subsequent Report to the Army Council in January 1917 recommended that women be employed behind the lines in France, organised into Units overseen by female officers. Following this, the establishment of the WAAC was announced in the press on 20 February 1917. The first draft of women, all recruited from the Women's Legion, arrived in France in March 1917.

From the outset the WAAC were clearly seen by the War Office as potentially problematic, and various attempts were made to ensure that the women were not thought of, and did not think of themselves, as soldiers. Helen Gwynne Vaughan, the Chief Controller of the WAAC in France, and Mona Chalmers Watson, the Director stationed in London, fought an ongoing battle with the War Office regarding the status of women in uniform. Officially, the WAAC remained a civilian organisation, attached to the army but not subject to army law. However, in practice, being in the WAAC was very much like being a member of the military. The women wore uniform, learnt to drill and parade, were organised by rank and were subject to strict rules regarding leave, behaviour and appearance.

All the minutiae of WAAC organisation had to be agreed within the War Office and obtaining agreement was often a long and fraught process. Gwynne Vaughan's initial suggestion that the general pattern of army organisation be followed caused consternation within the War Office. The compromise that was eventually reached meant that the women's ranks went from Chief Controller, the equivalent of Lieutenant Colonel, to Forewomen for Sergeants and Workers for Privates. Badges of rank were indicated by coloured shoulder straps and insignia of flowers and laurel wreathes. The conservative male institution that was the army needed women to undertake the non-combatant duties behind the lines. At the same time it was deeply suspicious of the emancipated women who were often attracted to such work. The subsequent organisation of the WAAC reflected the perceived need to maintain the femininity of women within a militaristic organisation.

By the beginning of 1918 rumours were widely circulating in Britain regarding the supposed immorality of the WAACs in France. The more far-fetched of the rumours included a maternity home specifically for WAACs, with a £50 bonus to each woman who became a mother. Newspaper reports of alleged prostitution led to problems in recruiting, and in an attempt to disprove these rumours the Ministry of Labour organised a Committee to investigate women's behaviour. Reporting in March 1918, the Commission concluded that not only were the rumours unfounded, but levels of unmarried pregnancy were lower in the WAAC than in the general population. In April 1918 the WAAC became Queen Mary's Army Auxiliary Corps (QMAAC) when Queen Mary became Commander in Chief in recognition of 'good services . . . both at home and abroad'.[1] The death and burial with full military honours of eight members of the QMAAC, when their camp at Abbeville was bombed, probably did more than anything else to change public perception of the women.

By the end of the war 80–90,000 women had served in the QMAAC, the WRNS (formed November 1917) and the WRAF (April 1918). In November 1918 31,850 women were serving with the QMAAC in Britain, 8,540 in France. When the last women were demobbed in 1921 they had earned the right to lay a wreath on the cenotaph. Despite this, many of the problems that faced the female 'soldiers' of the First World War were encountered again by their counterparts in the Second World War.

The interwar period was shaped almost as much by preparations for the coming war as it was by the needs of peacetime society. The apocalyptic potential of 'war in the air' was a recurring feature of interwar fiction and, increasingly, state policy. However, the wartime role of women in uniform became little but a memory, kept alive by Old Comrades Associations, until 1934 when Lady Londonderry suggested a scheme to unite all the women's voluntary services. From this emerged the Emergency Service, run by Gwynne Vaughan, founded in 1936 to train women officers for times of 'national emergency'. By 1937 the Emergency Service, the Women's Legion and the FANY were recognised by the Army Council and in 1938 it was proposed that the three organisations be amalgamated under the auspices of the Territorial Army. The Auxiliary Territorial Service (ATS), as it became known, with Gwynne Vaughan as Director, was created by Royal Warrant during the Munich crisis in September 1938.

Again the gender of the ATS shaped both the work undertaken and the organisation of the Service. The regulations for the ATS defined the organisation as non-combatant, stating that the primary function of ATS personnel was to replace soldiers. However, although the ATS existed, as did the women's services in the First World War, to release men for active combat, there was one key difference between the women's services in the two wars: in April 1941 the ATS was awarded full military status.

However, the increasing professionalisation of the ATS did little to enhance its reputation, particularly among men. When Mass-Observation asked soldiers whether they would object to their wives joining the service 36 per cent claimed they 'would stop her' while only 4 per cent 'wouldn't mind'.[2] Recruitment figures for the ATS had been lagging behind those for the other women's services as it was widely seen as 'unfeminine', so recruitment campaigns attempted to stress that being in the army could be a 'womanly activity'.

The boundary between masculinity and femininity was seen most clearly in the ban on women using weapons, maintained throughout the women's services. The women who came closest to using weapons were the members of the ATS detailed to work on the anti-aircraft sites with the Royal Artillery. After one, short-lived, experiment, allowing women to 'man' the guns, the rules excluding women from direct combat were strictly maintained, and during the V1 rocket campaign of 1944–45 women were not allowed to fire on unmanned missiles. This blanket ban on women's use of firearms sometimes placed women in dangerous situations. Ex-servicewomen remember going on guard duty with sticks – stick picket – while their male colleagues were issued with guns, and women replacing men on isolated and vulnerable searchlight positions arrived to find the Lewis guns being dismantled.

By June 1943, 214,420 women were in the ATS, the largest of the women's services. The ATS drew on women's work experience before the war – its demand for cooks, waitresses and clerks was insatiable – but also provided women with the opportunity to learn new trades. Training centres were opened to teach women skills such as shorthand, switchboard operation and motor mechanics. In addition to this technical training the Army Bureau of Current Affairs (ABCA) organised classes and lectures on citizenship for the army and the ATS. Again, prescribed gender roles in wartime can be read through the education provided for servicewomen. Classes and lectures for women were shaped by assumptions about their gender. Where men were lectured on political theory and current affairs, it was assumed that women would only understand these issues if they were put in personal terms. W.E. Williams, the civilian Director of ABCA, wrote that

> On many ABCA topics, e.g. Housing, Health, Schooling, the women's view is vital to the debate. Where the men tended to think in terms of arterial roads and underground garages the women wanted to argue about the best height for the kitchen sink, or the necessity for running hot water.[3]

Female interests were assumed not to focus on the public issues central to wartime citizenship such as the redistribution of wealth and the founding of a welfare state. Women were concerned with, and educated in, the minutiae, the domestic and the personal. Vocational education for women in the services also often provided a far less subtle education in the feminine. The ABCA scheme included one hour per week devoted to 'the man as soldier' which provided training in skills like map reading and mechanics. Courses available to women through this scheme included embroidery, soft-toy making, dressmaking and beauty culture. Education of women in the ATS thus countered the wartime disruption of home and family. These women may have been (auxiliary) members of the public, masculine world of the army, but they were educated for the domesticity to which it was hoped they would return.

Plate 20.1. Lance-corporal Joyce Culbard, Royal Military Police, West Berlin, 1962. After the Second World War women's new peacetime role in the British Armed Forces combined traditional notions of soldiering with feminine qualities and style.

Return to domesticity is exactly what the majority of servicewomen did at the end of the war. Demobilisation began six weeks after VE Day. Married women were the first to be discharged and numbers fell rapidly in both the male and the female services as the war ground to a close. However, although men continued to be 'called up' for five years, and young men completed two years' National Service between 1950 and 1960, there was little prospect of staying on for the majority of the half million women in the services. A much slimmed-down ATS continued to exist for four years after the war, with many of its members helping with the reconstruction of countries devastated by war. In 1949 this force was replaced by a new organisation: the Women's Royal Army Corps (WRAC).

The WRAC can, in some ways, be seen as a turning point. It represented the acceptance of women in the armed forces in peacetime and, by implication, the idea that military service could be an acceptable career for a woman. However, in many ways the old tension between soldiering and femininity remained. According to its charter, the WRAC was formed in order to replace officers and men in such employment as specified by the Army Council. The wartime role of women replacing men for more important and higher status occupations was written into the very fabric of the organisation.

From the outset the WRAC was conceived as not only a female organisation, but a feminine one. The uniforms were designed by Norman Hartnell, couturier to the Queen, whilst the Corps's motto, 'gentle in manner, resolute in deed' attempted to combine traditional notions of soldiering with the 'feminine' quality of gentleness. Concerns about the maintenance of femininity can be seen in the officers' training courses at Camberley where, as late as the 1960s, female officers were given lessons in beauty culture and flower arranging. Ideologies about gender shaped the operations as well as the training and appearance of the WRAC. Women soldiers were still barred from carrying firearms: the line between male and female, combatant and non-combatant, was still resolutely defended. The Corps was re-designated a combatant corps in 1977, but women did not begin weapons training until 1981. The controversial figure of the armed female soldier was to come under the spotlight during the Gulf War (1990–91), when many British newspapers questioned the wisdom of employing female combatants in wartime.[4] Although the majority of the approximately one thousand British female troops in the Gulf were employed in the medical and support services, many still came under fire and some had to leave children at home. Yet again, the presence of women in the military was seen as threatening the perceived linkage of femininity and the home.

Despite the dire predictions surrounding female service in the Gulf the army and the government found it to be a success, and in 1992 the WRAC was disbanded and women were fully integrated into the regular army. Three years later an independent review of the armed forces noted that the modern army was going to need fewer, but more highly skilled, soldiers. It went on to argue for an extended role for women, urging the armed forces to withdraw as many of the restrictions surrounding women's service as possible.[5] This was followed by a decision to increase the number of posts available to women in the army from 47 per cent to 70 per cent. All roles in the British army were now open to women except for service in the Infantry, the Household Cavalry and the Royal Armoured Corps.

The tension between femininity and armed combat continued to exist; the taboo on women as armed combatants – as killers – persisted. Army recruitment campaigns aimed at women continued to emphasise the femininity of female soldiers, and the nurturing possibilities open to them. The WRAC's last leaflet before disbandment referred to recruits as 'girls' and told them 'You will wear a well cut, feminine lovat-green uniform suit, dark green hat, court shoes, gloves, and you'll carry a handbag', referring apparently to an image of femininity from the 1950s, not the 1990s.[6] In a 1998 television recruitment campaign for the army, the only advertisement to feature a female soldier showed her comforting a rape victim in an unnamed, but presumably Balkan, country. Despite these attempts to show female combatants as feminine, there remains in the press a continued focus on the sexuality of the female soldier – repeatedly represented as either a lesbian or a sexually voracious devourer of male soldiers. The armed forces are a part of society and, as such, reflect social changes. They are also conservative institutions and, although affected by the battles fought and won by feminism, race and sexual politics, change within the forces lagged behind that within wider society. The military remained an essentially male institution; fighting, killing and dying for your country an essentially male rite.

IN FOCUS: The Modernisation Debate

The debate about women's role in wartime has been an ongoing one within all spheres of British historical research, forming a central strand in the thesis that war helps to modernise society. Broadly, proponents of this argument have pointed to the massive changes in women's lives during the First and Second World Wars, 'total wars' that have demanded the mass participation of the citizens of belligerent nations. While not contending that war itself brings about change, historians such as Arthur Marwick have argued that total war has tended to accelerate existing trends. The extension of the franchise to most British women in 1918, for example, has been widely interpreted as a result of a combination of suffragist agitation before the war and female participation in the war. Working on the land, in the munitions factories and in the Auxiliary Services, women could no longer be seen as the private, domesticated 'angel in the home' of the Victorian period. They had served their country in wartime and thus earned the right to political representation.

The two world wars have also been seen as modernising women's lives in less tangible and quantifiable ways. War work in both world wars provided women with increased access to public space as war work often took them away from the confines of the parental home for the first time. Women moved out of the 'traditional' fields of women's work into a variety of occupations which were previously the preserve of men. Female fashions changed as the practical needs of war work combined with fabric shortages to replace prewar frills and flounces with more practical, shorter, skirts and even trousers. With the absence of men, women took over all aspects of home management including child discipline and household repairs, which had traditionally been seen as falling within the male sphere. Most difficult to assess, but vividly represented in many of the diaries, autobiographies and spoken memories of women who lived through the war, is the increased confidence felt by many of them.

However, the expansion of feminist histories from the 1970s onwards saw a new and more critical approach to the modernisation thesis. Looking at the specific circumstances of women's war work and the employment patterns of women in the postwar years, historians such as Gail Braybon and Penny Summerfield argued that any wartime change in gender roles was short-lived and circumscribed by existing ideas about masculinity and femininity. In short, shifting gender patterns were strictly 'for the duration'. A central focus of the work of both Braybon and Summerfield was the process known as 'dilution', the mechanism by which women were employed to replace men.

In the First World War the 1915 Treasury Agreement between the government and thirty-five trades unions allowed women and boys into industries such as engineering on the understanding that they were trained

The Modernisation Debate (continued)

to do part of a skilled man's work, rather than taking over his whole job. In part this was a response to an immediate labour shortage: large numbers of skilled workers had joined the forces following the declaration of war and the need to replace them was greater than the time available to fully train their replacements. However, it also reflected existing ideas about women's work. The unions saw the entry of women into these previously male occupations as a threat to men's pay. Rather than fighting for women's pay to be brought up to the level of men, the unions used dilution to ensure that women remained as unskilled and semi-skilled workers, paid on lower grades than the skilled male craftsmen.

A similar pattern emerged during the Second World War. While there was not the immediate need to replace essential workers as there had been in 1915, it was still the norm for a woman to be paid only a fraction of the male rate. Although women were admitted to government training centres in 1941, they often found that when they emerged into the factories they were given simple, repetitive tasks, irrelevant to their training. Although there was no formal agreement on dilution as there had been in the First World War, women's pay remained on average considerably lower than men's. In 1942 women earned only 52 per cent of men's earnings. Despite widespread praise for women's wartime work, equal pay and conditions with men remained unobtainable for the majority of female workers.

Women's work in the forces was treated with the same essential ambivalence. While their presence in uniform was, for the most part, welcomed as visible and practical evidence of national unity and determination, concern was also expressed about women taking on the 'masculine' role of soldier. Recruitment posters encouraged women to enter the WRNS to 'free a man for the fleet' and the WRAF to 'serve with the men who fly'. Patrice and Margaret Higonnet have used the metaphor of the double helix to describe the position of women in total wars. The double helix is formed of two intertwined strands twisted in a pattern in which one strand remains permanently below and behind the other. This illustrates what they call 'the illusory nature of wartime change' where new roles for women such as those in the auxiliary services remain subordinate to the male role of fighting, killing and perhaps dying for his country.[7] Thus, although women took on work previously considered male, and therefore of higher status than 'feminine' occupations, they remained inferior to the male combatants.

The exemption of women from certain roles in the auxiliary services codified this gendered difference. The closest women in the ATS came to actual combat was working on the anti-aircraft sites in mixed batteries with men. Although the work carried out on these sites was equally dangerous for men and women, providing a key target for the bombers overhead, women's

The Modernisation Debate (continued)

status as non-combatant was preserved by the order preventing them from firing the gun. Similar orders, excluding women from the sharp end of the war – killing the enemy – were also enforced in the other services. One of the things that male combatants in both wars were told was that they were fighting to protect was women and the home. If women were fighting alongside them, what was there left to protect?

Demobilisation at the end of the Second World War was not as abrupt as it had been in 1918–19, beginning earlier and continuing for longer. Perhaps the main difference lay in the treatment of women in the auxiliary services. Although there was pressure on women in civilian employment to leave jobs open for returning men, there was no mass female unemployment as there had been in 1919. However, mothers with young children often found paid work difficult if not impossible to combine with childcare as wartime nurseries were replaced by nursery schools which only opened during school hours. Magazines for women encouraged a return to domesticity with fiction like 'I'll be Home on the First', and advice on 'Building up Beauty' before the men returned, while pictures of workers and servicewomen on magazine covers were replaced by more glamorous images.[8] The majority of women moved back into domesticity and 'women's trades' following both wars, indicating the continuity of traditional ideas about women's role.

Figures for the postwar employment of women are the tangible, quantifiable data available to the historian examining the argument that total war helps to liberate women. Less tangible is the effect of participation on women's self-confidence and self-esteem, and the place that their experience of warfare takes in their life experience. For feminist historians examining the limitations on women's wartime liberation the sense of pride and fulfilment that many women express when writing or speaking about their memories of war is a dichotomy. Penny Summerfield has explored this gap between theory and experience, providing a far more complex picture of the relationship between women and war than that found in the modernisation debates. While historians looking closely at the public discourse surrounding women in wartime may conclude that female liberation was always constrained, fragmentary and ultimately short-lived, the lived experience of wartime for many women was quite different. Summerfield found that many women believed the war had 'changed' and 'matured' them, opening new doors and providing 'freedom that we didn't really have before'.[9] Although the changes in women's wartime lives were always shaped by the often contradictory needs of wartime necessity and patriarchy, women often experienced and remembered these times as a period of liberation. For many women, the personal experience of change that war bought about, however limited and temporary, really did feel like being let 'out of the cage'.[10]

Women and pacifism

In direct contrast to the history of women in the military is the long and honourable tradition of female activism in the peace movement. Although the first widely recognised feminist-pacifist organisation was the founding conference for the Women's International League for Peace and Freedom (WILPF) at the Hague in 1915, female pacifist activism existed long before this. Since the seventeenth century female Quakers were committed to pacifism and helped to relieve suffering, for example, during the Crimean War and the Franco-Prussian War. The first-wave feminist movement also had a pacifist strand, seen most notably in Emily Hobhouse's Boer war peace campaign. Hobhouse travelled in South Africa, highlighting the plight of Boer women and children in the British prison camps and emphasising the common bonds between British and Boer mothers. Both in this internationalism and in the ways in which the arguments for and against the war divided the feminist movement, the Boer war peace campaign prefigured the 1915 Hague conference.

Plans for this meeting split the British suffrage movement, the pacifist members of the National Union of Women's Suffrage Societies resigning over their belief that the bonds of international sisterhood overrode national concerns. Because of the government's ban on British women travelling abroad, only three women from Britain were able to attend the conference, joining 1,200 delegates from other countries. The conference voted to send envoys to belligerent and neutral nations to stress the need for an early peace settlement. Although the envoys were generally well received the war continued, and the WILPF turned its attention to publicising the suffering of civilians in blockaded belligerent nations and to arguing that the enfranchisement of women would mean an end to all wars. The British branch of the League was led by well-known and respected activists such as Emily Pethwick Lawrence and Helena Swanwick, both of whom had been active in the suffrage movement before the war. By 1916 the League had 42 branches in Britain, with 3,576 members, committed to the belief that 'only free women can build the peace . . . themselves understanding the eternal strife engendered by domination'.[11]

Less well known than the Hague conference, possibly because its roots lay in working-class feminist and socialist networks such as the Women's Labour League, with less access to the public stage, was the Women's Peace Crusade. Formed by the Glaswegian radical Helen Crawford, the crusade was active between 1917 and 1918. The crusade was rooted in working-class communities in industrial cities like Glasgow and Manchester, and its activities included lectures, public meetings and demonstrations. Unlike the Women's International League, which concentrated on the impact of the war upon women, the Peace Crusade stressed its impact upon *working-class* women. At its height the Crusade was extremely well supported: 3,000 attended a meeting in Leeds and many other potentially large rallies were broken up by the police. Feminism, pacifism and socialism formed a potent combination of which the establishment was extremely wary.

Another working-class organisation, the Women's Co-operative Guild, was also active in the peace movement, twenty-three branches being affiliated to the

Plate 20.2. 'A Little Fit of the (H)ague', *Daily Express*, 28 April 1915. Because of a government ban on British women to travel abroad, only three British women were able to attend the founding conference of the Women's International League for Peace and Freedom at The Hague in 1915.

WILPF by 1923. As the majority of its members were mothers, the guild emphasised the maternal response to war, which placed the act of nurturing children in direct opposition to the destruction of warfare. The guild's best-known contribution to the peace movement was the white poppy campaign. The white poppy represented an alternative to the red poppy of the British Legion, worn to signify the wearer's commitment to remembrance of the war dead and provision for those injured by the war. The white poppy signified a commitment to peace and a remembrance of all those killed and injured by war; combatants and civilians of all nations, not just Britain.

The fear of a second world war, and the growing belief that the war would include the aerial bombardment of civilians, led to an upsurge in pacifist activity. The Peace Pledge Union collected 120,000 pledges to renounce war by 1937. 1938 saw the publication of Virginia Woolf's *Three Guineas* which examined the linkage between militarism and patriarchy, arguing that women, oppressed by both structures, should resist them. Yet, despite its enduring appeal, the book was widely criticised on its publication, appearing at a time when the threat of fascism was undermining peace movements throughout Europe. At the outbreak of war, the number of people committed to pacifism had shrunk, as the idea that this was a 'just war', significantly different from the First World War, became more widely accepted.

Pacifist activity in the years immediately following the Second World War remained limited, as the full horror of the holocaust became widely known. Although the WILPF opposed the foundation of NATO in 1949 the next great burst of pacifist activity didn't come about until the 1950s, in response to the increasing proliferation of nuclear weapons. The Women's Co-operative Guild was again at the forefront of this activity. The guild, although declining in numbers, campaigned to raise awareness of nuclear testing, publicising the particular vulnerability of children and the unborn to the effects of radiation. The Golders Green branch of the guild founded the National Council for the Abolition of Nuclear Weapons Tests in 1957, membership of which rapidly spread. Two thousand black-sashed women marched through London that year, culminating in a meeting in Trafalgar Square addressed by, among others, Vera Brittan and Edith Sumerskill. The success of the movement led to the foundation of the Campaign for Nuclear Disarmament (CND) the following year.

CND has been the most popular and widely supported peace group in Britain this century. Annual marches to Aldermaston, where Britain's nuclear laboratories are sited, and demonstrations in Trafalgar Square, regularly attracted tens of thousands of supporters. Within CND there was a small but active women's group, which worked to raise awareness of the dangers of radioactive contamination. 'Voice of Women', a small grassroots association, soon joined with CND, the Women's Co-operative Guild, WILPF and other groups in an umbrella organisation, the Liaison Committee for Women's Peace Groups. The 1963 Partial Test Ban Treaty, combined with the more pressing need to attack British support for American action in Vietnam, led to a decline in support and activity for CND in the mid-1960s. Although the women's peace movement never disappeared, it wasn't until the 1980s that it again occupied centre stage.

Feminist pacifism burst back into public view dramatically in 1980. The decision to site cruise and Pershing missiles in Europe led to a resurgence in support for CND. By late 1980 CND's membership had risen to over 9,000. As during the First World War, women's peace activity reflected and accentuated divisions and debates within the feminist movement as a whole. The maternalist strand of feminist-pacifism, seen in the earlier work of the Women's Co-operative Guild, was joined by highly politicised women from the 1970s' feminist movement who advocated separatism, and saw warfare as a male creation. A third strand identified itself with neither specific position, but felt happiest working for peace within a predominantly female environment. Despite these differences, women working for peace produced probably the best known and most successful example of direct action against warfare: the Greenham Common women's peace camp.

The peace camp emerged from a 'walk for life' from South Wales to Greenham in 1981. Although a small number of men went on the original march and stayed on at the camp which developed, by February 1982 the camp became women only. Women living in the camp, and the large numbers who visited, used a wide variety of imaginative and non-violent means of opposing the nuclear threat within the camp. There were echoes of the suffrage campaign as women chained themselves to the gates, photos of children, hair ribbons and baby clothes were tied to the fence to symbolise life, not death. By eschewing more traditional forms of protest the Greenham women emphasised their total opposition to the destructive weaponry inside the camp. At Easter 1983, for example, twenty-six women dressed as Easter Bunnies and teddy bears entered the base for a picnic; the language and imagery of Greenham inspired peace camps elsewhere. Camps and demonstrations were organised in many different places including three in London. In total Greenham inspired at least six hundred different local actions.[12]

In 1989 when the Berlin Wall fell and the immediate threat of nuclear war began to recede, there were still a dozen women living at Greenham. Although CND was no longer a mass movement, as it had been in the 1950s and the early 1980s, a strand of feminism strongly linked to pacifist activism continued to exist. Women have been active against the arms trade, for example attacking and disarming British jets about to be sold to the brutal regime in Indonesia. Numerous women's peace convoys made the often dangerous journey to Bosnia during the war there in the mid-1990s to distribute aid to women and children. In a wider sense, eco-feminism, which is internationalist and makes links between the destruction of the environment, government and business interests and masculinity can be seen as part of the continuing link between feminism and pacifism. Although missiles are no longer sited at Greenham the politics of the camp continued to influence feminist-pacifism until the end of the century.

Conclusion

In many ways the women's peace camp at Greenham brought together strands which had run throughout the women's peace movement in Britain this century: imaginative protests, maternalism and a determination among the protesters that, as women, it was their duty to oppose warfare. Ironically perhaps, the women of this century's peace movements and women in the military have more in common than first appearances may indicate. Both groups have struggled against the establishment to make their voices heard. Both have had to fight against prejudices which presume that women only have a limited knowledge of warfare and the public policy that governs it. But most strikingly, both groups have been overwhelmingly defined by their gender. Women in peace groups have often chosen to project a particular representation of femininity in order to stress their opposition to man-made wars. Women in the armed forces have found that the construction of their femininity by the military and political authorities becomes a means by which they are excluded from many activities. In war or in peace, women's relationship to militarism continues to be shaped by their gender.

Bibliographical Note

For initial reading on the war and modernisation thesis, A. Marwick, *Britain in the Century of Total War* (Basingstoke, 1968) still provides a good introduction, and exposition of the argument that total wars modernise society. More specifically focused on women is G. Braybon and P. Summerfield, *Out of the Cage: Women's Experiences in Two World Wars* (London, 1987). Individually, these authors have produced useful social histories of women's roles in the First and Second World Wars, G. Braybon, *Women Workers in the First World War: The British Experience* (London, 1981); and P. Summerfield, *Women Workers in the Second World War: Production and Patriarchy in Conflict* (London, 1984).

Cultural analysis of women in wartime can be found in M. Higonnet, J. Jenson, S. Michel, and M. Collins (eds), *Behind the Lines: Gender and the Two World Wars* (New Haven, 1987); and C. Gledhhill and G. Swanson (eds), *Nationalising Femininity: Culture, Sexuality and British Cinema in the Second World War* (Manchester, 1996). Recent work looking at the continuing impact of the war on women's lives includes L. Noakes, *War and the British: Gender and National Identity 1939–1991* (London, 1998); and P. Summerfield, *Reconstructing Women's Wartime Lives* (Manchester, 1998).

For a lively and thorough survey of women in the British peace movement, J. Liddington, *The Long Road to Greenham: Feminism and Anti-Militarism in Britain Since 1820* (London, 1989) remains unsurpassed. S. Oldfield, *Women Against the Iron Fist: Alternatives to Militarism 1900–1980* (Oxford, 1989); and R. Roach Pearson (ed), *Women and Peace: Theoretical, Historical and Practical Perspectives* (London, 1987) place the British peace movement within an international perspective.

Notes

1. J. Cowper, *A Short History of Queen Mary's Army Auxiliary Corps* (London, 1957), p. 48.

2. Mass-Observation, Mass-Observation Archive, University of Sussex, File Report no. 952, *The ATS*, 8 November 1941.

3. L. Noakes, *War and the British: Gender and National Identity 1939–1991* (London, 1998), p. 66.

4. See ibid., pp. 137–51.

5. M. Belt, *Independent Review of the Armed Forces' Manpower Career and Remuneration Structures: Managing People in Tomorrow's Armed Forces* (London, 1995), p. 43.

6. K. Muir, *Arms and the Woman* (London, 1992), p. 223.

7. M. and P. Higonnet, 'The Double Helix', in M. Higonnet, J. Jenson, S. Michel and M. Collins (eds), *Behind the Lines: Gender and the Two World Wars* (New Haven, 1987).

8. *Woman's Own*, 8 and 15 June 1945.

9. P. Summerfield, *Reconstructing Women's Wartime Lives* (Manchester, 1998), p. 276.

10. G. Braybon and P. Summerfield, *Out of the Cage: Women's Experiences in Two World Wars* (London, 1987).

11. Women's International League, *Monthly Newsheet*, November 1917.

12. J. Liddington, *The Long Road to Greenham: Feminism and Anti-Militarism in Britain Since 1820* (London, 1989).

21

THE STATE AND SOCIAL POLICY

Harriet Jones

Until quite recently, most of the historical writing on social policy was 'whiggish', optimistically assuming that the expansion of state welfare provision was accompanied by steady progress in the 'condition of the people'. But the persistence of poverty in Britain, and closer attention to the experiences of marginal groups in British society, has led to a more pessimistic approach. The condition of women is a good case in point, for the relative economic position of women in British society is not very different at the end of the century than it was at the beginning.

Social policy has had an enormous effect on women's lives, but the purpose behind it has varied. In some instances the state has attempted to influence and regulate female behaviour to fit moral norms or to address social concerns. In others it has attempted to address or alleviate a specifically identified cause of deprivation. The outcome has also been mixed. In some respects the state has assumed a jurisdiction and responsibility over spheres which had previously been considered private. In other respects, however, social policies have been instrumental in the achievement of equal rights and the emergence of women as full citizens of Britain. This paradox, of the restrictive and emancipating features of social policy is a key aspect of the subject.

Women and the Poor Law

Women at the beginning of the century, as today, were particularly susceptible to economic hardship, and formed the majority of those compelled to seek the assistance of the Poor Law authorities. Single parenthood was common in the early part of the century. Widowhood and desertion often left women in charge of their families, and their longer life expectancy meant that more women than men survived into old age and dependency. It was difficult, moreover, for women to earn adequate wages in a labour market which limited the type of work available, and which paid much lower wages to female than male workers. Even when in regular paid work, the majority of women did not have access to the kinds of mutual private insurance schemes which offered benefits to many male workers.

By 1911, the four largest Friendly Societies had only 2,235 female members between them. It was common for women workers to be barred from such schemes, or to be asked for larger contributions than men, in order to compensate for the irregular patterns of work and ill health that were inherent to the lives of most working-class women. For destitute immigrant women in Britain in this period, the situation was even worse. Poor immigrants were heavily reliant upon the charitable associations which existed to serve aliens in distress, and that provision varied widely both between different ethnic groups and geographically. Voluntary bodies and private charity played an important role in the relief of destitution, and coping skills often relied upon informal arrangements within families, among friends, or through the local pawnbroker.

It is not surprising, therefore, that more women than men were forced to turn to the Poor Law. But the Poor Law was not structured to meet the needs of destitute women, based as it had been since 1834 on the assumption that women were normally dependent on a male breadwinner (in spite of ample evidence that this was often not the case). Moreover, the provision of poor relief varied widely throughout the country because it was administered locally by elected Boards of Guardians, and financed through local taxation or 'poor rates'.

Both the majority and the minority reports of the 1909 Royal Commission on the Poor Laws were highly critical of this system, which treated women in the same situation very differently depending on where they lived, and on the views of local taxpayers as well as on the moral judgements of local officials. The minority report, reflecting the views of the Fabian socialists Sidney and Beatrice Webb, urged more compassionate treatment of all mothers in need, whether through widowhood, desertion, or 'illegitimacy'. The majority report was much harsher in its recommendations regarding the latter two groups, but shared the concern that 'deserving' widows should be treated with greater compassion and that it was desirable that families should be kept together when appropriate rather than being forced into segregated institutional care. These views did not significantly alter poor relief in practice before the First World War, but they were a reflection of the growing public debate surrounding the structural and economic causes of poverty and destitution.[1]

Maternalism and the Expansion of Social Policy

An increasing focus on female and child poverty was emerging in this period for a variety of reasons. Historians today stress the importance of competing 'maternalist discourses' in the origins of welfare policies in the late nineteenth and early twentieth centuries – not only in Britain, but in North America and Japan, as well as in other industrialising European states. These arguments elevated the qualities of nurturing and morality in women as mothers, and their wider value and importance in society as well as in the private sphere. Maternalist arguments emerged in Britain at a time when public and official anxiety was growing over economic competition from Germany and the United States, over the strength of the British Empire, and over the declining birth rate and persistently high levels of infant mortality. Many individuals and organisations were led in these years, often from radically different political points of origin, to support collectivist action in support of maternal and infant welfare. Whether in order to safeguard the future strength of the race and nation, to ensure the highest level of 'national efficiency' in industry and empire, or to improve the material conditions of the working class and redistribute national wealth, a broad consensus of opinion was moving in favour of state intervention to improve child health and fitness. This could only be accomplished by addressing the whole issue of motherhood as well.

Women played an enormously important role in this process, and it should be stressed that women of all classes and opinions were active participants in, rather than mere passive recipients of these developments. Philanthropic activity was a crucial channel through which middle-class women in nineteenth-century Britain had begun to assert a role in the public sphere, and the local nature of social welfare provision in Britain gave ample scope for the transmission of ideas and practice from the voluntary to the public sector. Voluntary initiatives and experiments, in which women played a leading role, were often in practice adopted by government, and performed a critical aspect of the early formation of the British welfare state.

Moreover, female political rights in Britain began at a local level, when in 1869 unmarried female ratepayers were allowed to vote in local elections and to stand for election on Boards of Guardians and, from 1870, on the new School Boards. By 1900 there were around 1,000 women serving as Poor Law Guardians and 200 on School Boards. Women often argued that their differences from men, as carers and mothers, uniquely qualified them to have a voice in social policy formation. Maternalism, in other words, was used as a wedge by early 'feminists' to expand their participation in public life and politics.[2] The expansion of state welfare also involved new opportunities for female employment – as teachers, nurses, health visitors and in other 'caring' professions.

By 1914 the state's role in welfare provision had expanded considerably as a result of these processes. The Midwives Act 1902, the Education (Provision of Meals) Act 1906, the Notification of Births Act 1907 and the Children Act 1908, were all intended to contribute to the improvement of child health and welfare. The cumulative effect of this legislation meant that the domestic realm was becoming less private for women who were now increasingly coming into contact with officials – health visitors or school inspectors, for example, whose intrusion was not always welcome.

The central welfare reforms of the 1906–14 Liberal governments, had a limited but significant impact on the lives of poor women. For instance, although the Pensions Act of 1908 offered only marginal help to a limited number of pensioners over 70 (excluding aliens, or the 'undeserving', among others),

62.5 per cent of the 490,000 claimants in 1909 were female. The scheme was redistributive in the sense that it was tax-funded, not based on contributions, and did not require claimants to retire from the labour market, making it arguably the most radically progressive welfare measure of the century.[3] Widows' and orphans' pensions were not included in the 1911 National Insurance Act, however, because of the high cost of contributions this would have entailed, although maternity benefits were included for wives of insured workers. In practice many women workers were not covered by the scheme, and many women colluded with their employers in avoiding the payment of contributions out of wages which were too low to allow for even a small weekly stamp.

The First World War

The First World War reinforced the maternalist and pronatalist preoccupation in welfare debates, as the fear over low birth rates and infant mortality was exacerbated by the high death toll among fit young men. The Local Government Board steadily increased the funding available for antenatal and mother and baby clinics after 1914. By 1918 the number of health visitors in Britain had more than doubled, and there were nearly 1,300 such centres, of which around 700 were funded by the local authorities. The 1918 Maternity and Child Welfare Act was intended to encourage the postwar continuation and expansion of this provision, requiring all local authorities to establish Maternity and Child Welfare Committees, which had to contain at least two women members.

There was, too, a maternalist component to the introduction of the Servicemen's Wife's Allowance of 1914. The allowances were intended to replace the role of the breadwinning husband while men were absent during the war, thus enabling married women to maintain a respectable home and family in spite of the strains of warfare. The allowances were universal but not generous and were conditional on good conduct. The Home Office relied upon police surveillance to ensure that servicemen's wives in receipt of allowances followed conventional norms of behaviour, and denied payment to women found to behave in an 'unwifely' fashion. In this way, the state undertook the moral supervision of servicemen's wives on behalf of the absent husband as well as taking over their financial maintenance.

Cash benefits paid directly to unwaged married women ended when the war was over, but the focus on pronatalist concerns gave increasing weight to calls for the 'endowment of motherhood' or for some sort of payment directly to mothers on behalf of their children. Family Allowances in some form had been advocated since before the war by some reformers, and in 1917 Eleanor Rathbone co-founded the Family Endowment Society to campaign for their adoption. Rathbone hoped that family allowances would enhance the power of women as mothers and as workers, and overcome one of the main objections to equal pay – the idea that male workers should be entitled to a wage large enough to support a family adequately, while women workers only needed a wage to supplement the family income. Unsurprisingly, the trade unions, and indeed, many women in the labour movement, were opposed. But the arguments in favour of family allowances gained in strength during the interwar years, as fears over the declining birth rate continued. Employers became increasingly interested in a scheme which could help to perpetuate a low-wage economy while simultaneously supporting large families, one of the principal causes of poverty.

Women and the Dole in Interwar Britain

Indeed, in spite of the fact that infant mortality rates had improved over the first three decades of the century, the social policy focus on mothers and children continued in the interwar period because of the sharp drop in family size. Persistent problems of structural mass unemployment from 1921 also meant that the state was not concerned to promote women's rights as paid workers. The female workforce which had expanded during the war was unceremoniously cast aside when the war was over.

One of the main effects of the 1922 Unemployment Insurance Act, for example, was to exclude married women from the insurance system, as it allowed extended unemployment benefits only to those who could prove that they were genuinely seeking full-time work. If a woman refused a job in domestic service, or working long hours away from home, she would be automatically disqualified. The Labour Government of 1924 actually tightened the implementation of this provision, and throughout the interwar years women's rights as insured workers were hampered by the persistent belief that married women in particular, were prone to 'scrounging'. Many of those disallowed under the genuinely seeking work test were forced to claim poor relief, or rely on family and friends for support. The onset of the Depression after 1929 only increased the determination to cut the costs of benefits, as numbers of claimants soared and, with them, the costs of the benefits system. Women, whose levels of benefit were already substantially lower than men, suffered particularly in this period as levels of payment were cut out of deference to Treasury orthodoxy.

The Second World War

On balance, British women benefited from the expansion of social policy during the Second World War, although historians do not agree on the extent to which wartime changes permanently altered the status of women in Britain. Nursery and daycare provision for women workers is a good example. Although 1,500 nurseries had been established through the efforts of the Ministry of Labour by 1944, most women still had to make do with casual childcare. Nursery subsidies were cut at the end of the war, so that this programme was of limited use for working mothers when it was in place, and had no long-term impact on daycare provision.

On the other hand, it could be argued that innovations such as the wartime Emergency Medical Service paved the way for the establishment of the National Health Service. In general, it is fair to say that the unprecedented extent of civilian participation in the war increased the likelihood that the wartime Coalition Government would have to pay serious attention to the subject of reconstruction and social policy after the war. This pressure was made all the more acute, given the abandonment of social reform following the First World War, and negative popular memories of the National Government's response to the mass unemployment of the 1930s. By 1945, there was tremendous political pressure to construct a more coherent and comprehensive system of social policies – which, taken together, would become popularly known as 'the welfare state'.

IN FOCUS: Women and the Beveridge Plan

Social Insurance and Allied Services was the formal title of the Report of a wartime government committee chaired by Sir William Beveridge, published in November 1942, on the future of the social security system in Britain. Generating an enormous amount of publicity and popular enthusiasm, the Beveridge Plan was an attempt to reform the patchwork of social policy provision which had grown up piecemeal over the previous fifty years, and to create a new comprehensive scheme of social insurance which in theory would abolish poverty.

Beveridge envisaged this system operating alongside a universal national health service, a system of family allowances, and in conditions of high levels of employment. Taken together, he believed that these measures would make it possible to eradicate what he termed as the 'five giants on the road of reconstruction': Want, Disease, Ignorance, Squalor and Idleness. In practice, Beveridge's Plan was altered substantially, but nevertheless formed the basis of the wartime and postwar legislation upon which the British welfare state was based. Many aspects of the scheme have been subject to criticism and analysis over the years. In particular, however, Beveridge's proposals concerning the problem of female poverty were problematic, and would have far-reaching consequences for women in postwar Britain.

Beveridge himself was well aware of the difficulties which faced both paid and unpaid women workers and was anxious to find a way around the particular problems of unequal and interrupted earning which characterised the lives of most women in Britain. It is not fair, therefore, to criticise him for deliberately imposing a patriarchal and discriminatory system, as in fact his views were quite in tune with progressive opinion at the time. Indeed, he was anxious to include as many women as possible in the insurance-based social security system that he designed: single and married, mothers and carers, waged and unwaged. As his biographer has stressed, 'in no area of

Women and the Beveridge Plan (continued)

the Beveridge Plan were greater efforts made to squeeze the knobbly foot of society into the narrow glass slipper of contributory social insurance'.[4]

But at the heart of the scheme lay an irreconcilable conflict as far as women were concerned. On the one hand, Beveridge was determined that the plan should be based on compulsory flat-rate insurance contributions and universal benefits, which he believed would lift the stigma which had been associated with the Poor Law and the means test. The contributory principle was thought essential to the fostering of social solidarity and the notion of citizenship. The essence of the scheme was that everyone would pay into it and everyone would be entitled to benefit from it. Good citizenship thus revolved around participation in the labour market, and the purpose of social security should be to protect the contributor from the risk of interrupted earnings due to sickness or unemployment, circumstances which were assumed to be infrequent and outside the norm.

On the other hand, Beveridge assumed that the overwhelming majority of women were likely to marry, and to become economically dependent upon their husbands' earnings when they did. The 1931 census had indeed demonstrated that 7 out of 8 married women were not in any form of paid work, although there were indications before the war that the number of married women in paid work was growing. Beveridge pointed out, however, that even when a married woman accepted paid work,

> she does so under conditions distinguishing her from the single woman in two ways. First, her earning is liable to interruption by childbirth. In the national interest it is important that the interruption by childbirth should be as complete as possible; the expectant mother should be under no economic pressure to continue at work as long as she can, and to return to it as soon as she can. Second, to most married women earnings by a gainful occupation do not mean what such earnings mean to most solitary women. Unless there are children, the housewife's earnings in general are a means, not of subsistence but of a standard of living above subsistence . . . the children's allowances proposed . . . will make this true in most cases in the future, even where there are children. In sickness or unemployment the housewife does not need compensating benefits on the same scale as the solitary woman because, among other things, her home is provided for her either by her husband's earnings or benefit if his earning is interrupted. She has not as a rule as strong a motive as other earners for returning to paid work as rapidly as possible.[5]

Beveridge's assumptions about married women were based on a 'companionate' view of marriage between equal partners working as a team. He was anxious to stress the value of women's unpaid work as carers in the

Women and the Beveridge Plan (continued)

home, and that women's unpaid contribution to the economy and society entitled them to a fair share of his social security system. Beveridge's view of marriage and the family was partly based on his lifelong concern with pronatalism and eugenics. His views now sound outdated, but were widespread at this time. 'The attitude of the housewife to gainful employment outside the home', he argued, 'is not and should not be the same as that of the single woman. She has other duties'; and further 'in the next thirty years housewives as mothers have vital work to do in ensuring the adequate continuance of the British race and of British ideals in the world'.[6] But at the heart of the Beveridge Plan lay this emphasis on paid work and regular contributions as the first badge of citizenship. The fact was that the inability of most women to pay equally into the insurance fund would inevitably mean that married women would be treated differently in the welfare state that he designed. Thus there was a clear conflict in his Report between the contributory principle and his view of married women.

The Beveridge Plan proposed that married women of working age should form a separate class within the insured population. Upon marriage, 'every woman begins a new life in relation to social insurance' which entitled her to a range of grants and benefits including marriage grant, maternity grant, widowhood and separation provision. But equally, on marriage the woman would lose the rights built up from previous contributions, and would have to build up those rights again on a fresh basis. Even when she did so, she lost entitlement to the full rate of sickness, unemployment benefit and pensions, to which a single working woman was entitled. On the assumption that a married woman's work was likely to be intermittent and low paid, she was given the option to opt out of the contributory scheme altogether, which in practice many women were tempted to do. Married women would therefore participate in the insurance scheme primarily through their husbands' contributions and benefits; the equal sharing of the latter, of course, depended upon Beveridge's idealised companionate model of marriage. For unmarried mothers who were not in paid work, or for women who were full-time unpaid carers, the situation was even less satisfactory, as they would be counted among those who fell through the social insurance system into the safety net of means-tested National Assistance benefits. Therefore, for a large number of women, the social citizenship conferred by insurance contributions, would simply not apply. The Beveridge Report was received with overwhelming enthusiasm when it was published in 1942. It became the centrepiece of the growing interest in postwar reconstruction at this time, and the basis of the postwar welfare state. But, from the outset, male and female participation in the welfare state would be based upon differing assumptions.

Plate 21.1. A school for mothers, 1907.

Women and the Welfare State, 1945–64

There is no doubt that on balance, women gained considerably from the welfare legislation which was enacted by the Labour Government between 1945 and 1951. The Family Allowances Act 1945 gave benefits directly to the primary carer (e.g. women in most cases) for the second and subsequent children. The National Health Service, which began to operate in 1948, was universal in its provision, in theory giving all women access to adequate health care for the first time. Moreover, the continuation of food subsidies and rationing until the mid-1950s, the existence of near full employment and the enactment (in modified form) of Beveridge's social insurance proposals, also contributed enormously to the improved health and welfare of women in Britain.

The great expansion in the social services after the war benefited women in other ways as well. The 'caring' professions had become a primary source of female employment, and in some instances opened pathways for promotion in local and central government agencies. For example, the 1948 Children's Act required that a Children's Officer be appointed in each council to take responsibility for children in care or otherwise at risk, and to oversee a staff of specialist social workers for that purpose. The developing profession of social work was dominated by women and the appointment of female officers was not uncommon. This army of female workers who staffed the welfare state were often confined to the lowest paid and least regarded jobs in the sector. This was particularly the case with women workers recruited in the 1950s to work in the

NHS from the West Indies. 'Our role', one group of women has explained, 'was to become the nurses, cleaners and cooks who would supply and maintain the service for others.'[7]

The contributory basis of the social insurance system introduced by the 1946 National Insurance Act was based on the Beveridge Plan, and thus problematic when applied to the needs of most women. Eligibility depended upon a consistent record of contributions, which most women gave up upon marriage. Thus access to the benefits available under the insurance scheme, including unemployment and sickness benefit, and pensions, was limited for many women. While married or widowed women could claim on the basis of their husbands' contributions, many women, including divorced or unmarried mothers, carers and the elderly, found themselves reliant upon the National Assistance Fund. This was a means-tested benefit system which was intended to provide a residual safety net for the small number of people who it was anticipated would not be eligible for social insurance. Beveridge had hoped that Assistance benefits would gradually dwindle, necessary only for the asocial, the disabled and the marginalised, and a certain stigma was meant to be attached to claimants (hence the retention of a means test). But in practice, the number of people compelled to seek the help of the National Assistance scheme grew rapidly after the war, and the majority of them were female. In other words, the welfare state excluded many British women from the central concept of 'social citizenship', articulated so enthusiastically by T.H. Marshall in 1950.[8]

The continued role for a means test in British welfare provision was confirmed after 1951, when the Conservatives returned to power. Although some benefits remained universal at the point of distribution – health, education, family allowances – successive Conservative administrations cemented the reliance on means testing and selectivity. Although this was partly ideologically motivated, it is also the case that the position of women in society as unpaid carers with interrupted earning patterns, would have made it difficult to pay for universal benefits on an insurance basis. Increasingly, both Labour and Conservative policy makers were beginning to think in terms of earnings-related contributions and benefits by the early 1960s, as one way of overcoming the problem of financing welfare.

Rediscovering Poverty and Reforming Welfare from the 1960s

The problem of female poverty and the Beveridge model for welfare was only deepened as time went on. Social policy historians associate the mid-1960s with the 'rediscovery of poverty' in Britain, as new social research undermined the complacency of the late 1940s and 1950s, to reveal hitherto unsuspected levels of *relative* poverty, particularly among children and pensioners. In the midst of full employment and consumer affluence, there were many who did not get a fair slice of the cake, and most of the poorest were female. Some modest attempts were made to correct this imbalance. In 1968 Family Allowances were increased substantially; the rise was targeted rather than universal in its effect, as the increase was taken away in higher taxes for the better off. Nevertheless, although child benefit (as it became known in the 1970s) has been shown to make a crucial difference in low-income homes, it never came to provide a wage to unpaid carers in the way envisaged by campaigners in the interwar years. In 1970, the National Insurance (Old Persons and Widows Pensions and Attendance Allowance) Act, introduced benefits for people needing constant care at home. This was the first time that the needs of unpaid carers were addressed seriously. Most radically, the State Earnings Related Pension Scheme (SERPS) was adopted in 1975 after two decades of debate over pensions reform. Significantly, the Labour minister responsible, Barbara Castle, fought successfully to incorporate the needs of women in its provision. Pensions contributions would be calculated on the basis of the twenty best years of work, and mothers staying at home to look after dependent children, and carers, were to be counted as contributors. The SERPS scheme was the most progressive of its kind in the world as far as women and carers were concerned, when it came into effect in 1978. But it was another female politician, Margaret Thatcher, who approved its dismantling in 1985. At that time, pensions were again reformed, and the pensions scheme for women dramatically cut.

Membership of the European Economic Community from 1973 had a significant impact on the relationship between women and the state. The 1975 Sex Discrimination Act was the product of EEC requirements as was the first legislation for equal pay between the sexes in British law. A series of Community directives aimed at women's employment and social security rights in the 1970s forced through tighter legislation in the years that followed. In 1982 and 1983 the Court of Justice ordered amendments to strengthen the 1970 Equal Pay Act. Social security regulations were also amended as a result of the European Court. European Community membership has played a hugely important role in establishing the legal rights of women to equal pay, working conditions and social security rights in Britain, a role that is often overlooked by British commentators.

Women, Demography and Social Policy since the 1970s

The dramatic increase in lone-parent families since the 1970s has placed the welfare system under increasing pressure and has come to be a focus of domestic political controversy, especially in the 1990s. The number of lone mothers has been significant throughout the century, increasing slightly after 1945 but never reaching double digits as a proportion of all households until the late twentieth century. It is also important to note the extent to which the composition of lone-parent households has shifted over time. Whereas the death of the spouse was an important contributing factor at the beginning of the century, it was a relatively small cause in 2000. During the 1990s divorce and separation were the principal factor. Between 1961 and 1994 the number of households

Plate 21.2. Nurse Takyiaw Prempeh at the Princess Alice Hospital, Eastbourne, Christmas, 1951.

led by lone mothers quadrupled, from 5 to 21 per cent of all families with dependent children; by the end of the century, over one third of all births in Britain occurred outside marriage (see Tables 5.3 and 5.4, pp. 73 and 75).

This phenomenon has caused concern since divorce and lone parenthood are statistically associated with poverty. Although fathers are legally obliged to provide maintenance, that has proved difficult to enforce. This meant that a growing proportion of young families in Britain were caught in a poverty trap, dependent upon state support and without any primary breadwinner, male or female. The state has been unsure how to respond. Traditionally, lone mothers have not been required to register for work, being treated as mothers first, and workers second. The chronic lack of childcare facilities in Britain makes it difficult to see how that definition could be overcome, even if it were universally thought desirable. Lone mothers have been increasingly the focus of popular hostility, identified as a central social 'problem' of the late twentieth century.

Another approach has been to target absent fathers to reimburse the state for the costs of maintenance. The 1990 Child Support Act, which established the Child Support Agency, initially required all lone mothers on benefit to authorise the state to recover funds from the absent father, with little regard to individual circumstances. The outcry which ensued was a source of scandal within the Conservative Government in the first half of the 1990s. This general approach, however, was not abandoned initially by the Blair administration after its election to power in 1997. Lone mothers were encouraged to seek work, new measures were envisaged to expand childcare facilities, and a range of new penalties were introduced for fathers refusing to cooperate with the CSA. It remains difficult to predict at the end of the century how this problem is to be resolved. The state in the twentieth century, while regulating many aspects of women's lives, has also enabled a great many to liberate themselves from unhappy or violent partnerships. That does not mean, however, that taxpayers will adjust easily to the responsibility for supporting unpaid mothers and raising a large proportion of children on benefit in the future. The great task of the welfare state in the twenty-first century is to resolve this dilemma.

Historical Debates

The orthodox historiography of the welfare state is optimistic in its assumption that women have universally benefited from the growth of welfare in this century. Similarly, some of the older studies of the social impact of the First and Second World Wars assumed that women were permanently empowered and liberated by their increased participation in the labour market and armed forces.[9] These simplistic interpretations were subjected to increasing scrutiny and criticism by Marxist and feminist scholars beginning in the 1960s.

According to Marxist commentators, women have been used as a reserve army of labour during the wars and times of full employment, forced out of paid employment when conditions were not favourable, and used generally to drive down male wages. Welfare rights for women were slow to develop because women had no direct value in the marketplace in the sense that male workers did. Feminist criticism has viewed social policy as part of the broader patriarchal aim of modern industrialised society. According to much left/feminist criticism, the development of the welfare state was an extension of the paternalist impulse within the family, regulating and constraining women's behaviour and, when necessary, replacing the role of male breadwinner. Welfare policy, in this analysis, has been central to the construction of 'social patriarchy', designed to extend and reproduce traditional gender and family roles so as to facilitate the continuation of traditional norms and values.[10]

More recently, there has developed a strand of neo-conservative criticism of welfare policy development which argues that the welfare state has undermined traditional social values by enabling women to leave the traditional family structure and to proceed with child rearing without the presence or financial support of fathers.[11] This approach was particularly noticeable, of course, during the period of Conservative administration between 1979 and 1997, and informed much policy development in those years. Thus, it has been possible to form plausible and convincing but nevertheless radically different arguments about the role of welfare policy in women's lives.

Much of this work has been rather polemical and superficial, however. More careful and considered academic analysis and debate has tempered the extreme interpretations in recent years, and as the body of rigorous academic literature has grown a more thoughtful and complex narrative has begun to emerge. For one thing, the more recent research has stressed the role of women and women-led organisations in the growth and development of social policy in this century. Maternalist language, as indicated earlier, was used by a variety of people to justify a variety of views. The 'welfare state' has been a central battleground of women's social and political rights and gender relations in British society have been determined in the gritty details of social and welfare policy. In that sense, elements of both right and left-wing interpretations are valuable, for, historically, social policy has been an arena in which a variety of agendas have been pursued, often simultaneously.

Bibliographical Note

The best of the historical surveys of social policy and welfare incorporate gender issues and debates. P. Thane, *Foundations of the Welfare State* (London, 2nd edn, 1996), covers the years 1870–1945, and includes documents. R. Lowe, *The Welfare State in Britain since 1945* (Basingstoke, 2nd edn, 1999); and H. Glennerster, *British Social Policy since 1945* (Oxford, 1995) cover the postwar period, incorporating recent developments. S. Pederson, *Family, Dependence and the Origin of the Welfare State: Britain and France, 1914–1945* (Cambridge, 1994); and J. Lewis, *Women in England, 1870–1950: Sexual Divisions and Social Change* (Brighton, 1984) contain much useful background and information on social policy in the first half of the century. J. Lewis, *Women in Britain since 1945* (Oxford, 1992) includes a chapter on women's welfare and the state.

G. Bock and P. Thane (eds), *Maternity and Gender Policies: Women and the Rise of the European Welfare States, 1880s–1950s* (London, 1991) is an important collection of essays. So too is C. Glendinning and J. Millar (eds), *Women and Poverty in Britain* (Brighton, 1987) and it is also worth reading their joint article 'Gender and Poverty', *Journal of Social Policy*, 18, 3 (1989). On maternalism the indispensable text is S. Koven and S. Michel (eds), *Mothers of a New World: Maternalist Politics and the Origins of Welfare States* (London, 1993) which includes several essays which apply to Britain specifically.

On the First World War see D. Dwork, *War is Good for Babies and Other Young Children: A History of the Infant and Child Welfare Movement in England 1898–1918* (London, 1987); P. Levine, ' "Walking the Streets in a Way No Decent Woman Should": Women Police in World War One', *Journal of Modern History*, 66 (March 1994); and A. Woollacott, 'Maternalism, Professionalism and Industrial Welfare Supervisors in World War I Britain', *Women's History Review*, 3, 1 (1994). On the interwar period see especially J. Macnicol, *The Movement for Family Allowances, 1918–45* (London, 1980); and also A. Deacon, *In Search of the Scrounger* (London, 1976). On the Second World War see D. Riley, *War in the Nursery: Theories of the Child and Mother* (London, 1983); and P. Summerfield, *Women Workers in the Second World War* (London, 1989). The Beveridge Report is analysed at length in J. Hills, J. Ditch, and H. Glennerster (eds), *Beveridge and Social Security: An International Retrospective* (Oxford, 1994). The most recent study of lone motherhood is K. Kiernan, H. Land and J. Lewis, *Lone Motherhood in Twentieth-Century Britain* (Oxford, 1998).

Notes

1. P. Thane, 'Women and the Poor Law in Victorian and Edwardian England', *History Workshop Journal* 6 (Autumn 1978).

2. See P. Hollis, *Ladies Elect: Women in English Local Government, 1865–1914* (Oxford, 1987).

3. J. Macnicol, 'Beveridge and Old Age', in J. Hills, J. Ditch and H. Glennerster (eds), *Beveridge and Social Security: An International Retrospective* (Oxford, 1994), p. 74.

4. J. Harris, 'Beveridge's Social and Political Thought', in Hills, Ditch and Glennerster, *Beveridge and Social Security*, p. 34.

5. Sir William Beveridge, *Social Insurance and Allied Services* (Cmd. 6404, London, HMSO, 1942), pp. 49–50.

6. Ibid., pp. 51, 53.

7. B. Bryan, S. Dadzie and S. Scafe, *The Heart of Race: Black Women's Lives in Britain* (London, 1985), p. 89.

8. T.H. Marshall, *Citizenship and Social Class* (Cambridge, 1950).

9. The classic account can be found in R. Titmuss, *Essays on 'the Welfare State'* (London, 1958); for a response see H. Rose, 'Rereading Titmuss: The Sexual Division of Welfare', *Journal of Social Policy* 10, 4 (1981).

10. See E. Wilson, *Women and the Welfare State* (London, 1977).

11. See, for example, G. Gilder, *Wealth and Poverty* (New York, 1981).

KEY DATES AND EVENTS

1867   Establishment of London and Manchester National Societies
for Women's Suffrage.
First women's suffrage petition presented to parliament.

1869   Oxford and Cambridge Local Examinations made available to women.
The Subjection of Women by John Stuart Mill published.
Women ratepayers eligible to vote in local elections under Municipal
Corporations Act.
Women ratepayers able to run for election as Poor Law Guardian
(women ratepayers had been able to vote for Guardians since 1834).

1870   Married Women's Property Act gives married women right to their own
earnings.
Establishment of Local School Boards; women ratepayers eligible to
vote and stand for election.
Edinburgh medical students riot in protest against proposed admission
of women.

1873   Girton College founded.

1874   Founding of London School of Medicine for Women.

1875   First woman Poor Law Guardian elected.

1876   Women gain right to register as physicians.

1878   Women admitted to degrees at London University.

1882   Married Women's Property Act allows married women to retain
property on marriage.

1883   Women's Co-operative Guild (WCG) established.
Repeal of Contagious Diseases Acts following agitation led by Josephine
Butler.

1884 Matrimonial Causes Act makes 'aggravated assault' grounds for judicial separation.

1885 Criminal Law Amendment Act raises age of consent for girls to 16 and provides for suppression of brothels.
Mothers' Union founded.

1889 First woman elected to London County Council.

1892 British Medical Association admits women doctors; about 100 women doctors in practice.

1894 Local Government Act enables women to stand for election to Rural and Urban District Councils.

1895 Term 'feminist' appears for first time.

1897 National Union of Women's Suffrage Societies (NUWSS) formed under leadership of Millicent Garrett Fawcett.

1898 Amendment to 1824 Vagrancy Act makes living on earnings of prostitutes an offence.

1899 Boer War begins.

1901 Death of Queen Victoria, accession of Edward VII.

1902 Boer War ends.
Midwives Act licenses midwives and improves standards in midwifery.

1903 Establishment of Women's Social and Political Union (WSPU) under leadership of Emmeline Pankhurst and her daughters Christabel and Sylvia.

1904 Establishment of British National Federation of Women Workers.
Report of Inter-departmental Committee on Physical Deterioration.

1905 Start of militant suffrage campaign.

1906 Liberal government elected, pledged to implement progressive reform.
Education (Provision of Meals) Act introduces principle of school meals subsidised by local authorities.

1907 Introduction of medical inspection of school children.
NUWSS launches first suffrage procession through London, the 'Mud March', so-called owing to poor weather.
Split within WSPU; start of Women's Freedom League.
First Aid Nursing Yeomanry (FANY), the first quasi-military organisation to recruit women established.

1908 Introduction of state old age pension at 5s. per week from age 70.
Gerald Mills and Charles Boon register their publishing house; their first romantic novel *Secrets* appears in 1910.

1909 *Marriage as a Trade* by Cicely Hamilton published.

1910   Liberal minority government re-elected in two general elections in
       January-February and in December.
       Death of King Edward VII, accession of George V.
       Suffragette campaign includes arson; suffragette prisoners mount
       hunger strikes.

1911   National Insurance Act introduces contributory health insurance for
       most manual workers but not their dependants; most married women
       and children excluded from scheme.
       Miss E. Davis-Colley becomes first female Fellow of Royal College
       of Surgeons.

1912   Criminal Law Amendment Act increased penalty for brothel owners
       to £100 or twelve months' imprisonment.

1913   Suffragette Emily Davidson killed after throwing herself under the
       King's horse during the Derby.
       Prisoners' Temporary Discharge for Ill-Health Act, the so-called
       'Cat and Mouse' Act.
       Mental Deficiency Act gave authorities power to incarcerate women
       believed to be 'feeble-minded'.
       The Great Scourge by Christabel Pankhurst published.

1914   Britain declares war on Germany, 4 August.
       Suspension of suffrage campaign for the duration.

1915   Women's international peace conference at the Hague results in
       founding of Women's International League for Peace and Freedom.
       National Federation of Women's Institutes (WI) formed.

1917   United States enters war on side of Britain and Allies.
       Russian Revolution.
       Establishment of Women's Army Auxiliary Corps (WAAC), renamed
       Queen Mary's Army Auxiliary Corps (QMAAC) in 1918; also founding
       of Women's Royal Naval Service (WRNS), and Women's Royal Air
       Force (WRAF).
       Women's Peace Crusade launched by working-class feminists to
       represent working-class women's opposition to war.

1918   Representation of the People Act gives vote to all men over 21 and
       to women over 30 who are ratepayers or wives of ratepayers,
       enfranchising majority of married women.
       Women entitled to become MPs.
       Reg 40 (d) (DORA) authorised compulsory medical examination of
       woman accused by member of armed forces of having infected him
       with VD; revoked after eight months.
       Maternity and Child Welfare Act extends maternity and child welfare
       services.

Women allowed to enter legal profession and to become JPs.
General election returns Conservative-dominated coalition.
School leaving age raised to 14.
Publication of *Married Love* by Marie Stopes.

1919   Nancy Astor becomes first woman MP to take up her seat.
Sex Disqualification (Removal) Act which made it illegal to deny
employment on grounds of marriage, enables women to enter
professions, become magistrates and sit on juries; nevertheless
marriage bars continue in many occupations, including teaching and
civil service.
NUWSS changes name to National Union of Societies for Equal
Citizenship (NUSEC) with Eleanor Rathbone as president.

1920   Oxford University admits women to degrees.
Time and Tide launched.

1921   End of postwar boom. Committee under Sir Eric Geddes appointed
to examine scope for public expenditure cuts.
Establishment of Six Point Group.
Marie Stopes opens first birth-control clinic in London.

1922   Implementation of 'Geddes Axe' programme of public
expenditure cuts.
Conservatives win majority in November general election.
Married Women Maintenance Act increased level of maintenance.
Infanticide Act eliminates charge of murder for woman found guilty
of killing infant if proved to be suffering from effects of childbirth.
Good Housekeeping launched.

1923   Matrimonial Causes Act enables wives to sue for divorce on same
grounds as men, adultery becomes sufficient grounds for female
petitioners.
Bastardy Act enables children to be recognised as legitimate on
subsequent marriage of parents and improves procedure to enable
unmarried mothers to claim maintenance from fathers.
Conservatives lose overall majority in December general election.

1924   Labour forms first minority government.
Margaret Bondfield becomes first female member of government
as parliamentary secretary at the Ministry of Labour.
Conservatives win October general election.
Katherine, Duchess of Atholl becomes first female member
of Conservative government as parliamentary secretary at the
Board of Education.

1925   National Insurance Pensions introduced, pensionable age reduced
to 65.
Introduction of pensions for widows.

Guardianship of Infants Act allows mothers equal access to
guardianship rights.

1926   Creation of Open Door Council promoting equal rights for women.
National Demonstration for equal suffrage held in Hyde Park.
Equal Political Rights Campaign Committee (EPRCC) set up,
organising protests meetings and parades in 1926 and 1927.
Establishment of Women's Service Library (later named the Fawcett
Library) in London.
Women's Cricket Association founded.

1928   Equal Franchise Act gives women vote on same terms as men.
Payment of contributory pensions to widows and elderly people
over 65.
NUSEC begins setting up Townswomen's Guilds (TG).
The Well of Loneliness by Marguerite Radclyffe Hall published and
banned.

1929   General election results in Labour's second minority government.
Local Government Act abolishes Poor Law Guardians and transfers
their functions to local authorities.
Margaret Bondfield becomes first female member of cabinet
as Minister of Labour.
A Room of One's Own by Virginia Woolf published.
Age at which marriage permissible raised from 12 to 16 for females.
Wall Street crash and beginning of depression.

1930   Poor Law renamed Public Assistance and Boards of Guardians
abolished.
Mary Bagot Stack founds Women's League of Health and Beauty.
National Birth Control Council established; after 1939 renamed Family
Planning Association.

1931   Financial and political crisis in Britain causes breakup of Labour
government; three-party National Government formed which wins
election with mainly Conservative support.

1932   Britain begins to recover from depression.
Woman's Own launched.

1933   Hitler becomes German Chancellor.
'New Deal' begins in USA.

1934   Dr Helen Mackay first woman elected to Fellowship of Royal College
of Physicians.

1935   General election returns National Government, dominated by
Conservative party, with increased majority.
Married women empowered to dispose of property by will on same
terms as single women. Husband's liability for wife's debts abolished.

1936 Death of King George V; Edward VIII accedes to throne, but abdicates after 10 months to marry American divorcee Wallis Simpson; accession of George VI.
Regular tv broadcasts begin.
Abortion Law Reform Association set up.

1937 Divorce reform extends grounds of divorce to include desertion, cruelty and insanity.
Woman launched.

1938 Auxiliary Territorial Service (ATS) founded; awarded full military status in 1941.
Three Guineas by Virginia Woolf published.

1939 War against Germany declared 3 September.
Women's Voluntary Service (WVS, later WRVS) formed by Lady Reading.

1940 Coalition government formed in May with Churchill as Prime Minister.
Food rationing begins.
Women to receive state pension aged 60.
Woman Power Committee established to co-ordinate campaigns concerning women's issues across party divide.

1941 German invasion of Russia (June) brings Soviet Union into war on side of Allies.
Japanese attack on Pearl Harbor (December) brings USA into war.

1942 Beveridge Report published.
Reg 33 (b) (DORA) empowered Medical Officers to request examination of woman suspected to be source of VD; repealed in 1947.

1943 Equal Pay Campaign Committee (EPCC) set up to co-ordinate campaign for equal pay.

1944 Education Act establishes free secondary education for all.
Marriage bar for teachers abolished by an amendment of the Education Act.
Equal Pay amendment to Education Bill passed in Commons but immediately overturned on confidence vote; Royal Commission on Equal Pay set up.

1945 War with Germany ends (May); and war with Japan ends (August).
Labour government elected with landslide majority.
Family Allowances Act provides cash benefit paid to the mothers for all but first children. Benefits paid from 1946.
Royal Society agrees to elect women fellows. X-ray crystallographer Kathleen Lonsdale (née Yardley) first female FRS.

1946   National Insurance Act, National Health Service Act and National
Assistance Act introduce comprehensive welfare state.
Royal Commission on Equal Pay recommends equal pay in public
sector, but Labour Government fails to implement reform which it
perceives as inflationary.
Marriage bar abolished in Civil Service.
Launch of *Woman's Hour* on BBC.

1947   School leaving age raised to 15.
Equal Pay Campaign mass meeting held, putting pressure on Labour
government.

1948   'Appointed day': National Health Service (NHS), National Insurance,
National Assistance implemented.
British Nationality Act allows British women to retain their nationality
on marriage to a foreigner.
Women admitted to degrees at Cambridge University; all medical
schools opened to women, but quota system (usually around 20 per
cent) continues to operate.

1949   Remnant of ATS replaced by Women's Royal Army Corps (WRAC)
which establishes a peacetime role for women in the armed forces.
Professor (later Dame) Hilda Lloyd elected President of Royal College
of Obstetricians and Gynaecologists, first woman president of a Royal
College.

1950   Labour government re-elected in February.
Korean War begins.

1951   Conservative government elected in October.

1952   Death of King George VI; accession of Elizabeth II.
Equal pay for men and women teachers in London.

1953   Korean War ends.
The Second Sex by Simone de Beauvoir published in English translation.

1954   Food rationing which was being phased out finally ends.
Equal pay for men and women in teaching, civil service and local
government introduced by increments.

1955   Conservatives win second successive general election.
Ruth Ellis hanged; the last woman to suffer the death penalty in
Britain.
ITV, the second (commercial) television channel, begins broadcasting.

1957   European Economic Community (EEC) founded.
Wolfenden Committee Report on homosexuality and prostitution.

1958   Life Peerages Act opens membership of House of Lords to women.
CND founded; first Aldermaston March.

1959   Conservative government re-elected with increased majority.
       Street Offences Act implements Wolfenden recommendations allowing
       women to be convicted for soliciting on uncorroborated evidence of
       single policeman; prostitutes forced off the streets.
       Obscene Publications Act relaxes publishing laws regarding
       pornographic material.

1960   Penguin Books prosecuted and tried for publishing *Lady Chatterley's
       Lover* by D.H. Lawrence. Jury of three women and nine men returned
       'not guilty' verdict.

1961   Erection of Berlin Wall intensifies Cold War.

1962   Contraceptive pill introduced.

1963   Britain's application for entry into the EEC refused on French veto.
       Robbins report advocates expansion of higher education.
       The Feminine Mystique by Betty Friedan published.
       Mary Whitehouse establishes Clean Up TV Campaign; later renamed
       National Viewers and Listeners Association.

1964   Labour wins general election on narrow majority.
       Dorothy Hodgkin (née Crowfoot) wins Nobel Prize for Chemistry.
       Second public tv channel, BBC2, begins transmission.

1965   Change of education policy promotes rise of comprehensive schools.
       Death penalty abolished.
       Miniskirt launched by Mary Quant.

1966   Labour wins general election with increased majority.
       National Assistance renamed Supplementary Benefit.
       Colour tv introduced.

1967   Second application to join EEC again vetoed by France.
       Abortion Act allows legal termination of pregnancy up to 28 weeks.
       Family Planning Act allows local health authorities to provide free
       family planning service, available also to unmarried women.
       Radio One launched.
       Laura Ashley opens first shop in Kensington.

1968   Start of London Women's Liberation groups and workshops.
       Pope Paul VI issues encyclical *Humanae Vitae* condemning artificial
       contraceptions.

1969   Voting age and age of majority lowered from 21 to 18.
       Divorce law liberalised by allowing 'irretrievable breakdown' of
       a marriage as grounds for divorce.

1970   Equal Pay Act outlaws discrimination in pay between men and women
       to be implemented on a voluntary basis until 1975.
       Conservatives win general election.

Matrimonial Proceedings and Property Act gives women increased share of matrimonial property by recognising the wife's non-financial contribution.

First National Women's Liberation Conference at Ruskin College, Oxford.

Feminists stage protest demonstration at Miss World contest at the Albert Hall, London.

The Female Eunuch by Germaine Greer published.

1971   Attachment of Earnings Act makes it easier to enforce court-ordered maintenance payments against husbands.

First major Women's Liberation street march.

Men banned from Women's Liberation Conferences; lesbian activists insist that sexuality be included in demands of Women's Liberation Movement.

1972   Establishment of Women's Aid.

School leaving age raised to 16.

First publication of *Cosmopolitan* and *Spare Rib*.

1973   Britain joins EEC.

Guardianship Act grants mothers equal rights with fathers in decisions over a child's upbringing.

First commercial radio stations begin broadcasting.

1974   Inconclusive general election in February; Labour minority government; Labour wins narrow majority in October.

Free contraception available on National Health Service.

1975   Referendum results in clear majority in favour of staying in the EEC.

Equal Pay Act comes into force.

Sex Discrimination Act establishes Equal Opportunities Commission.

Employment Protection Act establishes maternity rights for employed women.

Child Benefit Act provides tax-free, non-means-tested benefit paid directly to mothers and benefit for first as well as subsequent children for lone parents.

Margaret Thatcher becomes Conservative Party leader, the first woman to become leader of a major party in Britain.

International Women's Year. UN declares 1975–85 decade for Women, Equality, Development and Peace.

National Abortion Campaign to defend abortion rights founded and large-scale demonstrations held.

English Prostitutes Collective founded.

1976   Domestic Violence and Matrimonial Proceedings Act makes it easier to obtain an injunction to restrain a violent partner.

First rape crisis centre opened in London.
Anita Roddick opens first Body Shop in Brighton.

1977   Women's Royal Army Corps (WRAC) re-designated as a combatant corps although women do not begin weapons training until 1981.
Women's groups organise 'Reclaim the night' demonstrations in several cities.

1978   Legislation protects female workers against dismissal because of pregnancy and establishes right to maternity leave and maternity pay for six weeks at 90 per cent of normal pay.
Last National Women's Liberation Conference ends in disagreements and divisions.
First successful *in vitro* fertilisation or 'test-tube' baby Louise Brown born.

1979   Conservatives win general election; Margaret Thatcher first woman Prime Minister.
Dame Josephine Barnes becomes first woman president of British Medical Association.

1981   Establishment of women's Peace Camp outside cruise missile base at Greenham Common.
Jane Fonda's *Workout Book* published, stimulating aerobics craze of 1980s.
Prince of Wales marries Lady Diana Spencer.

1982   Unemployment rises above 3 million for first time since 1933.
Falklands War.
Massive demonstration at Greenham Common against siting of cruise missiles.
Second commercial tv channel, Channel 4, begins broadcasting.

1983   Conservatives re-elected with increased majority.
Equal Pay (Amendment) Regulation stipulates equal pay for work of equal value.

1984   Divorce allowed after one year of marriage rather than three.

1985   Sexual Offences Act for the first time criminalises male clients of prostitutes by outlawing 'persistent' kerb crawling.

1986   Sex Discrimination Act outlaws sex discrimination in collective bargaining agreements and extends anti-discrimination law to small businesses.

1987   Conservatives win third successive general election.
Diane Abbott becomes first black woman MP.

1988   Income Support and Social Fund replace Supplementary Benefit for low-income households.

Section 28, Local Government Act, prohibits 'promotion' of homosexuality by local authorities.

1989   Fall of Berlin Wall precipitates end of Cold War.
Publication of *Serious Pleasure* by Sheba, first generally available sexually explicit book written by lesbians for lesbians.

1990   Margaret Thatcher ousted from premiership; John Major becomes Prime Minister.
Gulf War begins.
Child Support Act establishes Child Support Agency.
Time limit for legal abortions reduced from 28 to 24 weeks in line with clinical practice.
Labour Party conference supports increased female representation in the party through quota system and aims for gender parity in the parliamentary party.

1991   Britain signs Maastricht Treaty; but opts out of single currency and social charter.
Gulf War ends.

1992   Conservatives win fourth successive general election on narrow majority.
Betty Boothroyd becomes first woman speaker in the House of Commons.
European Commission rules that gender differences in pension ages are to be eliminated.
WRAC is disbanded and women are fully integrated into regular army (by mid-1990s majority of posts in British army are open to women).
Women doctors account for nearly 30 per cent of registered doctors; just over half of all students entering medical schools female.

1993   EU (single European market) comes into existence.
Labour Party adopts positive discrimination in the form of all-female short-lists of parliamentary candidates to increase number of Labour women MPs; policy is subsequently ruled in breach of anti-sex discrimination legislation.

1994   Church of England accepts ordination of women and first women ordained.
Chief Medical Officer reports that men lead less healthy lifestyles than women.

1995   With 27.9 years average, age of women at childbirth is highest since 1957.
Equal Opportunities Commission Report shows that highly qualified ethnic minority women are twice as likely to be unemployed as whites.
Girls' schools take 18 of top 20 places in league table of 500 state and independent schools.

1996 Sex Discrimination and Equal Pay Regulations simplify proceedings in equal pay claims.

Pauline Clare becomes first woman chief constable (in Lancashire).

1997 Labour wins general election with landslide majority; Tony Blair Prime Minister.

An unprecedented number of female candidates results in the election of 101 Labour women MPs, highest number of female MPs ever with a total of 120.

With 29 female ministers, including 5 at cabinet level, record number of women in government.

Labour government accepts social charter.

Angela Eagle is first member of government to come out as a lesbian.

Women account for only 1.7 per cent of executives and 4.2 per cent of directors of FT-SE 100 companies.

Diana, Princess of Wales, dies in car crash.

Heather Hallett QC elected first female chair of Bar Council.

1998 Baroness Jay, Leader of House of Lords, appointed Minister for Women at Cabinet level, with Tessa Jowell representing women's interests in House of Commons.

Women's Unit, inside Cabinet Office, and Cabinet subcommittee on women established.

Britain has highest proportion of unmarried teenage mothers in the world.

Viagara, male potency drug, launched.

1999 Women students account for majority of undergraduate entry at universities; male professors outnumber female professors at rate of 10 to 1.

Minimum wage introduced.

2000 Government-backed study reveals that women suffer extensive discrimination in labour market; pay gap between men and women stands at 20 per cent.

Government launches ten-point plan for tackling domestic violence.

Jo Hale, 14, wins right to wear trousers in Equal Opportunities Commission-backed case against sex discrimination in school dress codes.

Worry about appearance is biggest concern in lives of majority of 12–15 year old girls; government summit discusses pressures on young women to conform to particular body image.

NOTES ON CONTRIBUTORS

Paula Bartley is Senior Lecturer in History at the University of Wolverhampton. She has written a number of history texts for schools, co-edited the Women's History series for Cambridge University Press, and is a reviews editor for *Midland History*. Her most recent books include *The Changing Role of Women* (London, 1996); *Votes for Women* (London, 1998); and *Prostitution: Reform and Prevention in England 1860–1914* (London, 1999).

Caitriona Beaumont is Lecturer in History at South Bank University, London. She has published a number of articles and essays on the history of women and the women's movement in Ireland and Britain, including 'Gender, Citizenship and the State in Ireland, 1922–1990', in S. Brewster, V. Crossman, F. Becket and D. Alderson (eds), *Ireland in Proximity: History, Gender, Space* (London, 1999). She is currently working on a book about the role of six mainstream women's organisations in the campaign for women's rights in Britain between 1928 and 1960.

Shani D'Cruze is Senior Lecturer in History at Manchester Metropolitan University. Her recent publications include *Crimes of Outrage: Sex, Violence and Victorian Working Women* (London, 1998) and an edited collection, *Everyday Violence: Gender and Class, c. 1850–c. 1950* (Harlow, 2000). She is also developing research on gender, class and 'serious' leisure in the twentieth century.

Carol Dyhouse is Reader in History at the University of Sussex. Her publications include *Girls Growing up in Late Victorian and Edwardian England* (London, 1981); *Feminism and the Family in England 1880–1939* (Oxford, 1989); and *No Distinction of Sex? Women in British Universities 1870–1939* (London, 1995).

Martin Francis is Lecturer in British and American History at Royal Holloway and Bedford New College, University of London. He is author of *Ideas and Policies under Labour, 1945–1951* (Manchester, 1997) and co-editor, with Ina Zweiniger-Bargielowska, of *The Conservatives and British Society, 1880–1990* (Cardiff, 1996). He is currently writing a book on emotion and politics in Britain and the USA since 1900.

Barbara Gwinnett is Senior Lecturer in Sociology at the University of Wolverhampton where she teaches sociological theory and criminal justice. Her research interests are in the policing of prostitution and social inequalities. She has published on prostitution and is currently co-editing an undergraduate textbook on social inequalities.

Lesley A. Hall is Senior Assistant Archivist, Contemporary Medical Archives Centre, Wellcome Institute for the History of Medicine, London, and Honorary Lecturer in History of Medicine, University College London. Her publications include *Hidden Anxieties: Male Sexuality 1900–1950* (Cambridge, 1991); with Roy Porter, *The Facts of Life: The Creation of Sexual Knowledge in Britain, 1650–1950* (New Haven, CT, and London, 1995); and, co-edited with Franz Eder and Gert Hekma, *Sexual Cultures in Europe: National Histories* and *Sexual Cultures in Europe: Themes in Sexuality* (Manchester, 1999). She is currently working on a biography of British feminist socialist sex-radical Stella Browne (1880–1955) and a volume, co-edited with Roger Davidson, on venereal diseases in a European social context since 1870.

Katherine Holden is Research Associate in History at the University of the West of England. She is author of, with Leonore Davidoff, Janet Fink and Megan Doolittle, *The Family Story: Blood Contract and Intimacy 1830–1960* (London, 1999); and editor of a multimedia CD-rom, 'Major Themes in Women's History from the Enlightenment to the Second World War', published by the TLTP History Courseware Consortium, University of Glasgow, 1999. She is currently working on a history of single men and women in twentieth-century Britain.

Sandra Stanley Holton holds an Australian Research Council Senior Research Fellowship at the University of Adelaide. She has published a number of articles and two books on the suffrage movement, *Feminism and Democracy: Women's Suffrage and Reform Politics, 1897–1918* (Cambridge, 1986); and *Suffrage Days: Stories from the Women's Suffrage Movement* (London, 1996). Presently, she is researching a cross-generational study of the Priestman–Bright circle of Quaker women, a number of whom helped form the women's movement and three generations of whom took part in the suffrage campaigns.

Harriet Jones is Director of the Institute of Contemporary British History at the Institute of Historical Research, London. Her edited publications include, with Michael Kandiah, *The Myth of Consensus: New Views on British History, 1945–64* (Basingstoke, 1996). She is completing a study of the Conservative Party and the welfare state between 1942 and 1958, which is forthcoming with Oxford University Press.

Helen Jones is Senior Lecturer at Goldsmiths' College, University of London. Her publications include *Health and Society in Twentieth-Century Britain* (London, 1994). She has written and edited numerous other books on politics, health and gender in twentieth-century Britain.

Jane Lewis is Barnett Professor of Social Policy, University of Oxford. She is the author of many books and articles on gender and social policy issues. Her most recent book, with Kathleen Kiernan and Hilary Land, is *Lone Motherhood in Twentieth-Century Britain* (Oxford, 1998).

Deirdre McCloskey is University Professor of the Human Sciences at the University of Illinois at Chicago, Illinois. Author of a dozen books on British economic history and economic philosophy, she is internationally known as a postmodern free-market feminist. Her book, *Crossing: A Memoir*, was published by the University of Chicago Press in 1999 and her latest book, *How to be an Economist ** Though Human* is forthcoming from the University of Michigan Press.

Billie Melman is Professor of Modern History at Tel-Aviv University, Israel. She is author of *Women and the Popular Imagination in the Twenties: Flappers and Nymphs* (Basingstoke, 1988); *Women's Orients: English Women and the Middle East 1718–1918: Sexuality, Religion and Work*, second edn (Basingstoke, 1995); and editor of *Borderlines: Genders and Identities in War and Peace 1870–1930* (London, 1998). She has written extensively on gender, British colonialism and orientalism, on nationalism and on women's historical writing in Britain during the nineteenth and early twentieth centuries.

Lucy Noakes is Lecturer in Cultural Studies at Southampton Institute. Her publications include *War and the British: Gender and National Identity, 1939–1991* (London, 1998). She is currently researching the relationship between women and war, focusing on the experience and representation of British and American women in wartime in the twentieth century.

Harold L. Smith is Professor of History at the University of Houston-Victoria, Victoria, Texas. In addition to editing *British Feminism in the Twentieth Century* (Aldershot, 1990); and *Britain in the Second World War: A Social History* (Manchester, 1996); he is author of *The British Women's Suffrage Campaign, 1866–1928* (London, 1998). He has also written numerous articles on twentieth-century British women's history.

Pat Thane is Professor of Contemporary History at the University of Sussex. She is author of *The Foundations of the Welfare State*, second edn (London, 1996); and *Old Age: Continuity or Change in English History?* (Oxford, 2000). She is also co-editor, with Paul Johnson, of *Old Age from Antiquity to Post-modernity* (London, 1998); and, with Lynn Botelho, of *Women and Ageing in Britain from 1500 to the Present* (London, 2000).

Penny Tinkler is Lecturer in the Department of Sociology at the University of Manchester. She has written extensively on aspects of twentieth-century girlhood including girls' popular literature, leisure, education, citizenship and consumerism. She is author of *Constructing Girlhood: Popular Magazines for Girls Growing Up in England, 1920–1950* (London, 1995). She is currently researching the feminisation of smoking in Britain, 1900–70.

Wendy Webster teaches history in the Department of Historical and Critical Studies, University of Central Lancashire. Her publications include *Not a Man to Match Her: The Marketing of a Prime Minister* (London, 1990); and *Imagining Home: Gender, 'Race' and National Identity 1945–64* (London, 1998). She is currently working on the impact of the decline of British colonial rule on gendered and raced narratives of Britishness and Englishness. She is a reviews editor for *Women's History Review.*

Ina Zweiniger-Bargielowska is Assistant Professor in Modern British History at the University of Illinois at Chicago, Illinois. Her publications include *The Conservatives and British Society, 1880–1990*, edited with Martin Francis (Cardiff, 1996); and *Austerity in Britain: Rationing, Controls and Consumption, 1939–1955* (Oxford, 2000). She is currently working on a history of the body in Britain since the 1950s.

INDEX

Notes: All references are to *women* and *Britain*, except where otherwise indicated. Page numbers in **bold** indicate **chapters**; *passim* is used where there are separate, not continuous, references on several pages.